Bridges of Reform

Bridges of Reform
*Interracial Civil Rights Activism
in Twentieth-Century
Los Angeles*

Shana Bernstein

OXFORD
UNIVERSITY PRESS

2011

OXFORD
UNIVERSITY PRESS

Oxford University Press, Inc., publishes works that further
Oxford University's objective of excellence
in research, scholarship, and education.

Oxford   New York
Auckland   Cape Town   Dar es Salaam   Hong Kong   Karachi
Kuala Lumpur   Madrid   Melbourne   Mexico City   Nairobi
New Delhi   Shanghai   Taipei   Toronto

With offices in
Argentina   Austria   Brazil   Chile   Czech Republic   France   Greece
Guatemala   Hungary   Italy   Japan   Poland   Portugal   Singapore
South Korea   Switzerland   Thailand   Turkey   Ukraine   Vietnam

Published by Oxford University Press, Inc.
198 Madison Avenue, New York, New York 10016

www.oup.com

Oxford is a registered trademark of Oxford University Press.

Portions of this book were published in an earlier form as "From California to the Nation:
Rethinking the History of 20th Century U.S. Civil Rights Struggles through a Mexican American,
and Multiracial, Lens" in the *Berkeley La Raza Law Journal* Vol. 18 (2007) and "From Civic Defense
to Civil Rights: The Growth of Jewish American Interracial Civil Rights Activism in Los Angeles"
in *A Cultural History of Jews in California: The Jewish Role in American Life, An Annual Review*,
Vol. 7, ed. by Bruce Zuckerman, and are reproduced here by permission of the *Berkeley La Raza
Law Journal* and Purdue University Press.

ISBN: 978-0-19-533166-0
978-0-19-533167-7 (pbk.)

Library of Congress Cataloging-in-Publication Data
Bernstein, Shana.
Bridges of reform : interracial civil rights activism in twentieth-century
Los Angeles / Shana Bernstein.
p.   cm.
Includes bibliographical references and index.
ISBN 978-0-19-533166-0 (hardcover : alk. paper)—
ISBN 978-0-19-533167-7 (pbk. : alk. paper)
1. Civil rights movements—California—Los Angeles—History—20th century.   2. Community
life—California—Los Angeles—History—20th century.   3. Los Angeles (Calif.)—Race
relations—History—20th century.   4. Cultural pluralism—California—Los Angeles—History—
20th century.   5. Los Angeles (Calif.)—Social conditions—20th century.   I. Title.
F869.L89A24   2010
979.4'94053—dc22

1 3 5 7 9 8 6 4 2
Printed in the United States of America

on acid-free paper

To Roberta Bernstein and Monte Bernstein

Contents

Abbreviations

ACLU	American Civil Liberties Union
AFL	The American Federation of Labor
CCC	Council for Civic Unity
CFCU	California Federation for Civic Unity
CIO	Congress of Industrial Organizations
CRC	Community Relations Committee
CSO	Community Service Organization
LACPFB	Los Angeles Committee for the Protection of the Foreign Born
NAACP	National Association for the Advancement of Colored People

Acknowledgments

I could not have written this book without the assistance, support, encouragement, and love of a wide community of institutions, colleagues, friends, and family. A number of fellowship programs provided me the time and funds necessary to research and write. They made this project possible and I am very grateful for their support. The Department of History, the Center for the Study of Race and Ethnicity, and the Taube Center for Jewish Studies at Stanford University awarded me generous fellowships and teaching assistantships. The Mellon Foundation sponsored a Stanford dissertation grant and later a postdoctoral fellowship at Northwestern University, while the Newberry Library provided work space at a crucial juncture. Grants and fellowships from the Historical Society of Southern California and the Haynes Foundation, the Huntington Library, Temple University's Feinstein Center for Jewish Studies, and Southwestern University enabled me to continue my research and writing. For the last several years Southwestern University has been my academic home. I am grateful for its support, including awarding me multiple grants from the Brown Foundation and the Cullen Foundation.

Many colleagues and friends have assisted me over the years, whether with this project specifically or with more general guidance and advice. I am indebted to the caring and inspirational professors in Stanford University's Department of History, where this book began as my dissertation. I have learned much from Estelle Freedman's deep dedication to social justice issues and to collaborative learning and from Richard White's wisdom and insight. My two advisors, Gordon Chang and Al Camarillo, nurtured this study from its beginning. Gordon helped sustain this project with his thoughtfulness, support, and common decency, while Al's model of socially engaged academia has set standards to which I aspire. I also benefited from professors outside Stanford University, especially Bill Deverell, who has been a wonderful friend, supporter, and mentor. Pedro Castillo, Mary Felstiner, Richard Roberts, and Krystyna von Henneberg have encouraged me with their enthusiasm and expertise. Others shone light on the then-mysterious publishing process, including Robert Devens, Tom Guglielmo, Becky Nicolaides, Renee Romano, Michael Sherry, Paul Spickard, and Judy Wu. I am particularly grateful to my fellow Stanford graduate students, especially Matthew Booker, Mark Brilliant, Michelle Campos, Roberta Chavez, Joe Crespino, Noemi García, Shawn Gerth, Gabriela González, Paul Herman, Rachel Jean-Baptiste, Shelley Lee, Martha Mabie Gardner, Gina Marie Pitti, Lara Moore, Ken Moss, Caitlin Murdock, Tara Nummedal, Monica Perales, Amy Robinson, Shira Robinson, Rachel St. John, Sarah Sussman, Cecilia Tsu, and Kim Warren. They pushed me to sharpen my arguments and their encouragement and friendship continues to deepen my belief in the power of collegiality. At various stages many other scholars and friends helped me think through my conclusions and provided support. They include Eric Arnesen, Henry Binford, Martha Biondi, Charlotte Brooks, Clark Davis, Mary Dudziak, Carolyn Eastman, Elizabeth Escobedo, Lori Green, Daniel Hurewitz, Ben Johnson, Robert Johnston, David Leonard, Alex Lichtenstein, Nancy MacLean, Gregg Michel, Julia Mickenberg, Dylan Penningroth, Vicki L. Ruiz, Roberto Ramon Lint Sagarena, Robert Self, Nancy Stalker, Mark Wild, and Ann Ziker. I especially want to thank Bill Deverell, Mario García, Bill Issel, Michelle Nickerson, Josh Sides, Allison Varzally, and the anonymous readers who read the manuscript in its entirety and offered crucial insights that significantly improved this book. Carolyn Chen and Devah Pager helped keep the research and writing engine running during my postdoctoral year, as did Daniel Castro, Steve Davidson, Lisa Moses Leff, Thomas McClendon, and Elizabeth Green Musselman, my fantastic history department colleagues at Southwestern University. Breck Foster, Michelle Nickerson, Allison Varzally, and Mark Wild graciously offered a couch or guest room during numerous research trips to Los Angeles. Comments from copanelists and audience members at talks enriched this study, especially those at the Huntington Library, the Los Angeles History Working Group, the Organization of American Historians, Northwestern University's Latino Studies Seminar, Southern Methodist University, Southwestern University's History Department Seminar, the Urban History Association, the Western Association of Women Historians, the Western History Association, and various invited conferences and seminars. I owe deep thanks to everyone who shared their ideas, and helped improve this book, on those occasions and others. Their contributions strengthened the manuscript, while mistakes and faults are mine alone.

Numerous archivists and librarians were essential to helping me uncover the evidence that provides this book's foundation. I thank the staff at the California State Archives, Stanford's Hoover Institution, the Southern California Library for Social Studies and Research, the University of Southern California's Regional History Center, the Library of Congress, the University of Illinois Chicago, and the Oral History Center at the

California State University at Fullerton. I am particularly grateful to Robert Marshall and Kathryn Cannarozzi at the California State University at Northridge's Urban Archives for their willingness to assist me so often, and for so long. I also especially thank Polly Armstrong and her colleagues in Stanford's Department of Special Collections; Jeff Rankin, Octavio Olvera, and their colleagues at the University of California Los Angeles's Department of Special Collections; the staff at UC Berkeley's Bancroft Library (especially David Kessler, whose delicious sandwiches made with homemade bread brightened some long days there); Mona Shulman, Susi Krasnoo, Robert Ritchie, Bill Frank, Brooke Black, and others at the Huntington Library; and Gretchen Laue at the University of California's Professional Development Institute, whose hard work has helped preserve the memory of the Community Service Organization. I thank David Deis, too, for his map.

Friends outside academia reminded me about life beyond books and teaching. Besides those good friends mentioned above, I thank Sarah Aird, Kathleen Dodge, Breck Foster, Angela Walker-Liang, Kristina Malsberger, Melisa Rossmeisl, Victoria Schlesinger, Susan Stolar, and Katherine Suyeyasu.

Many of my students, especially Ashly Hernandez, Angelica Castillo, and Erika Rendon, made my research more meaningful as I thought about its relevance to the future generation of scholars and citizens. I also thank the people of the past who fought long and hard in difficult times. Without them there would be nothing to write. Speaking of writing, to Susan Ferber, my editor at Oxford, I owe many thanks. Her editing skills improved this book greatly by cutting long sentences and unnecessary paragraphs, and also by asking sharp questions. I also appreciate the assistance of Oxford's production team, especially Marc Schneider, in making this book a reality. I thank too the countless other colleagues who I undoubtedly have accidentally neglected to mention.

My brother Dan and my sister Martine have supported me through this long process, and I appreciate their willingness to remind me when I'm taking it too seriously. My grandma Dorothy's support and love has always been a source of strength. Words cannot describe the love and appreciation I feel for both my parents, Monte Bernstein and Roberta Bernstein. My passion for history and commitment to writing this book was a product of their excitement: my mom's for ideas, creativity, and education and my dad's for hard work, discipline, and history itself. My new nuclear family has sustained me as well these past several years. My husband, Niko Matouschek, has offered steadfast support and cheerleading to get me around the final bend(s). His silly jokes take my mind off whatever might be weighing it down, while our intellectual debates motivate me to tell my story. And Ruby, your arrival has changed so much. My eyes are now on the future as well as the past; I look forward to seeing more of it through your fresh eyes. I also hope that the future you see, beyond my years, is brighter than what we have known.

Illustrations and Maps

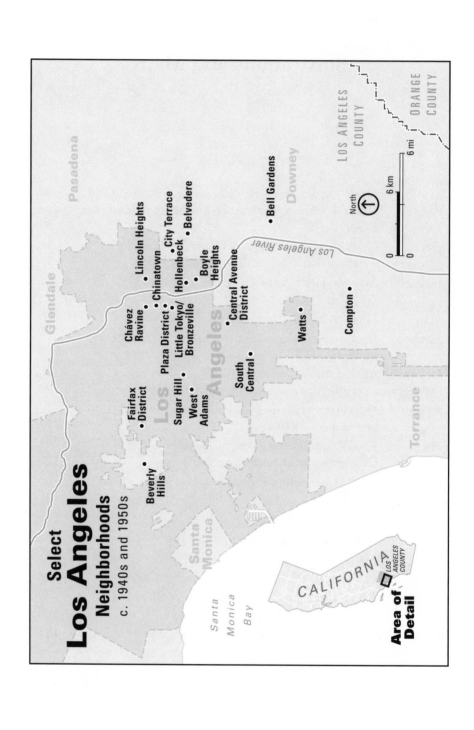

Select
Los Angeles
Neighborhoods
c. 1940s and 1950s

Santa
Monica
Bay

Santa
Monica

Beverly
Hills

Fairfax
District

Sugar Hill
West
Adams

Chávez
Ravine

Plaza District
Little Tokyo/
Bronzeville

Chinatown

Lincoln Heights

City Terrace

Hollenbeck

Belvedere

Boyle
Heights

Central Avenue
District

South
Central

Los Angeles

Glendale

Pasadena

Los Angeles River

Watts

Compton

Bell Gardens

Downey

LOS ANGELES
COUNTY

ORANGE
COUNTY

North

0   6 km
0   6 mi

Torrance

CALIFORNIA

LOS
ANGELES
COUNTY

Area of
Detail

Bridges of Reform: Interracial Civil Rights Activism in Twentieth-Century Los Angeles

Introduction

Antonio Villaraigosa's 2005 election as the first Latino mayor of Los Angeles since the nineteenth century was not just a victory for Latino Los Angeles. Riding into office on a wave of successful coalition building between Latino and African-American Angelenos that united voters in the pursuit of greater access and equality for the city's minority groups, Villaraigosa's election in many ways echoed the deliberate efforts by Jewish- and African-American organizations to propel the African-American Tom Bradley to the L.A. city council in 1963 and to the mayor's office ten years later. In mid-century interracial activism emerged as a powerful political force for civil rights in the city, as a diverse coalition of Mexican, African, Japanese, Jewish, and white Americans elected Edward Roybal in 1949 as the first Latino city council member of Mexican descent since 1881. The election of all three men signaled to the rest of the nation how productive interracial alliances could help transform politics from an arena of racial division and competition to one of cooperation.[1]

Progressive Americans turned their attention to politics in the multiracial metropolis of Los Angeles during World War II and the postwar era. As the city grew—by 1950 it had become the largest city in the West and the fourth largest in the United States—what had been a largely white Protestant city in 1930 became increasingly minority, composed principally of African Americans, Mexican Americans, Japanese Americans, and Jewish Americans.[2] Americans hopeful that cooperation rather than conflict would be a hallmark of a new era looked for signs of both the potential and the liabilities of a multiracial nation in the City of Angels.

Observers went west and trumpeted the fertile landscape for interracial political work there. In 1950, the New York office of the National Association for the Advancement of Colored People (NAACP) dispatched its African-American field secretary Lester P. Bailey to Los Angeles to assist with the local branch's membership drive. Bailey soon sent back an optimistic report. "Of all the major cities I have worked in, I feel that Los Angeles has the greatest potentialities for NAACP. Never before have I found as many interracial and white organizations sincerely interested in the wellbeing of the Association."[3] Even some

3

Japanese Americans returning from wartime internment camps remarked on the interracial communities that embraced their return. Mary Oyama wrote in *Common Ground* magazine, "Churches, clubs, and different organizations vie with each other in inviting Nisei [second-generation Japanese Americans] to join their groups."[4] A reporter for *Look* magazine, Sara Boynoff, announced to the nation in 1957 that Los Angeles was "a race relations success story." She believed, "The American city with perhaps the greatest potential for racial trouble [for its unusual diversity] is showing the country what people of different races can do to live side by side in harmony." She noticed that "the really striking thing about Los Angeles—attesting to the basic tolerance in this vast melting pot of Americans—is the proliferation of what might be called 'do-good' or humanitarian organizations."[5] The churches, labor unions, minority groups, public and private welfare agencies, youth groups, women's organizations, and veterans' groups, "all are doing their part," she proclaimed.[6] Boynoff's account may have been overly optimistic, but statements like hers and Bailey's, as well as those from other whites and African Americans, revealed a belief that Angelenos had made significant racial progress compared to other American cities.

While contemporary observers appreciated the importance of Los Angeles's collaborative initiatives, their prevalence, origins, and significance beyond a specific election or individual incident have been largely forgotten.[7] Civil rights struggles in mid-century Los Angeles were rarely the product of a single ethno-racial community. Instead, different racialized and subordinated groups, notably the city's Mexican-, Jewish-, African-, and Japanese-American populations, engaged one another and defined their strategies in relation to each other as well as to the dominant society. In mid-century Los Angeles civil rights activism was, by necessity, cooperative; collaboration was crucial for survival. Diverse residents of Los Angeles seeking greater equality came to recognize that shared goals frequently could best be pursued collectively.

Roybal's election illustrates that the roots of interracial civil rights campaigns in the city predate the high civil rights era of the mid-1950s to 1960s. In fact, this interracial political activism emerged in the 1930s and built momentum during World War II when clever activists used the country's wartime imperatives to facilitate their struggles. They joined forces to argue that winning the war in Europe and Asia demanded greater civil rights at home. Due to their deep roots in the L.A. political landscape as well as their tactical move to distance themselves from radical critiques about U.S. domestic and foreign policy, many individuals and organizations were able to continue their work even in the inhospitable environment of the Cold War. They did this in part by continuing to use the international sphere, arguing that winning the war for hearts and minds against communism abroad meant promoting equality at home.

Bridges of Reform focuses on this interracial political activism among the city's unusually diverse racial and ethnic communities that helped make Los Angeles a civil rights center. Interracial collaboration in Los Angeles nurtured an emergent civil rights activism that bubbled outward, helping to build a foundation for later ethnic group-specific efforts and shape an emergent national political and legal civil rights transformation. Recognizing the persistent work of these liberal civil rights activists rehabilitates the place of their city as an integral part of the national struggle for racial equality. Moreover, the city in its multiracial diversity served as a bellwether that gave Americans a glimpse of where their soon-to-be multiracial nation would head in decades to come.[8]

Los Angeles's emergence as a center of collaborative civil rights activism was intrinsically linked to the United States' budding international agenda during the "American Century." Los Angeles became a multiracial and interracial civil rights hub largely because of the city's, and the nation's, rising international prominence during World War II and the Cold War. Because of its residents' diverse international connections, race relations in Los Angeles had far-reaching implications in places such as Japan and Mexico. Angelenos' diverse cultural, linguistic, and family connections to various international locations made them particularly aware of a broad range of global issues and events and, particularly, of the ways these could be employed to both hinder and facilitate local civil rights struggles. For many, their international connections and experiences fueled their domestic equality campaigns. The city's Pacific and Latin American border location helped civil rights activism emerge as a political force. The equality struggles of its Mexican-descent population, for instance, built upon radical traditions of the Mexican Revolution. In the meantime, a rising tide of anti-Semitism that seeped into Los Angeles from Hitler's rise to power in Europe spurred the city's Jewish activists to action.[9]

Local activists were able to build upon the critical mass of diverse American and immigrant workers whom wartime mobilization drew to the Pacific-front city, and to the West in general, to fuel its booming defense industry. Migrants from the South, the Midwest, and the East, as well as immigrants from Mexico, flooded in to take advantage of the region's thriving economy. The federal government facilitated this growth in order to shore up defense fortification against Asia in the wake of Pearl Harbor and, later, the rise of Communist China. By the beginning of the Cold War, the United States had about 300 military bases and installations west of the Mississippi.[10]

As Los Angeles entered the national and international spotlight, conflicts among its increasingly diverse populations took on new significance, which multiracial activists used to make common cause and advance their pro-equality agendas. Mexican-, Jewish-, African-, Japanese-, and Anglo-American activists recognized that local and national officials feared that incidents of racism endangered the city's defense production capacities and damaged the United States' global reputation. The 1942 Sleepy Lagoon and 1943 Zoot Suit events exposed deep anti-Mexican discrimination and drew negative international attention, especially from Latin American countries. They jeopardized both domestic unity and the support of allies like Mexico for whom these incidents illuminated the United States' hypocrisy of fighting a "good war" against Hitler's racism yet permitting racial discrimination at home.

Members of the wartime African-American organization the Negro Victory Committee were among those who, recognizing such potential consequences, used the war as leverage for their civil rights demands. African Americans arguing for the Double V campaign against discrimination abroad and at home made increasingly common cause with their fellow Angelenos of all races. In this way, activists forged lasting interracial connections as they teamed up to use Los Angeles's and the nation's growing stature to advance an effective, collective pro-equality agenda. Their calls reached ever more receptive ears, as the pressure to support the war effort heightened white Angelenos' interest in preventing and resolving interethnic conflicts.

After the war ended, many activists adapted their domestic equality agendas to the Cold War climate, using language and approaches attuned to anticommunist imperatives as the United States asserted itself against the Soviet Union. Improving housing, education, and employment options as well as neighborhood conditions would bolster L.A. minorities against communist attempts at using discrimination to win support. Showing that democracy lived up to its own ideals would also help undermine Soviet propaganda in Latin America, Asia, and Europe, which used U.S. discrimination to make a case for communism's superiority. To survive the conservative scrutiny of the Cold War, these reformers distanced themselves from communists and fellow travelers (those who sympathized or cooperated with the Communist Party without actively joining) who had been welcome allies in earlier and more politically inclusive struggles. They continued to promote a domestic equality agenda substantially similar to earlier agendas, and maintained some old bridges while building new ones with "legitimate" (anticommunist) allies from other ethno-racial communities and from the staunchly anticommunist Catholic Church to reinforce their own reputation.[11] Roybal was one of the many Angelenos who used anticommunism to reinforce his calls for increasing minority rights as well as to reach across ethno-racial community divides for support.

Beyond its ethno-racial diversity and heightened national and global status, Los Angeles's cultural and political history also made it a fertile place for civil rights activism. The presence of Hollywood added to the city's domestic and international relevance and helped make it a civil rights center. The film industry—which played an important role in the United States' global struggles for ideological control against fascism and communism—provided ideological ammunition to local civil rights activists. Furthermore, Los Angeles had been a hub for activists from both extremes of the political spectrum, including fascists, antifascists, communists, and anticommunists since the early 1920s. The second largest communist population in the United States (after New York City) was based in Los Angeles during the early years of the Cold War.[12] The city was also among the first in the nation to pass a local communist registration ordinance, which required members, sympathizers, and affiliated organizations of the Communist Party to register with the government, supposedly in the interest of public safety. It became a major target of the California Legislature's Un-American Activities Committee, one of the earliest and most active such state committees in the country.[13] Such ideological intensity further complicated the lives of L.A. residents negotiating an already complex racial environment. The struggle to define an acceptable civil rights identity and politically feasible agenda in this hyper "all-American" context, often under the scrutiny of an international spotlight, was a particularly strategic—and potentially fruitful—endeavor.

Who exactly *were* the interracial civil rights activists at work in Los Angeles? Sometimes they were everyday people who shared neighborhoods, social venues, and workplaces. But more often cooperation occurred among leaders of community organizations who, in many cases, had greater political and economic resources than their fellow ethnoracial community members. Often neighborhood and informal social ties among the city's ethnic populations loosened over time as the city became increasingly segregated, particularly in the postwar period.[14] But political coalitions emerging from neighborhoods and workplaces continued even as social and neighborhood ties waned.

Activists who built bridges with other racial and ethnic communities were rooted in organizations like the National Association for the Advancement of Colored People (NAACP), the Jewish Community Relations Committee (CRC), the Mexican-American Community Service Organization (CSO), and the Japanese American Citizens League (JACL).[15] They included individuals like the attorney and NAACP member Loren Miller, who was raised in Nebraska and Kansas by a black (former slave) father and white mother and who migrated to Los Angeles in 1929 to pursue journalism after graduating from law school. Jewish Americans like CRC members Leon Lewis, a World War I veteran transplanted from Chicago, who became the organization's first executive director; World War II veteran Fred Herzberg who succeeded Lewis; and Joseph Roos, an

Austrian Jewish immigrant who inherited the position in the postwar era, also helped form this community of persistent activists. Mexican Americans like Edward Roybal and Anthony Ríos, whose early involvement with the Congress of Industrial Organization's Steel Workers Organizing Committee later launched him into activism with the CSO, were crucial players. Japanese-American representatives from the JACL participated too, though less frequently. Their trajectories were different from the other groups in part because of their wartime internment, which often made them wary about political involvement.

By the start of the Cold War, these civil rights activists and organizations had gained some access to mainstream politics and were accepted as the "legitimate" representatives of marginalized groups, which afforded them some degree of political leverage. They could not fully represent their diverse ethnic and racial communities, but people with dominant political power viewed them as representative. As a result, they had a voice, albeit an often small one, in local, state, and even national political circles. They generally operated within the established political framework to achieve their goals, rather than urging a change in the system itself. By contrast, more seemingly radical groups like the Civil Rights Congress and the Los Angeles Committee for the Protection of the Foreign Born, which also pursued collaborative interracial activism in the postwar era, had limited influence due to their close connections—and sometimes overlap with— communists and their associates. *Bridges of Reform* follows the paths of those who gained at least limited political access rather than their more marginalized counterparts. Many of its subjects were middle class, while others came from working-class backgrounds, revealing that civil rights initiatives in Los Angeles reflected collaboration not only among ethno-racial communities, but also to some degree between classes.

While this book brings together these various groups and individuals under one umbrella, it nevertheless recognizes their unequal power and influence. Their power depended on various factors including racial status, economic position, and geographic location. Los Angeles's Jewish Americans, for instance, usually had greater access to political and economic resources than African Americans, some of whom in turn had more access than Mexican Americans. The power imbalances they experienced partly explain their collaboration, as this story explains.

Though interracial civil rights coalitions were rather common in the city during the mid-twentieth century, they were not the most typical form of interaction among Los Angeles's various minority communities. Conflict frequently marked relations. Whether coalitions were rare or common is not the important question here, but rather their significance and long-term import. Interracial cooperation influenced civil rights outcomes and trajectories disproportionate to the number of people involved. Such cooperation shaped the public consciousness on civil rights, fostered careers, and generated influential local and national civil rights initiatives and even victories that, though limited, represented significant transformations.[16]

The African-American activist Loren Miller, the mainly Mexican-American civil rights organization the CSO, and the Jewish Community Relations Committee (CRC) illustrate particularly well the complex interconnections that characterized Los Angeles civil rights. Miller first found his civil rights footing in Los Angeles in the 1930s and increasingly collaborated across racial divides during World War II and the early Cold War. An NAACP member, he served as chair of the CSO's Legal Aid Committee and frequently collaborated with Jewish community organizations. Miller exemplifies the transition of a group of activists who worked with others across the left political spectrum, including communists, during the 1930s, but by the early Cold War came to establish their legitimacy by asserting anticommunism. While Miller praised the Soviet system after visiting the USSR in 1932, he adopted an anticommunist approach during and after World War II. This new stance gained him postwar political access and paved the way for his central role in achieving Supreme Court victories such as *Barrows v. Jackson*, the 1953 housing case that made it illegal to bring damage suits against those who broke restrictive covenants, and *Brown v. the Board of Education*, the decision that outlawed public school segregation. Miller's experience typifies the emergence of an anticommunist activist community that was increasingly cautious about political labels but that continued to work together to pursue long-time goals.

The CSO, formed in Los Angeles in 1947, was the first lasting civil rights organization serving the city's Mexican-origin population.[17] The collaboration that helped form and sustain the CSO reveals that its activism was substantially interracial, including African-American, Jewish-American, and Anglo-American members and supporters.[18] The CSO largely shared the agendas of the 1930s and World War II–era civil rights networks from which it emerged, including fighting for improved employment and housing and against police brutality. Like Miller, the CSO distanced itself publicly from previous allies whose sympathy for communists and fellow travelers cast them as unacceptably radical, including the well-known California racial justice activist Carey McWilliams.

The Jewish community's CRC was one of the organizations key to the CSO's emergence and survival in its early years. Founded in 1933, the CRC initially focused on defending L.A. Jews from rising anti-Semitism. By World War II its members recognized that joining forces with other struggling minority groups would help Jews better achieve shared goals, including eliminating housing and employment discrimination as well as combating racism and anti-Semitism in general, and they began to link themselves with the NAACP and other minority organizations. During the Cold War, the CRC maintained mainstream credibility for its interracial civil rights efforts by distancing itself from more radical-seeming organizations like the Jewish Peoples Fraternal Order (JPFO), a communist-affiliated workers organization.[19] At the same time, it continued to collaborate with "acceptable" organizations from other minority communities, including the NAACP and the newly formed CSO. In the postwar era the CRC assisted the CSO by providing financial assistance, counsel, and institutional support for its struggles against police brutality and political marginalization, and for neighborhood, housing, and employment equity.

The centrality of the CRC and the Jewish community more generally to L.A. civil rights struggles indicates the importance of including this ethno-racial group in this study. Jews were among the most active civil rights advocates in mid-century Los Angeles in part because of their status between mainstream society and more marginalized minorities, which they often used to their own, and sometimes other minorities,' advantage. By distinguishing between color and race, Jews' in-between status becomes clear.[20] While L.A. Jews were always colored white and therefore had privileges of whiteness such as full citizenship and naturalization, as late as the mid-twentieth century they continued to face exclusions in housing, employment, and other realms on the basis of their racial undesirability.

Moreover, recognizing Jews' role in cooperative mid-century civil rights campaigns helps uncover a previously hidden element of postwar American liberalism. Historians have tended to simply characterize Jewish Americans' participation as white involvement.[21] But lumping Jewish and white activism together has led to the conclusion that white Americans, especially outside the South, were becoming increasingly liberal on racial issues in this era. While this conclusion has merit—more whites *were* becoming more racially liberal—identifying substantial parts of this "white" activism as Jewish activism reveals that many of these initiatives were more pragmatic and self-interested than conclusions about a general mounting "white liberalism" would indicate. Without discounting liberal whites' efforts, this study demonstrates that some efforts previously interpreted as "benevolent" white initiatives symbolizing an increasingly liberal community were actually attempts by Jews reacting to discrimination. One of the overarching points of *Bridges of Reform* is that pragmatism characterized mid-century civil rights coalitions for all participants, Jewish, white, and otherwise.[22]

The paths of organizations and activists like the CSO, Miller, and others also underscore how the city's civil rights shaped the nation. Miller's central involvement in nationwide legal housing and education reforms, for instance, demonstrates the broader influence of Los Angeles's civil rights community and also exposes the interracial roots of what have been considered mainly African-American struggles. The CSO fostered the work of César Chávez and Dolores Huerta, two founders of the Chicano movement and driving forces behind the national farm workers' movement. The CSO's Anglo executive director Fred Ross trained Chávez directly.

Earl Warren's road from California governor to chief justice of the U.S. Supreme Court further illustrates the national significance of the interracial civil rights agenda emerging from Los Angeles and California more generally. Warren's 1954 role in overturning over half a century of "separate but equal doctrine" in *Brown v. Board of Education* needs no explanation. The California roots of his thought, however, are less well understood. As governor of the Golden State from 1943 to 1953, Warren witnessed the success of interracial coalitions in contesting Mexican-American schoolchildren's segregation. In 1947, he signed a law repealing the last California school segregation statute. Warren's support for racial reform in California stopped short of what many activists hoped for, and on certain issues in which he played a central role, like Japanese Americans' internment, racism clearly motivated him. Warren's career trajectory nonetheless makes visible the imprint of collaborative California initiatives upon national outcomes.

The stories of people like Miller, Warren, Roybal, Chávez, Huerta, and many others less well known reveal that the city's and state's struggles were central to the national narrative. Los Angeles and California fostered multiracial movements and the careers of individuals whose visions helped shape twentieth-century U.S. equality struggles and their policy outcomes. In this way, *Bridges of Reform* helps shift the history of race, and specifically civil rights, in the United States from its traditional black/white center to one that incorporates multiracial realities.[23] In the process it helps make the case for what one historian calls a geographically "wide," as well as a long, civil rights movement.[24]

Through the lens of Miller and the NAACP, the CRC, and the CSO's experiences, the relationship between civil rights and the Cold War becomes more complex than dominant understandings about it as a purely repressive era have allowed.[25] In many respects the standard narrative of repression and lost opportunities is accurate. The intensification of domestic and international anticommunism undoubtedly put pressure on existing coalitions, often tearing them apart by pushing fearful activists to marginalize or even purge onetime allies whose connection, or apparent connection, to the Communist Party made them "dangerous."[26] Many individuals and organizations were devastated, and careers and lives derailed. Countless numbers of people were alienated from friends and colleagues, never found work again, and even committed suicide after brutal red-baiting investigations into their political, professional, and personal lives. Los Angeles communists like Dorothy Healey and nine others—together called the Los Angeles Ten—were detained, and eight of them (including Healey) were sentenced to a year in jail for refusing to surrender information about the Communist Party. After CP activist Serril Gerber was fired from his job as a sixth-grade teacher for refusing to tell the House Un-American Activities Committee (HUAC) whether he was a communist, people threw things at his house, neighbors forbade their children from playing with his son, and his daughter became constantly fearful.[27] Even the city's longtime mayor, Fletcher Bowron, was voted out of office after almost fifteen years because he had supported public housing, which opponents cast as communist.

Furthermore, the liberal civil rights reformers who persisted during the Cold War strayed from earlier agendas and from their more "radical" counterparts in terms of their stance on civil liberties and foreign policy. They often acquiesced to civil liberties violations like free speech, freedom of expression, and freedom of political affiliation, and marginalized former allies further left on the political spectrum. Unlike more radical L.A. organizations like the Civil Rights Congress or the Los Angeles Committee for the Protection of the Foreign Born (LACPFB) they barely protested Cold War legislation such as the antilabor Taft-Hartley Act of 1947, the McCarran Internal Security Act of 1950, and city, state, and county loyalty oaths.[28] Their embrace of Cold War anticommunism led those who earlier had maintained anticolonial critiques of U.S. foreign policy to abandon this stance. The NAACP, for instance, shifted from critiquing imperialism in Africa to supporting, tacitly or actively, anti-Soviet, anticommunist, pro-western European democracy international policy stances like the Marshall Plan and containment more generally.[29] The CSO differed from the Asociación Nacional México-Americana (ANMA), another postwar Mexican-descent civil rights group, in this respect too. While the CSO used the Cold War as a tool for arguing for domestic equality, the ANMA flouted U.S. foreign policy by supporting the global peace movement and advocating an end to the Cold War. The ANMA opposed U.S. attempts to overthrow the popularly elected government of Guatemala and supported labor struggles in Chile, Bolivia, and Peru, as well as Fidel Castro's Cuban liberation movement. The marginalized radicals like those in the Civil Rights Congress, the LACPFB, and the ANMA were more willing than liberals to collaborate across the left spectrum—working with communists, socialists, and others outside the dominant two-party system—and more willing to critique U.S. foreign policy when it was at odds with their vision of global racial equality.

Still, nostalgia for a "lost left" has often blinded many from seeing nuances of what actually did occur during the Cold War era. If "liberals" and "radicals" diverged on civil liberties and foreign policy issues, they often were not so different in terms of their domestic racial equality agendas. The actual civil rights goals of Los Angeles's radical activists, who did not advocate overthrowing the U.S. government and followed a reformist rather than revolutionary civil rights path, resembled those of people considered liberals. If anything, the two differed in their approach to achieving such goals, with the radicals more likely to use direct confrontation tactics, such as street protests, and liberals more likely to work behind the scenes through politics, legislation, and the courts. But postwar liberal organizations like the NAACP, CSO, CRC, and JACL and their members, who believed minorities could be incorporated without major social or institutional change, significantly maintained earlier civil rights commitments despite their adoption of anticommunism. Their racial liberalism, in other words, did not reflect a drastic departure from the past, nor from their radical contemporaries.[30] Ultimately, postwar liberals' historical characterization as sellouts by radicals and by historians sympathetic to the radical perspective does not reflect their domestic civil rights stance, the profound effect that their tactics had on civil rights outcomes, or the reform-oriented nature of many of their predecessors. Their mask of global Cold War anticommunism enabled them to join forces and continue crucial elements of earlier domestic racial equality reform agendas and initiatives.[31] A persistent reform thread that emerged out of the 1930s continued during this "lost era" of civil rights supposedly marked only by decline and lost possibilities. *Bridges of Reform* in this way redefines and rehabilitates Cold War civil rights.

Racial equality activists were not the only ones to gain their footing in Los Angeles, and from there to disproportionately influence national civil rights developments. The gay rights movement, which emerged in significant ways from early 1950s Los Angeles, also exposes the role that city played in shaping national equal rights movements. The Mattachine Society, a key foundational organization in that movement, was created in the city during the winter of 1950–51. Moreover, Los Angeles's gay rights movement partially built its own struggle out of local racial justice networks, and gay activists modeled their calls upon L.A. racial minority activists' claims to full citizenship. Their activism also forces a rethinking of the early Cold War as a purely repressive era.[32]

Though Los Angeles was exceptional in its multiracial extremity and in its national civil rights influence, the city was not qualitatively different in terms of fostering an interracial community of activists during the early to mid-twentieth century. Evidence suggests that collaboration was a hallmark of nationwide urban civil rights activism. For example, the Congress of Racial Equality (CORE), one of the most important civil rights organizations to emerge from World War II, originated in black and white cooperation in Chicago in 1942.[33] The American Council on Race Relations, founded in Chicago in 1944, was also interracial.[34] New York, Denver, the San Francisco Bay Area, Miami, and other urban areas' histories hint at burgeoning mid-century interracial activism elsewhere.[35] Preliminary evidence suggests that northern and western American cities in particular operated as laboratories for cooperative civil rights campaigns.[36] But collaborative activism in Los Angeles was more marked than elsewhere given its unique patterns of wartime migration and resulting ethno-racial diversity, as well as the fact that no single minority group overshadowed the others in terms of numbers or influence. These diverse populations also undoubtedly found that they had more leverage than activists elsewhere, given the city's special importance as a defense production site and its exposed Pacific Rim location.[37] Los Angeles activists emerged from a particularly multiracial milieu and they seem to have influenced national trends more than their contemporary activists.

To trace this history, *Bridges of Reform* is organized chronologically. Chapter 1, "Los Angeles, the Early Years," provides a brief history of Los Angeles before the 1930s, setting the background for the city's rise to prominence in the region and nation and describing its racial landscape. Chapters 2 and 3 examine the World War II period, beginning with the wars in Europe and Asia in the 1930s and continuing through 1945. As chapter 2, "Shadows of War, Forces for Change," shows, the 1930s was a decade during which activists gained their civil rights footing and began cooperative initiatives. The mounting tide of racism and anti-Semitism heightened minorities' awareness of the threats facing them and increased their interest in protecting themselves individually and collectively. Chapter 3, "The War Comes Home," demonstrates how American entry into World War II accelerated domestic interracial civil rights activism, and the way the country's war aims provided leverage for domestic efforts.

Chapters 4 and 5 examine the early years of the Cold War, an era whose political context facilitated the activity of those reformers who decided to work within the confines of the U.S. political agenda. Chapter 4, "Cold Warriors of a Different Stripe," explores how activists collaborated less across the spectrum of left political labels in light of postwar demographic shifts, increasing discrimination, and especially growing anticommunist activities. Cold War coalition builders were careful to publicly welcome only those reformers willing to adopt an anticommunist stance, or at least distance themselves from communism, but they also challenged extreme red-baiters by formulating a persistent, all-American, democratic civil rights activism. "The Community Service Organization and Interracial Civil Rights Activism in the Cold War Era," chapter 5, illustrates through the CSO how this moderately framed Cold War civil rights activism was by definition collaborative, and how it carried on substantial elements of the racial equality agendas of reformers from earlier eras, involving some of the same activists.

The final chapter, "Los Angeles to the Nation," highlights the national significance of Los Angeles reform efforts. It analyzes how the city's interracial activists incubated strategies and agendas that shaped the contours of civil rights movements, reforms, and policy at the state and national levels. It also demonstrates how Cold War activism bridged earlier initiatives to the 1960s and afterward. The 1930s, World War II, and Cold War alliances later helped mold ethnic-specific local, state, and national developments, revealing the latter's interracial L.A. roots. The conclusion reflects on both the lasting significance and simultaneous shortcomings of this mid-century interracial activism, as well on challenges and opportunities modern Americans face as a multiracial nation.

This story of pragmatic interracial activists who emerged in Los Angeles during the 1930s and persisted during the early Cold War is not as heroic a view of civil rights history as protestors and sit-ins and nonviolent marches on Washington. Those activists unwilling to give in to Cold War pressures and/or abandon their former allies certainly seem more admirable. Yet those activists who built bridges with other minority groups and with the political mainstream quietly elucidate the relationship between wartime and conservative political climates and social reform. They also demonstrate how crucial L.A. alliances were to the mid-century emergence and perseverance of national civil rights struggles—and how pragmatic and interest-based such alliances were. How multiracial activist communities in Los Angeles strategized to achieve a society that would offer greater opportunities for peoples of all races and ethnicities may offer some examples for twenty-first-century Americans living in a multiracial nation that increasingly resembles mid-twentieth-century Los Angeles. As in the earlier period, the challenge for present-day social justice activists is to find common ground among diverse populations with often conflicting needs and demands. Americans once again wonder whether Rodney King and the 1992 L.A. riots—which seem to have continued the trend of race violence marked by the mid-century's Zoot Suit Riots and the 1965 Watts Riots—or the election of Villaraigosa and the rise to the presidency of a biracial black and white man named Barack Obama on a wave of multiracial support serve as clearer indications of our multiracial nation's future.

CHAPTER 1

Los Angeles, the Early Years

Mid-twentieth-century Los Angeles civil rights activism emerged in a city in conflict. Despite the city's historical reputation as a place of relative freedom—at least compared to the areas of the South and West from which many of its migrants came, Los Angeles's minority groups faced increasing marginalization during the late nineteenth century and the early decades of the twentieth century.

Southern California attracted many newcomers with its promise of cheap land, sunshine, beautiful beaches, and good health. What had been little more than a small western town grew in the late nineteenth century into an increasingly important population and business center. The Southern Pacific Railroad completed the first transcontinental connection to the city through San Francisco in 1876, and the Santa Fe Railroad arrived in 1886, linking Los Angeles with eastern markets. Lured by railroad promoters and other land speculators, many people, particularly native-born white Americans, flocked to the region. The city's population increased fourfold in the 1880s, from 11,183 in 1880 to 50,395 in 1890, a rate of growth higher than any other city in the country at the time. Then, between 1900 and 1930, Los Angeles grew from a town of 102,000 to a metropolis of 1.2 million people.[1]

The city's earlier racial landscape had been a collage of mestizos (the products of racial mixing in colonial New Spain), African-origin people, Europeans (including Jews), and Amerindians, even after the region's acquisition by the United States in 1848.[2] But by the 1860s white Americans became the majority and, in subsequent years, "minority" groups lost much of the influence they previously had asserted.[3] *Californios*, the ranch-owning class from before the Mexican War, lost cultural dominance and political power in the wake of the 1848 Treaty of Guadalupe Hidalgo. The treaty concluded the Mexican War and ushered in the United States' annexation of California and other current southwestern states. It also began the increasing social, political, and economic exclusion of Mexican-origin people by white migrants who soon became the dominant population.[4] Meanwhile, groups like Jews, who earlier had asserted some measure of social and political influence, lost stature as they became overwhelmed by large numbers of native-born white Protestants who inundated the region.[5]

The period between 1860 and 1930 brought mostly white, native-born migrants to southern California. The main population influx, especially by the first decades of the twentieth century, consisted of white Protestant midwesterners who "brought with them their middle western ties and their sentiments and habits, and changed the ethnic landscape of Los Angeles," according to Los Angeles historians Max Vorspan and Lloyd Gartner.[6] In this way, early twentieth-century Los Angeles was different from most industrialized cities in the East that had attracted large numbers of European immigrants and African-American migrants. Between 1900 and 1930 Los Angeles's foreign-born population never grew to more than 20 percent and its proportion of native-born whites was one of the three highest in the United States.[7] Seventy-seven percent of Los Angeles's population was native-born white in 1910. While that percentage decreased somewhat by 1930, it was still higher than most other cities, including San Francisco.[8]

Still, the nonwhite and immigrant populations began to grow in the early twentieth century, starting Los Angeles's transformation from a relatively homogeneous, native-born, white Protestant city to the multi-racial metropolis it became by the mid-twentieth century. The number of nonwhite or foreign-born white residents increased fifteenfold from 1900 to 1930 (from 22,000 to almost 350,000).[9] The region's economic growth drew African-American, Mexican, Asian, and European migrants to meet industrial and unskilled labor demands. They built the railroads, worked in construction, and planted the extensive agricultural land.[10]

Molokan Russians, Italians, and Chinese migrated to Los Angeles in the first decades of the twentieth century. From 1918 to the early 1930s, the population of Molokan Russians, observant Christians who fled Russian military conscription during the Sino-Japanese War and the upheaval of the 1905 Revolution, doubled in population (from 3,300).[11] The outbreak of the Great War in Europe sent over 10,000 Italian immigrants to the city. Even after the United States enacted legislation restricting immigration of Eastern and Southern Europeans in 1924, the Italian population kept growing, to about 36,000 by 1934.[12] By the early twentieth century, Los Angeles's Chinese population was still small, especially relative to San Francisco, where most of the American Chinese population settled after being lured to California by the 1849 Gold Rush. Moreover, the Chinese presence in Los Angeles paled next to other immigrant groups because of immigration restrictions and low birthrates. Los Angeles Chinese, however, did form a Chinatown near the center of town.[13]

Mexicans, Japanese, Jews, and African Americans were the most numerous and visible minority migrant groups to arrive in Los Angeles in this era. Mexicans were the largest, most geographically widespread, and fastest growing of these groups. The Mexican-origin population, already present in the region from the days it was part of the Spanish Empire, increased after 1900 when rising population pressures and unemployment in Mexico boosted the flow of Mexicans to the United States. The population exodus especially grew after the 1910 collapse of the Porfirio Díaz dictatorship and the start of the Mexican Revolution. A booming economy in Southern California and the increasing need for unskilled labor in the region attracted tens of thousands of Mexicans to the area.[14]

Japanese migration to the city began in the late nineteenth century. Although the 1907 Gentleman's Agreement and other immigration restrictions in the early twentieth century strictly limited the influx of Japanese to the United States, Los Angeles's population kept growing even after 1908 as Japanese from elsewhere in California and the rest of the country came to the city, in part because they were forced out of San Francisco by the 1906 earthquake and fire.[15]

Initially, many of the nineteenth-century Jewish migrants to Los Angeles had been better-off merchants, peddlers, and businesspeople. Those who came from the East Coast and from Europe between 1900 and World War II were poorer, especially after the 1913 opening of the Panama Canal allowed more impoverished European migrants access to the West. And an influx of poor Jews from the war-torn European continent continued to arrive in Los Angeles during World War I. But most Jewish immigrants to Los Angeles came first through eastern cities, particularly New York, rather than arriving directly from Eastern Europe.[16] By 1919, Los Angeles's Jewish population had shifted from largely West Coast–born to increasingly East Coast- and foreign-born.[17]

African Americans' presence in Los Angeles by the early decades of the twentieth century was small. Some arrived in the mid-nineteenth century with the Spaniards, others with the Americans in the war with Mexico, and still more came with the land boom after 1880. The Southern Pacific Railroad brought 2,000 more to Los Angeles in 1903 to break a strike by Mexican-American construction workers, but African Americans continued to comprise a small proportion of the city's rapidly growing population.[18] The city's black population nonetheless was the largest black urban community west of Texas as early as 1910, despite its relatively small numbers.[19]

By 1930, Japanese, Jews, Mexicans, and African Americans composed approximately 19 to 26 percent of the city's population (see chart). Around 60,000 southern and eastern Europeans also resided in the city.[20] Whereas most eastern and midwestern cities were largely divided between native-born white Americans and white European immigrants, in Los Angeles divisions were between an overwhelming native white

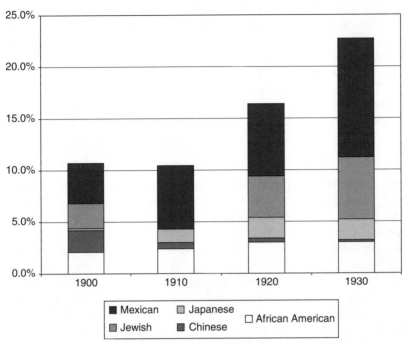

Sources: United States Bureau of the Census, *Twelfth Census of the United States Taken in the Year 1900, Population: Part I* (Washington, D.C.: U.S. Government Printing Office, 1901), 609; United States Bureau of the Census, *Thirteenth Census of the United States Taken in the Year 1910, Volume II: Population 1910* (Washington, D.C.: U.S. Government Printing Office, 1910), 180; United States Bureau of the Census, *Fourteenth Census of the United States Taken in the Year 1920, Vol. II: Population 1920, General Report and Analytical Tables* (Washington, D.C.: U.S. Government Printing Office, 1922), 47; United States Bureau of the Census, *Fifteenth Census of the United States: 1930 Population, Vol. III, Part 1* (Washington, D.C.: U.S. Government Printing Office, 1932), 61–3. It is difficult to attain an accurate Mexican population count for the early twentieth-century as, with the exception of 1930, they were not classified in a separate category. Scholars disagree as to the exact numbers of the Los Angeles population. Estimates in 1900 range from 3,000 to 5,000, in 1910 from 9,678 to 29,738, in 1920 from 29,757 to 50,000, and in 1930 from 97,116 to 190,000. The chart uses the average for each year. Estimates come from Camarillo, *Chicanos in a Changing Society*, 200. The figures for Jews are also estimates, as the census did not keep track of population by this characteristic; there are no figures available for 1910, so they do not factor into the chart that year. See Vorspan and Gartner, *History of the Jews of Los Angeles*, 109.

majority and a sizable nonwhite minority. European immigrants were not as noticeable a presence in Los Angeles as they were elsewhere, while nonwhite groups like Asians and Mexicans, as well as African Americans, were visible. Even on the diverse West Coast, Los Angeles was different, according to historian Robert Fogelson. "Nowhere on the Pacific coast, not even in cosmopolitan San Francisco, was there so diverse a mixture of racial groups, [and] so visible a contrast...as in Los Angeles."[21] In Los Angeles, these groups tended to live nearer to each other, in the same neighborhoods, and to attend the same schools than they did elsewhere. This proximity remained characteristic throughout the 1930s, and into the 1940s.[22]

Many newcomers came to the city for the chance to fulfill their dreams of greater opportunity and equality. Migrants from other parts of the country believed they would find less discrimination in the West, and scholars in recent years have shown that discrimination was indeed less fixed in the nineteenth- and early twentieth-century West than it was in the South, urban North, and Midwest.[23] African Americans migrating to Los Angeles found a less rigid and racially hierarchical society than the one they had known in Texas and Louisiana. African Americans who came to Los Angeles in the first decades of the twentieth century were lured by "lifestyle opportunities," while they tended to migrate to other cities for jobs.[24] Even through the 1930s, the city seemed like an improvement over southern areas from which black migrants came and northern areas where many friends had moved—it was not as racially segregated as southern, northern, and midwestern cities, homes were nicer and less expensive, and educational opportunities were better.[25] Los Angeles schools compared favorably to northern schools and provided better facilities (as well as integrated schools) for black children than those in the South. Los Angeles schools with large black student bodies received significantly more funding than predominantly black southern schools, even though schools in predominantly white L.A. suburbs received higher allotments.[26] Of all U.S. cities with more than 25,000 African Americans, Los Angeles had the highest proportion of black children in school. Approximately 34 percent of African Americans owned homes by the late 1920s, compared to 15 percent in Detroit, just over 10 percent in Chicago, and slightly more than 5 percent in New York.[27]

Upon arrival, though, racial and ethnic minorities found they had set their hopes too high. This was a "tenuous paradise," according to historian Josh Sides, because although African Americans in Los Angeles enjoyed certain advantages, they still confronted discrimination. The advantages they did find are attributable to plentiful urban space and low population density—and thus less competition—in this pre–World War II period, rather than to enlightened racial attitudes.[28] Jim Crow's presence and discrimination in general made themselves known to African Americans and the city's other diverse residents throughout the first decades of the twentieth century.

Widespread employment discrimination relegated minorities to the lowest occupational categories. Sixty-four percent of Mexicans worked in low-paying blue-collar jobs in 1910, 69 percent in 1920, and 68 percent in 1930. Mexican labor predominated in the railroad and electric railway systems, in construction and building supply industries, in public works and utilities industries, and in service industries, where they faced discrimination. The California Immigration Commission reported that in 1910 the railroads paid Mexican workers approximately 25 percent less than other workers including Greeks, Japanese, and others. A new commercial and industrial boom in Los Angeles during World War I brought Mexican labor into new areas of work, especially the rubber, steel, meat packing, food canning, and auto industries, but these were still blue-collar jobs. After the war most Los Angeles Mexican-origin men and women continued in the blue-collar sector, in bakeries, slaughter and packing houses, textile factories, paper and printing establishments, laundries, hotels, and wholesale and retail trade establishments. By 1930, while many worked in the nearby fields in agriculture at least some of the time, the majority were employed in urban occupations.[29]

African Americans faced even worse employment discrimination than Mexicans, because racist employers often preferred Mexican workers.[30] African Americans worked mostly as construction workers, maintenance people for the Southern Pacific and the Santa Fe Railroads, or as porters, cooks, waiters, and maids. Sometimes they worked in Hollywood in service jobs or even as actors, but always in roles that reflected their subservient work status.[31] Most unions excluded blacks, which compounded their limited job prospects.[32]

Asian-origin residents also faced employment discrimination that limited their employment options. Most Chinese by the early 1930s worked in the vegetable and fruit wholesale business, as domestic servants, or in stores, laundries, restaurants, and hotels. A few were professionals, while some owned small businesses.[33] Many of the original Japanese migrants to Southern California were railroad contract laborers on the Southern Pacific and Santa Fe railroads, but, as the railroads increasingly gave preference to Mexican workers, the Japanese community took root in Los Angeles and residents increasingly rented land and began vegetable farming. Some owned businesses in the Japanese neighborhood Little Tokyo. By the 1930s the majority in the Japanese-origin community of Los Angeles were farmers and farm laborers.[34]

Unlike Asians, Jews migrating to the area in the mid- to late-nineteenth century had enjoyed relative integration and participation in Los

Angeles business and politics. But this harmony was short-lived. The combination of an increasing conservative white population and an influx of poorer Jewish populations ended this era, and Jews too faced intensifying discrimination. After World War I, in Los Angeles as in the rest of the United States, anti-Semitic incidents became increasingly common, disrupting the sense of the city as a tolerant place for Jews. Social clubs previously open to Jews began restricting their membership. Angelenos increasingly exposed their anti-Semitic stereotypes. Jews became more marginalized and lost the social and political inclusion they once enjoyed.[35] Restricted mobility for minorities accompanied the city's increasing cosmopolitanism.[36]

Los Angeles's extreme antilabor environment compounded minority and other workers' suffering in the first decades of the twentieth century. The organized labor movement met with great resistance in Los Angeles, where the antilabor climate was so extreme that one study on this subject went so far as to claim, "it is doubtful if the labor movement has ever faced antiunion employer groups so powerful and well organized as in Los Angeles."[37] The city was notorious for its repressive crackdowns on labor protesters. The roots of the city's open shop system were deep in the late nineteenth century, when local developers and leaders believed that gaining a competitive edge on San Francisco—whose Gold Rush–era boom gave it a solid lead on Los Angeles as the economic and industrial capital of the West—meant management dominating Los Angeles's workforce. Business interests worked to eliminate all interference with their control of labor. They began in 1892 by breaking the printing trade union after a bitter two-year strike. Subsequently, L.A. employers established the open shop, and by 1910 they gained a 20 to 30, sometimes even 40, percent wage differential over San Francisco employers.[38]

Organizations like the Better America Foundation (BAF, founded by bankers, businessmen, professionals, industrialists, and Protestant preachers in 1920), the Merchants and Manufacturers' Association (M&M), the Chamber of Commerce, and the police department disrupted trade unions, spying and informing on their activities and provoking violence. Central to such efforts was the powerful publisher of the *Los Angeles Times*, Harrison Grey Otis. Otis remained committed to the idea that an open shop was a crucial precondition for drawing business to the city and turning it into a major metropolis. The influential publisher controlled the Merchants and Manufacturers' Association (M&M) and the Chamber of Commerce, and the police department was generally at the disposal of both. Otis worked together with the M&M and the chamber during the first decades of the twentieth century to make Los Angeles the "white spot" of the nation—or a place of intense local economic development—by suppressing organized labor and other dissenters to their development plans. "White spot" also referred to

Chandler and his associates' belief that the city was aesthetically, politically, and morally pure. For other white Angelenos, it also signified racial purity, meaning that theirs was a city built by and for white Americans. While the *Times* worked to turn public opinion against unions, the M&M used blacklists, lockouts, and other strategies to keep labor down. The Chamber of Commerce promoted Los Angeles to investors by selling its open-shop manufacturing potential. The police enforced an unconstitutional antipicketing ordinance that the *Times's* hand-picked city council voted into law, and locked up 470 picketers in the period preceding the 1910 *Times* bombing.[39]

When Otis died in 1917, his successor and son-in-law Harry Chandler continued to champion the open shop, along with the BAF, the M&M, and others. Such organizations and individuals worked hard collectively through the 1920s to enforce an antiunion, open shop environment, and suppress radical thought throughout the city, in the workplace, politics, and elsewhere. They made Los Angeles a dangerous place for any dissenters.

Labor activists, powerless in the face of government inaction against abusive corporations in this era, responded to such campaigns in Los Angeles as they did elsewhere, with public shows of violence. In 1910, they bombed the *Los Angeles Times* building, targeting the institution that symbolized their struggle. The blasts shortly after one A.M. on October 1, 1910, destroyed the building, which erupted into flames when the bomb hit a gas pipeline. The McNamara brothers—James was a union bomber and John the secretary/treasurer of the International Association of Bridge and Structural—eventually confessed to the crime. They said they had not known about this pipeline and meant only to damage the building. But the explosion and ensuing fireball resulted in the deaths of twenty-one *Times* workers and seriously injured sixteen. The McNamaras' conviction in 1911 marked the beginning of two decades of total powerlessness for organized labor in Los Angeles.[40] The bombing turned the public against labor activists and enabled the business class to tighten the clamp on unions, and the open shop became more firmly entrenched than ever. By 1930 the open shop system had brought about an industrial output in the city that outranked San Francisco's by $153.7 million, Seattle's by $929.6 million, Portland's by $1.1 billion, and Denver's by $1.2 billion.[41]

For white workers, labor suppression was bad enough. But for minority workers, racially restrictive housing covenants, which became widespread by the 1920s, restricted their freedoms even more. The California Supreme Court in 1928 upheld the legality of restrictive covenants and also declared that blacks who lived in restricted neighborhoods before their implementation must vacate their residences.[42] Covenants affected Mexicans as well as blacks, limiting their choice of neighborhoods in

nearly every section of the city and surrounding areas. Covenants especially restricted poor, working-class Mexican immigrants, because real
estate agents and homeowners sometimes bent segregation laws for
Mexican residents of the "proper" class. Affluent and elite Mexicans like
Hollywood movie stars Ramon Novarro and Dolores del Rio were able to
move into more affluent and fashionable west-side neighborhoods.[43]
Housing restrictions also forced Chinese-origin people into concentrated
areas that became known as Chinatowns.[44] White residents in the early
1920s reacted violently to Los Angeles Japanese who tried to move into
their neighborhoods. They posted notices that the neighborhood was
off-limits to Japanese and threw stones at the house of one Japanese businessman, eventually forcing him to move. They burned down another
Japanese man's house in a white suburb, and after the police refused to
help him, eventually forced him to leave. Whites beat another Japanese
man in the same neighborhood when he refused to move. Similar incidents occurred throughout Los Angeles.[45] Jews increasingly faced
restrictive housing covenants too.

To make matters worse for the region's minority populations, the
American government—local, state, and federal—often condoned
discrimination against them. Institutionalized discrimination against immigrants, particularly Asians, Latin Americans, and Southern and Eastern
Europeans, resulted from a rise in nativism in Los Angeles and around the
country in the early twentieth century and became the norm by the 1930s.
Increasing immigration restriction reflected this tendency. Direct federal
action against Asian immigration and, by implication, against Asians in
America, began in 1882 with the passage of the first significant restrictive
immigration law, the Chinese Exclusion Act, which suspended the immigration of Chinese laborers to the United States.[46] In 1907–8 the
"Gentleman's Agreement" between Japan and the United States continued
to restrict Asian immigration, this time against the Japanese, by limiting
the number of Japanese laborers immigrating to the United States. In 1917,
the United States advanced its anti-Asian immigrant policies by creating
the Asiatic "barred zone," which declared natives of certain (predominantly
Asian) regions inadmissible. In 1922, Congress extended eighteenth-cen-
tury laws denying citizenship to Asian immigrants also to American women
who married them. The 1922 Act (the Cable Act) stated that any American
women who married an "alien ineligible to citizenship" would have her
citizenship revoked. The 1924 Immigration Act codified and broadened
restrictions in the 1917 Act by adding Japanese to the barred list and placing quotas on southern and eastern European immigration, tightly sealing
the "golden door." In California, the legislature in 1920 closed loopholes in
the 1913 Alien Land Act, now preventing Japanese immigrants not only
from owning land in their own name, but also in their children's names.[47]
Mexican Americans became increasingly subject to immigration restric-

tions with the 1917 passage of another immigration act that excluded illiterates and required a head tax.[48] The federal government's ongoing enforcement of the Supreme Court's 1896 decision in *Plessy v. Ferguson*, which condoned separate facilities for blacks and whites, revealed its support for separate—and effectively unequal—treatment for African Americans.

Reactions to an increase in worldwide radicalism—including the Mexican and Russian Revolutions of the 1910s—fanned the flames of this rising nativism. Americans feared foreign radicalism would contaminate their country by way of southern European, Asian, and Mexican immigrants. They associated foreigners with radicalism and persecuted them, sometimes violently, as nationwide incidents during the Red Scare of the late 1910s and early 1920s and the trial and execution of suspected Italian immigrant radicals Sacco and Vanzetti reveal.[49] In California the repression of labor leaders and radicals intensified to extreme levels from 1910 to the mid-1920s. Police action against the Industrial Workers of the World, socialists, and the remnants of the Partido Liberal Mexicano (PLM), an anarchist group whose leaders had fled Mexico to the United States in 1904, reflected these crackdowns.[50]

Both officials and citizens directed their nativism at various immigrant groups in Los Angeles. They feared that the 1910 Mexican Revolution's radicalism would seep into the United States, spreading a rebellion among southwestern Mexican Americans. Angelenos also worried about possible collaboration between Mexican Americans and Germany during the Great War. Their memory of the 1917 Zimmerman incident, when the United States intercepted a German telegram to Mexico promising financial aid and the return of Texas, New Mexico, and Arizona in exchange for Mexico's World War I alliance against the United States, heightened their fears. Historian Ricardo Romo referred to this general fear and repression directed at Mexicans living in Los Angeles as the "Brown Scare" of the 1910s.[51]

The repression of immigrants and suspected radicals revealed itself most clearly through the activities of Los Angeles's infamous Red Squad, the Los Angeles Police Department's special unit created to deal with "subversive activities," especially by communists and other radicals. Historian Mark Wild called the squad the "enforcement tool" for the city's antiradical elite, which monitored Communist Party and other leftists' affairs in the 1920s and especially in the 1930s, until its elimination in 1938 by the newly elected mayor Fletcher Bowron.[52] Police chief James E. Davis and the squad's head William Hynes led the organization, which developed a spy system to infiltrate Communist Party clubs and other Los Angeles radical groups. The Red Squad often targeted, harassed, and persecuted "unwanted" minorities as it pursued alleged communists and other radicals.[53]

Racist and nativist citizens' group activities complemented the Red Squad's activities. Los Angeles organizations and individuals collectively formed in 1919 a Los Angeles County Anti-Asiatic Society, which primarily targeted the Japanese community. Participants included the Native Sons of the Golden West, the American Legion, neighborhood associations, organizations of county and city civil servants, members of organized labor, and a few representatives from the Democratic and Republican county central committees.[54] Hate groups like the Ku Klux Klan intensified their activities in the late 1910s and 1920s as well, reflecting rising tensions in the City of Angels that resulted from the influx of both native white Protestant and minority and other immigrant populations who all jostled to create a place for themselves in an increasingly settled city.[55]

Minority groups did not sit idly by in the face of growing hostility. In the first decades of the twentieth century they formed various organizations to help themselves. To varying degrees, these early twentieth-century institutions helped minority groups economically, worked to instill ethno-racial community pride, and to some degree fought discrimination. The first civil rights organization per se in Los Angeles was the Forum, created in 1903 by the pastor of the First AME Church, the editor of the black newspaper *The Liberator*, and a local attorney. The Forum both challenged white Angelenos' discrimination against African Americans and worked to incorporate new residents into the community.[56] Los Angeles blacks created other organizations, including a local branch of the radical, black nationalist United Negro Improvement Association (UNIA). Started by Jamaican Marcus Garvey in Jamaica in 1914 and in New York City in 1918, the organization moved in 1920 to Los Angeles, which soon became the center of western Garveyism.[57] The NAACP formed as the first California state branch of the organization shortly after a 1913 visit to the city by W. E. B. DuBois, the organization's founder.[58] The Japanese community founded the Japanese Association of Los Angeles (originally the regional Central Japanese Association of Southern California) in 1906, six years after San Franciscans created the first branch in response to discrimination against Japanese residents. Among the Japanese Association of America's initiatives was hiring lawyers to try to invalidate the alien land laws that prevented Japanese immigrants from owning land. In the early 1930s the Japanese Association of Los Angeles merged with the 3,000 member Japanese Chamber of Commerce of Los Angeles to become the community's civic body, the Los Angeles Japanese Chamber of Commerce.[59]

Various Mexican-American organizations worked to meet the immigrant worker's needs, including housing, employment, and health care, as well as to maintain Mexican culture and values by promoting patriotic and religious festivals. They also fought to improve the status of the community by challenging discrimination. Some were patriotic clubs that worked to maintain Mexican patriotism and to follow social and political issues in Mexico, such as the Club Independencia and the Comisión Honorífica. La Alianza Hispano Americana, a popular voluntary association in Los Angeles and the Southwest, supposedly worked to protect the rights of Mexican Americans, though it was criticized by community members for devoting too much attention to social affairs. Cruz Azul (Blue Cross) was an all-women's *mutualista* (mutual aid society) that gave charitable aid and attended to residents' medical needs in the city in the 1920s. Other mutualistas provided opportunities for residents to help their neighbors in various ways. Newspapers served as organizing and information centers for the Spanish-speaking community, and included *La Prensa*, *El Heraldo*, and *La Opinión*.[60] Residents formed trade unions as well, including the Confederación de Uniones Obreras Mexicanas (CUOM), which helped improve working-class conditions.[61]

Jews too created a community support and defense infrastructure. It included mutual aid societies and organizations, such as the Hebrew Benevolent Society, the First Jewish Polish Society, the Jewish Orphans Home, and women's organizations such as the Hebrew Ladies' Benevolent Society, the Ladies' Aid Society, and the Temple Sisterhoods. An organization called the Workmen's Circle provided moral and financial support to the widespread Yiddish culture and language. These agencies often helped newly arrived Jewish immigrants meet and socialize with one another and helped the unemployed look for work. The B'nai B'rith Lodge is one of the most well known of these, founded in Los Angeles in 1899. Over time, it increasingly incorporated monitoring anti-Semitism into its activities, especially through the Anti-Defamation League, or ADL.[62]

Most of these early twentieth-century organizations were not as politically and civil rights oriented as they and their successors would become in later years, as ethno-racial minorities mobilized to fight mounting discrimination and increasingly limited opportunities. As the 1930s approached, conditions for minority groups worsened. But the worsening conditions, together with a combination of other factors, also helped spur ethno-racial groups to further action in their own defense.

CHAPTER 2

Shadows of War, Forces for Change

In the spring of 1939, delegates representing 136 local, state, and national Mexican-American and Mexicano organizations with well over a half million members met in Los Angeles to found El Congreso de Pueblos que Hablan Espanol (Congress of Spanish-Speaking Peoples). They came together to develop strategies to seek greater equality for Mexican and Spanish-speaking people in Los Angeles and throughout the United States. Los Angeles became the organization's national headquarters.[1]

El Congreso represented a significant collaborative effort—among various members of the political center to left, and also among Mexican Americans and supporters from other ethnic and racial communities. Mexican Americans led and composed El Congreso's main membership, but African Americans, Jews, whites, and others sometimes cooperated with it. Its members and leaders came from a varied assortment of perspectives, including labor, Democratic Party sympathizers, communists, and socialists. The organization was a true product of the mid to late 1930s, when antifascism became a common cause for communist and noncommunist allies from the center to the left of the political spectrum to form a Popular Front to fight for racial justice and workers' rights, and against imperialism.

El Congreso was one of many new racial justice initiatives that took root in Los Angeles during the 1930s. Others included African Americans' Urban League and Jewish Americans' Community Relations Committee (CRC). This chapter explores how minorities formed such groups, both within and among their individual communities, during the Depression era as domestic and global sociopolitical conditions heightened their awareness of the threats facing them. The domestic economic downturn brought by the deepening worldwide Depression exacerbated preexisting sociocultural tensions in Los Angeles. The decreasing economic resources available to all Angelenos increased competition and heightened racist and anti-Semitic activity against minorities. Such dire conditions also facilitated the growth of activist initiatives as minority groups increasingly fought back to protect themselves, both individually and collectively. This intensifying activism was nourished on opportunities the New Deal provided, which included political organizations and strengthened labor

unions. The Communist Party also served as a training ground for collaborative minority racial equality activism. International developments
fueled Los Angeles's increasingly vocal minority communities, and these
domestic and global catalysts sparked local minorities to mobilize to fight
discrimination, often through a burgeoning interracial collaboration. In
other words, the Depression both heightened minorities' awareness of
racial discrimination and increased their possibilities for collaborative
political mobilization, specifically through the New Deal, Communist
Party, and labor unions.

THE NEW DEAL'S NEW OPTIONS

Franklin Delano Roosevelt (FDR) and his newly energized Democratic
Party, which rose to power on a wave of frustration with the former
Republican administration's laissez-faire approach as the global Depression
spread across the country and world after 1929, gave underrepresented
minority populations in Los Angeles a new avenue to express themselves
politically. It also provided new opportunities for them to engage with
each other and with white Angelenos. FDR's New Deal became an inherently multiracial arena that for the first time formally politicized various
ethnic and racial groups and brought disparate minority groups together
through a political party.

Many minorities rested their hopes for new economic growth for
California, and by extension for themselves, on the promise of the New
Deal, especially as worsening discrimination heightened their fears about
their future in Los Angeles. White Angelenos' anxieties about job competition intensified discrimination toward minority populations. Thirty-three
of every 100 workers in the city had been laid off by 1931, and most
remaining employees took pay cuts, time reductions, or both, according to
a survey of 1,500 businesses employing fifteen or more people. Los
Angeles's suffering was particularly severe. Per capita wages fell there by
one half between 1929 and 1933, bank debits decreased 71 percent, retail
sales fell 56 percent, and bankruptcies in Southern California were more
common than elsewhere in the nation. Half of California's unemployed
population lived in Los Angeles.[2] Los Angeles's unemployment rate was
higher than other large American cities' during the early years of the
Depression: by January 1931, it stood at 17 percent, compared with an
average of 15 percent in other large cities. Although unemployment
declined throughout the 1930s, it was still at 15 percent of the labor force
in 1940.[3]

Continuing migration to California, particularly Los Angeles,
heightened worker competition. Dust Bowl migrants from the central

states left their drought-stricken homes and joined migrants from elsewhere seeking opportunities in the Golden State.[4] California attracted
three times more migrants than any other state in this decade, even
though its population grew more slowly than before.[5] Los Angeles experienced a 22 percent population increase between 1930 and 1940, sur-
passing the 1.5 million mark.[6]

Portions of this surge of newcomers were minorities, who encountered even worse conditions than other Angelenos. While African
Americans stopped moving to cities like Chicago, New York, and Detroit
during the Depression, their presence in Los Angeles grew throughout
the decade, by 67 percent. This represented a higher growth than in the
1920s. The Jewish population almost doubled from 1930 to 1941.
Scholars estimate that at least two-thirds of the newly arrived Jews came
from cities throughout North America rather than from abroad.[7]

Other minority groups in the city remained relatively stable, such as
Asian-origin populations, while the Mexican and Mexican-American
community declined. The Asian population had largely stagnated in earlier decades because of restrictive immigration legislation, and increased
only slightly during the 1930s due to natural population increase. Ongoing
restrictive immigration legislation prevented new arrivals. The Japanese-
origin population in the city of Los Angeles increased by just over 10 percent from 1930 to 1940, while the Chinese-origin population grew by
only 1,727 people (which actually represented over 50 percent growth in
such a small population).[8] The Depression depleted the Mexican-origin
population. Throughout the 1920s, while nativists had succeeded in limiting Asian and European immigration, employers—particularly those
with agricultural interests—had pressured policy makers to exempt
Mexicans from immigration restrictions. In the 1930s, as the job pool
dwindled and the demand for unskilled laborers diminished, white native-
born residents turned against Mexican immigrants too as they increasingly
viewed immigrant labor as competition rather than as necessary cheap
labor. Officials encouraged, and forced, Mexicans to return to Mexico,
resulting in about 500,000 leaving the country between 1929 and 1939.[9]
Many of the early deportees returned voluntarily, especially those who
had attained some financial success. But most of the Mexicans who
returned to Mexico by 1931 did so under pressure. Often American-born
citizens of Mexican descent were "returned" to a country that never had
been their home, as federal officials together with local leaders tried to
address unemployment problems by deporting Mexicans. In many cases
the government paid their passage to the border. Los Angeles officials
made deals with the Southern Pacific, according to the well-known local
civil rights activist Carey McWilliams, to "ship Mexicans back to Mexico
at a wholesale per capita rate of $14.70."[10] Los Angeles County organized
the most ambitious repatriation program in the country, in large part

because it had the highest concentration of Mexicans outside Mexico. Los Angeles became the first city in the country to use local and federal tax money to conduct the repatriation.[11]

All minority populations who remained or arrived in Los Angeles faced extremely difficult economic conditions, as their ethno-racial status made their prospects even more dismal than other residents.' Thirty percent of the African-American population and 19 percent of other "nonwhites" in Los Angeles were on unemployment relief by October 1933, compared to only 7 percent of the white population. Mexicans comprised 16 percent of California relief applicants in the year 1929–30 and 13 percent in 1930–31.[12] Unemployment disproportionately affected certain minority groups. An estimated 20 to 50 percent of Mexican families still in Los Angeles in 1931 were unemployed, and a Mexican consular official reported that the latter percentage likely was more accurate.[13] African Americans' unemployment rate was twice as high as the general population's. By contrast, Japanese unemployment was far lower than other groups.' Only 3 percent of all Japanese in Los Angeles County were on relief or seeking work in 1940, compared with 12 percent of all workers. These low figures can be explained, according to historian John Modell, by the Japanese community's ethnic economy spreading work very thinly and accommodating its workers more successfully than other communities did. The community's large percentage of self-employed workers also helps to explain its low unemployment rate. It is clear, though, that the Depression still limited Japanese Americans' employment options severely as it did for other groups.[14] Jews, too, faced growing employment discrimination in the 1930s, though conditions for them were not as bad as they were for their fellow minorities. They were effectively barred from certain kinds of jobs; law firms, except Jewish ones, were generally off-limits, as were public schools.[15]

African Americans confronted many varieties of discrimination. They continued to find economic conditions in Los Angeles better than elsewhere in the United States. For instance, Los Angeles blacks had better access to federal relief work than their counterparts in most southern states and found better housing than in many other cities.[16] Nonetheless, discrimination was the rule rather than the exception in Los Angeles; restrictive employment practices in place from the 1920s continued to keep blacks out of many industries. The city's demand for unskilled industrial workers was smaller than many northern cities' until World War II, and the constant influx of white workers usually filled the limited jobs that did exist. Opportunities for African Americans in clerical or professional jobs were few and far between. Black teachers were not hired in Los Angeles junior and senior high schools until 1936 because of objections from white parents and white teachers' refusal to share eating and bathroom facilities. The Department of Water and Power justified its refusal to hire blacks for a city construction project in 1931 with the excuse that it lacked separate black and white camp facilities.[17]

Such especially severe economic troubles made minorities hopeful that the New Deal would help remedy their situation. FDR did bestow growth on the Golden State in part as a reward for California capitalists' support for his reform programs. New Deal projects built an infrastructure for more development, including the Hoover Dam (Boulder Dam at the time), the Golden Gate Bridge, the San Francisco Bay Bridge, irrigation projects, and shipyards, which generated jobs for the state's numerous unemployed.[18] Yet, like elsewhere, New Deal programs denied minorities many of the benefits that other Californians and Angelenos reaped. Depression-era growth project work contracts, implemented by local government officials who in Los Angeles were mostly Republican, mainly benefited white workers. Mayor Frank Shaw oversaw 444 New Deal projects in the city, which employed about 40,000 individuals and spent $54 million of mostly federal money, most of which was not available to African Americans.[19] The Social Security Act of 1935, which for the first time mandated federal payments for pensions, unemployment insurance, and benefits to dependent mothers and children, excluded most African Americans. It did not apply to positions they were most likely to hold, as state, county, and city employees, and especially as field workers, domestic workers, and casual laborers. Although the number of African-American leaders appointed to government posts in state and local agencies increased during the New Deal era, some of these appointments reinforced African Americans' frustrations. The State Emergency Relief Administration (SERA) prohibited Floyd Covington, the African-American executive director of the Los Angeles Urban League, from visiting white aid applicants' homes when he became a caseworker and later a director of caseworkers. Many of the New Deal's benefits did not reach Mexican Americans either, in large part because they too were concentrated in occupations not covered by New Deal legislation. The Wagner Act, officially the National Labor Relations Act (NLRA), for the first time protected the rights of many workers to organize labor unions, engage in collective bargaining, and take part in strikes, but excluded agricultural workers from its provisions concerning collective bargaining. The Agricultural Adjustment Act (AAA), which subsidized farmers to reduce crops in order to eliminate the surplus (which was driving down produce prices), indirectly subsidized antiunion elements and enhanced industry's economic control. This disproportionately affected the African Americans and ethnic Mexicans who frequently toiled in American fields.[20]

The New Deal did assist Los Angeles African Americans and other racial minorities in limited—but important—ways. The Federal Theater Project helped some members of Los Angeles minority groups become stage and screen stars. The "Who's Who" of Hollywood subsequently listed African Americans like John Larkin, a Los Angeles comedian, and Mildred Washington gained acclaim for her many theater performances, where she worked alongside stars like Claudette Colbert and Bing Crosby.[21] The New Deal sent strong messages to Mexican Americans too that their support and votes were important for its success. It provided housing relief for Mexican Americans. The Federal Emergency Relief Administration (FERA) also furnished some relief payments and created a de facto minimum wage.[22]

FDR's programs aided European-descent minority groups to a greater degree. They transformed Jewish activism nationwide as Jews, like many white Americans, began to make demands on what they saw as a more receptive government. Jewish activists increasingly built bridges between their neighborhood concerns and the local and federal governments, and came to expect government intervention and assistance. The New Deal began to provide services to local white ethnic communities, such as providing rent consultants to help prevent eviction.[23] In Los Angeles, New Deal funds supported education programs at the Menorah Center, an important Jewish social center. The Emergency Educational Program and the Works Progress Administration (WPA), which provided jobs and income to the unemployed, sent teachers there several times a week to teach elementary and advanced English; Americanization lessons on history and civics to immigrants preparing for naturalization tests; music; contemporary Jewish history; physical education; child care; home visitation; cooking; and nutrition.[24]

Perhaps most significant, the New Deal realigned party affiliation and loyalty among minority communities. Minorities in Los Angeles and around the nation joined the tide of Americans supporting the New Deal with the hope that it would help them achieve more sociopolitical and economic equality. Though the New Deal's promise did not extend as far to groups like African Americans, Mexican Americans, and Asian Americans as it did to other segments of the population, the 1930s nonetheless marked a profound political shift for many of them in Los Angeles and nationwide.

Many African Americans switched their traditional allegiance to Lincoln's Republican Party to become Democrats loyal to Franklin Delano Roosevelt. Though Los Angeles blacks were ahead of other urban California blacks in their support of the Democratic Party, which for some had begun as early as the 1920s, the decisive shift happened—as it did elsewhere—during the Depression and particularly during the election of 1936. Increasing political involvement accompanied this shift. This realignment represented more than a symbolic party shift, as the New Deal mobilized many *new* voters in general, some of whom were African American. The number of registered Republicans in L.A. County declined in the 1930s by 180,202, while the number of registered Democrats grew by a tremendous 1,963,533.[25] Since the total county population grew by only 577,000, this marked a huge increase in Democratic Party voters among the previously settled population.[26]

Los Angeles Jewish Americans also became more politically involved as many rallied behind FDR even though they—like other minorities in this period—remained largely outside official city politics. Running a Jewish candidate for elective office in 1920s and 1930s Los Angeles would have been unrealistic. But Jews did make gains in appointed offices, especially in the legal realm. They also received recognition at the state level, where a good number served in the administration of Governor Culbert L. Olson, a liberal governor elected in 1938. Some of these political appointees later became prominent in the Community Relations Committee (CRC), an important local Jewish civil rights organization formed in the 1930s. Among these was Isaac Pacht, whom Olson named president of the State Board of Prison Directors. In later years Pacht became the leader of Los Angeles's organized Jewish community and a central player in Jewish and cooperative interracial civil rights campaigns.[27] More recent Jewish arrivals to Los Angeles tended to support FDR in the 1940 presidential election, while the established community, especially among the long-term residents who held much of the community's wealth, supported the Republican candidate, Wendell Willkie.[28] Mendel Silberberg, the CRC's longtime chairman, was among local influential Republicans. The powerful Jews in Hollywood, most of the heads of the major studios, supported the Republican Party, with a few exceptions like Dore Schary. Other Hollywood Jews joined non-Jews in the movie industry to support FDR and the New Deal, both for personal beliefs and also because New Deal policies, which increased the public's purchasing power, left money for going to the pictures.[29]

Japanese Americans asserted themselves more visibly in the U.S. political arena during the 1930s as well. Like Jewish Americans, L.A. Japanese Americans joined both parties, and it is unclear whether they supported FDR to the same degree as other minority groups. In the late 1930s they formed a Japanese-American branch of the Republican Party and Democratic counterparts like the Japanese American Young Democrats, which appeared all over the state, especially in cities like Oakland, San Francisco, and Los Angeles. The Young Democrats represented L.A. Japanese Americans' first time participating in what historian John Modell calls "the Rooseveltian world of minority-group politics."[30]

As a community, those of Mexican origin had relatively little contact with or participation in the two-party system and did not become a visible political force in Los Angeles and other southwestern cities more generally until the post–World War II era. Their social and political exclusion, disfranchisement, substantial ongoing orientation toward

Mexico, and the absence of patronage or precinct organization in Los Angeles contributed to their political marginalization. Not until 1949 did significant numbers of Los Angeles Mexicans register to vote, when the Community Service Organization (CSO), a civil rights organization that focused heavily on increasing Mexican-American voter registration, swept through East Los Angeles neighborhoods.[31]

Still, Mexican and Mexican Americans' formal political activity grew noticeably during the 1930s as Franklin Delano Roosevelt's New Deal energized disfranchised, discouraged people nationwide.[32] Mexican immigrants' sharply increased requests for naturalization in Los Angeles between 1934 and 1936, representing a 34 percent increase from any earlier period, suggest a surging interest in American politics. Since this surge undoubtedly reflects a response to continuing threats of deportation and repatriation, it is hard to conclude that it reflects Mexican Americans' actual interest in American politics. Moreover, Mexican immigrants' naturalization and voting rates still remained relatively low in the 1930s. But the New Deal strongly affected Mexican Americans in Los Angeles.[33] Eduardo Quevedo Sr. became the first Mexican-American candidate in the twentieth century to vie for local political office when he ran unsuccessfully in 1938 for city council. Some Mexican Americans, including Quevedo, Manuel Ruíz Jr., and Edward Roybal, worked in the 1930s to gain support among the Mexican-origin population for FDR's Democratic Party. Roybal, for instance, worked for the New Deal's Civilian Conservation Corps, while Quevedo campaigned for FDR in his 1932 presidential bid and later worked for the federal Works Project Administration (WPA).[34]

These Mexican Americans' burgeoning political activities in the 1930s segued into important political initiatives, many of which were interracial. Quevedo became the president of El Congreso and later chaired the 40th District Democratic Council and was a member of the L.A. Democratic Advisory Committee. Quevedo's rise to leadership positions was especially impressive given the fact that he was largely self-taught, having left school at the age of fourteen to work in a New Mexico mine with his father. In later years Manuel Ruíz became chairman of the Citizens' Committee for Latin American Youth and formed the Coordinating Council for Latin American Youth. Ruíz actively participated in interracial coalitions like the California Committee on Youth in Wartime to ensure fair employment throughout the state of California. Roybal was the most important Mexican-American political figure to emerge from Los Angeles in the first half of the twentieth century. He became the first Mexican American on the city council since the late nineteenth century, elected in 1949 by a multiracial coalition of Mexican Americans, Jews, Japanese Americans, African Americans, and whites, a position he held until 1962 when he won a seat in the U.S. Congress.

New Deal realignments facilitated growing interracial political coalitions that resulted in the election of other minority representatives too. A coalition of largely black and white voters swept African-American Augustus Hawkins into a state assembly district seat in 1934. Hawkins had arrived in Los Angeles from Shreveport shortly after World War I. He entered politics when he found that the stock market crash had ruined his and other black college graduates' chances of attending graduate school, as he had planned after finishing his economics undergraduate degree at UCLA. He and other African Americans blamed the Republicans and looked to improve their conditions through the Democratic Party. Hawkins' victory depended as much on white Westside votes as on his black support, since other African-American candidates who failed to gain white votes lost the election. Black Democrats joined "white liberals" in this period to push minority civil rights to the center of their joint agenda. Hawkins' election marked a shift in the nature of black politics because a biracial coalition elected him, and because he hoped to enact changes with a broader aggregation of pro-labor constituents. His white support was particularly interesting given that he represented the predominantly minority area of South-Central Los Angeles, where he served until becoming the first African-American member of Congress from California in 1962, the same year that Roybal was elected.[35] The ascendance of Roybal and Hawkins in local and state, and eventually national, politics highlights the larger impact of the interracial New Deal Democratic Party.

LABOR ACTIVISM

Minorities revealed their increasing commitment to organized civil rights struggles, and came into contact with each other, in more ways than party affiliation and electoral politics. Labor unions also provided a venue for increased interracial activism. Support for labor union activity swelled in the 1930s as multiethnic workers joined the white working class to make their voices heard. The New Deal was relatively receptive to union labor. For example, in 1935 it passed the Wagner Act, which guaranteed workers the right to collectively bargain, prohibited employer interference with their organizing activities, and gave them the right to select their own bargaining representatives through voting. Workers of many backgrounds took advantage of these conditions in Los Angeles and elsewhere, and in the process often encountered each other for the first time.

Labor activism was particularly challenging in Los Angeles, an open shop city where the weak state of organized labor compounded the discrimination that Los Angeles minorities faced. Business interests' tight control made victory difficult for organized labor to achieve, whether among the white working class or minority workers. But in spite of the hostile climate, workers made substantial efforts to organize and fight for their rights. In 1933 at least thirty-seven agricultural strikes swept across California, some in the Los Angeles area.[36] Trade unionism in L.A.'s Jewish community surged in the mid-1930s, as workers joined the International Ladies' Garment Workers Union (ILGWU), the Bakery Workers, the United Hat, Cap and Millinery Workers, the Fur Workers, and the Amalgamated Clothing Workers. In an important victory, the Amalgamated Clothing Workers effectively demonstrated its strength with a 1933 strike against Kurtzman Brothers, and by 1935 had achieved many of its goals. Clothing workers, a high proportion of whom were Jewish, were among the first to win advantages from the New Deal's receptiveness to union labor, and to crack the open shop somewhat successfully.[37]

Mexican Americans in Los Angeles also were fairly active in strike activities.[38] At the same time Mexican Americans remained largely disconnected from formal politics, the children of Mexican immigrants became involved in union activism.[39] Some of Mexican Americans' strikes and labor campaigns were ethnic group specific, while others increased their contact with other ethno-racial groups like Jews, African Americans, and whites. Women in particular became active in such interracial workers' movements. Approximately 1,500 largely Mexicana but also Jewish and Italian dressmaker members of the ILGWU struck in September 1933 for union recognition, a thirty-five-hour workweek, a guaranteed minimum wage, a shop chairman, and other demands. They achieved some significant success, though they did not attain all of their demands. Rose Pesotta, one of the Russian Jewish ILGWU leaders who came to Los Angeles to work on the strike, spoke in her memoir about the Mexican women's commitment to the strike, even at great costs like hunger, losing their jobs, threats of deportation, and others. In August 1936, 3,000 garment workers of different ethnic and racial groups, many of them ILGWU, struck again and came close to establishing a closed shop. The United Cannery, Agricultural, Packing and Allied Workers of America (UCAPAWA)—another interracial and heavily female union movement—likewise made some gains. Mexican, African-American, and white workers joined forces to strike against conditions in the fields, canneries, and elsewhere.[40] This union's biggest moment was an interracial victory achieved by predominantly Mexican and Russian Jewish women strikers in the early fall of 1939 over one of the biggest L.A. canneries, the California Sanitary Canning Company. After a three-month strike, a secondary boycott, and intervention by the New Deal's National Labor Relations Board, UCAPAWA established itself as a union and attained higher wages in the canning industry. The union gained recognition and continued to fight the persistence of highly unfair practices such as the piece-rate system of payment.[41]

Unlike Jewish and Mexican Americans, and compared to the rest of the country, black participation in Los Angeles organized labor was particularly limited. The Teamsters were one of the few Los Angeles unions to accept blacks before World War II.[42] Many of the organizing drives that addressed local African Americans' concerns originated within their own community. In 1930 African Americans formed the Women's Industrial Council, which worked specifically to ensure black workers' equality—though it was part of the larger labor movement. The council included representatives from churches, clubs, and business groups. Black workers in organizations such as the Red Cap Station Porters made some headway against employers. It organized in 1932, gained an AFL charter in 1933, and eventually succeeded in overturning the Southern Pacific's refusal to pay them wages (their income previously came entirely from tips). But since the Porters were merely eighty-strong in Los Angeles in 1938, the organization represented only a small portion of Los Angeles's black population.[43] Still, even their limited participation in labor activism increased African Americans' contact with other ethno-racial groups.

Much of the initiative for the strikes came from within the ethnic communities themselves, but support from various organized labor groups was crucial to their strength. The Congress of Industrial Organizations (CIO), which after breaking away from the more conservative American Federation of Labor (AFL) in 1935 became a separate, more left-leaning union in 1936, played a particularly vital role. The CIO's organizing principle, that the most deprived workers needed the most help, was unusual even in the 1930s. The CIO helped motivate and support many strikes by Mexicans and other minorities in the late 1930s. By the end of the Depression it had organized over 15,000 Mexican-American workers in the Los Angeles area. For instance, UCAPAWA was a CIO organization. The L.A. CIO involved itself in Mexican community issues like transportation, gangs, police relations, health care, discrimination, citizenship, youth, education, and legal defense. It organized the Committee to Aid Mexican Workers, conferences on Mexican workers' plight, and wrote about Mexican community issues in its California paper, the *Labor Herald*, with the hope of educating other workers about Mexicans and their concerns.[44]

Despite instances of interracial organizing, the support the CIO and other mainstream labor groups provided fell short of minorities' hopes of inclusivity. The CIO and the AFL incorporated Japanese Americans better than they had before the 1930s, but they continued to organize them in segregated units.[45] Los Angeles minorities received less union support than minorities elsewhere. The powerful open shop system weakened organized labor to the point that it was in no position to be very helpful to—or even very interested in—the struggles of African Americans, Mexican Americans, and other minorities. According to historian Josh Sides, the relationship that emerged in northern industrial cities in the 1930s between organized labor and racial minority communities, a relationship that sparked early civil rights battles elsewhere, did not emerge in Los Angeles until the end of World War II. In contrast to places like Chicago during the Depression, Sides argues, blacks, whites, and Mexicans in Los Angeles did not find "a workers' common ground."[46] While this may have been true relative to elsewhere, multiracial workers nonetheless forged among themselves links that became important to later burgeoning civil rights struggles. UCAPAWA, ILGWU, and various CIO-sponsored activities increased cooperation among Los Angeles communities, providing a foundation and launchpad for later activism.

Much interracial civil rights leadership in Los Angeles emerged from the CIO movement, especially among Mexican Americans. Union ties to later civil rights activism are less visible in the African-American community, in no small part because of its relatively loose ties to organized labor. Jewish-American labor activity produced leaders, too, but those leaders tended to remain more involved specifically in union work than in civil rights per se. Among Mexican-American union activists, though, prominent emergent figures included Bert Corona of the International Longshore and Warehousemen's Union; Frank López, Anthony (Tony) Ríos, and Jaime González of the Steel Workers Organizing Committee; Rosendo Rivera from the United Electrical Workers; Jess Armenta of the United Transport Workers; and María Durán, an International Ladies' Garment Workers Union leader.[47] Many of these people used this early labor experience as a springboard for their later involvement with other Mexican-American community and political organizations and with interracial civil rights initiatives. Ríos later became president of the postwar collaborative civil rights group, the Community Service Organization (CSO), Maria Durán became the CSO's treasurer, and Rosendo Rivera became president of the Spanish-Speaking People's Congress. Bert Corona, born in El Paso in 1918 to immigrant parents, became one of the most prominent labor and civil rights activists shortly after he moved to Los Angeles for a basketball scholarship at USC. He became involved in numerous Mexican-American and interracial civil rights initiatives, including El Congreso, the CSO, and many others.[48]

THE COMMUNIST PARTY

Organizations besides FDR's New Deal and labor union activity offered further avenues for redress during the difficult Depression decade and, relatedly, for interracial collaboration. The Communist Party (CP), which played a particularly important role in Los Angeles's open-shop environment, brought together Los Angeles workers and civil rights–oriented activists, providing them with a third alternative for collaborative political engagement. During the Depression, dire circumstances facilitated minority communities' heightened involvement with the Communist Party, as they did with their labor organization activities. The Los Angeles branch of the Communist Party (L.A. CP), which had formed in 1919, made strides toward developing an interracial, working-class coalition of activists.

The L.A. party tried to become more inclusive and reach out to other minorities during the 1930s. Previously it had been almost exclusively Jewish and did not have the broad ethnic diversity that characterized the CP in San Francisco and elsewhere. In the late 1920s, though, L.A. members changed their names so they would seem less like Jewish immigrants and more like "Americans," presumably widening the CP's appeal. Moreover, Depression-era CP protests evolved out of a number of ethnic protest traditions, including those of its Japanese-American, Mexican-American, and African-American members, even though its membership and leadership were heavily Jewish. Depression-era members included Japanese labor organizers and socialists; Mexicans inclined toward unionization and others who brought socialist, anarchist, and radical traditions from the Mexican Revolution; and African Americans who brought experiences ranging from the NAACP to black nationalism to the emergent Sleeping Car Porters Union.[49] CP leaders in Los Angeles spoke in or translated their speeches into Spanish, Italian, and Japanese and posted signs and handbills in various languages. The party sponsored demonstrations on issues that concerned these diverse groups, including rallies in support of the Scottsboro Boys—the nine black boys from Alabama accused of raping a white woman, striking Mexican Imperial Valley farm workers, and Tom Mooney—a white radical labor activist who appealed to old-line union members. It demonstrated against antialien fishing laws that concerned the Japanese community, and against the Nazis, an issue of particular interest to Jewish members.[50]

The party did important work for unions with large Mexican memberships, and represented the community in its battles with welfare offices, the police, and immigration authorities. It staged demonstrations for thousands of Angelenos, such as the "Hunger March" in the center of town's Plaza area, where many Mexicans were concentrated. It claimed that 40,000 people participated in this march on October 2, 1933, including fifteen units of a Mexican community club called the Mexican Liberal Club.[51] The CP assisted Mexicans in ways beyond labor organizing, for example by helping to establish organizations such as the International Labor Defense (ILD) and the Workers Alliance. The ILD emerged to counter the activities of organizations like the Ku Klux Klan and to defend workers and radicals in court. It worked with Mexicans to fight inequities in welfare distribution in the 1930s and assisted them in numerous other social justice struggles. It also provided legal assistance to L.A. unions, including Mexican unions.[52] The Workers Alliance, which emerged in the 1930s, was dominated by the Communist Party. It sought to organize WPA project workers to demand higher wages, to help relief recipients demand more support, and to empower tenants facing eviction. Some branches on the eastside held meetings in Spanish, while several Mexican-origin people assumed leadership positions.[53]

The L.A. CP encouraged nonwhites to assume leadership roles, which they did, not only in ethnic-centered activities but also in the organization's very structure. There were Jewish, Italian, Japanese, and Spanish-surnamed "chiefs," according to a police sweep in January 1931.[54] Karl Yoneda, a Japanese-American longshoreman, became a CP leader who organized among Mexican and African Americans as well as Asian Americans. Sen Katayama, also a Japanese-American labor organizer and socialist, was a cofounder of both the CPUSA and Japanese community organizations.[55] Pettis Perry, a poor and uneducated Southern black migrant, became the most influential African American in the CP during the Depression. Perry joined the CP shortly after his arrival to Los Angeles in his early twenties, after a Jewish immigrant named Sadie Goldstein convinced him to join the party's campaign defending the Scottsboro Boys.[56]

The CP also attracted Loren Miller, a transplant from Nebraska and Kansas whose father was black—a former slave—and mother was white, whose activities are central to this story of change and continuity in Los Angeles civil rights efforts from the 1930s through the early Cold War. Miller came to Los Angeles in 1929 to pursue journalism the year after he graduated from law school in Topeka, Kansas.[57] He visited the Soviet Union in 1932 and, upon his return to the United States, praised the communist country in a speech at Los Angeles's Second Baptist Church. He also joined the John Reed Club, a racially integrated group mostly filled with Communist Party members, and supported the Communist Party's cause through his staff work on black Los Angeles newspapers like the *California Eagle* and the *Sentinel* (though neither was pro-communist in tone or content).[58] His support for the CP in the 1930s drew fire from Angelenos like the *Eagle*'s owner Charlotta Bass, who at the time was a staunch Republican. Miller also joined the communist-affiliated National Negro Congress for a while.[59]

Like many of those who assumed leadership roles in Communist Party activities, members also came from various ethno-racial backgrounds. The combination of organizational secrecy and the scarcity of certain ethnic communities' sources make it difficult to attain accurate information on ethnic membership composition. But it is clear that approximately 10 percent of the Communist party's recruits in 1936–37 were Mexican workers. Historian Zaragosa Vargas suggests that there were 435 Mexicans in the L.A. CP.[60] Japanese-American membership was high too: nationally, while roughly only 1 out of every 5,000 persons in the United States was a member of the CPUSA, nearly 1 in every 600 Japanese Americans joined, and Southern California had the greatest concentration of Japanese-origin CPUSA supporters in the country.[61] Japanese members in Los Angeles numbered about 60 to 100 according to one estimate.[62]

By the late 1930s and early 1940s, the Los Angeles Communist Party had at least partially achieved its goal of broadening its membership base. It recruited significant numbers of non-Jewish, American-born members including teachers, journalists, lawyers, doctors, movie studio workers, and university students. It became the second largest Communist Party section in the country, reaching an official membership of approximately 3,000 by the late 1930s.[63]

African, Mexican, and Japanese-origin people did not join in numbers as great as the party had hoped, though. Newspaper accounts, which published accounts of and arrest lists from demonstrations, suggest that these groups were much more likely to participate in Communist-sponsored activities than they were to actually join the party.[64] While it achieved the participation of many groups, the CP did not successfully retain most of its recruits as members. Such people as Bert Corona and Carlos Bulosan, a Filipino activist, worked with the CP through informal alliances rather than formal affiliation.[65] Though many Mexican activists worked with the CP in the 1930s, most did not join. At least one scholar argues that the CP's failure in the Mexican community resulted in part from its inability to understand the community's traditions and political approaches.[66] African Americans' experience with the CP was similar. Even those African Americans who wanted to join often faced resistance from elites within their own ethnic group who viewed the CP as an economic threat or as competition for community members' allegiance. The majority of African Americans in Los Angeles were either ambivalent or hostile to the CP in the 1930s, and black membership in that decade remained relatively low.[67] The Los Angeles Communist Party never quite managed to transform itself from a Jewish/white centered institution into a broader multiracial alliance throughout the Depression and the World War II years.[68]

Furthermore, despite its role in mobilizing various communities, the Communist Party ultimately failed to achieve any lasting political victories. This failure partially resulted from its inability to attract and retain enough diverse recruits.[69] The limited diversity it did achieve ultimately impeded the party's success, for its membership's multira-cialism caught the attention of anticommunists. Anticommunist activity by business interests and public officials, best epitomized by the Red Squad, limited the L.A. CP's effectiveness tremendously in the 1930s, the heyday of the national and other regional CPs. Other groups also actively fought and hindered the Communist Party in Los Angeles in the 1920s and 1930s, including the Better America Federation, the Merchants and Manufacturing Association, and the *LA Times*. As Carey McWilliams lamented, "The *Los Angeles Times* and energetic anti-Communist organizations were determined to make Los Angeles the 'white spot' of the nation."[70]

Despite the party's incomplete successes, though, members of some Los Angeles ethnic and racial minority communities who did not join the CP still worked closely with it on various issues, participating in Communist-sponsored activities at much higher rates than their membership indicated.[71] This varied participation shows that in spite of its hindrances and limitations, the Los Angeles Communist Party further introduced diverse groups of Angelenos to each other in the 1930s, providing a foundation for later interracial, cooperative civil rights initiatives.

COMMUNITY POLITICS ON THE RISE

Depression-era conditions intensified Los Angeles minorities' involvement in independent antidiscrimination initiatives, too, many of which involved interracial collaboration and built upon connections established through New Deal, labor, and Communist Party activities. El Congreso, a short-lived but important organization, was one of these organizations. The group represented a significant effort by Mexican Americans, in tandem with progressives in other communities, to build a working-class movement that fought to attain basic rights for Mexican and Spanish-speaking people in Los Angeles and throughout the United States. Members strategized for causes including supporting federal housing projects, improving sanitation and medical care through federal assistance, fighting race discrimination, improving education and pay, unionizing workers, securing jobs for the unemployed, abolishing the poll tax, fighting deportation, and advocating for citizenship and naturalization, among others.[72] El Congreso also made fighting policy brutality and juvenile delinquency central to its programs. It protested unjustified killings of Mexican-American men by the police, as well as police attempts to pressure Mexican-American women for sexual favors after arresting them on false prostitution charges.[73]

El Congreso was different from other Mexican-American civil rights organizations like the League of Latin American Citizens (LULAC), which until that point was the most prominent organization fighting for the rights of Mexican-descent people in the United States, though it was less prominent in Los Angeles than in Texas. El Congreso's battle for increased equality engaged more with the international arena, and it was more inclusive across gender, nationality, and left-to-center political delineations. While El Congreso focused more on domestic equality issues, it kept one eye on international issues of concern to Mexicans and Mexican Americans, particularly in Mexico and Spain. It voted at its national convention to support Republican Spain against Franco and the fascists in the Spanish Civil War, which lasted from 1936 to 1939. Congreso members passed a resolution critiquing Roosevelt's administration for blockading Spain and for not opposing Hitler and Mussolini's provision of arms to General Franco, who eventually won the war. In terms of Mexican affairs, El Congreso gained support for Lázaro Cárdenas' administration's expropriation of American and other foreign oil in 1938. It organized a protest march of 9,000 people through downtown Los Angeles, along Broadway, to oppose possible American attempts to intervene to get back their oil concessions in Mexico. El Congreso officials supported Cárdenas in no small part, according to Bert Corona, because he was a champion of the people and embodied the ideals of the Mexican Revolution.[74]

Other aspects that differentiated El Congreso were its commitment to gender equality and its struggles on behalf of immigrants as well as citizens. Unusually, approximately 30 percent of its members were female, including prominent leader Josefina Fierro de Bright. Elsewhere, women were less involved in such organizations and, when they were involved, their leadership was rare. One of El Congreso's primary concerns was fighting gender discrimination.[75] Also, while most other Mexican-American civil rights organizations at the time focused strictly on citizens' rights, El Congreso fought discrimination against noncitizens, an especially salient issue in this decade that had witnessed massive deportation of Mexicans. Its work included fighting proposed bills that would deny them relief unless they worked toward citizenship. El Congreso also opposed state legislation that would deport noncitizens receiving state welfare and offered counseling on immigration and naturalization issues. El Congreso helped immigrants fill out forms for resident or citizenship status and job applications, offered lawyer services, and called for language and other prerequisites for citizenship to be relaxed. It supported continuing and expanding relief programs in the late 1930s, in part by attempting to establish an old-age pension system in California. While El Congreso defended the rights of noncitizens, it also called on Mexicans to become American citizens and encouraged Mexican Americans to vote and engage in political action against discrimination because it believed the community's strength depended on political action.[76]

El Congreso also embodied the collaboration between communist and noncommunist allies from the center to the left of the political spectrum in this Popular Front era. Its leaders, members, and supporters emerged from traditions both within and outside the mainstream two-party political system. El Congreso included local Mexicanos motivated, inspired, and catalyzed into mainstream political campaigns by the New Deal. Among these New Deal Democrats was El Congreso's first president Eduardo Quevedo Sr., who actively supported FDR in 1932 and again in 1936, and also helped elect the New Dealer Culbert Olson to become California's governor in 1938. Quevedo also worked for the New Deal agency the Works Progress Administration (WPA) from 1934 to 1937. Congreso received support from prominent politicians like Governor Olson, State Attorney Robert Kenny, Carey McWilliams—who at the time was State Housing and Immigration director, L.A. County Supervisor John Anson Ford, and Fletcher Bowron, the mayor of Los Angeles from 1938 until 1953. Other members, including communists, socialists, and others who sympathized with such perspectives affiliated outside the two-party system. One of the main forces behind El Congreso's organization, Luisa Moreno, was a former Communist Party member and UCAPAWA organizer who had worked in Florida, Texas, and elsewhere organizing multiracial populations of workers. She took the lead organizing the 1939 national meeting.[77] El Congreso's executive secretary Josefina Fierro de Bright also brought an "outside the system" perspective from her upbringing in a family of Mexican radicals. The heavily Jewish and white CP supported El Congreso and provided it with ideological and political reinforcement.[78] These elements within and outside the mainstream political infrastructure worked together to reform society to bring greater equality to Mexicans and Mexican Americans by incorporating them under the democratic umbrella.[79]

Labor's important role in El Congreso further reveals its collaborative Popular Front orientation. Workers' rights were one of its main focuses, although El Congreso was not specifically a labor organization and did not directly participate in the union movement. CIO organizers like Luisa Moreno and Harry Bridges of the International Longshoreman Workers' Union and the CIO, among others, worked closely with El Congreso. El Congreso worked for liberalized wage and hour laws. It also encouraged Mexican Americans to join unions by educating Spanish-speaking workers about their rights to bargain collectively, strike, and picket, and emphasized that union meetings held in Spanish and English would bring more Mexican-descent workers into the union movement.[80] Congreso members drew support from CIO unions, using their growing activism in the union movement to help fortify this Mexican-American organization and revealing the connections between the various forms of activism the 1930s catalyzed.

El Congreso's relationship with the Communist Party, the CIO and other labor unions, and Democratic Party political activists illustrates how minorities' own intensifying civil rights initiatives drew from the other tides of activism which the decade fostered. It also reveals how minorities' own campaigns were intertwined with the decade's mounting interracial collaboration. Congreso organizers explicitly stated that one of their goals was to build unity among groups and nationalities with the same objectives, demonstrating Mexican-American activists' increasing awareness that interracial coalitions were essential for fighting discrimination.[81] The participation of the Urban League's African-American leader Floyd Covington at El Congreso's founding convention in Los Angeles underscores this interracial interest. Covington, who had been working with Mexican Americans on the city's east side to build relationships with African Americans, chaired a session at this three-day convention.[82] El Congreso continued to work with African-American organizations like Covington's Urban League. In one example, it teamed up with the Urban League, the NAACP, and other organizations on a statewide committee organized to defend Fetus Coleman, a black man unjustly accused of rape after he stumbled upon a white policeman having sex with a white woman in San Francisco's Golden Gate Park. The stunned policeman jumped to his feet, pulled up his pants, and arrested Coleman, while the woman later testified against him in court. The interracial defense committee managed to secure Coleman's freedom later, after he already had been sentenced to San Quentin.[83]

In addition to participating in such interracial activist endeavors, El Congreso received financial support from diverse ethno-racial groups. These included the League of Women Voters, B'nai B'rith and other Jewish organizations, African-American organizations, Hollywood stars like Anthony Quinn and Dolores del Río (both Mexican American) and John Wayne, and CIO labor unions.[84] An important component of El Congreso's activism, interracial cooperation led to connections that lasted beyond the organization's short life. As with the Democratic Party, the Communist Party, and labor unions, the interracial and cross-left political cooperation embraced by Depression-era minority institutions like El Congreso resulted in increasing numbers of fruitful initiatives. These Depression-era minority institutions also became training grounds for community-based leadership and incubators for the collaboration that helped initiate later civil rights struggles.

Interracially inclined organizations like El Congreso built upon the decade's rising tide of ethno-racial community activism. Los Angeles minorities had built antidiscrimination watchdog organizations for decades. Conditions in the 1930s, though, intensified such activity and oriented it increasingly toward organizations that fought specifically for political and civil rights. Los Angeles minority groups confronted multiple varieties of discrimination during the Depression decade. For instance, white Angelenos excluded blacks and Mexican Americans from many restaurants and theaters in spite of a law that guaranteed equal access to public facilities. Predominantly white suburbs such as Pasadena enacted particularly egregious restrictions. In the 1930s the city opened only one public swimming pool to blacks, which it allowed nonwhites to use merely one day each week. The L.A. Fire Department segregated blacks in separate units.[85] Japanese immigrants continued to find they were restricted from owning land, while Mexican immigrants and even Mexican Americans faced deportation.

For Mexican Americans, new strong defense agencies that emerged to battle worsening conditions included El Congreso as well as the less well known Federation of Spanish-Speaking Voters, which formed for the first time during the 1930s, though they built upon existing institutions like mutual aid societies.[86] The timing of their emergence is due in part to the Depression-era deportation of influential members of the community's Mexican-born leadership, which shifted the community's orientation to Mexican Americans more interested in fighting for their rights as American citizens.[87] The deportation also raised the community's awareness of the dangers they faced in a hostile society.

Japanese-, African-, and Jewish-American defense organizations grew more active during the Depression era. The Japanese American Citizens League (JACL), which became known as the Nisei (second generation) community's civic body, became a national organization in 1930, though its roots stretched back to San Francisco in the 1920s. The Los Angeles branch hosted the 1932 national convention, attended by over 500 delegates. The national JACL and its regional branches increasingly worked in the 1930s to eliminate discriminatory legislation against Japanese and Japanese Americans.[88] In 1931, it helped repeal the Cable Act, which stipulated that female U.S. citizens who married aliens ineligible to citizenship—effectively Asians—would lose their own citizenship. The JACL assisted in obtaining naturalization rights for about 500 Issei, or first-generation Japanese immigrants, World War I veterans. At its national convention in 1938, it confronted issues of employment discrimination and vocational problems. By 1940 it had fifty chapters with about 5,600 dues-paying members.[89]

The activities of the Los Angeles branch of the NAACP, which had formed in earlier decades and which along with the national organization became the main instrument of legal protest against increasing segregation and discrimination, illustrate how African-American defense institutions' work also intensified during the 1930s.[90] The Los Angeles NAACP heightened its reform activities as it brought discriminatory institutions to court, fought to gain black women admittance to L.A. County Hospital's nursing school program, pushed for safer schools for black and Mexican kids in the area, and worked to place more blacks in New Deal programs like the Civil Works Administration. Together with the Northern

California branch, the L.A. branch quickly became one of the two biggest branches in the West.[91]

The African-American community also formed new civil rights organizations in the 1930s, including the Urban League of Los Angeles and the Los Angeles Council of the National Negro Congress (NNC).[92] The local chapter of the newly formed National Negro Congress was headed by Augustus Hawkins just two years after a coalition of largely black and white voters had elected him to the state assembly. The importance of a multiracially elected politician like Hawkins to ethno-racial community organizations like the NNC highlights the relationship between interracial coalitions and individual communities' initiatives.

For Jewish Americans, too, the 1930s deepened their commitment to fighting for their rights and catalyzed the formation of new defense organizations. While Jewish Americans faced increasing exclusion and anti-Semitism, conditions for them were more bearable than they were for other Los Angeles minorities. Jews faced different circumstances in that their rights were never openly attacked in any "reputable quarter," according to historians Max Vorspan and Lloyd Gartner, and no significant public figure or major party spoke out against them.[93] But despite this "façade of safety," Los Angeles Jews faced anti-Semitism, especially from groups like the Ku Klux Klan that used so-called gentlemen's agreements to exclude Jews from home ownership and social groups in Los Angeles neighborhoods. Restrictive covenants completely closed many areas to Jews, as they did their fellow minorities. Elite social and business clubs and even the chamber of commerce, which had had Jewish founders and officers, began to exclude Jews. Myths circulated on Los Angeles radio that Jews had caused the Depression and war.[94] Furthermore, a small group of active local Nazis, including the numerous fascist organizations that operated in Los Angeles like the German Bund, made their lives increasingly difficult.[95] Nazi activity combined with domestically rooted Depression-era conditions in 1933 to spark Los Angeles Jews to create their first self-defense organization, the Community Relations Committee (CRC), which eventually became the L.A. Jewish community's most important civil rights vehicle—especially for collaborative work with other ethno-racial communities.

THE INTERNATIONAL INFLUENCE

The Jewish community's formation of the CRC in response to mounting internationally sparked domestic discrimination exposes the role of international events, along with domestic issues, in heightening minorities' commitment to protect themselves through intensified civil rights activism. International conflicts compounded American minority groups' already precarious situations. They both raised some minorities' aware-ness of their globally unstable positions and exacerbated discrimination against them by triggering it at home.

In the case of Los Angeles Jews, as word of the dangers facing European Jews from Hitler reached the United States, and as fascists began to make inroads at home, they became increasingly aware that an Axis victory would bring severe consequences to them as well as to their compatriots abroad. This recognition inspired them to greater activism not only on behalf of their "kinfolk" in Europe, it also mobilized them to be more vig-ilant about their own security and well-being in the United States. Jews had created a community infrastructure in earlier years, including many mutual aid societies and organizations and workers' groups. But the CRC was the first agency of its kind in Los Angeles, and in the nation, specifi-cally created to monitor domestic anti-Semitic activities and to respond to the growing fascist threat.[96]

Nazi activities in Los Angeles sparked new action in a Jewish community that previously had not focused significant energy on fighting domestically rooted anti-Semitism. Jewish community leaders called meetings to discuss the issue and from one such meeting emerged the Community Relations Committee (CRC)—called the Community Committee until 1941—to monitor local fascist and anti-Semitic activities.[97] The CRC drew participa-tion from a wide array of influential Jewish Los Angeles civic, business, and cultural leaders, including war veterans. Its membership was largely middle class, but Hollywood figures supported the organization, for the most part providing financial backing rather than day-to-day involvement. Prominent participants included the Warner brothers, MGM's president Louis B. Mayer, Paramount Pictures founder Adolph Zukor, and Dore Schary, RKO Pictures screenwriter and producer, and later the president of MGM. Schary remained more active in the CRC's day-to-day affairs than most of its other Hollywood members. Executives of large department stores like the May Company and Bullocks and Barkers were among the CRC's business community representatives.[98] Leaders of the Jewish legal community became especially active, including federal judge Harry Hollzer and the prominent attorneys Isaac Pacht, Loeb and Loeb, and Mendel Silberberg. Pacht became an important member of the Jewish community, as well as a prominent figure in interracial organizing efforts in the 1940s and 1950s.[99] Silberberg, who came from an old-line Los Angeles Jewish family, became the organization's chairman and remained in that position through 1952, when he replaced Isaac Pacht as the president of the Los Angeles Jewish Community Council, the organized Jewish community's umbrella organi-zation. His close ties to the soon-to-be governor Earl Warren, the Chandler family of *Los Angeles Times* fame, and many other local and state politicians and leaders proved very useful to CRC civil rights organizing. Silberberg's strong Hollywood connections also served the organization well for fund-raising and networking purposes.[100] The varied membership of the CRC included veterans of World War I, such as its first executive director from 1933 to 1946 Leon Lewis, who had relocated from Chicago to Los Angeles for health reasons, specifically due to battlefield gas exposure. Lewis and others encouraged the involvement of veterans to help provide the CRC with an element of all-American legitimacy.[101]

Visibly growing and pervasive Nazi activity in 1930s Los Angeles catalyzed these local Jews to organize the CRC as a "civic protective" group. "Profiting by the experience of our unfortunate co-religionists in Germany," Lewis explained to other Jewish community officials, "small committees in several of the larger cities [including Los Angeles] have operated quietly and efficiently since the early part of 1933 to stem a mounting wave of organized activity against the Jew [in the United States]."[102] At the end of the CRC's first year, Lewis reflected upon the Los Angeles Jewish community's sudden awareness of the danger it faced. While "American Jews [had] been confronted with no serious problem of this character" in previous years, he explained, "suddenly the inspiration of Hitlerism resulted in the mushroom growth of a movement" of anti-Semitism.[103]

Los Angeles Jews like those who joined the CRC were particularly aware of the threat fascism posed, since their city was a hotbed for

Figure 1: Nazi Flag outside Downtown Los Angeles Businesses, 1938(?), Folder 8, Box 2, Photo Collection, The Jewish Federation Council of Greater Los Angeles's Community Relations Committee Collection, Urban Archives Center, Oviatt Library, California State University, Northridge.

German nationalist and Nazi activity in the 1930s. Los Angeles Nazis formed the Friends of New Germany, which held its first open meeting during the summer of 1933 in a room next to the Aryan Book Store. Members of the organization, whose major objective was to build anti-Jewish hatred in America, wore brown shirts with red, white, and black swastika arm bands. The secretary of the German-American League of Los Angeles spoke at the meeting, urging the city's fifty German organizations to cooperate in order to "enlighten" the city's approximately 150,000 Germans and German-descent people about the Nazi program.[104] "Nazi or Nazi-phile groups" in 1930s and early 1940s Los Angeles "expended...a great deal of effort...to spread anti-Jewish feelings," according to Leon Lewis. These groups included organizations like the Nazi-affiliated German-American Bund and Silver Shirts, as well as the Ku Klux Klan, along with some members of America First and "numerous 'splinter' organizations operating under a religious, political or patriotic camouflage inspired by selfish ambitions of their leaders who were not above using Nazi 'divide and conquer' techniques to accomplish their ulterior un-American objectives," according to Lewis.[105] In a raid on the German House (Deutsche Haus), the building that housed both the Bund and the Aryan Book Store, authorities confiscated 10,000 pieces of anti-Jewish literature and detained the secretary and four other followers of the Bund.[106] Support for Nazis was so accepted that Angelenos even flew Nazi flags over their downtown businesses.[107]

One particular incident belied the lurking anti-Semitic dangers. On September 19 and 30, 1935, fascist sympathizers inserted approximately 50,000 copies of an anti-Semitic pamphlet into home editions of the *Los Angeles Times*, the largest newspaper in the Southern California region. They also posted the pamphlets on Southern California telephone poles, slipped them under doors, left them on street corners, and tossed them into automobiles. Some *Times* employees apparently had sneaked them into the paper, allegedly without management's knowledge. The pamphlet accused Jews of "show[ing] complete disregard of our law" and "evidenc[ing] a positive contempt for every element of our Christian morality and common decency." Furthermore, it charged that Jews display "unspeakably bestial degeneracy." They supposedly had a "distinctly racial program" which called for "the seduction of a SHIKSE (any Gentile girl, young or unprotected)" and performed "lewd and lascivious acts...intended to introduce vice and perversions into the lives of small children." Among many other attacks, the pamphlet charged that Jews "have promoted a widespread contempt for the ordinary virtues of honor and honesty in business," and asserted that Jews owned the movies, radio, and many magazines and newspapers—which all was part of an attempt to control access to "our people." The pamphlet accused Jews of "fomenting discontent, radicalism, and Communistic revolution." It cited a survey that stated that 95 percent of all Communist agita-

Figure 2: Nazis Meet at Los Angeles Deutsches Haus to Celebrate Hitler's Birthday, April 20, 1935, Folder 8, Box 2, Photo Collection, The Jewish Federation Council of Greater Los Angeles's Community Relations Committee Collection, Urban Archives Center, Oviatt Library, California State University, Northridge.

tors and propagandists in America were Jews and encouraged all Americans to boycott Jewish businesses, explaining that money "spent at the movies may endorse and support further Jewish attacks upon our Christian morality."[108] In the wake of this incident, and in response to the rise of local fascism generally, Carey McWilliams published a booklet titled *It Can Happen Here: Active Anti-Semitism in Los Angeles* in which he reproduced the anti-Semitic pamphlet and issued a call to arms against fascism in Los Angeles and California more broadly. "I undertook the investigation," McWilliams wrote, "because I have come to believe that California is that state of the union which has advanced furthest toward an integrated fascist setup."[109] Such local incidents of fascism compounded the fears of Jews in Los Angeles and across the country.

Investigations in Southern California revealed an extensive network of people and even in-depth plans to support the Germans militarily. According to a former German-American Bund member's testimony before a committee investigating "subversive activities," Bund members discussed plans at their 1936 meetings to "paralyze the Pacific Coast from Seattle to

San Diego." The witness testified that 100 Bund members, including many who were machinists or mechanics with the requisite skills, declared they were willing and able to do this work. The Bund functioned as "an arm of the Nazi government for espionage purposes," according to the informant, who also explained that in 1936 he and other L.A. Bund leaders had helped a German espionage agent photograph U.S. submarine and destroyer bases in San Diego for the Nazis. The witness emphasized, moreover, that the group's secretary Herman Schwinn described himself as a "representative of the German government."[110] The problem, of course, was not limited to Los Angeles. Growing numbers of Americans nationwide attended German-American Bund and other anti-Semitic rallies, and an estimated 14,000,000 Americans listened to Father Charles Coughlin's anti-Semitic weekly radio addresses.[111]

Evidence of Nazi activity in Los Angeles revived Americans' residual fears of German infiltration through Mexico. Americans' World War I–era discovery of Germany's Zimmerman telegram, which made overtures to Mexico to ally against the United States, initially sparked these concerns. Los Angeles newspaper articles in the late 1930s spread the alarm that this time, Germany would successfully defeat the United States. One such article reported that 116 leaders of the West Coast "Hitler movement" were in Southern California planning to make contacts with other Nazi organizations in Mexico and eventually Canada.[112] Others speculated that negotiations between the two countries to exchange Mexican oil for fifty German "passenger" planes were a prelude for Mexico's entry into the war.[113] Another 1940 newspaper article reported that Nazis recently had hung posters around Mexico City promising Germany's help returning California, New Mexico, Arizona, Texas, and part of Colorado to Mexico in exchange for Mexican support.[114]

It is difficult to explain this high level of both Nazi activity and fears of Nazi infiltration in a location so far from Europe. Joseph Roos, an Austrian Jewish immigrant who had been raised in Germany and became the CRC's executive secretary in the postwar era, later offered one plausible explanation. Roos believed that Joseph Goebbels, Hitler's propaganda minister, chose Los Angeles as a point of entry for the Nazi Bund's propaganda because "he figured that in New York—they never called it New York, they called it 'Jew York'—there were so damn many Jews, they'll go and throw it into the ocean." Jewish Americans' investigations determined that Goebbels sent material first to Los Angeles for subsequent distribution to all other Bunds across the United States.[115]

Jewish community leaders originally formed the CRC to monitor and report on the activities of local groups like the Bund perceived to be threats to Jews and to democracy more generally. Consequently, in its early years the CRC focused primarily on monitoring fascist, pro-Nazi, and anti-Semitic groups, gathering and processing information about them and countering their propaganda through public education.[116] The CRC sent spies to infiltrate Nazi and pro-German organizations' meetings, monitored their publications, followed their public activities, and gauged their influence throughout the city. Spies reported back about Bund and Friends of New Germany members' activities, including what cars they drove, where they drove them, whom they talked and associated with, and what transpired at their meetings. The CRC published extensive reports in its affiliated News Research Service and developed relationships with local Jewish press and other publishers in an attempt to persuade them to expose the groups' activities in their newspapers. The CRC also sponsored educational workshops and pressed law enforcement officials and politicians to be more vigilant about anti-Semitic activity.

While groups like the Friends of New Germany and the Silver Shirts lost membership and power, CRC attempts to curb Los Angeles Nazi and other anti-Semitic activities by exposing them to the public and to law enforcement officials met with many challenges.[117] Problems especially

Figure 3: Anti-Nazi Rally in Los Angeles, August 1938, Folder 7, Box 1, Photo Collection, The Jewish Federation Council of Greater Los Angeles's Community Relations Committee Collection, Urban Archives Center, Oviatt Library, California State University, Northridge.

arose as Los Angeles law enforcement officials' own anti-Semitism became evident. Los Angeles Police Chief Davis granted CRC executive director Leon Lewis a meeting in 1933 but rebuffed him after merely three minutes, as Lewis began to explain his hope that the CRC and police department would share information and coordinate monitoring activities. Davis curtly explained that the police department would do its job to protect life and property, but that he would not disclose information about its activities. As Davis continued, he shocked Lewis by revealing his own anti-Semitic views: Germany had been forced into action because Germans could not compete economically with Jews. Furthermore, he said, Henry Ford had found the same difficulty in competing with Jews, so he had "gone after" them as well, but had not been able to get away with it.[118] Whether because of officials' anti-Semitism or mere apathy, throughout the 1930s such local officials largely ignored the CRC's pleas to increase their vigilance against fascists and anti-Semites in Los Angeles.

After Pearl Harbor and the United States' entry into World War II, though, CRC members found themselves relieved of some of this monitoring work. Officials began arresting numerous Angelenos and charging them, as Nazis, with subversive activities.[119] A federal grand jury indicted Herman Schwinn, the former West Coast chairman of the German-American Bund and a Silver Shirt member, on charges of conspiracy and sedition. It also indicted Frank K. Ferenz, who had been distributing Nazi films, and Hans Diebel, the Aryan Book Store's operator.[120] An early 1942 *LA Examiner* newspaper headline blared, "'Baby Bunds' Shown Still in Existence." The article reported that federal officials had located these organizations that helped aliens and naturalized Germans work for the German Reich. It also cited the U.S. attorney general John Martin Dean as saying that the U.S. government had sent these pro-Nazi members of the West Coast Bund to eastern concentration camps.[121]

The federal and local government's more active involvement in these groups' activities, which officially became subversive once the United States entered the war against Germany, enabled the CRC to shift to other issues important to the Jewish community, primarily building bridges with other communities. In this way, the coalescence of domestic and international threats in the early 1930s marked the official beginning of the Los Angeles Jewish community's struggle to fight for its own rights and, later, for other minorities'.

Like Jews, the West Coast Chinese-American community was propelled into deeper activism by events in the global sphere. For Chinese Americans, World War II began after the 1931 Manchurian Incident. The Chinese argued that the Japanese army provided a justification for attacking Manchuria by destroying a few feet of track on the Japanese-owned South Manchurian Railway, while the Japanese argued they moved into Manchuria to "restore order" after a staged Chinese attack on the railway.

The incident marked the start of the war between China and Japan and immediately sparked Chinese Americans' increased involvement in the Asian conflict and, along with it, their more active involvement in domestic American politics.[122]

Chinese Americans were a small percentage of the Los Angeles population, especially relative to places like San Francisco, but the way the international war affected their larger community illustrates very well the confluence between international events and domestic ethnic activism in the 1930s. Chinese and Chinese Americans in the United States found ways to support China against Japan's aggression. In communities across the United States, concentrated on the West Coast but also in eastern urban areas like New York City, Chinese Americans organized demonstrations and mass meetings, raised relief funds, called for a nationwide boycott of Japanese goods, and spread propaganda against Japan.[123] After the United States entered the war in 1941, they continued to support China.

The Chinese-origin community's involvement in China's affairs stemmed not only from an interest rooted in familial and nationalist ties to the country, but also from a sense of marginalization and exclusion in their adopted country. Beginning in the mid-nineteenth century, white Americans abused Chinese immigrants and their descendants, particularly on the West Coast. For instance, laws forbade Chinese immigrants from naturalizing, and beginning in 1882, the government began to exclude Chinese immigrants from the United States.[124] Long-term racism and lack of acceptance in the United States helped push even American-born Chinese and long-term Chinese immigrant residents to orient themselves toward Chinese politics. Some Chinese newspapers went so far as to advise American-born Chinese to "return" to China because of the discrimination they faced in the United States. The exclusion made many of them feel like immigrants, causing them to identify with China during Japan's invasion.[125]

Because some members of the U.S. Chinese community believed that a strong China could help guarantee their rights in America and that they would not gain respect until China itself did, strengthening China became a step along the path to equality at home.[126] Chinese Americans who held this view saw their struggles for equality in the United States as inextricably tied to China's victory against Japan.

The connection between war abroad in the 1930s and building momentum for civil rights at home is most clearly illustrated by Jewish and Chinese Americans' experience. But international circumstances compelled other groups to domestic civil rights action too. For Mexican-origin people, the link between the quest for civil rights in the United States and struggles in Mexico was rooted in a period before the 1930s, and was less connected to events associated with the global Great War than with the Mexican Revolution. The ideologies and skills some immigrants had developed and used across the border, fighting in the Mexican Revolution of 1910–20, helped shape the community's struggles for justice in the United States. Josefina Fierro de Bright, whose parents' involvement fighting in the Mexican Revolution influenced her activist ideologies and commitment that she applied to El Congreso and elsewhere, demonstrates this connection. Her mother had supported Ricardo Flores Magón, one of the most radical revolutionary leaders, while her father fought with the revolutionary general Pancho Villa.[127] While the Mexican revolutionaries fought for different goals than they and their counterparts did in Los Angeles rights struggles, their experience in the revolution nevertheless shaped a tradition of struggle that helped inspire the Mexican-origin community's American involvement. Moreover, because before the 1848 Treaty of Guadalupe Hidalgo the American Southwest had been Mexican, it is hard to separate Mexican Americans' "domestic" struggles from the international.

For Los Angeles African Americans too, international events during the 1930s inspired growing domestic commitments. Loren Miller, one of the main actors in this story of burgeoning Los Angeles civil rights activism, explained in a 1933 essay titled "Goodbye to Isolation" that his recent visit to the Soviet Union had helped convince him that communism offered an avenue for world cooperation and for the advancement of black people everywhere, including the United States and Africa.[128] Miller had sailed the preceding summer to the Soviet Union, traveling under Soviet sponsorship with nineteen other African Americans, including Langston Hughes and other less famous travel companions who represented a cross-section of the African-American population. The Soviets had planned to sponsor a film about African-American life in the United States, with the intent of portraying the Soviet Union in a positive light. The film never materialized. But the experience shaped Miller's views for the next half-decade. Miller explained that his travel in the Soviet Union convinced him that the Communists had been able to "reconcile the age old difference between more than a hundred once hostile groups, [and] have hit upon the doctrine that will satisfy the historically rooted urge for national greatness at the same time it builds internationalism."[129] This Soviet experience helps explain Miller's commitment during the 1930s to cooperating with communists in Los Angeles for civil rights and other causes.

Incidentally, domestic commitments also in turn fueled African Americans' international involvement. In his essay, Miller urged his fellow black Angelenos to not only pursue their struggle at home, but also to become more engaged in the international realm. He explained, "A bound-together world is birthing internationalism." Especially concerning the Soviet Union and Ethiopia—where Haile Selassie I was leading the country to greatness as a model for all black people, "The Negro must bid goodbye to Isolation."[130] Nationally, African Americans increasingly looked abroad during the 1930s and recognized that black struggles extended beyond American borders, especially as Ethiopia struggled for freedom against Italian colonial domination from 1935 to 1936. Ethiopia's battle sparked American blacks' noticeable entry into foreign policy activism, especially as they became frustrated with the United States' decision to take a neutral stance in the conflict. From the time of Ethiopia's invasion through the immediate postwar years, many black civil rights organizations, including the NAACP, adopted an antico-lonial critique of U.S. foreign policy.[131] Italy's invasion of Ethiopia sparked antifascist activity in Los Angeles generally. The American League against War and Fascism organized a meeting in Los Angeles soon after Mussolini's invasion of Ethiopia, which marked what Carey McWilliams believed to be "the beginning of the antifascist phase of the politics of the 1930s" in Los Angeles. McWilliams also remarked upon the large sum of money California raised for the battle against fascism.[132] Los Angeles African Americans, who were in constant contact with national African-American colleagues through local branches of organizations like the Urban League and the NAACP, and whose Loren Miller displayed an interest in Ethiopian affairs and independence only two years earlier, likely joined their L.A. neighbors and African Americans nationwide in supporting Ethiopia's antifascist campaign.[133]

The connection between international consciousness and domestic activism is less obvious for Los Angeles's African-American and Mexican-descent community than it is for its Jewish population. Regardless, the 1930s were a key era for many Los Angeles communities' civil rights developments—many of which were increasingly collaborative—in no small part because of international conditions. The 1936 formation of the Hollywood Anti-Nazi League for the Defense of American Democracy illustrates this rising interracial civil rights tendency and its connection to the international events which increasingly came home to Americans. As members of the league explained to County Supervisor Ford, they cre-ated an interracial commission of "Hindus, Negroes, Whites, Japanese, Chinese, Koreans, Filipinos, and others" to fight against rising domestic Nazism, which they viewed as a "vital threat" to racial tolerance.[134]

Activists mobilized to fight for their rights as discriminatory conditions became increasingly apparent in the 1930s. A combination of factors, including the intensity of discrimination and new options provided by the New Deal and other forms of political engagement like labor unions and the Communist Party, motivated ethno-racial groups' civil rights efforts. El Congreso and the other organizations that crystallized during the 1930s embody the ways the decade sparked civil rights activism.

Some of these nascent movements reflected cooperation across the center-to-left political spectrum and among ethno-racial communities, which formed lasting networks that became springboards for later activism, as subsequent chapters will explore. These initiatives and organizations demonstrate how international factors also inspired this heightened civil rights activism. The international realm played an increasingly important role in domestic civil rights efforts as the United States entered the global arena in full force in the years that followed, marching onto the battlefields of World War II in Europe, Asia, and elsewhere, and taking the stage as a developing world power. The U.S. entry into World War II provided activists with ammunition to justify their battles and to ensure results, as the next chapter will reveal.

CHAPTER 3

The War Comes Home

As the United States entered World War II in 1941, many Los Angeles minorities, like Americans nationwide, joined the road to economic recovery by getting jobs in the war industry and by joining the military. While wartime put them on more equal footing with the majority population in some ways, it exacerbated preexisting problems of discrimination, as well as gave Los Angeles's marginalized groups new leverage in their ongoing struggles for equal treatment. It ushered in increased civil rights awareness, activities, and legislation around the city and the country.[1]

Local minorities' growing leverage came in part from Los Angeles's increasing national prominence and importance to the U.S. war effort. The city's own wartime transformations reflected the nation's changing status: its mounting national importance as a center of wartime production paralleled the United States' growing international role. And, as the United States became more globally prominent, national attention shifted to this southwestern city whose stability affected the war effort. Los Angeles's unique location as a crossroads for people from Latin America and Asia made race relations there particularly crucial to the U.S. war effort, both in the European and Pacific theaters. National attention especially focused on the city as international observers zeroed in on the discrimination there against increasingly diverse, multinational populations—discrimination that called into question the United States' commitment to fighting for democracy against Hitler's racial supremacy.

Two well-known wartime incidents and their aftermath illustrate how the war brought new leverage for social justice, particularly how international events facilitated the building of domestic interracial struggles. The Sleepy Lagoon murder case and the Zoot Suit Riots reflected a city exploding with racist incidents against Mexican Americans. These domestic eruptions drew negative attention to Los Angeles from both national and international audiences at the same time the United States relied more on its alliances with Latin America, China, and the European powers. When exposed to an increasingly attentive world, discrimination in Los Angeles created an international public relations fiasco and

60

jeopardized U.S. alliances, making local discrimination not only a national but an international issue. The negative spotlight forced the hand of previously reluctant local officials, who increasingly focused their attention on minorities' plight. Events like these also brought the relatively parallel struggles of minority groups into greater contact with each other, thereby facilitating an increasingly interracial, coalitional activism. Part of this increasing contact came in the form of interracial organizations created by city and county officials and those white citizens who recognized the importance of easing discrimination, while some of it originated in minorities' own initiatives that emerged from the opportunity provided by the international fight against the Axis powers. Minorities strengthened existing interracial efforts like El Congreso, and instigated new ones like the Sleepy Lagoon Defense Committee, the coalition that came together to address the nationally and internationally visible racial injustice in Los Angeles. This chapter explores how the war legitimized civil rights reform as a goal, creating a window of opportunity for diverse activists to join forces and push for change.

A NATIONAL AND INTERNATIONAL CROSSROADS

Los Angeles's centrality to wartime production transformed it into a racially and ethnically diverse city whose newcomers and long-term residents were forced to confront each others' differences. The city became an even greater draw for migrants during the war years. Its booming defense industry beckoned diverse populations to take advantage of these and other employment opportunities.[2] Los Angeles's population increased by a dramatic 14 percent during the early war years—from 1,504,277 in 1940 to 1,718,000 in 1943—as it lured migrants with its abundant jobs. Second only to Detroit, it received over $11 billion in war contracts, which fostered more jobs than any other western or northern wartime production center.[3]

Minority groups composed much of this newcomer population. African Americans from the South and Southwest, Mexican-origin populations from across the international border and Southwest, Jews and other European-origin "ethnic" groups from Europe, the Midwest, and the East Coast, and Midwestern whites flocked to the region. African Americans migrated to Los Angeles in record numbers, more than doubling between 1940 and 1950.[4] Six thousand African Americans arrived in Los Angeles each month at the peak of migration in 1943.[5] The city's Mexican-descent population grew 46 percent between 1940 and 1950 as newcomers joined the city's long-term population, many of whom had been there since before the 1848 war with Mexico.[6] Its Jewish-American population increased by 15 percent from 1941 to 1945, and by 1948 it had grown by a stunning 92 percent from the prewar period.[7] By some estimates 168,000 Jews, 200,000 African Americans, 235,000 Mexican-origin people, 5,000 Chinese-origin people, and 12,000 Japanese-origin people lived in Los Angeles by 1946. Some locals estimated that minorities composed 40 percent of the city's population by 1950, though 30 percent is probably a more accurate figure.[8]

This tremendous population growth severely strained Los Angeles's infrastructure. Housing shortages became a particularly difficult problem. Los Angeles was more spread out than other cities like Chicago or New York, but a wartime overcrowding crisis developed despite its expansive geographic landscape. Newly built public housing was insufficient to meet demand. Even the L.A. Housing Authority's move to double its capacity from 13,000 people in 1941 to 27,000 by 1943 barely helped the over 200,000 people who relocated to Los Angeles in the early years of the war.[9] The housing crisis affected L.A.'s minority communities most severely, since pervasive restrictive racial covenants that persisted from earlier in the century prevented minority migrants from moving into white neighborhoods and kept them confined to the growing ethnic ghettoes, barrios, and other increasingly crowded areas. A 1945 city report estimated an 11,000 person housing deficit for African Americans—approximately 10 percent of the city's total black population. Overcrowding was so bad in one predominantly African-American neighborhood that an area previously housing 30,000 residents contained over 70,000 by 1944.[10]

During the war various ethnic and racial groups shared common space. Multiracial neighborhoods, particularly on the east side of the city in places like Boyle Heights, counted among their residents Mexicans and Mexican Americans, African Americans, immigrant and American Jews, Italians, and other eastern European ethnic immigrant groups like Molokan Russians. Residents mixed at dances, shared community centers, and attended the same high schools. The student body of Roosevelt High School, an east side school, was extremely multiethnic. The area's mixed populations swam together at the Menorah Center, a Jewish community institution opened in 1928 in the east side's City Terrace neighborhood, in the only swimming pool available to them within five square miles.[11]

Increasing violence and harassment from whites accompanied the growth, diversity, and mixture of races.[12] The Zoot Suit Riots which erupted throughout the city in June 1943 illustrated these tensions most dramatically. From June 3 through June 13, violence between the Mexican-origin community and servicemen from local military installations raged on the streets of downtown and East Los Angeles. White servicemen looking for young men wearing zoot suits, a style of clothing popular in the Mexican community, rode streetcars through the city, jumping off and beating their chosen victims. Mexican-American (as well as some African-American) men—including many not wearing zoot suits—were stripped and beaten by mobs and later unfairly arrested as the instigators. Although nobody died, many Mexican Americans suffered violence. In one instance, white servicemen looking for Mexican "zoot suiters" yanked Pedro García, a graduating senior at an east side high school, out of a seat at a movie theater and dragged him outside into the street. While a large group of white bystanders watched, they tore off his clothes, kicked, and beat him until he was bloody and unconscious. Policemen witnessed the scene but did nothing to intervene.[13] Contemporary press reports blamed Mexican-American "zoot suiters" for the violence. But racist servicemen provoked the riots against Mexican-origin men wearing zoot suits, and local authorities did little or nothing to help stop the violence.[14] Relations between whites and minorities were strained throughout the period. John Anson Ford, a prominent white ally of civil rights activists on the L.A. County Board of Supervisors from 1934 until 1958, later recalled the unusual severity of tensions in wartime Los Angeles. "Perhaps never before had so large a population in America experienced the variety and intensity of racial friction that marked World War II and its aftermath in Los Angeles County," Ford wrote in his memoir.[15]

Ideological tensions in Los Angeles magnified the turmoil in this heterogeneous, overcrowded environment. Immigrants, migrants, and native Angelenos encountered each other in a fear-ridden, suspicious environment, particularly in the wake of Pearl Harbor. The city's importance to the defense industry made it a potential target for both Axis powers abroad and "subversive forces" at home, including Axis sympathizers, communists, and other perceived enemies. Widespread concern spread as fears of attack from within Los Angeles permeated daily life. The local American Legion declared that Southern California was "spotted with subversive organizations aggressively spreading dissention [sic], defeatism, obstruction to our war effort and open disloyalty to the United States of America."[16] The region was an "Achilles' heel" of enemy propaganda and the possibility of enemy attack, the legion explained, because of its extensive defense industries.[17] Such fears indicate the high levels of stress many Los Angeles residents experienced.

The American Legion, along with other private and governmental groups, monitored the regional activities of these "alien" influences and issued a pamphlet on how to identify subversives. Groups being watched included newly formed organizations like the Friends of Progress and the World Events Forum, as well as preexisting ones like the Friends of New Germany and the German Bund. Domestic-oriented groups like the KKK and America First were observed too because, though they did not necessarily have foreign ties, their white supremacist activities divided the American population and were believed to harm the war effort.[18]

The migration of many German intellectual exiles to Los Angeles fed public suspicions of dangerous foreign influences too. Los Angeles's warm climate and the possibility of finding work in the film industry attracted émigrés such as authors Bertolt Brecht, Lion Feuchtwanger, Heinrich and Thomas Mann, Erich Maria Remarque, and Franz Werfel. Federal and state agencies monitored them and others for suspected subversion in this "key area for exile surveillance," as historian Alexander Stephen dubbed Los Angeles. German refugees were particularly monitored for communism by the FBI, the Office of Strategic Services (the CIA's forerunner, which intercepted and examined mail), the Department of State, the House Un-American Activities Committee (HUAC), and the California version of HUAC known as the Tenney Committee, one of the earliest, most powerful, and active state un-American activities committees in the country.[19]

Fears of an attack on Los Angeles and of internal subversion mushroomed in the wake of the December 7, 1941, surprise attack on Pearl Harbor. Edgy Angelenos expected that the Japanese might just as easily target their vulnerable Pacific port city. Reports of submarines "lurking" off the coast, of Fifth Column activities, and of Japanese infantry units "poised for attack" were common in California.[20] One false alarm especially intensified these fears. The U.S. Army warned at 2:25 A.M. on February 26, 1942, that unidentified aircraft approached the city. Antiaircraft batteries fired rounds against what turned out to be empty sky. "Roaring out of a brilliant moonlit western sky, foreign aircraft flying both in large formation and singly flew over Southern California early today and drew heavy barrages of antiaircraft fire—the first ever to sound over United States continental soil against an enemy invader," the *Los Angeles Times* incorrectly reported.[21] The population at large particularly suspected minorities, whose racial backgrounds supposedly associated them with enemy forces, of conspiring against them. Further inflaming racial and xenophobic hatred, one typical headline in the *Los Angeles Times* proclaimed in 1943, "Startling Jap Spy Activity Here Told."[22]

THE WAR TRANSFORMS OFFICIALS' APPROACHES TO MINORITIES

As global war tensions mounted, Angelenos realized that their own neighborhoods became battlefields in the Allied effort. Disturbances at home threatened both to undermine the United States' international reputation and to weaken the home front unity crucial to an Allied success. Concern that discriminatory treatment of minority groups might jeopardize the United States' international status and security resonated throughout Los Angeles and moved white Los Angeles officials to improve race relations by increasingly supporting civil rights.

The fear that exposed racism would weaken support from U.S. allies was particularly salient with respect to Latin America, given the city's large Latin American-origin—particularly Mexican—population. Retaining Latin American support meant treating the United States' Latin American–descent population decently, or at the very least disguising discriminatory treatment from public view. A worried County Supervisor Ford explained to Attorney General Biddle in 1942 that discrimination against West Coast minority groups jeopardized Latin American support. Ford mentioned to Biddle that a State Department representative had warned him that Axis propagandists in South America used the U.S. failure to give minority groups equality and democratic justice to gain support for their cause.[23]

Newspapers around the globe publicized the racial discrimination exhibited in Los Angeles in the Sleepy Lagoon and Zoot Suit incidents. Axis agents in Latin America used evidence of American racism as a tool to sway Latin Americans toward the fascists. Their radio broadcasts publicized the northern city's Sleepy Lagoon transgressions when, in late 1942 and early 1943, seventeen Mexican-American boys were tried and unjustly convicted for the death of teenager José Díaz. Díaz was discovered on August 2, 1942, lying unconscious on a dirt road near the Sleepy Lagoon, a water-filled gravel pit used as a swimming hole on the largely immigrant and minority east side of Los Angeles. He later died of wounds whose cause was never actually determined. Police arrested the entire group of seventeen boys (in addition to five others whom they later released), who had attended a party with the victim the night before he died. Anti-Mexican sentiment helped convict the boys. Local papers, including the *Los Angeles Times*, whipped up anti-Mexican hysteria by calling them members of the 38th Street gang. According to one neighborhood observer, though, it was really a group of kids who "just hung out together."[24] The police submitted a report to the grand jury that declared Mexicans inherently criminal and biologically prone to violence, and irregularities marked the trial. Despite months in jail, the judge would not allow the defendants to cut their hair or change their clothes. A guilty verdict on Jan 12, 1943, resulted in the largest mass conviction in California history to that point. The judge sentenced three of the boys to life in prison for first-degree murder, and found nine guilty of second degree murder and five of assault.[25] Latin American radio reported on the case in broadcasts such as the following on January 13, 1943: "In Los Angeles, California, the so-called City of Angels, twelve Mexican boys were found guilty today of a single murder and five others were convicted of assault growing out of the same case. The 360,000 Mexicans of Los Angeles are reported up in arms over this Yankee persecution. The concentration camps of Los Angeles are said to be overflowing with members of this persecuted minority," it continued. "This is justice for you, as practiced by the 'Good Neighbor,' Uncle Sam, a justice that demands seventeen victims for one crime."[26]

A report prepared for the House of Representatives cited forty-nine instances of negative Mexican reactions to incidents like the Sleepy Lagoon case and the Zoot Suit Riots. These included refusing to send farm laborers to Texas because of "unjust discriminations and other violations of the Good Neighbor Policy," according to President Camacho's addresses to the Mexican people. The report warned, "Failure to continue to do our utmost to reduce race discriminations against [sic] Mexicans here and to build mutual understanding will mean more effective Axis propaganda broadcasts beamed to Mexico and the rest of Latin America."[27]

Within days of the Zoot Suit Riots' outbreak, Francisco Castillo Najera, the Mexican ambassador to the United States, requested that Secretary of State Cordell Hull publicly condemn the riots. Najera warned Hull that news of the riots would travel quickly throughout Latin America and strengthen Axis propaganda against the United States.[28] Najera's prophecy came to fruition. One Mexico City publication charged that at the same time the United States opposed "the racial theories of Germany, [it] feeds, sustains, and cultivates this racism in its own territories against Mexicans."[29] The coverage of these racist events introduced Mexico and Latin America's general public to the social and political realities faced by Mexican-origin people in the United States.[30]

Federal, state, and local officials scrambled to repair the country's tarnished image in the wake of these exposures of Los Angeles racism, fearing that evidence of discrimination would reverse years of U.S. efforts to strengthen alliances with countries in the Southern Hemisphere and pave the way for enemy countries to gain influence in Latin America.[31] Within two days of his meeting with the Mexican consul Najera, Secretary of State Hull promised that the United States would investigate the matter fully. Hull assured Najera that if investigations revealed that the riots victimized Mexican nationals, the United States would proceed according to international law and appease the Mexican people and government. The State Department revealed its ongoing concern by sending William Blocker, the U.S. consul general in Ciudad Juárez, Mexico, to Los Angeles in July 1943 to investigate the riots. Blocker interviewed Mexican consular officials and local American authorities, including the mayor and the sheriff.[32] Apprehension about potential negative foreign reaction to news of the Zoot Suit Riots motivated California senator Sheridan Downey and other U.S. officials to urge the government to investigate even before rioting had stopped.[33]

The United States' dependence on support, resources, and manpower from Latin America, particularly Mexico, to sustain its wartime agenda made addressing discrimination against Mexican-origin people especially urgent. Latin America was a frontline of defense against fascist expansion, and the United States needed Latin American alliances to prevent Axis incursions in the Western Hemisphere. Strengthening the Pan American system could help counterbalance events in Berlin, President Roosevelt and Secretary of State Cordell Hull believed from as early as the mid-1930s. The United States declared at the 1938 Pan American Conference in Lima, Peru, that Latin American groups "akin" to the National Socialist Party in Germany, and receiving supplies of German arms or Axis propaganda, represented "Axis penetration" into Latin America.[34]

American officials and citizens feared Axis incursions into the Western Hemisphere would undermine the Allies' war effort, a situation that Los Angeles's anti-Mexican discrimination only exacerbated. FDR warned the American people in that same year that Germany might seek economic control over Latin America and use hemispheric military bases to launch attacks against the United States. In one of his famous fireside chats in December 1940, FDR warned, "There are those who say that the Axis powers would never have any desire to attack the Western Hemisphere. That is the same dangerous form of wishful thinking which has destroyed the powers of resistance of so many conquered peoples." Roosevelt cautioned that Axis forces might pursue Latin America's resources, which he called "the most tempting loot in all of the round world."[35] Seventy percent of people surveyed in a *Fortune* magazine poll in the summer of 1940 believed the United States would have to fight Germany to prevent it from trying to gain control of Latin America.[36] FBI Special Intelligence Service personnel returned from Central and South America in July 1940 with what they reported as a great deal of evidence of fascist activities.[37]

Signs of fascist advances in U.S. Mexican communities like those in Los Angeles seemed to validate these worries, and heighten concerns that discrimination would fuel the Mexican-American community's anger against the United States. The sinarquistas, a pro-fascist organization founded in Mexico in 1937 by a German Nazi and his Mexican sympathizers, made inroads in L.A.'s Mexican barrios that same year. The group, which had 500,000 supporters in Mexico, promised Mexican Americans that returning the Southwest to Mexico would accompany a Nazi victory. Estimates of the group's support in California vary, from 50,000 supporters in the state to only 2,000 in the Southern California region.[38] But regardless of the actual numbers, the organization gained supporters and instilled fear in local and federal officials.

The United States relied upon Latin American support during the war for other reasons besides preventing an Axis takeover from within the hemisphere. The "Bracero Program" (officially the Emergency Farm Labor Program) supplied much-needed agricultural and railroad workers while the armed forces and war industries diverted American labor.[39] Latin American raw materials including metals and agricultural products also fueled the Allied war effort, since war production diverted most North American resources and the fighting disrupted traditional supply lines between the United States and much of Europe, Asia, and Africa.[40] Mexico's military assisted the United States too. Mexico allowed the United States to build military bases on its soil, and its military supplied air forces—the 201st Air Squadron—to fight in the Philippines in 1945. Perhaps most significant, the Mexican government permitted Mexican citizens living in the United States to be drafted into the U.S. armed forces—without reciprocal rights applying to U.S. citizens living in Mexico. As many as 250,000 Mexican citizens served in the U.S. military during World War II, in addition to an estimated 500,000 to a million Mexican Americans.[41]

Despite Mexico's declaration within days of Pearl Harbor of its unconditional support for the Allies and these activities, racism against Mexican-origin people in the United States jeopardized the country's support.[42] American authorities knew that Mexico's population remained unconvinced that its government made the right choice in supporting the Allied war effort. Many Mexicans felt detached from the war, uncertain that the cause justified sacrifices. A minority of Mexicans even supported the Germans.[43] As Latin American countries, particularly Mexico, voiced their concern, local and federal U.S. officials recognized the strategic international importance of remedying perceptions of discrimination against Los Angeles's Mexican-origin people.[44]

Federal and local officials worked to counter portrayals of American racism. Representatives from the Office of the Coordinator of Inter-American Affairs, created within the Department of Commerce in the fall of 1941, asked Los Angeles–area newspapers soon after the Sleepy Lagoon arrests to tone down their negative coverage of Mexican Americans. Such efforts were effective, according to observer Carey McWilliams, as much of the coverage quieted or disappeared from October to December.[45]

Moreover, recognizing that race relations in Los Angeles played a key role in building and maintaining Latin American good will, local and federal governments used the city to promote positive relations with its southern neighbors. The Office of the Coordinator of Inter-American Affairs cosponsored (with the Western College Association) an Institute on Inter-American Relations and Post-war Planning in early 1943 that emphasized the importance of the "Latin culture" in the United States. Organizers hoped it would further the Good Neighbor Policy and Pan-Americanism. Los Angeles was an obvious choice of location because of its pervasive "Spanish background [population] and infusion of Latin culture."[46] The institute recognized that improving Mexican Americans' status, specifically in terms of youth, housing, labor, and education, would help ensure smooth relationships with Latin America.

Local government officials, who could no longer trivialize the problems of groups like ethnic Mexicans in the city that they had promoted for many years by labeling it "more Anglo-Saxon than the mother country today" with the hope of encouraging Anglo-American migration and economic investment, conducted a wartime campaign to educate Angelenos about Latin America in the interests of promoting a good neighborly relationship.[47] The Los Angeles County Public Library published a pamphlet called *Republics of the Western Hemisphere* in which it provided a reading list to "help Americans gain insight into the history, politics, resources, and customs of the countries of Latin America and an understanding of the problem of hemispheric defense."[48] Mayor Fletcher Bowron emphasized that Los Angeles welcomed "all U.S. neighbors," including Mexicans, South and Central Americans, and Canadians. His denial that wartime circumstances motivated his emphatic welcome could not mask the obvious connection. Shortly after Mexico declared its support for the Allies, Bowron explained, "I hope that our southern neighbors do not feel that we are now attempting to court their affections because of present world conditions. We will remain friends and continue the spirit of neighborliness long after the dark clouds of war have drifted away." But Bowron betrayed his own intentions by indicating that the threat of Axis infiltration into the Western Hemisphere did in fact motivate his attempt to solidify bonds between North and Latin America. "Just now we all realize..." he explained, "that we must stand shoulder to shoulder for the protection of the Western Hemisphere and the principles of democracy."[49]

Bowron also began speaking at celebrations around Los Angeles in 1941 in honor of Mexican Independence Day and in 1942 for Cinco de Mayo. The timing of Bowron's appearance at these events was more than coincidental. At a 1943 Mexican Independence Day celebration, he proclaimed, "We all love freedom and we are fighting side by side against common enemies to protect our independence from any vestige of domination by the forces of military might and aggression on the other side of either ocean."[50] Bowron celebrated another holiday in 1944 using similar language: "We rejoice with those to whom Cinco de Mayo symbolizes the spirit of freedom for which Mexican patriots fought 82 years ago. On that day, in the decisive battle with the French forces at Puebla, the Mexicans rejected for all time the idea of any foreign intervention."[51] Needless to say, Bowron did not mention the "foreign intervention" displayed when the United States wrenched California and other parts of the Southwest from Mexico in 1848.

Federal officials pressured local officials to ameliorate conditions to help ensure the success of the war effort. The Office of War Information in Washington D.C. reiterated to Mayor Bowron that discrimination (or even merely the impression of it) against Mexicans and Mexican Americans in

Figure 4: Mayor Bowron Celebrates Cinco de Mayo on Olvera Street, Los Angeles's Historic and Tourist Mexican Heritage Site, ca. 1952 (similar events took place during World War II), Los Angeles Daily News Collection, Department of Special Collections, Charles E. Young Research Library, UCLA.

the United States jeopardized military success.[52] Its inquiry after the Sleepy Lagoon arrests prompted Bowron to coerce local agencies and institutions into remedying discriminatory conditions. Bowron urged L.A. school superintendent Vierling Kersey to use the schools to improve relations in Los Angeles. Schools' attempts to help Mexican youth avert gang violence and arrest, he told Kersey, would play an important role in the Allied war effort and would appease the federal government. Bowron then appointed a committee composed of local residents of Mexican ancestry and other local officials to help "make those of Mexican blood living in Los Angeles feel that they are Americans rather than Mexicans," to inspire patriotism, and to help "break down the barriers between races as far as possible."[53] To prove that local officials were "competent to take care of the situation locally," and that Los Angeles did not need "Federal interference," Bowron pointed to committees he established—which included participation from Mexican Americans and from high officials like the superintendent of schools, Protestant ministers, and the city's archbishop.[54]

Days after the Zoot Suit violence broke out, County Supervisor Ford wrote to Nelson Rockefeller, who at the time was at the Office of the Coordinator of Inter American Affairs, to explain the efforts local officials were making to improve Mexican populations' conditions and to "ameliorate regrettable results of an international character."[55] Ford explained to Rockefeller that the Board of Supervisors was joining with local community organizations to create "a program . . . which will seek to give added impetous [sic] to various constructive efforts in the neighborhoods with large Mexican population," including recreation programs, good will meetings, and other projects.[56] Ford also asked California's U.S. senator Sheridan Downey to urge the federal government to continue funding the Inter American Center, also known as the Southern California Council of Inter-American Affairs. The center worked to facilitate race relations in Southern California as well as to foster good international relations, advancing its organizers' belief that "the Good Neighbor policy begins at home." It emphasized that "the welfare of hundreds of thousands of Americans of Latin culture in Southern California is indissolubly [sic] linked with that of Anglo-Americans" and its role to help "develop common interests between the peoples of the United States and those of the twenty neighboring republics, now and after the war."[57]

Officials' intensified efforts to lessen discrimination against Los Angeles's Mexican-origin population were largely utilitarian by-products of the newly sparked concern about the national and international implications of such discrimination. Most investigations of the Zoot Suit violence and its causes largely failed to acknowledge the very real racism and discrimination that provoked the riots, focusing instead on trying to prevent damage to the war effort. Mayor Bowron demonstrated this official lack of conviction that minorities' conditions needed improvement. Though many constituents viewed Bowron as a racial liberal due to his higher receptivity to minorities' needs than other candidates, concern about race discrimination itself was not the primary motivation for his wartime focus on race relations. Bowron believed conditions were less dire than reports indicated, and addressed Angelenos' race concerns mainly in the interest of improving international and national opinion of his city. He explained to the national Office of War Information that coverage of the riots misrepresented the way Los Angeles treated its minority groups and had caused "irreparable damage" to the city, which did not have a large-scale race problem. The supposedly faulty coverage also caused "misunderstanding" on the part of Mexican officials, he explained. Bowron asked the federal government to help ascertain the truth so that the "garbled, highly colored, wholly misleading and detrimental news accounts that went out to the entire country and relayed to the people of our neighboring American Republics could be corrected."[58] Bowron even went as far as asking Police Chief C. B. Horrall to write him a report to defend the city to the State

Department, the Office of the Coordinator of Inter American Affairs, and the Office of War Information, as well as to Latin America.[59] Bowron instructed Horrall to emphasize that the Zoot Suit Riots resulted from Mexican-origin people breaking laws rather than from white prejudice against Mexicans, and to be sure to mention that Mexicans in the "colonias" had asked the police to step in. He told the chief to indicate that "the Police Department has merely attempted to enforce the laws and keep the peace and this requires vigorous action because of the nature of the activities of the young hoodlums involved."[60] In a letter to the State Department, Bowron reiterated that neither prejudice nor "unfriendly feeling" toward Mexican-origin people had prompted the acts of local citizens, police and armed forces.[61]

The United States' international agenda helps explain the changing official approach to the civil rights of two other West Coast minority groups, Japanese and Chinese Americans. White Americans previously had grouped these two together as reviled "Orientals" whom they excluded from West Coast communities and victimized with discriminatory legislation. But during the war, Chinese Americans' civil rights status improved, while Japanese Americans' became increasingly constricted. *Time* magazine highlighted the suddenly different status of each group in an article published two weeks after the Japanese attack on Pearl Harbor. The December 22, 1941, article, "How to Tell Your Friends from the Japs," explained how to distinguish between a Chinese "friend" and Japanese "enemy."[62] An article in *Life* the same day, titled "How to Tell Japs from the Chinese: Angry Citizens Victimize Allies with Emotional Outburst at Enemy," did the same.[63] "Previously maligned as the 'heathen Chinee,' 'mice-eaters,' and 'Chinks,' the Chinese were now," as historian Ronald Takaki explains, "'friends' and allies engaged in a heroic common effort against the 'Japs.'"[64] One Japanese-American soda fountain clerk who recognized this sudden transformation wryly commented the day after the attack on Pearl Harbor, "I guess I'll have to change my name to Wong, now."[65] Chinese Americans sometimes clarified to white Americans that they were not Japanese by wearing buttons that announced, "Chinese Reporter *Not Japanese* Please."[66]

International wartime circumstances catalyzed changes in the longtime exclusion of Chinese Americans from full national participation. The United States risked undermining cooperative efforts with China by continuing to refuse Chinese immigrants naturalization rights and to all but prohibit Chinese immigration. A congressman warned Congress that because the "salvation of the white race" depended on continued Chinese friendship and military cooperation, Chinese exclusion must be eliminated.[67] In late 1943, the government overturned the 1790 Naturalization Act that denied nonwhites the right to become citizens and liberalized the 1882 Chinese Exclusion Act, which had limited Chinese immigration for decades. Chinese Americans could for the first time join the armed forces on an equal basis, work in white-collar jobs, skilled trades, and the civil service, and live outside Chinatowns.[68] Social attitudes toward Chinese Americans "changed overnight," according to historians, though of course race continued to mark this population well beyond the 1940s.[69] Ultimately, international expediency determined the timing of the transformation. Japanese propaganda, which played upon American racism to gain pan-Asian support, stimulated American officials to liberalize policies toward Chinese immigration and Chinese-descent American residents, as did U.S. wartime enthusiasm for China and American commercial interests there.[70]

Chinese-American activists facilitated these changing attitudes too by rallying throughout the war to support China, seeing this support as synonymous with American patriotism. After Japan's attack on Pearl Harbor, Chinese Americans aided the combined China and U.S. fight against Japan. They bought National [U.S.] War Bonds, served in the U.S. Army, raised funds for China, and boycotted Japanese goods.[71]

The wartime status of Japanese Americans, whom Americans affiliated racially with a U.S. enemy, deteriorated at the same time that Chinese Americans made civil rights gains. Japan's enemy status combined with deeply rooted racial stereotypes, fears, and discrimination toward the Japanese-descent population to create a context for the United States to further abrogate civil rights and liberties.[72] FDR signed Executive Order 9066 on February 19, 1942, authorizing the evacuation and internment of 120,000 Japanese-origin people—citizen and immigrant. Governmental and special interest groups' arguments that internment was necessary to protect the United States from feared internal attacks persuaded most Americans.[73]

California officials like Mayor Fletcher Bowron and Attorney General Earl Warren, who was elected governor that same year, actively supported internment. Warren encouraged the federal government's decision makers, who relied heavily on information coming out of his office to intern West Coast Japanese-origin residents. Racism motivated Warren, who viewed Asian-origin people, Japanese in particular, as foreign, inscrutable and, especially after Pearl Harbor, treacherous.[74] German Americans and Italian Americans were not interned to the same degree, in part due to the logistical difficulty of imprisoning such a large number of people, but also because they were viewed as white.[75] Some people undoubtedly welcomed internment as a way to fulfill a long-term goal of ridding their communities entirely of the Japanese, while a very small minority protested the evacuation.[76]

Even the most otherwise progressive civil rights activists supported internment, with a few brave exceptions. These included Carey McWilliams, new California attorney general Robert Kenny, and Al Wirin of the Southern California American Civil Liberties Union (ACLU), who spoke out individually even as the ACLU supported internment. The communist newspaper, the *People's World*, an otherwise strong voice against injustice, supported internment. As the L.A. Communist Party's Dorothy Healey later reflected, "So unquestioning was our support for the war that…we raised no objection when Japanese American citizens, including some of our own comrades like Karl Yoneda, along with his non-Japanese wife, Elaine Black, were sent to relocation camps in the western desert." Healey remembered sadly, "The *People's World* fired its sole Japanese-American employee in those early months of the war."[77]

Other minority groups' organizations did not oppose internment, either, though in some cases they did express concern about the way the evacuation and internment were conducted. The chairman of the NAACP's Legal Committee of the Alameda County branch (in Northern California) and the vice president of the prominent black union the Brotherhood of Sleeping Car Porters, C. L. Dellums, wrote to the national NAACP's executive director Walter White expressing concern about the evacuees' poor treatment. He explained to White that they suffered terribly from the heat in the railroad coaches, which were not air-conditioned and had only "two old-time small fans," and protested that the passengers were not allowed to open any windows. Dellums wrote, "[M]any of them became ill. Several fainted." He also alerted White about the discrepancy between the treatment of Japanese and Italian and German descent people—that the former were interned en masse while the latter two groups were not.[78] White did not explicitly oppose the internment, but he did express his thoughts to Assistant Attorney General Wendell Berge. In White's view, once internees had been deemed loyal, they should be allowed to return to their homes.[79] But his was a minority opinion. Not even the vocal African-American newspaper the *California Eagle* opposed the internment until 1943.[80] Nor did Los Angeles Jews and their agencies oppose internment, but like select African Americans, some worked to lessen its devastating impact. Members of the L.A. Jewish Community's Community Relations Committee (CRC) tried to convince officials at Los Angeles's Hall of Justice to secure better prices for the businesses and property Japanese Americans were forced to sell at extremely short notice.[81]

Despite some critiques, other minorities remained publicly silent about the constitutionality of internment, and some even privately supported it. African Americans and Jews may have feared appearing disloyal or have been preoccupied with their own pressing wartime concerns. But racism, especially long-term tendencies in American society, and particularly in the West, to affiliate Asian-origin people with foreignness, also seems to have played a role. These other minorities may also have kept quiet as they

Figure 5: Japanese Americans Submit Their Personal Property to the LAPD Three Weeks after Pearl Harbor, December 29, 1941, Los Angeles Daily News Collection, Department of Special Collections, Charles E. Young Research Library, UCLA.

themselves benefited from the treatment of Japanese Americans. Historian Daniel Widener argues that the removal of Japanese Americans created a prwofit for those African Americans who occupied their homes and took over their businesses.[82] Historian Ellen Eisenberg shows that some CRC leaders even helped orchestrate internment behind the scenes as they allowed their fears of global and domestic fascism and anti-Semitism to overshadow their commitment to racial equality and social justice. Joe Roos, for instance, worked in secret with other CRC leaders through an investigative organization called the News Research Service to spy on foreign and domestic "un-American" organizations they saw as part of the Axis war effort, and to share their information with government agencies. Targeted organizations included some Japanese organizations, as well as Nazi organizations and the KKK, and their information helped convince government officials that a portion of the West Coast's Japanese-descent population was dangerous.[83]

Officials often explained their support for internment in security rather than racial terms, although the absence of internment from Hawaii—the

site of the Pearl Harbor attack—and of large-scale German or Italian internment belied such claims. Mayor Bowron insisted that the "prosecution of
the war" justified both his support for internment and his reluctance later
in the war to return the internees to Los Angeles. Such a return, Bowron
warned in early 1945, could harm the war effort by compounding the
city's wartime housing shortage and lead to violence and disunity.[84]

The national security argument changed course in the next few years,
revealing how Japanese peoples' fates depended on American policy
makers' reading of the international environment. Ironically, over time
Americans advocated ending internment as they proclaimed the racial
discrimination it embodied damaged the United States' international
reputation and indirectly gained support for Japan in countries where
America's racial minorities were majorities. Some people articulated their
concern about internment's negative international consequences soon after
the program began. County Supervisor John Anson Ford, for instance, did
not oppose internment itself, but he did express fear that the United States'
failure to act with restraint toward the internees would jeopardize the war
effort. He urged U.S. attorney general Francis Biddle to resist being persuaded by people who viewed internment as an opportunity to remove
Japanese Americans, since treatment of this population "may have a very
marked effect on the attitude of the hard-pressed millions of China."[85]

This position gained currency as the war progressed, especially as most
Japanese Americans "proved their loyalty" by supporting the American
war effort. Thirty-three thousand Japanese Americans served in the
armed forces during the war. Hawaiian Nisei—second-generation Japanese
Americans—served in the 100th Battalion, while interned mainland
Nisei joined Hawaiians in the most decorated unit in U.S. military history,
the 442nd Regimental Combat Team.[86] Discriminating against such a
"loyal" population strengthened Japan's war efforts by playing into the
hands of Japanese propagandists, a speaker at a 1945 Los Angeles Rotarian
meeting emphasized.[87] When the War Department began allowing large
numbers of internees deemed "loyal" to leave the camps, civil rights organizations like the NAACP used the international argument in part to
convince reluctant local governments to welcome the ex-internees into
their communities. The NAACP emphasized the negative international
consequences of such discrimination to New York City mayor Fiorello
LaGuardia. National NAACP official Roy Wilkins explained in a news
release, "The treatment of these peoples has been one of the major items
cited by those [abroad] who would interpret this terrible war as a war of
color and race."[88]

Besides jeopardizing international support, race discrimination threatened to destroy the home front unity necessary to wage the war. Angelenos
feared race riots such as those near home and deadly and destructive ones

in Detroit and New York in the summer of 1943 would disrupt America's ability to sustain war production levels. These conflicts scared some official Angelenos into making concessions to cement unity that they had not been willing to make before.

Nervous Angelenos often referred to Detroit to explain their concerns for ameliorating conditions in Los Angeles. Representatives from the county supervisors, the City Housing Authority, and local social agencies met in Mayor Bowron's office with federal agents of the Housing Administration, National Housing Agency, and War Manpower Commission to discuss preventing similar deadly race riots by alleviating the tight housing situation for minority residents. Bowron explained that "after the very disgraceful incidents in Detroit, some of us" at this meeting "felt that it was far wiser to take precautions before rather than after."[89] These officials worried that if conditions did not improve, the continuing inflow of African-American migrants would subject Los Angeles to "disease, epidemics, race riots and a general breaking down of the home front in this area."[90] Mayor Bowron assured the secretary of the Navy in the wake of the Zoot Suit Riots that Los Angeles, "with its many important war industries, can ill afford to have production disrupted by any disturbances and we are striving by every means to prevent such disturbances."[91] Bowron emphasized in a rally speech that his city "is alert to the importance of home front unity as a weapon for successfully fighting the war and assuring a peace that is real and lasting."[92]

John Anson Ford remembered the role the Zoot Suit Riots played in awakening concerns all over Los Angeles about race, especially concerning Mexican Americans' plight. "Proposals for an allocation of extra Community Chest money to finance special youth projects in 'blighted' areas of the county had been denied" in previous years, Ford recalled. "But those dark days in early June 1943 awakened the entire metropolitan area and reversed the decision of the Community Chest."[93] Subsequently, it added $300,000 per year for five years to the previous budget of $364,000 per year it allocated to youth-serving agencies, almost doubling this budget, much of which was directed to minority communities. Mexican Americans were the main recipients of the money, though African Americans and Asian Americans benefited as well, Ford explained. While Ford's belief that "the tide of lawlessness and bitterness in Los Angeles was turned" was overly optimistic, it nonetheless highlighted the Zoot Suit Riots' important role in awakening the city's concern about discrimination.[94]

The wartime convergence of domestic race tensions and international imperatives stimulated local city and county officials like Bowron and the Los Angeles County Board of Supervisors to sponsor new interracial civil rights–oriented organizations, some of which became permanent. White citizens often joined officials in these cooperative efforts, particularly in the wake of the urban race riots' wake-up call. Meanwhile, minorities seized upon the window of opportunity presented by the wartime imperatives, hopeful that their longtime efforts to improve civil rights would finally succeed. Sponsors and members repeatedly referenced the importance of these official interracial organizations in maintaining a unified home front and broadcasting an image of a racially just democracy to the world.[95]

One organization still active today, the Los Angeles County Committee on Human Relations, took root during World War II as an effort to help maintain domestic unity. Originally called the Los Angeles County Committee for Interracial Progress, the County Board of Supervisors formed the organization in January 1944, in response to the Zoot Suit Riots, to "improve intercultural and intergroup relations among the citizenry of this County."[96] The Board of Supervisors hoped the group would counter "racial tensions" that were a "hindrance to the progress of the war, and...[a] menace to the spirit of unity in our community."[97] A diverse group of community members helped convince the supervisors to create this interracial wartime organization, including Catholic, Protestant, and Jewish religious leaders like Bishop Joseph T. McGucken, Reverend Willsie Martin, and Rabbi Edgar Magnin. The Committee for Interracial Progress aimed to centralize the many individual efforts focusing on the city's race issues, especially concerning the Latin American and African-American populations, of which people in the field counted twenty-two groups dealing with the former and seven dealing with the latter.[98] The committee planned to deal with changing community conditions such as the new populations, especially minorities, lured to the city by the industrial expansion. These Asians, African Americans, and Mexicans, in the board's words, "contribute[d] to the fascinating, cosmopolitan character of this community."[99]

Prominent Angelenos interested in antidiscrimination, labor, business, and other issues eventually joined the Committee for Interracial Progress. Members included representatives of the chamber of commerce; Carey McWilliams; Manuel Ruíz Jr., a prominent Mexican-American activist and attorney who chaired the Citizens' Committee for Latin American Youth and the Coordinating Council for Latin American Youth (CCLAY); Phillip M. Connolly, the well-known activist president of the California CIO; Floyd Covington, the Urban League's executive secretary; and George Gleason, an advocate for minority groups since the 1920s.[100] Covington, Magnin, McGucken, Martin, and Gleason's involvement point clearly to the continuities between efforts in the 1930s and 1940s. These men knew each other from their work on the Committee for Church and Community Cooperation, appointed by the County Board of Supervisors in 1937, which seems to have been the first official interracial organization in the Los Angeles area. Gleason, the Committee for

Interracial Progress's executive director, was the executive secretary of the earlier organization. Monsignor Thomas J. O'Dwyer, who became involved in other later interracial initiatives, also played an important formative role in the Committee for Church and Community Cooperation. In the years before internment, members from the Japanese-American community like Masao Satow, from the Japanese YMCA, attended meetings of this group, which addressed both interfaith and interracial issues.[101] The Committee for Interracial Progress, as its name implies, focused most explicitly on interracial issues, reflecting the increasing prominence of race in the new wartime circumstances. A highlight of its activities was the 1945 Institute on Community Relations it cosponsored with the Chicago-based American Council on Race Relations (ACRR). This institute aimed to alleviate racial tensions by training more than 15,000 county officials and employees to provide better service to all population groups, specifically minorities.[102]

In addition to county-sponsored agencies, city organizations also emerged during wartime. The Official Interracial Committee, which Bowron appointed in September 1943, is one example. This group's largely African-American leadership included Los Angeles NAACP president Thomas L. Griffith Jr., Los Angeles Urban League president Floyd Covington, the CIO's Revels Cayton, and Norman O. Houston, the secretary-treasurer of the Golden State Mutual Life Insurance Company, one of L.A.'s most prominent black businesses. They all worked with the mayor, Covington explained, to "deal with the immediate problems cutting across the areas of police protection, housing and transportation."[103]

While the Official Interracial Committee seems to have had a heavily black membership and to have focused more on African Americans' issues than on a multiracial community, Bowron formed a more racially inclusive Mayor's Committee for Home Front Unity in January 1944 for the express purposes of working on "war efforts" and solving the city's "problems leading to inter-cultural conflicts."[104] Twelve prominent community leaders—six blacks, two Jews, one "Latin-American," one businessman, and two clergymen—composed the committee, which addressed specific problems among the city's minorities like transportation, housing, police, and "delinquency." Some of its African-American members, including Covington, Cayton, Griffith, and Houston, had been on the Official Interracial Committee formed four months earlier, while white clergyman McGucken had served on the Committee on Church and Community Cooperation. The addition of more diverse representatives from the Jewish and Mexican-American communities makes clear that the wartime conditions forced Bowron to realize the city's multiracial population mandated multiracial representation. Organizers highlighted the participation of Jewish community leaders on the twelve-person committee. They were Community Relations Committee's chairman

Mendel Silberberg and Universal Pictures producer Walter Wanger. They also highlighted the involvement of prominent Mexican Americans such as Armando G. Torrez, the director of the Mexican Chamber of Commerce.[105]

Other official interracial initiatives arose out of the wartime riots, such as the California Committee on Youth in Wartime, which first met in November 1943. Active members included prominent Mexican-American community activists Manuel Ruíz of the Citizens' Committee for Latin American Youth and the Coordinating Council for Latin American Youth (CCLAY), African-American community representatives Norman Houston, representatives of official wartime agencies like Walter McKibben of the California State War Council office, and Los Angeles area judges. Governor Earl Warren formed the agency to address the "much-publicized juvenile delinquency problem" by creating, in Warren's words, "proper social conditions for our children to live in." Warren was concerned about tensions surrounding minority youth, specifically their potentially negative impact on the war effort. Tellingly, he set up a structure whereby the Committee on Youth in Wartime advised the War Council, which then advised the governor. Warren's creation of the committee reveals that he attributed the tensions to juvenile delinquency rather than to military and police racism. But Warren nonetheless realized that Mexican Americans' conditions needed improvement. After the war, he turned the California Committee on Youth in Wartime into the California Youth Committee to continue its work. The ongoing participation of members like Manuel Ruíz highlights such efforts' continuity.[106]

Such official committees often served as discussion forums for community representatives to meet with each other and with officials more than they actually found solutions to the problems they targeted. The efforts more often than not inadequately addressed discrimination and racial inequality in Los Angeles. But they also created an official avenue for minority community representatives to voice their concerns to city, county, state, and even national policy makers. Moreover, they reflected an altered racial climate.

NEW CITIZEN-BASED INITIATIVES

The strategic international urgency of addressing discrimination helps explain the timing of officials' interest in minorities' plight, but growing civil rights activism had nonofficial origins as well. Minority activists and their white allies seized the opportunity to use the threat racism posed to the international war to mobilize new activist initiatives and strengthen old ones, increasing numbers of which involved interracial coalitions.

Civil rights crusaders made important strides at home as the Allied forces battled on the European, North African, and Pacific fronts. The Chicago-based American Council on Race Relations (ACRR) declared that 1943 had been a key year for the growth of new voluntary groups on the West Coast.[107]

Among the most prominent of the new voluntary interracial initiatives were the councils for civic unity, which emerged out of an emergency citizens' meeting during the Zoot Suit Riots, developed chapters in various California cities during the war, consolidated in 1946 as the statewide California Federation for Civic Unity (CFCU), and lasted well into the postwar period. The councils for civic unity emerged from the Hollywood Democratic Committee, a largely white coalition of local activists initiated by movie industry members, but the groups came to include much more multiracial participation. They brought together representatives of California's racially diverse organizations—including the NAACP, CRC, and multiple other Jewish and African-American organizations, religious organizations, and eventually Japanese-American and Mexican-American organizations.[108] The Council for Civic Unity's executive committee reflected African-American and Jewish involvement in such interracial initiatives. Two of its seven members were Jewish, one of whom was the CRC's executive director from its founding until after World War II, Leon Lewis. Another member was the African-American lawyer and civil rights advocate Loren Miller. But the remaining four committee members were white Angelenos, underscoring whites' heavy involvement in the organization.[109]

White citizens' involvement in wartime civil rights initiatives resembled officials' in the sense that both explicitly stemmed from the wartime context. Many of the newly formed interracial groups, especially those with large white memberships and organizers, sought—at least initially—to improve race relations in order to strengthen the war effort. The Council for Civic Unity was formed initially to "take steps toward eliminating the disease of racial incitement and discrimination which threaten the war production of this vital area." Those attending the organization's initial meeting decided to start immediately "in order to prevent another 'Detroit' in Los Angeles."[110] This interracial organization's heavily white leadership was motivated in large part by wartime defense concerns. Increased civil rights activism, particularly through interracial efforts, became an important result of white citizens' wartime concerns.

Minorities, who became increasingly involved in wartime civil rights initiatives, some of which were racial group-specific and others of which involved collaboration across racial divides through organizations like the Council for Civic Unity, often used wartime justifications more strategically. Like other Americans, they feared the consequences of an Allied loss, but they used these fears tactically to justify their arguments for improved civil rights. They seized the opportunity presented when both government officials and other Americans less concerned about discrimination for its own sake argued that improving race relations was crucial to the war effort.

The L.A. organization the Negro Victory Committee, formed in April 1941, reflected how some minorities co-opted wartime rhetoric of fighting for victory for democracy abroad to insist the United States live up to its ideals at home. They strategically protested injustice by calling attention to the hypocrisy of fighting Hitler's racism in Europe but not fighting discrimination in the United States, particularly in war industry employment.[111] African Americans labeled their two-pronged fight against Hitler in Europe and against Jim Crow at home the "Double V" campaign.[112] Los Angeles African Americans joined the national campaign by waging local battles through organizations like the Negro Victory Committee, which argued that discrimination threatened America's international security by weakening the war effort. Its first chairman, Reverend Clayton D. Russell, who at the time was also the local NAACP's vice president, reflected in later years about the self-conscious nature of the strategy. "In order to gain employment which was the number one need for blacks at the time we exploited the war," Russell remembered. "We charged those who were discriminating with hurting the war industry. And we notified the War Manpower Commission, President Roosevelt, and Senators and Congressmen from California that the War effort was being hurt by their failure to utilize full manpower."[113]

The Negro Victory Committee revealed its strategy again at a mass rally on April 12, 1942. Its pamphlet, *America! This Is Our Stand*, urged blacks to participate simultaneously in the war effort overseas and at home. The committee also warned the country that a full patriotic mobilization would be difficult without the enforcement of equal rights at home. African-American speakers emphasized that bitterness about domestic discrimination threatened to undermine the war effort. "When we read of attacks against Negroes at Tuskegee, Fort Dix, Fort Bragg, Fort Bennings, Sikeston, discrimination in the Navy," Russell explained, "our morale is injured and consequently the nation's war effort is injured."[114] Russell and other speakers urged blacks not to accept their fate as second-class citizens, appealing to the audience to "remember it is [in] America that we can fight for our rights, that we can fight against such treatment, that we can fight for the extension of democracy." But Russell urged them at the same time to resist succumbing to the disunity caused by racial discrimination because this "will destroy America and this is just what Hitler wants; to create disunity. The Negro people will not and must not allow themselves to be the pawns of Hitler."[115] A victory for Hitler would mean that "the same slavery that now holds the conquered of Europe will be the fate of America and we Negroes in America will face racial extinction. It will be as if the K.K.K. had taken over the White House and Congress and lynching instead of being a blot on the nation's honor will be the lawful practice of the land as is the persecution of the Jewish in Germany." America's shortcomings did not compare to what an Axis victory would bring.[116] Even a Japanese victory would endanger blacks in this view, since although the Japanese were also a "colored group" victimized by white colonial countries, their role as imperialists guilty of oppressing their Asian neighbors on racial grounds did not bode well for African Americans.[117] African Americans must, the Negro Victory Committee advocated, support the American war effort while seizing this opportunity to protest unfair treatment, enforcing and upholding American ideals.

The Double V approach—a two-pronged attack against Hitler in Europe and racism at home—implicitly if not explicitly infused the language of specific local struggles. Black shipyard workers in Los Angeles used it during World War II to gain support for integrating unions and fighting employment discrimination. They picketed the Boilermakers' International Union, which attempted to establish separate black and white unions and provided few benefits and no role in decision making to African Americans. The picketers carried signs with slogans like "Jim Crow Belongs to Germany!" and "We Won't Pay Dues to Hitlerism!"[118] Opponents of restrictive covenants emphasized white Americans' hypocrisy for supporting them during a war that diverse Americans fought together to destroy Hitler's racist "empire."[119]

Double V campaigns that came closest to undermining the war effort provoked the most significant civil rights gains. Activists recognized that their potential to weaken the war effort by threatening domestic unity gave them great bargaining power. In one of the most well known cases, FDR established the federal Fair Employment Practices Committee (FEPC) in direct response to African Americans' activism. The head of the all-black railroad workers' union the Brotherhood of Sleeping Car Porters, A. Philip Randolph, warned he would initiate a 100,000-strong African-American march on Washington D.C. to protest discrimination in the defense industry, armed forces, and other government agencies. This proposed march, scheduled for July 1, 1941, six months before the United States even entered the war, would jeopardize the domestic unity Franklin Delano Roosevelt needed to mobilize the country for the war effort. Six days before Randolph's planned march, FDR issued Executive Order 8802, which declared illegal all employment discrimination concerning workers in defense industries or government because of race, creed, color, or national origin.[120] African Americans had pushed the federal government to implement this significant program, which became the first federal antidiscrimination legislation since Reconstruction. FDR hoped it would strengthen domestic unity by encouraging minorities to support the Allied effort, but the FEPC was largely ineffective. It could not hope to keep up with nationwide discrimination with its first-year budget of only $80,000 and subsequent yearly budget of $431,609, and a mere seven field officers and five clerical workers. Nonetheless, the combination of the FEPC and the wartime labor shortage resulted in the hiring of 2,000,000 blacks in defense plants nationwide and 200,000 more in the federal civil service. And it set an important precedent and paved the path for later civil rights reforms.[121]

Local African-American activists' most effective efforts also promised to undermine crucial domestic wartime functions. Their threat to disrupt service on the Los Angeles Railway, thereby preventing adequate transportation for city workers, forced the company to hire black workers, in compliance with FDR's Executive Order. African Americans received support from white workers who opposed the railway's policy because the wartime white manpower shortage left them overworked. The African-American newspaper *The California Eagle* and the Negro Victory Committee jointly proposed a mass march on the railway, an idea cheered on by 1,500 black and white attendees at an interracial meeting. In the face of this protest, the railway altered its policy.[122]

In this way, the war opened a window of opportunity for minorities' increased activism, and the result was particularly noticeable in the African-American community. The Congress of Racial Equality (CORE) formed in 1942 to challenge Jim Crow in the South and Urban League chapters burgeoned in Portland and San Francisco in 1945. National NAACP membership multiplied almost ten times (to half a million) during the war, while the Los Angeles chapter grew from 2,000 in 1941 to over 11,000 in 1945, making it the fifth largest chapter in the United States.[123]

Mexican Americans also used the window of opportunity by couching their war on discrimination in Double V language. Their heightened awareness of and anger about discrimination mounted as the war progressed, decreasing their tolerance for segregated swimming pools, schools, and cemeteries.[124] They encouraged the federal government to protect their rights by strategically using the connection between domestic equality struggles and international alliances, particularly with Latin American countries. By linking improved treatment of Mexican Americans with wartime victory, these activists partially instigated the federal and local governments' increasing focus on Mexican Americans' civil rights. Eduardo Quevedo and Manuel Ruíz, leaders of the Coordinating Council for Latin American Youth (CCLAY), used language of "war-imposed necessity" to petition officials to support their requests for better facilities, incorporation into defense industry jobs, Spanish-speaking law enforcement officers, enforcement of antidiscrimination ordinances, access to federal housing projects, and many other issues. They demanded that President Roosevelt issue executive orders "relaxing restrictions on *friendly and allied aliens* [emphasis added]." Discrimination against the Mexican-origin population, they warned, all combined with the work of the enemy to create "a situation that may become very serious if remedies are not immediately put into effect."[125] The Coordinating Council applied for funds from the California State Treasury with the justification that "juvenile delinquency among American youngsters of Latin-American extraction has inspired Nazi and Fascist sources to adversely exploit Inter-American relations."[126] They received the requested funds.

In another instance of Mexican Americans' increasing strategic wartime activism, the Citizens' Committee for Latin American Youth also was formed in part to emphasize the negative impact of anti-Mexican discrimination on the international war effort. Manuel Ruíz chaired, and other familiar activists joined this committee, including the Mexican Americans Bert Corona and Eduardo Quevedo, and white advocates such as Monsignor Thomas J. O'Dwyer of the L.A. Catholic Archdiocese. Official members included Sheriff Eugene Biscailuz and Police Chief C. B. Horrall. Frequent visits from the consul of Mexico reinforced the committee's arguments about the international consequences of discrimination. The consul explained at Citizens' Committee's meetings that problems in Los Angeles concerned him because Mexican-American youth problems frequently involved Mexican-born parents.[127] Frustrated members discussed the government's willingness to draft them into military service at the same time defense industries excluded them.[128] As violence flared during and after the Zoot Suit Riots, Quevedo, Josefina Fierro de Bright, and other concerned Mexican Americans and some white allies such as John Anson Ford criticized police and press treatment of their community during meetings attended by the Mexican consul, Chief of Police Horrall, and representatives from the sheriff's office. They emphasized that the situation was especially urgent because of its implications for American professions of goodwill to Latin America.[129]

Even though Mexican-American activists' efforts fell short of their hopes, their collective efforts resulted in concrete investigations into remedying unequal conditions. Concern that poor conditions in the Southwest might foster the attempts of Axis propagandists and "proto-fascist *nacionalistas*" to encourage anti-American sentiments, undermining FDR's domestic and foreign policies, prompted federal investigators to conduct three studies in the early spring of 1942. The Office of War Information's report concluded that "institutionalized discrimination" against several million "Latin-Americans in the American Southwest represents a serious waste of potential manpower. It is also a constant irritant in hemispheric relations, a mockery of the Good Neighbor Policy, an open invitation to Axis propagandists to depict us as hypocrites to South and Central America."[130]

While some Mexican Americans linked their campaign for equality to wartime imperatives by emphasizing that equality would increase international support for the United States, others highlighted its importance for achieving the domestic unity necessary for victory. Members of El Congreso followed this tack during the war, at least until the organization dissolved in 1942. They argued that if the government hoped to retain Mexican Americans' wartime assistance, it must eliminate housing, school, public, and job discrimination against them. El Congreso reasoned that if "aliens"—Mexican nationals—were fit for the draft, they also ought to be eligible for defense employment. The organization brought charges of discrimination in war industries to the War Manpower Commission and formed the Hispanic Committee on Defense Jobs (Comité Hispano de los Empléos de la Defensa), which cooperated with the War Manpower Commission and California officials to help Mexican-origin people secure defense jobs.[131]

African and Mexican Americans' Double V argument that their assistance achieving victory abroad depended on antidiscrimination victory at home persuaded government officials, who borrowed Double V language to seek greater white support for wartime antidiscrimination policies. But whites inverted minorities' Double V language, emphasizing that fighting racism assisted the war effort, while African and Mexican Americans often argued that supporting the war effort was instrumental to fighting discrimination at home. Eugene Davidson, an FEPC representative, explained to one predominantly white Los Angeles citizens' group that FDR initiated the FEPC to maintain U.S. international security. Other governments were overrun by Hitler because they ignored "the problem of minority groups," Davidson explained. "Your government," he continued, "does not intend that this shall happen in America." Davidson reassured his audience that by taking a "strong position on the place of minority groups in a Democracy," their government had fortified the United States against an Axis invasion.[132] Davidson used Double V rhetoric, explaining, "We are fighting for America and fighting against Nazism in America. You ought always to remember that we are engaged in two fights—not just one fight....Today we are fighting a battle here just as much as are the boys in khaki on the other side."[133]

Davidson attempted to scare whites into supporting civil rights legislation by emphasizing that they too had a concrete stake in the battle against discrimination. He suggested to his largely white audience that they should not sympathize with Jews and "Negroes" merely because they were victims of discrimination. Davidson explained that the matter was "much deeper." He asked his audience, "Have you ever stopped to think that in the world the majority of people are of the darker races?" If

Japan succeeded in separating the world on the basis of color, he warned, "the white race would be a minority group and it might even be that some future President's Committee would have to be set up to protect white people from discrimination on account of their race and color."[134] An Allied loss, in other words, could turn the racial tables, making whites the oppressed minority. Supporting antidiscrimination legislation would both increase the chances of an Allied victory and potentially spare whites in the wake of an Axis victory.

African and Mexican American-inspired Double V language also assisted other whites' antidiscrimination efforts. For example, local school reformers borrowed such language to buttress their wartime work. The Los Angeles Federation of Teachers proposed to counter domestic discrimination by integrating multiracial issues into the school curricula. Five of the seven rationales the federation used to convince the Board of Education to adopt a Resolution on Inter-Racial Democracy in the Schools emphasized the nexus between international security and domestic racism. The teachers argued that addressing race relations in the schools would help counter Fifth Column agents' attempts to prop-agate "anti-Mexicanism, anti-Semitism, and anti-Negroism." It would encourage minority groups to mobilize for war production and civilian defense. Such efforts would simultaneously strengthen the United States' world leadership. The teachers cited the U.S. attorney general's argument that ending race prejudice would counter threats to the United States' position at home and abroad. Finally, the Federation of Teachers cited wisdom from Wendell Wilkie's *One World*, which explained that one could not fight imperialism abroad while maintaining it at home.[135] Supervisor Ford also used Double V language to respond to a petition circulated by one of his neighbors that asked residents to exclude non-whites from the neighborhood. Connecting the war abroad with the un-Americanism of restrictive housing covenants, Ford stated, "When our boys are fighting Hitler so heroically, I cannot bring myself to take the step you ask because it certainly is walking on the same path of racial intolerance that his bloody feet have trod."[136]

Much of minorities' increasing activism took the form of collaborative interracial efforts as they came to recognize the mounting importance of collaboration to their equality struggles. Mexican Americans, for in-stance, increasingly created diverse coalitions. The Sleepy Lagoon Defense Committee (SLDC), a group of people that joined forces to defend the Mexican-American boys unjustly incarcerated on murder charges, illustrates this collaborative development particularly well. Historian David Gutiérrez has argued that the committee "represented an unprecedented coalition of articulate, forceful Mexican-American advocates and liberal Anglo community activists."[137] This committee reflected even more widespread cooperation, though, than between Mexican Americans and Anglos.

Mexican-American leaders including Josefina Fierro de Bright, Anthony Quinn, and Eduardo Quevedo originally brought the committee together. But progressive whites, Hollywood representatives, Jews, blacks, and others joined them in their struggle to bring these boys justice. Progressive white attorneys Robert W. Kenny, Carey McWilliams, and Clore Warne joined Jewish attorneys Ben Margolis and Abe Isserman and the Arab-American lawyer George Shearer. Many Mexican Americans whose activism was rooted in various 1930s labor efforts—particularly through the CIO—participated, including Bert Corona, Frank López, and Eduardo Quevedo. Other Mexican Americans like Richard Ibañez joined the coalition, as did African Americans—including most prominently Charlotta Bass, then editor of the African-American newspaper *California Eagle*. Labor union representatives from the AFL, CIO, and independent unions pitched in, too. The well-known local activist from the CIO Phillip "Slim" Connelly represents such collaboration. Connelly had been elected the first president of the California CIO Council in 1938, and in 1939 he became the secretary of the Los Angeles CIO Council, where he remained until 1949 when the anti-communist climate led to his removal from office. By then Connelly had married the prominent Los Angeles communist Dorothy Ray Healey and taken over as the editor in chief of California's communist newspaper *The People's World*. During Connelly's tenure the LA CIO Council became an important center for African Americans' emerging equality campaign. Members of other Los Angeles left organizations, including LaRue McCormack of the International Labor Defense, a communist front organization, joined, and even seem to have been centrally involved. Hollywood celebrities Orson Welles, Guy Endore (a member of the Communist Party), Collier Rogers (Will Rogers Jr.'s wife), and the Mexican Americans Rita Hayworth and Anthony Quinn gave their support along with Hollywood producers, screenwriters, and others including John Bright. Three of the Hollywood figures who supported the SLDC, Dalton Trumbo, John Howard Lawson, and Ring Lardner, were later blacklisted members of the Hollywood Ten, their careers ruined after they refused to testify before the House Un-American Activities Committee's anticommunist investigations.[138] Besides Mexican Americans, Jews were particularly prominent in the coalition and helped raise much of the committee's funding. Harry Braverman, a Jewish Community Relations Committee member who became a central figure in postwar collaborative civil rights initiatives between Mexican Americans and Jews, served as the Sleepy Lagoon Defense Committee treasurer.[139]

The Sleepy Lagoon Defense Committee reveals how such wartime collaboration continued to cross not only the racial spectrum and the center to left of the political spectrum, but also the class spectrum. Participants came from a broad range of backgrounds, from union members to lawyers to Hollywood stars, among others. The rights of working-class people were front and center in the agenda of such organizations, and, as historian Zaragosa Vargas argues, labor rights were civil rights.[140]

Mexico's concern for domestic American race relations, and its stake in this high-profile case, helped facilitate the success of such collaborative efforts. The Mexican Consulate supported the Defense Committee by retaining a lawyer who assisted at the defendants' trial, and the SLDC used this foreign country's interest as fodder for its cause. Like other activists in the Mexican-American and African-American communities had done, SLDC members argued that the defendants' unjust treatment hurt the international unity necessary to defeat fascism. The committee's lawyers opened the trial by highlighting how the racism revealed by the Sleepy Lagoon trial, the mass arrests of Mexican Americans in the Zoot Suit Riots, and the all-around anti-Mexican hysteria jeopardized the United States' previously successful efforts to create hemispheric goodwill and solidarity against the Axis powers. The SLDC emphasized that in addition to these Mexican-American defendants, standing trial were "the whole Mexican people, their children, and their grandchildren. It was the whole of Latin America with its 130,000,000 people. It was the Good Neighbor Policy. It was the United Nations and all for which they fight."[141] The fight for civil rights was, members argued, "an integral part of the welding of Allied unity for the winning of the war."[142]

Not surprisingly, the eventual victory secured by this interracial, transnational effort further drew the attention of Latin American governments. In the wake of the decision, the consul general of Mexico wrote a letter to Alice Greenfield (later McGrath), one of the committee's Jewish activists, thanking her for her work.[143] The Mexican press covered the court victory extensively and "very favorably in terms of U.S.-Mexican relations," according to SLDC member Carey McWilliams. One Mexican magazine, *Hoy*, even published a three-page spread in its September 10, 1944 issue, reinforcing the importance of domestic civil rights successes to U.S. international relations.[144]

Soon after overturning the Sleepy Lagoon verdict, some of the same people involved in the Sleepy Lagoon Defense Committee collaborated to respond to the Zoot Suit Riots. They formed the Los Angeles Committee for American Unity. Chaired by Harry Braverman, the committee included other familiar figures: Charlotta Bass, Carey McWilliams, Clore Warne, Eduardo Quevedo, Manuel Avila, Al Waxman, and Ben Margolis. While the riots were still raging, the committee petitioned local, state, and national officials to intervene. Members demanded that government officials conduct thorough investigations, in no small part because of what they called the riots' "profound" international implications. Committee members cautioned that the riots provided the Axis with a "new weapon against the unity of the United Nations. The Good Neighbor Policy has been struck a severe blow. The portion of the United States in relation to the colored people of the world has been prejudiced."[145] The committee expressed concern about the riots' anti-African American implications too.

Braverman and Quevedo's involvement in both the SLDC and the Los Angeles Committee for American Unity foreshadowed their later involvement in Mexican-American issues. After the war, Braverman became the chairman of the Jewish Community Relations Committee's (CRC) subcommittee dealing with the Mexican-American civil rights organization, the Community Service Organization (CSO). Quevedo eventually rose to appointed positions within Governor Brown's administration, after which he became the president of the influential Mexican-American Political Association (MAPA).

International and other wartime circumstances also increased African Americans' interracial networks, as the participation of Charlotta Bass and other blacks in the Sleepy Lagoon defense effort revealed. The newly arrived African-American population, which wartime labor needs drew to the West Coast, brought "able and sophisticated Negro spokesmen. For the first time," the American Council of Race Relations' (ACRR) 1946 report, *Race Relations on the West Coast*, explained, "the colored minority groups of the West Coast had spokesmen who clearly envisaged the problem of racial discrimination." The report specifically noted these leaders' awareness of the needs of the region's multiracial population. "It is to their credit that they did not confine their interest to Negroes alone," it explained, "but in a sense became spokesmen and advocates for the entire colored, minority groups."[146] The report recognized both minority activists' increased visibility as well as their increasing tendencies toward cross-racial political cooperation.[147]

Floyd Covington, the head of the local Urban League in the 1930s and 1940s, confirmed African Americans' growing political alliances. His 1942 report on racial tension areas in Los Angeles remarked upon Mexican and black youths increasingly mixed socializing in "gangs" and at dances. Politically, local blacks tried to gain more influence by building a "Negro-Mexican bloc in the areas where both races are concentrated," Covington explained, and the two communities also jointly formed a leadership roundtable to help integrate blacks into neighborhoods. Blacks also cooperated with other groups. A "Negro-white" committee formed to "champion the cause of the dis-enfranchised [*sic*] Americans of Japanese ancestry," Covington wrote. Overall, what he called "Pan Colorism" was increasing in Los Angeles.[148]

Like the African-American and Mexican-American communities, L.A.'s Jewish-American community also began to strengthen relationships with other minority groups. The Community Relations Committee (CRC) led the way. Its wartime executive secretary Leon Lewis contacted Jewish communities nationwide in the summer of 1942 in search of ways to persuade rank-and-file Jews why they must "champion the rights of other minority groups."[149] By mid 1943, Los Angeles Jewish community organizations increasingly discussed strategies for improving relations with other minority groups, especially African and Mexican Americans. They offered assistance to groups like the Fellowship Center, which sought to establish a community center in eastern Los Angeles that would provide "some effective help...to the Negroes."[150] Lewis and the CRC also initiated a campaign with the County Committee for Interracial Progress to persuade local department stores to include non-Anglo-Saxon, blue-eyed children in their Christmas displays, an interesting choice of focus for Jewish activists.[151] The Jewish Community Council (JCC), the Jewish community's umbrella organization, encouraged its members to join the local Urban League to show support for its work and the black community. The league's president, Floyd Covington, welcomed the support and wrote to the JCC, "I am sure that this inter-agency project is the beginning of even a wider sphere of cooperation between our mutual groups."[152] The CRC also first recognized and became interested in the severity of Mexican Americans' plight during this period, specifically in the wake of the wartime Sleepy Lagoon case and Zoot Suit Riots, discussing the issue at meetings in June 1943. Many attendees concluded that the media and police had unfairly blamed Mexican Americans and considered forming groups to investigate the situation. Though it took no specific actions at the time, the organized Jewish community's memory of the violence helped inspire its postwar interest in aiding Mexican Americans' Community Service Organization (CSO).[153]

By mid-1943, Jewish Americans often led interracial civil rights efforts. According to Ted LeBerthon, a columnist for the local newspaper *LA Daily News*, Jewish community leaders "have been in the forefront of this significant movement" to create antidiscrimination committees composed of people from all areas and communities of Los Angeles. These interracial efforts incorporated religious, labor, and industry leaders as well as "representatives of all antidiscrimination committees that have heretofore been representative of single social groups, such as Jews, Mexicans, Negroes and Filipinos," LeBerthon explained. In his observation, members now worked to present "a powerful united front against discrimination wherever found."[154]

The CRC in particular became one of the most active catalysts for civil rights coalition building, drawing on its members' powerful political and community connections. Silberberg, Pacht, and other CRC members persuaded Mayor Bowron in 1945 to propose a permanent Mayor's Community Relations Board to assist L.A. minority groups, help ease racial tensions in the Mexican and "Negro" communities, and ameliorate local anti-Semitism and anti-Catholicism. The ordinance, which would have been far from transformative, ultimately failed despite Bowron's support for it. Still, it marks an increase in Jewish interests in interracial antidiscrimination efforts.[155] The CRC was heavily involved, for instance, in the creation and maintenance of the Los Angeles County Conference for Community Relations (LACCCR) and other similar city and county groups.[156]

Jewish organizations' decision to team up with other minorities was neither easy nor unanimous. Community members wrangled with each other over the desirability of aligning with other, "worse off" minority groups. Their interracial involvement by the middle—and especially by the end—of the war represented a clear shift from earlier stances. In 1941, for instance, CRC members debated joining African Americans also working to fight state employment discrimination by establishing a California race relations commission. Though many meeting attendees in principle supported legislation proposed by Augustus Hawkins, the African-American assemblyman, the dominant perspective that "we should not get behind so-called racial bills as Jews and classify ourselves with the colored group," triumphed. CRC members "unanimously opposed...the sponsorship of any legislation at this time."[157] Both prejudice and an aversion to public association with such a clearly down-trodden group, given their own precarious status, explains some of Jews' resistance.

By the end of World War II, many Los Angeles Jewish community organizations had done an about-face on building coalitions with other, more racialized minorities. The CRC's postwar stance on cooperating with African Americans to fight employment discrimination illustrates this shift. By the late 1940s the CRC listed establishing a statewide Fair Practices Committee (FPC) as a top priority. The two secretaries of the new California FPC were Max Mont of the Southern California Jewish Labor Committee and Bill Becker of San Francisco's Jewish Labor Committee. Isaac Pacht, the past president of the Los Angeles Jewish Federation Council and past chairman of the CRC, joined C. L. Dellums, a prominent leader of the Brotherhood of Sleeping Car Porters, to cochair the statewide committee.[158] Observers credited both the African-American and Jewish communities with initiating this effort.[159]

Jewish involvement in cooperative interracial efforts was also seen elsewhere, in the West and throughout the nation. In San Francisco, Jews, along with Catholics, were prominently involved in building coalitions that incorporated African Americans, Mexican Americans, Chinese Americans, and other local minority groups. These included the Bay Area Council against Discrimination (BACAD), formed in 1942, and the Council for Civic Unity, in 1944. In New York City, three important national Jewish organizations, the American Jewish Committee, the Anti-Defamation League, and the American Jewish Congress, campaigned vigorously for civil rights in cooperation with African Americans, and non-Jewish whites. During World War II, such organizations began to believe that the best way to pursue safety for Jews was to pursue equality for all groups.[160] It is important not to overestimate the extent of such collaboration and sympathy. Jews' ambivalence toward African Americans, and toward aligning their interests, persisted into the war era. Jews both sympathized and related to African Americans at the same time they also distinguished themselves from them. But the increasing cooperation among segments or representatives of the Jewish and African-American population during the war era marked an important transformation.[161]

For African Americans, too, the collaborative foundations of their growing activism were visible around the country. In 1942 NAACP branches nationwide proclaimed the importance of seeking broader support from members of other races. Their priorities for the year included developing an "inter-racial program...to seek a more active participation in our organizations of desirable and influential white people."[162] The Congress of Racial Equality (CORE), the prominent wartime and postwar organization that focused on African Americans' civil rights, hints at African Americans' wartime cooperation. CORE was interracial from the time of its 1942 founding by members of the Fellowship of Reconciliation at the University of Chicago. As early as the fall of 1942, black and white CORE members protested blacks' exclusion from restaurants like Stoner's in the Chicago Loop. When the interracial protesters sat to eat, servers brought them meat covered with egg shell, oversalted food, and garbage sandwiches. CORE members responded with a mass sit-in, which they replicated in 1942 and 1943, years before African Americans in the South protested similarly. This organization produced prominent African-American activists whose trajectories carried them far into twentieth-century civil rights movements, including James Farmer and Bayard Rustin.[163]

In other regions, wartime interracial cooperation usually meant black and white, and often black and Jewish, and did not involve Mexican Americans as much as it did in Los Angeles. In part, this was due to the fact that Mexican Americans could not yet rely upon such a strong national civil rights support network. African Americans and Jewish Americans' prominence in local and national antidiscrimination efforts partially reflects their ability to draw support from strong national organizations. Mexican Americans had southwestern or national organizations like the League of United Latin American Citizens (LULAC), founded in 1929 and particularly active in Texas, but in regions outside Los Angeles these groups remained rather isolated from the civil rights initiatives of other nearby minorities. Some scholars attribute this distancing to Mexican Americans' interest in claiming whiteness and avoiding those groups like African Americans who might "downgrade" their racial status.[164] The national Mexican-American population's high levels of poverty and relatively small middle class, as well as language barriers—especially among the immigrant Mexican population—also undoubtedly contributed to the isolation and lack of resources necessary to conduct collaborative civil rights campaigns.[165] Los Angeles was the first place that Mexican-American civil rights advocates coordinated significantly with other ethnic and racial populations, through El Congreso, the Sleepy Lagoon Defense Committee, and CCLAY, and, to some degree, labor groups like the CIO and governmental agencies such as the Coordinating Council for Latin American Youth.

Even in Los Angeles, though, cooperative wartime efforts incorporated Jewish Americans, African Americans, and their white allies to a greater extent than Mexican Americans and Japanese Americans. While Japanese Americans' internment explains their wartime absence, Mexican Americans' marginality is less straightforward. Despite their large numbers in the area, they remained relatively outside many interracial efforts until the postwar era. They were active in efforts arising out of specific instances of anti-Mexican racism, but the groups that formed to combat discrimination more generally, like the Council for Civic Unity, collaborative CRC-NAACP efforts for local and state fair employment committees, and committees formed by the mayor, the county supervisors, and interfaith groups, tended to include relatively few Mexican Americans until the postwar years. Various factors might include the community's depleted resources from the 1930s deportations, a long-term ambivalence about their permanence until the 1930s, and the absence of strong local and national advocacy organizations. Like the Mexican-origin population nationwide, Los Angeles's largely immigrant Mexican-origin population struggled with linguistic and cultural barriers. The heavily Spanish-speaking population was even less politically integrated than African Americans despite their larger and longer-term presence in the city.[166] Not until the postwar era, through the Community Service organization (CSO), did Los Angeles's Mexican Americans become even more significantly integrated into long-term collaborative efforts.

INTERRACIALISM AS PRAGMATISM

Los Angeles minorities' increasing interracial tendency in the wartime period is clear, but the reasons behind it are less apparent. Many minority activists were like other Americans in that they increasingly organized against discrimination because they feared the consequences of an Allied loss, but they joined interracial antidiscrimination efforts for other reasons too. For one thing, they hoped to increase their political effectiveness. Shared community space also facilitated cooperation between the groups concentrated in World War II Los Angeles's east side neighborhoods. Even more than cooperation, though, such close contact bred interracial friction, which became its own impetus to interracial collaboration. Tension, and outright hostility, originating from within minority communities—as well as from the surrounding white society—reveal the hurdles coalition-minded minorities faced. They also help explain the motivation behind many such coalition-building attempts. For the largely minority residents of mixed-race neighborhoods, such conflict had more immediate consequences than the threat to home front unity and to the war effort: it directly threatened their physical and material well-being. These residents sought to soothe interminority tensions which often led to interracial violence and jeopardized their common well-being. In this way, wartime friction ironically helped inspire collaboration.

Such friction particularly arose in neighborhoods where Mexicans, African Americans, and Jews competed for status and resources. A 1945 report by the Chicago-based American Council of Race Relations (ACRR) pointed out representative Los Angeles neighborhoods, including the east side neighborhood Hollenbeck, the well-known multiethnic, multiracial eastside neighborhood Boyle Heights, and Watts, a south central section. *The Problem of Violence: Observations on Race Conflict in Los Angeles* reported that, in neighborhoods like these, African-American and Mexican-American residents were faced with low income and few employment, educational, and housing opportunities, while an irresponsible press, discriminatory real estate and mortgage company practices, and a prejudiced police force exacerbated white residents' insecurities and prejudices.[167]

Youth violence was also a serious issue. In one illustrative case, what started as an "altercation" between two junior high school girls, one black and one Mexican, spread to the surrounding black and Mexican Hollenbeck community. In Watts, where black/white tensions were most common, violence also resulted from insulting exchanges between white youths from surrounding neighborhoods and Watts' Mexican youths. Jewish conflicts with Mexican Americans were also apparent in neighborhoods like Hollenbeck, where tensions between middle-class Jews and working-class Mexicans were common. The ACRR report stated that in schools like Hollenbeck Junior High School, one of "four major tinder boxes" in the L.A. school system, "the great barrier to the acceptance of Mexican children by Jewish children is in the middle-class bias of the Jewish parents, expressed in excessive concern over dirt and disease." Rather than helping overcome these biases, teachers were often driven by their personal prejudices against both Jewish and Mexican children.[168]

Class differences sometimes caused divides among minority communities. Aspiring middle-class Mexican-American organizations, such as
the Mexican Affairs Committee, reinforced prejudice against African
Americans by refusing to cooperate with them, the ACRR reported.[169]
Such fear that affiliating with African Americans would detract from
these Mexican Americans' own tenuous status reflects how entwined
notions of class and race were during this era. Many Mexican Americans
in the first decades of the twentieth century tried to claim a white identity in order to make socioeconomic and political gains and in the process
shunned cooperation with even more racially marked minority groups.[170]
Class tensions operated in other ways as well. Mexican Americans, African
Americans, and other groups sometimes directed their animosity and
frustration at Jews, whom they viewed as more successful. In one instance, the ACRR reported that Mexican-American groups were outspokenly anti-Semitic as well as antiblack.[171]

Minimizing interracial tensions particularly motivated Los Angeles
Jews, who worked to improve relations with other minority groups in
part to counter what they viewed as rising anti-Semitism. This motivation was visible in the assistance Jewish Americans provided to Japanese-
American internees. There were rumors of general anti-Jewish sentiment
among Japanese Americans, particularly after an editorial in a Los Angeles
Japanese newspaper soon after FDR issued the internment order identified one of Mayor Bowron's key advisers on internment as a Jewish man
named Cohen. The editorial also protested the rationale behind internment that grouped all Japanese-origin people together as possible subversives and ominously suggested that, by the same logic, one might
conclude that all Jews were untrustworthy and should be thrown in a
camp too, especially given charges "against your [Jewish] race regarding
business ethics and dishonesty."[172]

Jewish community members tried to counter perceptions of a disproportionately Jewish role in orchestrating internment by working to
decrease Japanese Americans' suffering. The Community Relations
Committee wrote to officials at the Hall of Justice asking them to secure
better prices for the businesses and property Japanese Americans were
forced to sell. The CRC's executive director Leon Lewis emphasized that
the Hall of Justice's actions would help to "remove...once and for all any
indiscriminate charges of exploitation by Jews." A group of Jewish
attorneys also offered, through the CRC, to "assist by legal and moral sua-
sion, and without fee, any Japanese who claims he has been exploited by
any Jewish purchasor [sic]."[173]

Jewish community members hoped to combat perceived wartime
anti-Semitism in the African-American community too. Tensions between blacks and Jews also had class undertones. Jews countered accusations of discrimination against blacks, emphasizing that they were

isolated examples rather than indicative of a larger Jewish antiblack rac-ism. Rabbi Edgar Magnin, a local social activist rabbi who sat on many interracial committees, responded to a request from Lucius Lomax, the editor of the African-American newspaper the *Los Angeles Tribune*, for his help "eliminating some of the causes of [anti-Semitism]" in regions like East Los Angeles and other heavily black neighborhoods. Lomax suggested that "A large part of the enterprise in the Negro neighbor-hoods of the country is Jewish-owned. With little exception, this enterprise exploits the Negro, over-charges him for inferior merchandise and returns little of the profits to the community." Lomax cited the case of one Jewish landlord who had overcharged his black tenants and had incited resentment. Lomax cautioned that although *he* knew this in-stance reflected "carelessness" rather than racism, the average Negro "sees only that he is ill-used and that so many of his exploiters are of a particular race or religion....The result of this is an inclination toward group prejudice." Lomax requested Rabbi Magnin's help in rectifying both this particular situation and the larger issue of black anti-Semi-tism.[174] The rabbi replied that although he was sympathetic to African Americans' concerns, discriminating against blacks was not specific to the Jews. He and many other Jews, Magnin told Lomax, actually resisted other whites' insistence that they enforce restrictive covenants against blacks. But Magnin also explained that "this is not a virtue on our part. I mention it merely to show that Jews should not be pointed out as though we had all the faults in the world."[175]

Significant numbers of Los Angeles Jewish Americans remained working class and their immigrant status often added to their marginal-ization. But these fraught situations hint at underlying class differences between Los Angeles Jews one the one hand and African Americans and Mexican Americans on the other. The city's Jewish population was increasingly upwardly mobile. And while the city also had a sizeable middle-class black population, many of whom populated the Urban League and the NAACP, the black population brought by the wartime migration was increasingly working-class and politically disenfran-chised. Los Angeles's middle-class Mexican-origin population was even smaller. Tensions resulting from this growing class divide surfaced in interactions between Jewish Americans and both African and Mexican Americans.

Jewish Americans' concern about racial violence potentially being directed at them increased their orientation toward interracial civil rights coalition building. Despite their increasing material progress, Jews were forced by wartime events to recognize their own vulnerability in the world, in the United States, and in Los Angeles. Hitler's European activ-ities, rising domestic anti-Semitism and fascism, and an awareness that some Americans blamed them for U.S. involvement in the war intensified

Jewish Americans' sense of their precarious status.[176] In 1943, CRC
members recognized that "the links already obvious between anti-Negro
and anti-Japanese agitators will inevitably be extended...to other groups
against whom hatred can easily and safely be directed, including the
Jew."[177] The United States' entry into the war freed time and energy for
Jews to focus on interracial projects—"building bridges" with other
minorities, as they called it. Previously, Los Angeles Jews, through the
CRC, directed most of their antidiscrimination energy, time, and money
to surveillance of fascist and other anti-Semitic subversive groups, work
taken up by U.S. government agencies and citizens' groups after Japan's
attack on Pearl Harbor drew the United States into the international
crossfire. After 1941, CRC leaders believed they no longer needed to
monitor the Nazis and their allies to the same degree "because by then
our own government agencies, the intelligence agencies, the FBI,
the Office of Strategic Services [OSS], all of those were watching," the
CRC's postwar director Joseph Roos later reflected.[178] Reflecting on
the CRC's changing purposes during the war, Isaac Pacht noted that by
1951, previously Jewish "defense" agencies instead called themselves
"Jewish *public* and *community* relations agencies."[179] A letter from the
wartime director Leon Lewis to CRC members explained that all "good
citizens" bore the responsibility of fighting bigotry which targeted any
and all Los Angeles residents. According to Lewis, because bigots tended
to "rely upon the existence of ancient prejudices and...make Jewish
groups the first point of attack," Jews could most effectively fight prejudice against themselves by helping promote public education about all
racial and religious groups.[180] The CRC and other Jewish groups continued
to fight anti-Semitism, but now they did so collaboratively, viewing anti-
Semitism as part of the larger issue of racism or discrimination. This
earned the CRC a reputation throughout the nation as a leader of interracial efforts in Los Angeles. Of course, the CRC's stance concerning the
Japanese-descent population marks an exception to this mounting interracialism, but was consistent with L.A. Jews' focus on what they believed
to be the best way to fight fascism and anti-Semitism, and general threats
to Jews' global security.

With the exception of Japanese Americans, silenced by internment, Los
Angeles minority groups' antidiscrimination efforts increased during the
war, in no small part because the war itself opened a window of opportunity through which they could maneuver to advance their causes.
International events framed all these efforts, creating a climate that facilitated their effectiveness and made civil rights advancement, at least on
some level, expedient. Wartime circumstances motivated groups differently. Fears of Axis infiltration into the United States and anti-Semitism
more generally largely motivated Jews' interracialism, while impending

home front disunity and loss of international support better explains officials' and white citizens' motivation. Maximizing their political strength more directly helped motivate African and Mexican Americans' alliances. Combating neighborhood violence motivated majorities and minorities alike. Working through coalitions was made both possible and mandatory by the war-induced influx of racially diverse populations that strained local resources and revealed a stark option: work together or suffer from the resultant discord. Postwar activists continued to build upon the efforts of those who chose the former path.

CHAPTER 4

Cold Warriors of a Different Stripe

Uncertainty about the future of civil rights accompanied the end of World War II. Lawrence Hewes of the American Council for Race Relations reflected on the way it had influenced his and other activists' understanding about race relations on the West Coast. Their realization "that many fellow citizens sincerely identified 'Americanism' and 'democracy' with white supremacy and keeping weaker people 'in their place'" frightened them. "Whites who held different views were promptly discounted as 'nigger lovers,' 'Jap lovers,' and Communists," Hewes explained, "even by some responsible union, business, and community leaders."[1] Distraught by feelings that many Americans revealed about race during the war, Hewes could not have foreseen that the situation would deteriorate as the Cold War chill settled over Los Angeles, the West, and the rest of the United States.

Returning minority servicemen's expectations of better treatment in light of their service to their country shattered after the war as it became clear that drastic inequality persisted—and even worsened—in the face of a retracting economy and housing crunch. Mounting anticommunism exacerbated racial tensions caused by the war, Los Angeles's demographic transformations—particularly its growing minority populations, and the transition to a peacetime economy. Cold War fears of global communism and various forms of domestic radicalism made pursuing racial justice an even more difficult task in the postwar era. Red-baiters increasingly undermined social reformers' legitimacy by pointing to the similarities between the platforms of civil rights activists and communists. Conservatives frequently labeled racial reformers un-American, thereby thwarting racial justice efforts. As a *Los Angeles Daily News* editor sympathetic to the civil rights cause astutely observed, irresponsible anticommunist accusations had succeeded in forming "a wholly erroneous public conception—a conception that every organization working for reform or change or betterment is honeycombed with disciples of Karl Marx." Such indiscriminate accusations endangered civil rights progress, the editor explained, because they "bring disrepute to the forces of progressivism" and "frighten many progressive citizens who are not Communists but who don't like to be branded and ostracized and thereby discourages them from joining organizations working for the public good."[2] This observation illustrates the mounting opposition to communists and their allies, even from Americans sympathetic to some progressive causes. It also encapsulates the Cold War's challenge to civil rights activists: to pursue their goals in the face of accusations linking all social reform attempts to global communism.

Cold War crackdowns on civil rights in the name of anticommunism marginalized many activists who had been involved in Los Angeles civil rights coalitions since the 1930s. Governmental pressure led to the exile or deportation—for their supposed radicalism—of some activists who helped shape coalitions like the Sleepy Lagoon Defense Committee and El Congreso. Luisa Moreno left under threat of deportation, in order to avoid testifying against the famous Longshoremen union leader Harry Bridges. Shortly after refusing the U.S. government's offer of citizenship in exchange for her testimony, Moreno and her husband moved permanently to Guatemala. Josefina Fierro de Bright also left "voluntarily," for fear of being arrested or subpoenaed and incriminating her friends and colleagues.[3] Fellow activists sidelined others who had been integral to earlier coalitions because they believed the Cold War mandated a cautious approach and associations.

The end of the war removed important fuel from civil rights arguments' fire, rendering irrelevant justifications that civil rights were necessary to protect the home front and the Allied effort. "While these problems [intergroup tensions] could be solved during the war with comparatively little effort because of the desperate need for unity," the Los Angeles Council for Civic Unity (CCU) presciently, if a bit over simplistically concerning the past, noted, "they have become exceedingly difficult and serious since V-J day."[4] Transformations the city had undergone made postwar problems particularly severe, as CCU members observed: "The inflammable inter-racial and inter-cultural problems of most American cities are combined and concentrated in the Los Angeles area: mixed population increases; an excess of new, as well as old, ideological organizations; extremes—tensions—intolerance—disturbances—incipient riots—racial, religious and cultural misunderstandings; the insidious doctrines of race and group hatreds—and the efforts of subversive and hate-mongering groups to ignite them."[5]

In the face of these setbacks, the CCU and many of its civil rights allies remained active and strengthened their resolve during the early Cold War. Some activists worked within the constraints of the conservative era by framing their efforts in anticommunist terms. Reformers hoping to maintain mainstream support justified their activities with anticommunist goals, arguing that their civil rights agenda was essential to preserving democracy because eliminating discrimination would foil communists' attempts to gain a foothold in marginalized communities. Among the organizations that effectively retooled their message in this way were the Jewish Community Relations Committee (CRC), African Americans' National Association for the Advancement of Colored People (NAACP), Mexican Americans' Community Service Organization (CSO), and the Council for Civic Unity (CCU). Leaders including the African American Loren Miller, the Jewish American Isaac Pacht, and the Mexican American Edward Roybal rose to influence in this way, but conducted a careful balancing act. Communists and their sympathizers accused them of selling out, while red-baiters and conservatives accused them of betraying American democracy through their supposed communist-influenced radicalism. Cold Warrior activists hoped to juggle their concern for civil rights and other community struggles with their support of civil liberties. They generally concluded that too adamantly supporting civil liberties and radicals' rights in the early Cold War would jeopardize their effectiveness in other struggles, and they chose their battles carefully in the hopes of maintaining as much legitimacy and influence as possible.

Council for Civic Unity members expressed the problem such activists believed they faced: their postwar effectiveness depended upon "the difficult task of repudiat[ing] the Communists on the extreme left, and the Fascists on the extreme right." In their view, organizations like the CCU then could devote "[themselves] to constructive programs in race relations."[6] A Jewish Community Relations Committee (CRC) press release articulated well this dual struggle: they tried to remain vigilant against "radical" infiltration while defending the "innocent" from extreme anticommunists' "unjust and false accusations."[7]

It is significant that some Cold War activists managed to pursue any civil rights agenda or attain any social justice during the height of Cold War repression. Struggling to maintain their relevance, some degree of effectiveness, and their personal safety, they charted a path between anti–civil rights red-baiters on the extreme right, whose conflation of all reform agendas with communism endangered their progress, and "tainted" groups and individuals on the extreme left, whose nonconformist approaches and affiliation jeopardized their efficacy in such a climate. They believed that achieving civil rights results meant establishing a middle position of pro–civil rights anticommunism.[8] As they did so, they articulated policies and agendas that in some ways *were* more moderate than their predecessors, as this chapter will explore. Specifically, anticommunism led them to limit their alliances across the political left by marginalizing former allies. Anticommunism also led many to abandon earlier critiques of U.S. foreign policy, and expressions of solidarity with oppressed groups elsewhere in the world. In terms of their domestic equality agendas, however, they maintained much of the thrust of earlier critiques. Before examining how they charted their path and what it entailed, we must first establish why in the early Cold War they felt pressured to moderate elements of their earlier activism.

A RISING ANTI-RED, ANTI–CIVIL RIGHTS TIDE

The growing estrangement between the United States and the Soviet Union raised fears about worldwide communist domination, including its potentially corrosive effects on American democracy, and heightened suspicion of those who sought to reform U.S. society.[9] Racial equality activists, particularly susceptible because of similarities between communist and civil rights agendas, operated in an environment permeated by suspicion. Some anticommunists viewed civil rights advocacy as a subversive activity—whether the activists were communists or not—because "stoking the fires of racial unrest" would disrupt American society.[10] Candidates vying for the presidency in 1948 fired accusations of communism at each other, often connecting it to civil rights. Candidate J. Strom Thurmond accused incumbent Harry Truman of attempting to heighten class and race hatred in order to "create the chaos and confusion which leads to communism."[11] Truman protected himself by deflecting the anticommunist rhetoric onto another target, Henry Wallace. He asserted that a vote for Wallace's third-party ticket—the Progressive Party—was "a vote for all the things for which Stalin [and] Molotov . . . stand."[12]

Fearful Americans blocked attempts to pass liberal "un-American" legislation, including civil rights, at all levels of government. In California, efforts to pass state legislation creating a Fair Employment Practices Committee (FEPC) failed repeatedly until 1959. The U.S. Senate filibustered President Truman's 1945 attempt to pass a national Fair Employment Practices (FEP) bill. The U.S. Congress gutted liberal versions of an employment bill and in 1946 passed a conservative act that deliberately omitted mention of federal commitment to full employment and to provisions that would mandate public spending to supplement private expenditures.[13] Fearful of the increasingly conservative climate, the president was reluctant to act on his civil rights investigative committee's calls for legislation eliminating discrimination and segregation in employment, housing, health facilities, interstate transportation, and public accommodations; to pass a law criminalizing lynching; and to issue executive orders against racial discrimination in the federal civil service and armed forces.[14]

California and Los Angeles developed their own particularly conservative legislation. California became the first state to pass loyalty oaths and Los Angeles County the first county in the nation to do the same, both in 1947. The L.A. City Council followed suit in 1948.[15] Conservative

Richard Nixon replaced longtime liberal Los Angeles Congressman Jerry Voorhis in a 1946 campaign in which he accused Voorhis of being "soft on Communism." Four years later, Nixon used the same anticommunist platform to beat the popular liberal congresswoman Helen Gahagan Douglas, whom he labeled "the pink lady."[16] Nixon rose to national prominence on an anticommunist Southern California platform, revealing both the power of such an approach and the difficulties civil rights activists in the region faced.

Red-baiting in Los Angeles increased in the postwar years. Conditions in Los Angeles were among the worst in the country, in part because they built upon the city's long tradition of radical repression. Southern California's "acute fear of communism" can be attributed to its economic reliance upon large defense contracts and its fear of being a target for foreign attack, most visibly during the Korean War.[17] The presence of communists, socialists, and other "undesirables" in the Hollywood community and in the mixed multiracial, immigrant population fed Cold War fears, too. Politicians, governmental institutions, and fearful citizens were poised to attack any group supporting ideas even remotely resembling communist platforms.

The anticommunist tide in Los Angeles, as in California and nationwide, swept up many people, including a fair number with no association to communism. A 1948 report from the California Un-American Activities Committee, the state's powerful version of the national anticommunist House Un-American Activities Committee, which explained that "the conflict between Americanism and Stalinism is irreconcilable and cannot be compromised," reflected this dangerous climate. It continued by explaining that "the secret and conspiratorial nature of the Communist Party" made identifying a Stalinist individual or organization difficult and justified extreme vigilance against any possible suspects.[18] Furthermore, it stated that "U.S. Communists, as part of the program of world Communism, continuously and consistently operate behind the facade of front organizations."[19] The committee's working definition of communism, which included anyone "who knowingly and voluntarily assembles with a group of persons at which meeting communism is advocated," revealed that even people who merely attended meetings with communists were suspect.[20]

The committee, also known as the Tenney Committee after its first leader, Jack B. Tenney, an active leftist turned vigilant anticommunist and increasingly zealous "witch-hunter," particularly focused its investigations on the Los Angeles region.[21] Tenney believed the area harbored a disproportionate amount of radical activity. Tenney's committee assisted FBI and HUAC investigations in California, compiled countless pages of information, and printed numerous reports on "subversive" activities in California.[22]

In 1947, HUAC also made Los Angeles a primary target. It zeroed in on the city because of the Hollywood film industry's influence on a nationwide and worldwide audience. It investigated alleged communist activities among producers, directors, screenwriters, and actors. HUAC's blanket targeting was misguided even though some influential Hollywood figures were communists or fellow travelers, especially among Hollywood's Jewish community.[23] HUAC also focused on Los Angeles because of its belief, as member representative John McDowell (Pennsylvania) explained, that "large numbers" of foreign communists streamed into the United States across the Mexican border.[24]

Anticommunist attacks originated in nongovernmental circles, too. Los Angeles newspaper articles with titles like "Red Spies Sneaking in from Mexico" whipped up fear of Mexican immigrants.[25] White middle-class mothers and wives joined and even instigated many campaigns to purge Los Angeles of anticommunist "un-Americanism." Angelenos from a broad range of backgrounds, and for a broad range of motives, embraced anticommunism. These included women and men, elites and nonelites, and both racists/anti-Semites and nonracists.[26]

An eloquent letter from a noncommunist Hollywood progressive to a friend in New York City illuminates the atmosphere reform-minded Angelenos experienced. "Sometimes I doubt if you people in the more liberal atmosphere of New York...have any idea at all of how bad, how really fearful behind the scenes, the Hollywood milieu is for an unconfused [noncommunist] liberal," Dudley Nichols wrote to Freda Kirchway, the editor of the Nation before Carey McWilliams. Nichols lamented, "The super loyalists, the bigoted and ignorant, the scared reactionaries, the corrupt and militant totalitarians, the men using patriotism as an ugly club to cow or kill whoever doesn't knuckle under to them—these people are bent on blacklisting every decent free-minded man who works in the Hollywood field."[27] Nichols highlighted the Tenney Committee's particularly repressive tactics: "Anyone these people don't like is labeled a Communist, and it has become a dangerous word—like tsetse fly that can kill you even after you've swatted it down."[28]

Civil rights activism became a prime target for Los Angeles anticommunists. Even before World War II ended, the Tenney Committee attacked the multiracial activists defending the Mexican American Zoot Suit defendants. Tenney dismissed racial tensions and harsh living conditions—what activists identified as the root causes of the riots—as communist fabrications. "The Communist Party press, pursuing the party line on racial agitation, continually fed the fires of racial antagonism by charging that Mexican youth in the United States was being subjected to police brutality, race-discrimination, segregation and humiliation," a fifty-page segment of the committee's 1945 report claimed. It charged that communist-inspired and communist-dominated organizations, "trained rabble-rousers," defended the Mexican population. The committee determined in public hearings shortly afterwards that Communists had deliberately fostered the racial agitation that caused the Zoot Suit Riots.[29]

Targeting civil rights reformers, particularly minorities, as suspected communists increased as U.S.-Soviet relations deteriorated. Postwar documents including Tenney Committee reports reveal that virulent anticommunists targeted minority organizations seeking greater equality for their communities. Some of the groups Tenney's postwar reports identified had openly communist members, including former Popular Front–era organizations like the Sleepy Lagoon Defense Committee and El Congreso, but many other groups were cited despite their deliberate attempts to frame themselves as anticommunist.[30] These noncommunist—and even anticommunist—targets included organizations like the Japanese American Citizens' League (JACL) and the African-American National Association for the Advancement of Colored People (NAACP), which Tenney's report described as "Communist Infiltrated, but neither Controlled nor Dominated."[31] Tenney also targeted individual activists whose past associations with communists and communist affiliates rendered them "suspect." One such target was African-American activist Loren Miller, who upon his return from travels in the Soviet Union during the 1930s had praised the communist system in speeches and writings, and who belonged to the National Lawyers' Guild.[32]

Los Angeles Jewish community groups featured most prominently in Tenney's reports.[33] Tenney frequently conflated Jewish organizations— especially those in Los Angeles—with radicalism, despite the noncommunism and even anticommunist bent of most. His committee's 1947 report listed fifteen of the fifty members of the local Jewish Community Relations Committee as "tainted." In June 1949, Tenney accused the prominent Jewish community member and leader Isaac Pacht of being "in the Stalin orbit."[34] Pacht, who soon became cochair of the statewide committee for Fair Employment Practices and the president of both the California Federation for Civic Unity (CFCU, the CCU's statewide organization) and the Jewish community's umbrella organization, the Jewish Community Council, ironically helped craft these groups' anticommunism. Tenney's characterization of Pacht in later years hinted that more than anticommunism motivated Tenney's heavy focus on the Jewish community; anti-Semitism shaped it too.[35] Tenney recollected other minorities' anticommunist civil rights groups and individuals too, but far less than he discussed their equivalents in the Jewish community. He referred in his oral history one time each to the NAACP and the Urban League, and not at all to the Mexican-American community's Community Service Organization (CSO).[36] In later years Tenney blamed Jews for his downfall.[37] In 1953 he published *Zion's Fifth Column*, a book intended to expose political Zionism as dangerous to "our American way of life."[38] Tenney defended himself from accusations of anti-Semitism by protesting that he was merely anti-Zionist.[39] Tenney was not alone: the connection between Jews and Communism figured prominently in California's anticommunist crusade, as well as in the minds of many white Americans since the time of the 1917 Russian Revolution. White Americans also often associated African Americans, though a bit less so, with disproportionate communist associations.[40]

But the atmosphere was dangerous for all civil rights activists, especially minorities, whether communist or not. Accusations conflating civil rights activism with communism and other forms of subversion, which Californians were quick to believe, threatened to undermine any and all civil rights agendas.

AN AMBIGUOUS VICTORY

Widespread and growing discrimination in postwar Los Angeles dismayed those who had hoped that World War II and its global fight for democracy would transform the home front permanently for the better. Minorities who migrated to Los Angeles during the war, when they found unprecedented job opportunities, found their postwar options severely limited. Racial tensions intensified as the city converted from a war to a peacetime economy and competition increased for even more limited housing and employment. Reformers seeking greater racial equality found themselves caught between anticommunists' accusations and growing societal racism.

Attempts to build public housing in Los Angeles after the war especially illuminate the dilemma reformers faced. "Antisocialized housing" campaigns and anticommunist investigators' accusations that housing reformers were "red" impeded such initiatives.[41] The well-known case of the destruction of Chávez Ravine in the late 1940s and early 1950s to make way for Dodger Stadium illustrates particularly well how anticommunism impeded the construction of public housing. Anticommunists' accusations against Frank Wilkinson, the Anglo-American assistant director of the L.A. City Housing Authority, derailed attempts to build public housing for the area's mainly Mexican-origin populations. Once plans to build public housing on the land, which by 1952 had been cleared of its inhabitants—by persuasion and by force—were cancelled, the eager Dodgers snatched the land for their new stadium. Wilkinson remembered with bitterness how anti-red crusades destroyed his plans, ruined his career, and landed him in jail for a year. His blacklisted status made it hard for him to get a job when he was released from prison and forced him to work as a janitor in a business owned by Quakers while volunteering for the ACLU as a civil liberties researcher. The experience also left Wilkinson angry and guilt-ridden that the city never followed through on its promises to the neighborhood's poor inhabitants, who found themselves permanently displaced.[42]

Obstruction of these inaccurately billed "socialized housing" reform campaigns presented an especially grave threat to Los Angeles minorities, whose housing woes worsened as military personnel and Japanese American internees returned to the city. The Los Angeles Housing Authority sheltered just over 13,000 people at the time of the U.S. entry into World War II, but by 1943 over 200,000 migrants had moved to the city and the agency had only doubled its capacity to 27,000.[43] The city faced "an overall housing shortage unequaled in any other city in the United States," the agency's director explained, "conservatively estimated as a need of approximately one hundred thousand units of housing."[44]

Restrictive covenants made the housing crisis especially acute for minorities.[45] These barred African Americans from 95 percent of the city's housing.[46] They limited even famous minority residents, including the entertainer Nat King Cole, who was prevented from moving to a property he bought in an "exclusive" section of the city by threats, letters, and calls. Warnings sometimes threatened violence against residents and prospective residents. "One of your coons came here in Sherman Way, Van Nuys, offering $1,000 over price to a family to buy a home here and just to get your black animal cross breeds into our white neighborhood. Just try to come," menaced one note left for an African-American family trying to move into a restricted neighborhood. The note, published in the *Los Angeles Daily Tribune*, threatened, "We will burn you out. You filthy intruders.... There is nothing so nasty on two feet than you niggers. You bitch in our civilization, stay on your own side."[47] Most of the 170,000 African-American residents of Los Angeles were confined to three communities—the Central Avenue district (south of downtown), which came to encompass the former "Little Tokyo," Watts (seven miles south of downtown Los Angeles), and the West Adams neighborhood (five miles southwest of downtown).[48] Mexican Americans confronted similar problems, which forced many of them to working-class, segregated barrios, especially on the eastside, which became largely Mexican-origin.[49] Racial covenants did not affect Jews as severely, but anti-Semitism continued to limit their housing choices even as increasing numbers found ways to move to the city's more affluent Westside.[50]

The return of approximately 12,000 to 15,000 Japanese Americans to Los Angeles, where they found their former homes occupied by recent migrants, primarily African Americans, exacerbated racial tensions.[51] Japanese Americans confronted mixed reactions to their resettlement in Southern California. Mayor Fletcher Bowron believed that the majority of Angelenos did not favor their 1945 return. "I feel that these gentlemen [of the War Department and other Washington D.C. officials] have made an honest mistake in misjudging public opinion," Bowron explained, "and that they are in error when they believe that the majority of the people favor the return of the Japanese."[52] Signs menacing, "No Japs Allowed, No Japs Welcome" greeted some internees; others found themselves welcomed by former neighbors.[53] Resistance often came from minority neighbors as well as from white Angelenos, especially in neighborhoods like the former "Little Tokyo," renamed "Bronzeville" after over 6,000 Japanese-origin people were evacuated in May 1942 and approximately 5,000 African American (and other) migrants moved in.[54] A report on police brutality blamed mounting tensions in the city on the recent population boom. "Tremendous population shifts during and following World War II," the report stated, "created such problems as competition for jobs, housing, recreation and transportation which, together with other factors, threatened or resulted in open antagonism between racial, religious and national groups."[55]

Figure 6: African American Life in Little Tokyo/Bronzeville after Internment, 1943, Los Angeles Daily News Collection, Department of Special Collections, Charles E. Young Research Library, UCLA.

Employment discrimination, like housing discrimination, also plagued Los Angeles minorities. The transformation to a peacetime society meant the end of the employment boom the war had brought to the City of Angels. Without war fueling demand, jobs disappeared and unemployment rose. The contraction hit the defense industry particularly hard. By 1948, unemployment had, in the words of Governor Earl Warren, "assumed serious proportions." Ten percent of unemployed Americans were in California in May, 1949, making it one of the hardest hit areas in the country, and more than half of these unemployed Californians resided in Los Angeles.[56] Minorities, especially African Americans and Mexican Americans, were the last hired and first fired. Los Angeles employers earmarked 70 percent of 1946 job requests for whites only.[57] The L.A. Sears Roebuck hired African Americans only for "menial" positions.[58] Downtown stores relegated blacks, according to a study conducted by the Southern California Anti Defamation League (ADL), to "stereotyped jobs" including stock clerks, janitors, and elevator operators. Sales clerk positions were off-limits to African Americans, though some stores hired Mexican and "Oriental" people in this capacity.[59] Discriminatory language appeared in as much as 6 percent of the employment advertisements placed in the five major Los Angeles metropolitan daily newspapers, according to another ADL study.[60] The Los Angeles Fire Department remained racially segregated as late as 1956.[61] Auto and life insurance policies regularly refused minorities coverage, and the banking industry barred them from employment.[62] Many postwar restrictions also applied to Jews. Between August 1946 and June 1947, the Bureau of Jewish Economic Problems received 103 complaints from Los Angeles Jews who experienced employment discrimination.[63] Jews faced difficulty securing certain kinds of jobs, including those in insurance, banking, finance, mining, petroleum refining, and heavy manufacturing industries. Many private employment agencies refused Jews' applications, claiming they could not place them.[64]

Postwar employment discrimination against minorities mounted, although unemployment was lower after the war for some groups than it had been before the United States joined the fighting in 1941. Black Angelenos' unemployment dropped, for instance, from 18 percent in 1940 to 12 percent in 1950.[65] Mexican Americans in California gained skilled job positions in the 1940s. Over 7 percent of all employed Mexican-American males worked in professional and other white-collar jobs by 1950, compared to less than 3 percent in 1930.[66] Many barriers to unions and training programs fell, and government positions, especially in military bases, post offices, and local governments, provided expanding work opportunities. Mexican Americans nonetheless continued to occupy low occupational positions relative to the white population. The Bracero Program (which continued through 1964) compounded the local Mexican-origin community's postwar problems by allowing employers to hire less expensive foreign labor instead of American residents.[67] African Americans filled the lowest occupational rungs and their outlook compared to white workers' was grim, despite gains in employment, particularly manufacturing. Approximately one-fourth of the city's black population was unemployed.[68]

Other forms of discrimination permeated postwar Los Angeles communities, reinforcing minorities' outrage that injustice at home outlasted the Allied victory. The Los Angeles Bar Association prohibited African-American membership. Los Angeles recreational bowling leagues restricted membership to "whites only."[69] Racists burned crosses on the lawns of Los Angeles African Americans' homes, especially when they moved into previously "lily-white" neighborhoods. Police were often "indifferent" to these acts of terror, African Americans explained in frustration.[70] Public swimming pools excluded Mexicans and African Americans, theaters separated them, and some businesses refused to serve them.[71]

Figure 7: Demonstrators Protest Discriminatory Housing in Los Angeles, 1946, Los Angeles Daily News Collection, Department of Special Collections, Charles E. Young Research Library, UCLA.

Jewish Americans' increasingly middle-class status compared to African Americans and Mexican Americans did not shield them from discrimination either. Jews had difficulty breaking into local politics, early 1950s disputes about the Board of Education were framed in anti-Semitic terms, and radio sermons by the Congregationalist Reverend James W. Fifield and other local anti-Semites reached receptive audiences.[72] The American Automobile Association listed certain hotels as "restricted" from Jews.[73] Vandals marked anti-Semitic symbols on Jewish establishments, including painting two swastikas on a Los Angeles temple and six swastikas on stores and walls in one East Los Angeles area, painting crosses on two families' apartment doors, vandalizing a Jewish cemetery in Bell Gardens, and shattering the windows and destroying the Torah of a Jewish community center.[74] Teachers at one eastside junior high school were both "outspokenly anti-Semitic as well as anti-Mexican," according to the American Council on Race Relations, which reported that "the Jewish adolescent discovers that his middle-class status gives him no immunity."[75]

THE COMMUNIST CONNECTION

Anticommunism became only one of various weapons wielded against minorities to exclude them and prevent them from attaining equality. But despite the pervasive discrimination and deep Cold War fears that facilitated countless false charges of communism, some anticommunist accusations had a basis in reality. Communists were often at the forefront of civil rights struggles in Los Angeles and nationwide. The presence of communists in civil rights communities fueled and reinforced anticommunists' attempts to marginalize struggles for equality in Los Angeles.

Noncommunist minority activists recognized an element of truth in accusations that communists made headway in their ethno-racial communities. Zane Meckler, the western director of the noncommunist Jewish Labor Committee's antidiscrimination department, explained the "threat" which noncommunist civil rights organizations believed the Communist Party posed: "Within recent years...the Communist Party in America, and its Jewish section as well, has presented a mortal threat to all decent democratic and educational movements." Meckler continued to explain, "The threat has been all the more serious within Jewish life as it has been within other minority communities where the temptation has always been present to accept support from whatever sources and to use whatever tactic is necessary to achieve public attention and specific objectives."[76]

During the early Cold War, Los Angeles housed the second largest communist population in the country after New York City. Los Angeles party membership grew from 2,500 in the mid-1930s, to 3,200 in 1945, and increased to its late 1948 high point of 5,000, while national membership simultaneously dropped in half, from 100,000 in 1939 to 50,000 in 1949. Los Angeles accounted for 10 percent of national postwar membership.[77]

Communists were particularly present among civil rights and minority communities, though members' cautious secrecy makes membership numbers difficult to ascertain. The Los Angeles CP actively recruited minorities, appealing to their concern about the disjuncture between the promise and reality of equality in American democracy. Local Jews maintained a large communist population, particularly in the community's eastside stronghold. Workers' groups like the Jewish People's Fraternal Order (JPFO) and its Emma Lazarus women's division associated with communists, whether or not members were communists themselves. Los Angeles Jewish Americans continued to be drawn to and influential within the CP.[78] Local African Americans' association with the CP actually increased in the postwar era. While ambivalence—and sometimes hostility—characterized prewar blacks' approach to the L.A. CP, by 1949 several hundred blacks had joined the organization, representing 10 percent of the local membership. The Communist Party's promise of social justice persuaded them, as it did their national counterparts. Sixty-one percent of African Americans interviewed for a national study were sympathetic to communism in 1955, and blacks composed one-fourth of the Communist Party's Central Committee by 1961.[79] Mexican Americans' participation is especially hard to gauge, but Dorothy Healey, a prominent member of the L.A. party, placed their membership in the L.A. CP at about 300 to 400 members in the early 1940s. The overall L.A. CP membership gain by the late 1940s suggests that the Mexican American representation likely also increased.[80] Though reliable figures on Japanese-origin CP membership are elusive, memoirs by party members like Karl Yoneda make clear that Japanese Americans joined the Communist Party earlier in the twentieth century and remained members.[81]

Communist Party involvement in local minorities' activities sometimes warranted anticommunist investigators' suspicions of its role in civil rights endeavors. It is likely, for instance, that the director of an eastside Jewish Community Center allowed communist front organizations to meet there. This caused problems because it meant that the Los Angeles Community Chest, which partially funded the center, indirectly paid for the front organizations' meetings. An internal Jewish community investigation concluded that center members likely assisted communists, if they were not communist themselves.[82] And Mexican-American organizations like the Associación Nacionál México-Americana (ANMA), a national organization with several branches in Los Angeles, also worked closely with communists.

Some members even seem to have been CP.[83] Many members of organizations like the Los Angeles Committee for the Protection of the
Foreign Born, an interracial organization that formed in 1950 to fight
deportations sanctioned by the McCarran Internal Security Act that
same year, were also CP members.[84]

Cases like these do more than reveal the merit of some suspicions
about communist involvement in Los Angeles equality struggles. They
also help explain that anticommunists who truly feared communist
involvement in American society did not merely seek to derail civil rights
progress, using anticommunism as an empty foil to do so. But despite the
fact that it was accurate to assume CP involvement in some equality
struggles, conflating all civil rights activism with communism was misguided. Moreover, anticommunism cruelly devastated many individuals
and organizations and derailed careers and lives of communists and non-
communists alike who fought for a more equal society. Countless numbers of people were alienated from friends and colleagues, never found
work again, and even committed suicide after brutal red-baiting investigations into their political, professional, and personal lives.

MINORITIES RESPOND: A CRITIQUE OF
ANTICOMMUNISM

Civil rights reformers who hoped to maintain their efficacy in the face of
mounting anticommunist suspicions struggled to articulate a racial
equality agenda more widely "acceptable" during the Cold War. To do so,
they reinvented themselves using anticommunism, articulating a middle-
ground anticommunism that carved a space for civil rights. They argued
that extreme anticommunism that targeted anything remotely similar to
communist platforms jeopardized democracy, while simultaneously
fighting for civil rights and targeting "actual" communists would help
advance democracy. They defined their pro–civil rights approach as the
most American Cold War path because it was an antidote to communism
that could help democratically minded Americans counter both un-
American conservatism and radicalism.

Cold War activists charged that indiscriminate anticommunists used
the radical label to suppress legitimate struggles to build a more egali-
tarian society, and thus a better democracy. Isaac Pacht expressed this
concern in his opening speech at the Jewish community's 1951 Workshop
on the Problem of Communism. In his speech Pacht stated, "I do not
believe that Communism in America is a threat. I believe Senator
McCarthy is a greater threat to the democratic way of life—which we
cherish—than the Communist Party."[85] Pacht clearly exaggerated, since
at other times he clearly expressed his concern that communism was a

threat. But still, his point about the anticommunist threat is clear. Cold War activists opposed the proposed 1948 Mundt Bill, too, because the bill's "Subversive Activities Control Act"—which would render the Communist Party illegal—would target civil rights organizations en masse. NAACP members opposed it, and the American Jewish Congress cautioned that the bill's intention to curb the activities of groups "loosely described as 'Communist-front organizations'" threatened to entrap all organizations working to extend democracy in the United States by "eliminating discrimination, protecting civil rights, and promoting equality of opportunity," including goals such as ending "lynch terror," protecting and extending the right to vote, and providing decent housing and education for all Americans.[86] The CRC declared that the Tenney Committee's false accusation against the American Jewish Congress was "in keeping with [its] unsavory record...since its inception—a record replete with instances of the Committee's use of its power to smear liberal American organizations and individuals."[87]

Cold War reformers used language of un-Americanism to carve a space for their agenda. The CRC labeled red-baiters who targeted Jews as both "antidemocratic" and "anti-Semitic."[88] Jewish community organizations expressed growing opposition to Tenney in "un-American," especially anticommunist, terms more than in anti-Semitic terms. They argued that Tenney's 1949 accusation that Judge Isaac Pacht was in the Stalin orbit functioned to "aid and encourage Communism in our State."[89] They also claimed that Tenney's downfall would bring a "nation-wide victory for democracy and decency," and joined forces first to defeat his 1952 bid for the 22nd U.S. Congressional District (the San Fernando Valley) and later (1954) his state Senate re-election campaign.[90] The NAACP's director of national branches, Gloster Current, criticized the House Un-American Activities Committee (HUAC) in 1948 with similar language of un-Americanism. If HUAC really wanted to "perform a useful function," Current declared, "it should indict those Southerners who oppose the civil rights program and expose them as being dangerous to the security of the United states and the American way of life."[91] The California Federation for Civic Unity (CFCU) accused Tenney of following "the current Communist Party line" when he introduced his 1953 "Freedom of Choice Initiative," which would effectively legalize discrimination by permitting employers and landlords to hire, rent, or sell to whomever they chose. While Tenney insisted that encouraging individual choice was all-American, the CFCU countered by charging that limiting Americans' freedom to *escape* discrimination was un-American.[92] In cases like this one, Cold War civil rights strategy succeeded, and the initiative died.

Reformers further strengthened their cause by highlighting red-baiters' especially un-American discrimination against minorities fighting the Korean War, whose defense of their country against communism proved their Americanism. Edward Roybal, who in 1949 became the first Mexican-American member of the city council in almost seventy years, supported his critique of extreme anticommunists this way. In 1950, Roybal drew attention as the sole member to oppose the council's decision to implement a citywide communist control ordinance, which he feared would especially target civil rights activists. Cognizant that he might be "signing [his] own [political] death warrant," he told the council he persevered partly because the ordinance would wrongly target and punish Los Angeles "Negro, Japanese American, and Mexican American GIs" who upheld American ideals by challenging discrimination at home, where they could find no place to live, when they had had "all the space between the 38 parallel and Puzan [sic] in which to die."[93]

Their fight against red-baiters who targeted racial equality advocates epitomized Americanism, Cold War activists argued. They stressed that their opposition to racism helped ensure domestic security by preventing communists from stealing the hearts and minds of minorities. Roybal justified his lone opposition to the communist-control ordinance by emphasizing that improving minorities' conditions would eliminate the "breeding ground for Communism" and strengthen democracy. Roybal explained that he too "despised" communism, but that discriminating against the wrong people through such ordinances would hinder rather than help the international struggle against it. The ordinance would wrongly target "a large number of little civic organizations in my district and elsewhere...who are interested in their own neighborhood problems, with civic betterment, with participation in municipal affairs, and with the protection of civil rights—in a word, with the preservation and advancement of our Democracy."[94] In addition to failing to "curb the Communist danger," it also would pose new dangers that would destroy democracy even more surely than Communism itself. It threatened to repress legitimate, *democratic*, civil rights activists whose antiracist platforms resembled communist agendas, placing them "at the mercy of any biased crackpot who may decide to report [them] to the Police Department as subversive."[95]

Roybal's stance against the ordinance, and his careful assertion of both his own anticommunism and his Americanism, drew significant public support from Los Angeles residents representing a wide range of the civil rights advocacy political spectrum. A group of 700 Angelenos representing "almost every racial and religious group in the community and a considerable variance in political thinking," according to a local newspaper editorial, honored him at a large banquet in November 1950.[96] Roybal received letters praising his courageous defense of civil liberties from communists and fellow travelers and from more moderately positioned groups and individuals. These included people who did not see eye to eye on the communist issue, such as members of the Jewish Peoples Fraternal

Order (JPFO) and Judge Isaac Pacht, who helped lead organized Jewish community efforts to expel the communist-affiliated JPFO.[97] Left-leaning activists supported Roybal's opposition to the ordinance, if not his anti-communist justifications. But more cautious community members who also praised Roybal must have felt protected enough by Roybal's language to speak at an event attended and supported by such a broad spectrum of the civil rights left. For example, Pacht spoke on behalf of 300,000 members of the organized Jewish community during the height of an internal community controversy over communists' and fellow travelers' membership. In their speeches, Pacht and Roybal both buttressed their Cold War legitimacy by emphasizing the religious—Christian and Jewish—roots of their commitment to fighting for the peoples' rights.[98]

Activists sometimes went a step further by arguing that explicitly antiracist legislation would "defeat Communism by extending democracy" and "preserve and further the American ideal."[99] The American Jewish Congress urged the U.S. Congress to pass legislation for voting rights, decent housing and education, and against racial and religious employment discrimination and lynching, believing this would be more effective than passing explicitly anticommunist legislation like the Mundt Bill.[100] All "loyal Americans" who hoped to "combat Communism," Jewish Community Council members explained, must help extend civil rights for all Americans, since "communism tends to flourish wherever segments in our population, sometimes referred to as minority groups, are subjected to limitations by virtue of their racial, creedal or national origin identities." In these terms, not addressing racial, religious, and national origin groups' "just grievances" endangered democracy.[101] The president of a Southern California NAACP branch similarly urged Americans to keep communism at bay through fair housing, integration, and alleviation of poverty.[102]

The language of Americanism permeated the arguments of both civil rights opponents and advocates during the early Cold War. Restrictive covenant supporters argued in favor of amending the U.S. Constitution to legalize the covenants, which served to "protect American family life, stabilize home values, . . . avert racial tensions and particularly safeguard the rights of families." While covenant supporters argued that they were merely doing their "duty as a patriotic citizen," civil rights proponents countered that refusing minorities' rights to live in "the home they buy with their hard-earned cash" was "un-American," as an article in the L.A. African-American newspaper the *California Eagle* explained.[103] Minorities seeking to buy unrestricted homes merely hoped to attain "a measure of wholesome democratic living," a report on restrictive covenants written by the Jewish community's Milton Senn explained.[104] An article in a local Catholic newspaper strategically titled "'Homes for Veterans': But Not Just Any Vet" highlighted the un-Americanism of restrictive covenants by exposing the plight of one "young ex-paratrooper" whose hopes to buy a home in Los Angeles were dashed when a salesman told him: "We don't do business with Mexicans, buddy. This is a restricted community."[105] The Mexican-origin man was a good father, a regular churchgoer, and a veteran (codes for a good American), the article explained, and pointed to the injustice that a city with such a "lovely Spanish name" prohibited men such as Adolph Soria, who had "done their share in building America," from buying homes because "their people didn't come over on the Mayflower." Discrimination against minority veterans represented an especially cruel betrayal by "the comrades beside whom [they] fought— and who now won't rent or sell [them] a home."[106] Flyers from the NAACP's 1947 membership campaign emphasized that the organization's fight for African Americans' civil, economic, and social rights advanced the "American way of life" and encouraged membership among "all loyal American citizens of every race and creed."[107]

Deciding to use anticommunist language only came after intense community debates over acceptable critiques of anticommunism. Members of civil rights organizations trying to claim Cold War legitimacy by selectively opposing extreme anticommunism disagreed with each other about the appropriate path to follow. Jewish community organizations argued internally, for instance, over how to articulate their opposition to anticommunism. A local B'nai B'rith chapter's 1948 decision to assist Tenney, which it believed to be politically expedient and even necessary in such a dangerously conservative atmosphere, provoked an outcry from other chapters and other Jewish community members. Critics representing a large percentage of Southern California membership in B'nai B'rith accused those who assisted Tenney of violating democratic principles. While many supported the idea of "proper" monitoring of subversives, which was important in order to "expose the true enemies of the state and make more tranquil our lives and more secure the democratic liberties we all enjoy," they argued that anticommunist organizations like Tenney's committee dangerously disregarded "individual and groups' rights and reputations." "By our silent participation" with the chapter's decision, the chapter's critics protested, "[we] are ... vilifying our own affiliated organizations, sister organizations, members and friends—and crying aloud to the world, 'You cannot call us communists. We are advising the Tenney Committee.' "[108] Such critics ultimately shaped the policy of the Jewish community, which decided against playing an advisory role to Tenney.

Other episodes in the Jewish community also reveal the nuance and careful consideration that shaped civil rights advocates' anticommunism. Internal CRC discussions in 1947 exposed widespread opposition to the County Board of Supervisors' loyalty tests by those who believed they would silence all antidiscrimination struggles. But they also believed that "clearly defined and specifically restricted" oaths which would distinguish legitimate minority rights organizations were acceptable. Despite their opposition to the supervisors' loyalty tests, though, Jewish community members expressed little enthusiasm about taking a public stand, fearing that doing so would implicate them as communists.[109]

Braver community members, like Milton Senn from the Southern California Anti-Defamation League (ADL), urged California Jews to communicate their opposition to their elected representatives. He acknowledged that "championing the rights of minorities and fighting for the removal of discriminatory measures directed against them [might] convey the impression that we are defending the Communist movement simply because it, too, appears to be interested in these objectives." But Senn believed that Jews should risk the danger. "We are doing what is right," he said, "and...we should not permit our faith or our courage to be withered by an appellation which might be attached to us [Communist sympathizers]."[110] And a few Jewish community organizations like the local and national branches of the American Jewish Congress publicly denounced the presidential loyalty oaths, explaining in a joint resolution that "the procedures embodies [sic] in the Executive Order are totally inconsistent with democratic methods and that anti-democratic influences cannot be countered by devising an administrative and executive totalitarianism of our own."[111]

But most Jewish community organizations ultimately decided that expressing even nuanced and careful opposition to such loyalty oaths posed too many risks. "Fear that our protest would be construed as an implied defense of the communist movement" led the national ADL in 1947 to silence nationwide protest. The CRC shied away from supporting American Civil Liberties Union litigation testing loyalty oaths' legality.[112]

Similarly situated African-American organizations also expressed opposition to the loyalty oaths and similar issues. Despite its mounting anticommunism, the NAACP did not remain silent on what it perceived as clear violations of a democratic society. For instance, during the height of the controversies over anticommunism in 1949, the national NAACP declared that it opposed "wholeheartedly" the President's Loyalty Program and the Mundt-Ferguson bills. On the one hand, it recognized the important challenge the government faced in making certain its employees were loyal and patriotic. However, the resolution explained, "we feel that the present program has helped create national hysteria and fear and is a greater danger to the strength and integrity of our democratic ideals than is the danger which the loyalty program was designed to cure."[113]

But as the Cold War deepened, the NAACP too increasingly limited its public actions against such violations of democracy. Earlier in the Cold War, the L.A. NAACP joined a multiracial community that included Jewish Americans and others to oppose the Los Angeles post office's decision to fire Frank Barnes, the head of the Santa Monica NAACP branch. The post office fired Barnes for allegedly cooperating with "subversive" organizations in a protest he helped organize in November 1947 against the Santa Monica Sears store's discriminatory hiring practices. Among the supposedly subversive groups with which Barnes cooperated were the Jewish Peoples Fraternal Order (JPFO), the American Jewish Congress, and the Progressive Citizens of America. A memo written by Los Angeles NAACP legal staff member Loren Miller, together with documents from the CRC and other organizations, shows that the NAACP and other increasingly anticommunist allies protested the injustice of the dismissal. They were careful, though, to protest in terms of how the dismissal violated fundamental *American* principles like freedom of speech and the Constitution rather than in terms of supporting the communist groups' right to participate.[114]

But NAACP cooperation with "dangerous" groups, even when they justified it under the banner of such American principles, became increasingly rare. In 1950, the Los Angeles NAACP's chairman of the Legal Redress Committee gave a speech at an anti–Mundt Bill event co-organized by the Communist Party, the Civil Rights Congress (a "communist front" organization), and various union, civil rights, and church organizations. The speech catalyzed discussions between Los Angeles NAACP president E. I. Robinson and the national office's Gloster B. Current about removing the official from his post.[115] It was no longer seen as possible for an NAACP official to participate in an event involving the same kind of collaboration across the political left that happened during the Sears protest three years earlier. With African Americans as with Jewish Americans, fear trumped bravery in most cases.

Charting an all-American Cold War civil rights path meant on the one hand helping democratically minded Americans counter un-American conservatism, specifically extreme anticommunism which left no room for fighting discrimination. On the other hand, though, it also meant navigating away from un-American radicalism, especially anyone or anything too closely associated with, or sympathetic to, communism, both on international and domestic issues. Domestically, Cold Warrior racial equality activists shied away from associating with former allies whose communism, or refusal to adopt anticommunism, endangered their legitimacy. Internationally, they aligned with U.S. foreign policy, specifically global anticommunism.

TOEING THE COLD WAR FOREIGN POLICY LINE

Clever Cold Warriors buttressed their Americanism by tapping into the increasingly important global arena. They built upon strategies developed in World War II, which first drew reinforcement from the United

States' burgeoning international agenda to facilitate campaigns for greater equality. Now they argued in postwar terms. Instead of legitimating civil rights by arguing that maintaining the home front would help beat the fascists abroad, they justified their collaboration as an antidote to global communism. They used international imperatives, specifically the United States' mission of swaying the rest of the world away from communism and toward democracy. For instance, national NAACP leader Walter White argued that supporting housing desegregation could help the United States win the support of third-world nations by proving it was not backwards in terms of race relations.[116] The *Daily News*, a Los Angeles newspaper sympathetic to civil rights reforms, joined the chorus of voices publicizing the international democratic imperative of enforcing civil rights. "At a time when we are preaching Americanism and democracy we need to bolster our preaching with some positive proof that we are doing something about it," the editorial pleaded, otherwise the Russians could point to U.S. failures as evidence of U.S. hypocrisy. "No nation can long last as a first class nation if it tolerates within its confines such a thing as second class citizenship," it emphasized.[117]

Using the international sphere to justify civil rights at home had a new impact on activists' stance on racism abroad. In earlier periods, many Los Angeles minorities and their counterparts nationwide linked their critique of racial inequality at home with international anticolonial struggles, which often meant they criticized U.S. foreign as well as domestic policy. They had condemned unequal relations at home alongside colonialism in places like Mexico, Ethiopia, Spain, and elsewhere in Europe, while occasionally expressing support for other governments, including the Soviet Union, Mexico's Cárdenas administration, and Republican Spain. In Los Angeles, Loren Miller praised the Soviet Union after his trip there in the early 1930s. He also urged African Americans to support Ethiopia in her "dream of national greatness" while fighting for increased equality at home.[118] El Congreso criticized the Roosevelt administration for blockading Spain and for not opposing the provision of arms by Hitler and Mussolini to General Franco and the Spanish fascists. El Congreso also praised the Cárdenas administration's resistance to U.S. imperialism and protested attempts to recover U.S. oil Mexico had expropriated. Jews in Los Angeles and elsewhere worked behind the scenes to raise voices against Hitler's expansionist, anti-Semitic European campaigns while they also struggled to fight domestic anti-Semitism.[119]

During the Cold War, adopting anticommunism largely severed the struggle for civil rights at home from critiques of racism and colonialism abroad.[120] Many domestic equality activists submerged their earlier foreign policy criticisms of the United States and its allies, including their critique of international racism, to the U.S. foreign policy goal of fighting communism. Activists who remained committed to anticolonial causes and to other critiques of U.S. foreign policy discovered that Cold Warriors no longer welcomed them into their coalitions. Fissures in the African-American community reflected this break. Groups like the NAACP marginalized members who had been influential in earlier decades, in large part because of disagreements over whether to make battling racism and colonialism abroad a key goal. Civil rights activist W. E. B. DuBois, one of the NAACP's co-founders, and others criticized U.S. foreign policy makers for deliberately overlooking western European allies' imperialism to keep them from falling to communism while sacrificing colonized countries in Africa and elsewhere. Walter White and other Cold War NAACP leaders ousted DuBois from the organization in 1948 in no small part for these views. If the NAACP addressed racism abroad, it was in the context of maintaining the United States' Cold War leadership, rather than in the terms DuBois wanted: supporting African demands for freedom and autonomy.[121]

Anticommunist civil rights campaigners like those who dominated the Cold War NAACP, on the other hand, came to accept anticommunist U.S. foreign policies. NAACP members in branches nationwide, including Loren Miller and others from Los Angeles, adhered to the national organization's stance, believing that the best way to fortify domestic civil rights reform agendas was to embrace the argument that discrimination undermined the legitimacy of the United States to lead the "free world." For instance, the NAACP supported the 1947 Truman Doctrine, which upheld containment as the best way to prevent the spread of global communism—even at the cost of supporting undemocratic regimes like in Greece and Turkey. It also supported U.S. policies that helped the "third world" make the transition to modernity and eased the way for private American investment. This often meant maintaining former imperial powers' oversight of much of Africa and Asia at the cost of these regions' indigenous people.[122] The NAACP also condoned the 1947 Marshall Plan, through which the United States provided billions of dollars in economic and technical assistance to its anticommunist European allies.

A radio discussion during the NAACP's 1948 West Coast conference in Los Angeles with the managing editor of the African-American *Los Angeles Sentinel*, national NAACP officer Gloster Current, West Coast regional NAACP secretary Noah Griffin, and Los Angeles NAACP officials emphasized that improving civil rights would strengthen U.S. anticommunist foreign policy. Current maintained that "America's strongest defense against Communism [in the world], is to make Democracy work here in the United States." Part of making democracy work at home—and by implication abroad—meant monitoring the antidemocratic behavior of institutions like HUAC. But it also meant enforcing civil rights, Current continued. "Civil Rights is America's challenge to prove to all of the people of the world that Democracy is the best form of government." He explained over the air waves that "Democracy must be made to work now, or atomic war-fare will forever destroy it." Legislation against lynching, the poll tax, and Jim Crow, and measures passed for fair employment, educational assistance, increased displaced persons immigration, minimum wage, social security insurance, and national health insurance, Current argued, were all part of "America's strongest defense against Communism."[123]

Foreign policy became the most controversial topic between commu-nists and anticommunists at the NAACP's national convention in Los Angeles in 1949. NAACP official Roy Wilkins recalled in his autobiog-raphy that when communists tried to infiltrate the meeting, they focused on pushing the NAACP to condemn Truman's Cold War foreign policy. They specifically wanted the NAACP to "repudiate its endorsement of the Marshall Plan and to condemn the Atlantic Pact." According to Wilkins, the communists and their supporters tried to make the NAACP look as if it was "going pink" by bringing an "applause section" to the meeting and clapping whenever "their lines were touched upon."[124]

Deep fissures over Cold War U.S. foreign policy appeared in the Mexi-can-American community too, as divergences between the Community

Figure 8: Roy Wilkins Speaks at the National NAACP Convention in Los Angeles, 1949, Los Angeles Daily News Collection, Department of Special Collections, Charles E. Young Research Library, UCLA.

Figure 9: CFCU Convention at Asilomar, on California's Central Coast, December 1954, Carton I, California Federation for Civic Unity Records, 1945–1956. Courtesy of the Bancroft Library, University of California, Berkeley.

Service Organization (CSO) and the Asociación Nacional México-Americana (ANMA) reveal. The ANMA emerged in Arizona out of Henry Wallace's 1948 Progressive Party presidential campaign against Democrat Harry Truman, Republican Thomas Dewey, and Strom Thurmond of the segregationist States Rights Democratic Party. The CSO emerged in Los Angeles from 1947 efforts to elect Edward Roybal to city council.

The CSO pursued an anticommunist tack similar to the NAACP. CSO leaders and their allies buttressed their Americanism by explaining that their efforts would help ensure a U.S. Cold War victory and promote democracy internationally. Roybal, for instance, used the United States' international struggle in the Korean War to argue against housing discrimination at home. "How ironical," Roybal observed. "We send billions of dollars and tens of thousands of men across the seas to prevent the spread of communism and at the same time allow destructive forces among us to subject these men to the humiliation and insult of being rejected when purchasing homes because their names or complexions differ from those of other applicants."[125]

The ANMA, on the other hand, did not hesitate to critique U.S. foreign policy. This organization, which quickly established chapters in Los Angeles and across the Southwest, flouted U.S. policy by supporting the global peace movement. The ANMA urged Mexican Americans to stand up for peace in Korea and for easing U.S.-Soviet tensions. In 1950, it participated in a two-day mobilization to circulate the Stockholm Peace Appeal, which called for an end to the Cold War. Popular struggles in Latin America also became an ANMA cause. The ANMA opposed U.S. attempts to overthrow the popularly elected government of Guatemala and supported labor struggles in Chile, Bolivia, and Peru, as well as Fidel Castro's Cuban liberation movement. It also supported efforts by Spanish refugees to obtain amnesty for political prisoners who had been condemned to death by Franco. Furthermore, the ANMA tied domestic reforms for Mexican Americans to the issue of ending the Cold War and to world peace more generally.[126] On foreign policy issues, the ANMA rather than the CSO followed in the internationalist footsteps of 1930s and World War II–era civil rights organizations.

Such differences over foreign policy between anticommunists and communists in organizations like the NAACP, and between organizations like the CSO and the ANMA, reveal that part of creating a "liberal" Cold War civil rights identity meant diverging from "radicals" on international issues. Liberals reclaimed civil rights from the red baiters and made them "American" and a democratic Cold War imperative in part by submerging international critiques to a domestic focus. Radicals risked alienation at home by challenging U.S. foreign policy.

COLD WARRIORS: THE LEFT IS OUT

Conforming to moderate anticommunism also led Cold War civil rights campaigners to distance themselves from some of their radically identified colleagues. In the past, supporting the United States' international agenda (defeating fascism) had been conducive to joining forces across the left. But battling global communism tore such alliances apart. As Cold War reformers recognized their precarious status and fought the public's tendency to inextricably link civil rights with subversive activities, they responded to Cold War pressures by marginalizing former allies whom they believed would undermine their Cold War efficacy. The belief that the "communist enemy" was omnipresent triumphed, in many cases, over careful preservation of democratic principles, as organizations sidelined anyone suspected of being communist.

In extreme cases vigilance meant expelling those who did not decry communism from organizations that previously had included activists of varying political orientations. In 1946, the Los Angeles Council for Civic

Unity culminated a struggle of several months by ousting such members in order to gain credibility.[127] The Los Angeles County Conference on Community Relations (LACCCR), an interracial group of government officials and representatives of local housing, employment, and other civil rights groups, did the same. The Conference in October 1947 modified its operating rules to strip groups, including the American Jewish Labor Council, the Civil Rights Congress, Mobilization for Democracy, the National Negro Congress, and others, of their voting rights. It allowed them to remain in the organization as observers but not as participants. The LACCCR took this action, its director Dale Gardner explained, because "Communists or Communist front organizations joining the Conference...threatened[ed] to destroy the progress made during the last year."[128]

Labor organizations followed similar paths in the late 1940s. Representatives of the L.A. Central Labor Council believed that "subversive groups" whose "Red Fascist ideologies and attempts to undermine the efforts of sincere democrats in the race relations field" threatened their own success.[129] The CIO cleansed itself of these supposedly radical, disruptive influences in the late 1940s.[130] Among the unions the CSO expelled was the International United Mine, Mill and Smelter Workers Union (Mine-Mill), the group that helped organize the ANMA.[131]

The NAACP's path illustrates particularly well how much internal turmoil these communities experienced, specifically how the Cold War encouraged previously more inclusive organizations to sideline former allies. Cautious African-American Angelenos confronted the dilemma of how to deal with communist influences in the late 1940s and early 1950s, when they attempted to purge the local NAACP. Matters came to a head when two developing and opposing tendencies in the African-American community clashed: African Americans' growing interest in communism and their increasing tendency to conform to anticommunism.

Internal dissent racked the NAACP in 1947 and 1948, in part over the African-American community's disagreements about the role communist sympathizers should play in the organization. Los Angeles branch membership declined from 14,000 in 1946 to fewer than 6,000 in 1949. This marked a sharp decline for the organization that had been the fifth largest NAACP branch in the country.[132] Branches nationwide suffered declines in the postwar years, and national and West Coast branch officials viewed the L.A. branch communist threat as part of a larger West Coast "epidemic" in particular.[133] As early as 1946, the NAACP's West Coast regional director Noah Griffin explained to Walter White that "many" West Coast branches were "fully aware of the threat that is offered from infiltration by certain party members into important positions in the branches," and that they planned to stop "further infiltration."[134] Communist involvement seemed even more pronounced in other West

Coast branches like Richmond, where the national office's Roy Wilkins explained that "the Reds have completely taken over the branch."[135] On the issue of anticommunist fractures, Los Angeles was not unique, though it was among the branches with the most pronounced problems.[136]

The turmoil stemmed in part from suspicions that the branch's president, Thomas Griffith, had allowed communists to influence the organization. The national and regional offices worked with local members to depose Griffith, whom they suspected had brokered deals with communists and their affiliates for their support of his 1949 reelection bid. Griffith's actions, if true, violated the NAACP's nationwide policy on "communist infiltration." By 1950, the national NAACP resolved that the board of directors must investigate and eradicate communists and communist sympathizers.[137] The high tensions and the organization's "bitter factionalism" over the branch presidency rendered it nearly dysfunctional by 1948 when, according to the organization's West Coast director Noah Griffin, many members wanted to split into two organizations.[138]

The African-American community split along many axes, and the NAACP strife involved criticism both that it was not radical enough and that it was too radical. Disagreements over whether the NAACP should sever—or foster—its communist ties reflect an ideological conflict over whose influence should set the organization's agenda. Yet it reflected only part of the branch's difficulties. Other issues, including "general community apathy" and "do-nothingness," also contributed to the controversies surrounding the membership decline.[139] The membership drive in late 1948 only worsened the situation. Close to 200 of the L.A. organization's newest members were "members of the Communist Party, or so-called extreme Leftists," according to the branch's executive secretary Mary Alton Cutler. Cutler wrote to Roy Wilkins urging him to assist the L.A. branch's anticommunists. Cutler estimated that approximately 400 of the organization's members in late 1948 were Communists, information that President Griffith "laughed off as a matter of no great concern" when she discussed it with him.[140] Whether or not her figures are accurate, the issue led to even greater divisiveness.

The stakes were high, since members hoping to retain civil rights influence believed that establishing the organization's credibility depended on holding firm against communist influence. Local and national newspaper coverage publicizing the suspected infiltration made resolving the matter particularly urgent for the local, regional, and national offices. Articles such as the Los Angeles Tribune's "Communist Threat to 'Take Over' Local NAACP Fought" and national coverage by the Pittsburgh Courier and other African-American newspapers revealed that the negative publicity was widespread. Mary Alton Cutler enclosed clippings like these in her letters to embarrass the national office into action on behalf of the Los Angeles anticommunist contingent. She hoped these would give officials "some idea as to how bad our public relations are in L.A." and predicted that the branch's troubles would only escalate without the national office's intervention.[141]

Responding to Cutler's pleas, the West Coast regional and national NAACP offices, reportedly "gravely concerned" over the Los Angeles situation, investigated the branch's suspected communist ties. They worked to undermine local leaders, instead supporting candidates they found to be more acceptable and plotting with local allies to vote suspected communists and communist supporters out of office. NAACP policy stated that the national office must allow the L.A. branch self-determination in selecting its officers, as Roy Wilkins explained to Norman Houston, a sympathetic L.A. branch member and prominent local businessman, while also urging Houston to act with other local members to ensure that the association's national policy against communist and other fellow travelers' infiltration was upheld. "I could write more frankly on the subject," Wilkins explained, "but I am sure you can read between the lines." Wilkins encouraged his ally to "work to elect an executive committee which is non-communist" to counter Griffith's alleged deal with "left-wingers." Nobody "must be permitted to serve as a front for those who seek to take over an NAACP branch and make it a mouthpiece for policies foreign to those of our Association," Wilkins declared.[142] Gloster B. Current also directed West Coast officials that "it is time for the National Office to step in in a quiet way to direct the strategy behind the scene . . . [by using] diplomacy and tact because we are dealing with an explosive matter." Current continued, "There can be no doubt that the Communist element is supporting Thomas Griffith."[143]

In Los Angeles, NAACP members seeking to defeat Griffith included Loren Miller, the prominent NAACP attorney whose record of communist sympathy from the 1930s haunted him in the postwar era. Miller participated in a committee headed by Houston to restrict communist elements from Los Angeles minority politics.[144] Committee members signed a declaration stating, "We the undersigned members of good standing of the Los Angeles Branch N.A.A.C.P., and eligible to vote, do hereby register our protest against the irregular and unconstitutional manner of the annual election." Miller and company accused Griffith of allowing a Communist Party member to speak. This member had prefaced her remarks by "admitting" that she was a communist, and then she went on to "defend the Party with such vehemence that more than half of the audience left the meeting in protest." The only meeting attendees remaining were "fellow travelers," who consequently became the voting majority.[145]

George Thomas, a former Portland NAACP president and leader of the LA County Conference on Community Relations, observed the election and declared that "[t]he manner in which it was held was a disgrace to the

Association." He claimed that nobody clarified who was eligible to vote or who was a legitimate member, and that Griffith glossed over the West Coast Regional Conference's statement concerning communism, especially the part that restricted communist membership. Thomas called for the national office to intercede by scheduling new elections.[146] Griffith ultimately won reelection, but the showdown forced him to distance himself from communists, disclaim any connection between them and the NAACP, and ensure adherence to NAACP procedures.

Those like Loren Miller who wanted to maintain a place in the NAACP distanced themselves from past associations with the CP and established reputations as anticommunist civil rights advocates. In 1952, a year after Miller acquired Charlotta Bass's African-American newspaper the *Eagle*, he looked back at the institution's history and criticized Bass for having turned the *Eagle* into an "extreme left-wing newspaper." Miller argued that it did not become a respectable paper until 1951, when he bought it and shifted it to advocate "Fair Deal–New Deal policy."[147] Interestingly, Miller and Bass crossed paths between the 1930s, when the latter was a staunch Republican who ran the *Eagle* rather conservatively, and the early Cold War, by which time she had moved to the left and developed associations that made her less publicly acceptable in the Cold War climate. As Miller had done in the 1930s, she traveled to the Soviet Union in 1950 and wrote rave reviews of the country as free of racial discrimination. In 1952, she became the first female black vice presidential candidate for the United States Progressive Party, which became the party of political refuge for communists, socialists, and fellow travelers during the Cold War.[148]

Whether true disillusionment or Cold War strategy motivated him, Miller asserted in later years that by the late 1930s and early 1940s, he had come to believe that "there was a great deal of fraud in the Communist claims." He explained that he and other African Americans especially became critical during World War II, as the party abandoned them by disbanding its units in the South in order to avoid undermining American wartime political unity by offending whites.[149] By 1949, Miller felt the need to distance himself from his former affiliations, as he revealed in a letter to U.S. Representative Helen Gahagan Douglas. "I think that you have a right to know that I am not now nor have I ever been a member of the Communist Party although it is certainly true that in the past I did cooperate with it and some of its front organizations, a course of action that I deliberately forsook in 1938 out of a conviction, born of some experience, that it was an anti-democratic force and that it was activated by sometimes bad, sometimes insincere motives." He further emphasized, "I think that I should add that my experiences have given me a deep and abiding faith in the democratic processes and have convinced me that the solution of present day problems, whether racial or of a general social nature, requires the extension, rather than the repudiation, of those processes."[150] Wilkins' private letter to Norman Houston also suggests that an ideological rather than merely pragmatic anticommunism motivated at least some NAACP members and leaders. Wilkins encouraged Houston to "work to elect an executive committee which is non-communist," since nobody "must be permitted to serve as a front for those who seek to take over an NAACP branch and make it a mouthpiece for policies foreign to those of our Association."[151]

Though tensions dissipated for a while after the election, the communist issue continued to draw suspicion to the Los Angeles branch. Three years later, the NAACP's national president Walter White warned the West Coast director that unless the L.A. branch was free of communist influence, he would not stop there during his upcoming West Coast tour. White hoped to build support in Los Angeles for NAACP protests against racial bombing in Florida but feared that accusations of left-wing influences would "give a kiss of death to efforts to attain justice."[152] From the late 1940s through the mid 1950s, the L.A. NAACP struggled continuously to counter communist attempts to overtake the organization. Members distributed flyers with titles like "Keep Your Eyes Wide Open: Don't Get Sucked In!" to defend the NAACP's credibility. The flyers warned members to protect themselves against civil rights organizations, including the California Labor School, the Civil Rights Congress, the Negro Labor Council, the *Militant*, the *People's World* (a California communist newspaper), and *Political Affairs* (a magazine), which worked in the "interest of the Communist Party or other subversive and un-American movements."[153]

Parallel conflicts manifested themselves in the organized Jewish community. The Jewish community campaign to root out communist influence began in the same year the NAACP campaign gained steam, 1947, as it responded to mounting anticommunism around it. The campaign gathered speed shortly after Tenney pinned the subversive label on the American Jewish Congress in 1948. Committees appointed by the CRC studied both the larger anticommunist campaign (and its implications for Jews) and Jewish Community Council organizations that were potentially "Communistic," making recommendations about how to deal with them.[154] One organization targeted to be ousted from the Jewish Community Council, the umbrella organization for the organized Los Angeles Jewish community, was the Jewish Peoples Fraternal Order (JPFO). The organized Jewish community's anticommunist purges went a step further than others, as it conducted internal trials to determine whether to allow groups like the JPFO to remain in the community. Fissures developed with particular frequency in Los Angeles's organized Jewish community, which reacted in part to the particularly intense scrutiny it faced from red-baiters like Tenney. The JPFO, a workers' group with about 5,000 Southern California members, engaged its own legal counsel to defend itself, but was unsuccessful after many months of internal investigations, discussions, and hearings. The failure of the JPFO to prevent its expulsion in 1951 is not surprising in the face of powerful Community Council prosecutors including Lester Roth, a former judge and lawyer for various motion picture industry interests.[155]

The organized Jewish community justified the trials on the grounds of the danger it believed the JPFO posed. Advocates of expulsion feared that eventually the JPFO would spread communist influences throughout the Jewish community at large. A CRC member cautioned at a meeting on the subject that the "communist cause...would gain increasing strength in the Community Council...through *gullible liberals* [emphasis added]" who, by their unawareness, would sabotage the Jewish community from within.[156] The CRC's chairman Mendel Silberberg explained in his organization's meeting that growing anticommunism, which seeped into Los Angeles from the international Cold War, made allowing radical influences to remain in the Jewish community particularly dangerous. Silberberg emphasized that the JPFO's suspected ties to communists and other radical organizations "has the seeds of great injury to the Jewish Community."[157]

Many Jews feared that negative publicity concerning communism would compound the mounting anti-Semitism they faced. The Jewish Community Relations Committee (CRC) published a study, "Report of New Anti-Semitic Organizations Being Formed in Los Angeles," that revealed its heightened sense of insecurity as early as September 1945.[158] A CRC meeting in 1947 discussed the "intensification of anti-Semitism," especially the reappearance and strengthening of prewar anti-Semitic groups and the anti-Semitic tone of some newspapers.[159] An L.A. Jewish group cited a national survey in *Fortune* magazine in October 1947, which revealed that about 40 percent of Americans think that Jews have more "economic power...than is good for the country," to support its argument that Los Angeles Jews must fight back against anti-Semitism.[160] Such fears drove organized Jewish community members' reaction to radicalism in their midst.

The JPFO ouster consumed significant internal community energy. The JPFO protested that the decision reflected the will of merely a "handful of men" who had gained control of the Jewish community by "damn[ing] as un-Jewish all who disagree with them." To emphasize the decision's antidemocratic nature, the JPFO compared Jewish community leaders with both Hitler and Tenney, two of Los Angeles Jews' villains. "Shall we go down the path of German Jewry who, before they stepped into the gas chambers, turned on their fellow Jews in a purge of 'undesirables'?" queried a JPFO letter pleading for support, "Or shall we hew a new path with the democratic weapons we have learned?"[161] A JPFO report asked, "Shall we take our philosophy from Jack Tenney...? Shall we take our philosophy from the House Un-American Activities Committee, whose John Rankin has filled the pages of the Congressional Record with anti-Semitic, anti-Negro, anti-Italian filth?"[162]

It is no coincidence that this internal community tension over the JPFO in Los Angeles was magnified into a matter of national Jewish concern during the Korean War. An article in the New York–based Jewish newspaper, *The Jewish Daily Forward*, criticized the L.A. community for not being vigilant enough against communists. "Think of the effect of a Jewish organization bearing the brant [*sic*—brand], 'traitors to the United States,' especially in view of the Korean situation," it cautioned. The article urged Jews to intensify their anticommunist vigilance as their country engaged in war in the Pacific. "When one bears in mind that the Pacific Coast is the gateway to the Asiatic countries and that there is intensive propaganda here against the interests of the United States," it explained, "one realizes painfully that the Los Angeles Jewish Community Council cannot afford the luxury of harboring the Communist vandals who today or tomorrow may be pointed out as spies and traitors."[163] The Los Angeles Jewish community's proximity to the Pacific front, combined with its already vulnerable situation given anticommunist tendencies to link Jews with communism, convinced members that its vigilance was imperative.

Campaigns to negate communist associations sprang up among Jewish and other minority communities nationwide, but Angelenos often were at the forefront of such activities, given both the strong presence of communism and anticommunism in the L.A. area and the Pacific-front location. The local Jewish community became involved in some of the most heated anticommunist campaigns in the country. The Los Angeles CRC's series of 1951 workshops on the Jewish community's relationship to communism were the first nationwide. At these workshops, community members discussed strategies to deter the identification of Jews with communism, appropriate attitudes to adopt toward communist organizations, and acceptable stances on legislation like the communist registration ordinance (laws passed in 1950 at the national, county, and city level requiring Communists and communist-front organizations to register). Letters between Los Angeles and other branches indicate that Jewish communities nationally modeled similar workshops upon these.[164]

Pragmatic Jews sought to negate the association between Jews and communists by exposing groups that used the label "Jewish" to "serve their own devious purposes," as a CRC press release explained. The CRC assumed the position of "sentinel organization," the release explained, "to keep our Jewish community alert to any and all organizations that pose as one thing and are in fact something else."[165] The Jewish Labor Committee, for instance, fought what it viewed as attempts by the American Jewish Labor Council (AJLC), a supposedly communist-affiliated organization, to confuse the public about the two. It explained to the CRC that "Jewish Communists and their temporary allies" had created the AJLC "to exploit the trade union field for political advantage."[166] In his opening speech at the "Workshop on Problem of Communism," Isaac Pacht explained that, while he did not think communism in the United States was a big threat, "I see danger, however, in the unceasing efforts of Communists and their dupes to bore into our organizations and their attempts to use our institutions and agencies to further their own ends."[167] Jewish community representatives who attended the conference on communism reinforced that the Jewish community was like the majority of the American people, in that it was not "Communistic or Fascistic and that it is devoted to the American democratic ideals, Constitution and Bill of Rights." As they had since the founding of the Republic, Jews would continue to fight for "the American heritage."[168]

Jewish community representatives tried to protect the community's reputation in ways that drew nationwide attention even beyond Jewish circles. In one infamous instance, House Un-American Activity Committee pressure on Hollywood led many prominent Los Angeles Jews to participate in November 1947 in blacklisting the Hollywood Ten. The House of Representatives claimed these screenwriters, producers, and directors were in contempt of Congress for pleading the First Amendment in refusing to respond to whether they were or ever had been a member of the Communist Party. Shortly thereafter, the CRC's chairman and chief attorney for the Motion Picture Producers Association Mendel Silberberg chaired a committee that met at New York City's Waldorf-Astoria Hotel to draft a position statement on these industry members. Silberberg and forty-eight motion-picture company executives, including another prominent CRC member, Dore Schary, created a two-page press release, known as the Waldorf Statement, which announced they would not knowingly hire communists. They also agreed to discharge the Hollywood Ten until they purged themselves of their contempt citations or renounced communism under oath. The executives, prominently Silberberg, had been reluctant up to that point to have a blacklist, but the fifteen producers signing the statement, of whom ten were Jewish, came to believe that falling in line behind HUAC was the best way to maintain Hollywood—and Jews'—image in the public mind.[169] Other CRC members, including the organization's soon-to-be executive director, Joseph Roos, and attorney Martin Gang, also participated in improving Hollywood Jews' image this way. Roos, an Austrian immigrant raised in Germany who became the CRC's director in 1950, worked with Jews who believed they had been accused unfairly, or who wanted to "repent" before HUAC, by combing their records to build cases for their "innocence," and Gang acted as their defense attorney.[170]

In the face of these national debates, some CRC members opposed stances such as the ousting of the JPFO on the grounds that such a politically diverse community mandated political diversity in its organizations. Some argued, "If they are communists 'So What?' The Jewish community is not a political organization and it has a responsibility to include all ranges of Jewish interest."[171] Others emphasized that the community was obligated to fight all forms of discrimination—political as well as racial. Still others criticized the decision as fundamentally anti-democratic, arguing that "a liberal today must decide" to commit to democracy over succumbing to anticommunist fears.[172] Many of these Jews believed their community had caved in to political pressures.

These counterarguments reveal strong internal Cold War disagreements within the Jewish community similar to those within the NAACP. Internal dissent is an important reminder that organizational leadership and policies are not synonymous with the will of the entire membership. Nonetheless, such disagreements do not diminish the significance of the decision, which helped shape greater Los Angeles's perceptions of the Jewish community and the Jewish community's trajectory.

The JPFO ouster did not end the internal community turmoil, as local attitudes toward the 1952 Rosenberg trial reveal. The CRC labeled as illegitimate all local efforts to defend Ethel and Julius Rosenberg, Jewish Americans accused by the federal government of spying for Russia. It claimed their communist affiliations deprived them of the right to defense and accused groups defending the Rosenbergs of playing the "anti-Semitism card" to gain public sympathy for these undeserving people. "The Rosenbergs were not convicted because they were Jews," the CRC emphasized, "but because they were bad Americans."[173] The CRC and other anti-Rosenberg Jewish organizations admonished supporters that by highlighting the Rosenbergs' Jewishness, they reinforced the public's penchant for linking Jews to communism and endangered the entire community. The CRC declared in no uncertain terms that "Communism and Judaism are diametrically opposed and do not mix."[174] Organized Jewish community members' fear of anticommunism and desire for Cold War efficacy left them unable to openly consider the possibility that the Rosenbergs had been unjustly accused and merited defense.

These Jews similarly downplayed the role anti-Semitism played in other anticommunist attacks. They protested the State Department's decision to dismiss employees, the majority of whom were Jews, for alleged communist involvement, but they remained silent about possible anti-Semitic motives. "To inject the Jewish issue, unless we have some concrete evidence of anti-Semitism," an official from the national office of the American Jewish Committee explained to CRC director Fred Herzberg, "would merely bring upon the Jews the kind of Jewish-Communist-tieup [sic] in the public mind that would be most damaging to us."[175]

Jewish community members were so skittish about being associated with communism that they avoided calling attention to their fight *against* it, despite their realization that such publicity could help invalidate the misperceptions. For instance, the CRC rejected an appeal for support from an organization called the American Jewish League against Communism, fearing this could backfire and "only strengthen the impression already held by some that there are so many Jews who are Communists that it requires a separate organization to stamp them out." They instead emphasized that "Americans as Americans [must] fight Communism."[176] Philip Connelly, the prominent (non-Jewish) leftist formerly associated— before its antiradical reorganization—with the Los Angeles CIO, accused the Jewish community of letting anticommunism undermine its commitment to progressive causes. He lamented that it recommended that member organizations "embrace the policy of 'hush-hush'... [and] shun struggle, [to] disassociate themselves from everything progressive."[177]

But Connelly and other disenchanted activists' criticism captures only part of the story. Cold War civil rights reformers believed that adopting a moderate version of anticommunism was crucial to their survival and to maintaining support for their equality agenda, which led them to depart in two important ways from their predecessors, many of whom were the same individuals and organizations. They reconsidered their alliances and their international orientation. The anticommunist campaign made domestic civil rights in the name of global anti-Communism—and often at the expense of global racism—the new cause célèbre among Cold Warrior reformers. It also clearly made some cooperation off-limits, severing partnerships and fragmenting efforts from an earlier era by creating a divide between activists many Americans deemed too radical and others trying to frame themselves as more politically acceptable in the current climate.

But at the same time that Jews and African Americans involved in groups like the CRC and NAACP sought to put distance between themselves and activists too closely connected to communism, they were careful not to let what they saw as overblown fears of communism divide their communities. In 1952 the CRC's executive director Roos warned some members of the Jewish community against letting unjustified fears of communism interfere with important, legitimate civil rights protests. He urged that "the psychology of fear must come to an end soon lest we lose the very thing which we say the Communists want to destroy."[178] Roos spoke in response to some Jews' decision not to participate in a joint Jewish- and African-American protest of bombings and other attacks on Jews and blacks in Florida.

In fact, the anticommunist climate in some ways cemented Cold War reformers' resolve, fortifying their ongoing commitment to antidiscrimination efforts. The organized Jewish community in Los Angeles and nationwide responded to communist threats—which jeopardized "the integrity and reputation of the Jew in America"—by voting to "strengthen and arm itself against Communist infiltration while building legitimate progressive movements seeking genuine social and economic betterment," as the Jewish Labor Committee's Zane Meckler explained.[179] Meckler, who represented the same organization that made every possible effort to separate itself from the communist-affiliated American Jewish Labor Council, encouraged Jews to challenge social inequality, but only through "building *legitimate* [emphasis added] progressive movements." This distinction, no matter how subjective, provides a key to understanding the relationship between Cold War anticommunism and ongoing multiracial equality struggles.

CONCLUSION

Disputes about acceptable incarnations of anticommunism show how Cold War civil rights activists articulated a nuanced position—against communism and for civil rights. This vision did more than make civil rights activism merely acceptable; it made upholding American ideals imperative for fortifying the country. Correspondence between national NAACP officials Henry Lee Moon and Walter White encapsulated this "middle-ground" Cold War strategy. "Any middle ground program, it seems to me, need not only to disavow McCarthyism on the one hand and Communism on the other but also to present a positive program in concrete terms," Moon explained. "It is not enough merely to be for democracy. The meaning of democracy has to be spelled out, and a consistent strategy for attaining this goal needs to be blueprinted."[180] Moon argued that civil rights groups' Cold War agendas needed to encompass three components: criticizing democratic violations on the left, being effective watchdogs for violations on the right, and articulating a positive program for "democratic" change.

Mary Hornaday, writing in *The Christian Science Monitor* about the struggle for civil rights in Los Angeles, explained: "The Communists' efforts to identify themselves as the racial saviors of mankind is [*sic*] forcing Americans who have postponed clarifying their views on this issue to take a stand."[181] But this keen observer overlooked how virulent anticommunism, as well as communism, motivated many Americans to define the shape of Cold War civil rights. The NAACP, CRC, and CFCU, certain labor organizations, city and county commissions, and others articulated an all-American civil rights position as an antidote to both communism and "unjustified" anticommunism. These activists used the political climate to their advantage to chart a moderately framed, what they called democratic path, between un-American radicalism and conservatism.

Hornaday's observations about the relationship between the Cold War climate and the development of a civil rights agenda suggest yet another civil rights consequence of Cold War anticommunism, embodied by the persistence and evolution of the collaborative organization the Council for Civic Unity. Hornaday emphasized that such a council faced an important task in a racially diverse city like Los Angeles, which had "the racial problems of most American cities put together" due to the growth of its African-, Mexican-, and Jewish-American populations and returning Japanese-American populations. The tensions resulting from such increased racial diversity, Hornaday explained, heightened the need for such multiracial efforts.[182]

What Hornaday did not recognize, though, was the relationship between such collaborative organizations and the Cold War political climate. A statement from CIO leader Albert Lunceford shortly after his organization marginalized "dangerous" activists hints at what these coalitions had in common. "Since the reorganization of the Council, CIO in Los Angeles'...role in the community consists of working with all other *liberal* groups on the basis of a progressive program," including a "thorough civil rights policy," he explained.[183] Following the purge of more seemingly radical members from the organization, the CIO looked especially to other "liberal" (anticommunist) groups to build collaborative strength, as did other organizations. These coalitions of Cold Warriors found common ground in their anticommunist civil rights agenda. The Cold War in this way facilitated cooperation among multiracial anticommunist organizations that joined forces in order to carry on an interracial reform thread that had been building since the 1930s. Such interracial civil rights efforts evolved—and emerged anew—not in spite of the Cold War, but partially because of it, as the next chapter will reveal.

CHAPTER 5

The Community Service Organization and Interracial Civil Rights Activism in the Cold War Era

A group of east side Los Angeles residents—poor, disenfranchised, and mostly Mexican American—met in 1947 to brainstorm ways to elect a city council representative who would advocate for them. This group failed on the first attempt to elect Edward Roybal, a local social worker and community organizer whose family had moved to Los Angeles from Albuquerque in 1922. But their efforts had lasting significance.

These Mexican Americans, together with ethnically and economically diverse allies from the surrounding Jewish-American, African-American, Japanese-American, and white communities, helped Roybal win election two years later. Roybal became the first Mexican American elected to the city council since 1881—and the council's only nonwhite member—in a district where fewer than one-fifth of voters were Mexican-origin.[1] Mexican Americans' small presence in Roybal's district made interracial and cross-class coalition politics crucial to securing his victory. Mexican Americans, including the community's few doctors and few attorneys like Richard Ibañez, turned out to support Roybal, as did numerous unions with heavy Mexican support. Roybal's campaign chair Balt Yañez, also the United Steel Workers' Business Agent, integrated his union into the campaign. The auto and rubber unions also joined, as did the CIO-PAC, the political arm of the CIO. Mexican Americans worked with Jewish community organizations like B'nai B'rith and Southland Jewish Organization to build connections between the communities. The International Ladies' Garment Workers' Union (ILGWU), whose members included many Jewish and Mexican Americans, helped activate the Jewish Labor Committee and other Jewish workers' organizations. The AFL's Jewish Carpenters and Painters unions also helped, as did Jewish business and professional people like the owner of Phillips Music Company, who organized his fellow merchants' support. Jewish attorneys donated money and helped organize the campaign, while theater owner

Jack K. Berman and *Eastside Journal* publisher Al Waxman threw their support behind Roybal too. Roybal also drew African Americans, earning the support of *The California Eagle* and the newly formed Committee for Equality in the City Council, led by Loren Miller and the young police officer and future L.A. mayor Tom Bradley. Japanese Americans like attorney John F. Aiso (who also worked with the ILGWU) supported Roybal as well.[2] Eventually the CIO Council of L.A. and the Independent Progressive Party joined in endorsing Roybal through their own campaigns.[3]

The interracial, cross-class coalition behind Roybal's campaign also planted the seed for the Community Service Organization, or CSO, a civil rights organization that focused on Mexican-origin Angelenos but also served the east side's other diverse residents and, significantly, depended upon cooperation from racially diverse Cold Warrior activists for its foundation and early sustenance. The CSO replaced El Congreso as the most important civil rights group for L.A. Mexican Americans, and became the first enduring civil rights organization for the largest urban Mexican-origin population in the United States. The CSO effectively brokered relationships between Los Angeles's Mexican-American people and the city and county of Los Angeles, and its success depended in no small part upon forging relations with other ethnic and racial minority groups.

Minority activists aimed to achieve more than equality *for* multiracial populations; they worked through organizations like the CSO to achieve this vision through multiracial populations at times acting in tandem. The red scare led Cold War reformers to fortify alliances with well-reputed minorities, religious institutions, and labor organizations at the same time it forced political purges within civil rights communities and the reframing of civil rights agendas in Cold War terms. The Cold War proved a catalyzing force for communities as they saw crossing ethnic and racial divides as the avenue of most likely success for civil rights reform. Such intercommunity networks hint at a substantial continuity between earlier activism and its postwar incarnation, as many of the activists involved in such postwar initiatives emerged from 1930s and World War II endeavors, and many of their racial equality agendas continued from the earlier eras even if their language changed to conform to the Cold War anticommunist climate.

AN INTERRACIAL ORGANIZATION EMERGES

The CSO formed when the largely Mexican-American but diverse Roybal election coalition joined forces with a prominent Jewish-American community activist from Chicago. Saul Alinsky visited Los Angeles during the war both as a good will ambassador for the Department of State (to build national morale and raise support for war bonds) and in response to Mayor Bowron's summons in the Zoot Suit Riots' aftermath. These trips sparked his interest in the local Mexican-American community and led him to help it gain organization and tap funding sources after the war. He used funds he raised in Hollywood—much of it from film star Melvyn Douglas and his wife, the "pink lady" congresswoman Helen Gahagan Douglas—and in the Los Angeles Jewish community to hire a white man named Fred Ross to be the West Coast regional director of his Chicago-based Industrial Areas Foundation (IAF). Douglas became one of the members of the Southern California Advisory Committee to the IAF, as did fellow Hollywood figure and Jewish community activist Dore Schary. Other Jewish community members also joined the committee, including Isaac Pacht (who became the chairman of its board of directors) and Rabbi Edgar Magnin, as did Catholic representatives like Monsignor Thomas O'Dwyer. Law enforcement officials like Sheriff Biscailuz served on the committee as well. Ross approached his new role with commitment and energy, eventually becoming the CSO's executive director, in which capacity he worked alongside prominent local Mexican Americans including Anthony (Tony) Ríos and Gilbert Anaya.[4]

Mexican Americans initially were skeptical of this outside agency's support and a white man's leadership role, but they accepted the assistance, Ross believed, because it provided them with "what the Negroes and Jews had had for years, a field organizer who would work night and day, week in and week out for months on end to help them build a real foundation."[5] Ross, whom Mexican Americans came to hold in high esteem, spent the next five years helping east side Mexican Americans and their multiracial allies channel their activism through the CSO. Ross's support and organizational know-how fortified Mexican Americans' door-to-door organizing, and he eventually became the CSO's executive director.[6] By 1963 the CSO had established thirty-four chapters across the Southwest, primarily in California, with over 10,000 paid members. Most members were factory and field workers, though a small minority of professional and small business people joined too. The majority—about three-fourths—were citizens, with as many women as men.[7]

Encouraging civic participation among east side residents, who increasingly were Mexican-origin (American-born and immigrant) but also Jewish, Japanese, Italian, Filipino, and African American, as well as white, became the CSO's main purpose. The organization hoped to improve conditions for these diverse communities east of the L.A. River by influencing city politics (though to guarantee funding technically it remained a nonpolitical organization). It concentrated on issues like health care; neighborhood improvement projects (like adding street lights to the

Figure 10: CSO Halloween Party; undated, Folder 2, Box 32, Fred Ross Papers, 1910–1992. Courtesy of Department of Special Collections and University Archives, Stanford University Libraries. Tony Ríos is third from the left, Edward Roybal is fifth from the left; Fred Ross is in the center; Hope Mendoza Schechter is sixth from the right; and Eliseo Carillo is fifth from the right.

area's dark, often unpaved roadways); housing, including fighting against restrictive covenants and developing public housing; fair employment; voter education and voter registration; fighting police brutality; and assisting immigrants, with agendas such as obtaining old-age assistance for them.

The CSO did not always succeed, as its efforts to save the east side Chávez Ravine neighborhood and to prevent freeways and urban renewal from splitting neighborhoods illustrate. CSO members like María Durán Lang, Henrietta Villaescusa, Ralph Guzmán and others petitioned in vain to try to keep Chávez Ravine intact.[8] Still, significant victories marked CSO efforts in the late 1940s and 1950s. An eight-year campaign culminated in the 1961 passage of state old-age assistance for elderly noncitizens.[9] Organizers also saw their efforts to pave east side streets, build sidewalks, and add streetlights and traffic signals in an area that previously had been mostly dirt roads come to fruition.[10]

The CSO achieved two particularly important civil rights victories concerning police brutality in its first decade. In the first, the CSO helped secure the conviction of five Los Angeles police officers and dismissal or suspension of seventeen others after they severely beat seven young men, five of whom were Mexican American, during a 1951 Christmas Day party at the police station. The men were brought to the station after a fight with police officers at a local bar, and officers beat the men during this "Bloody Christmas" incident in response to false rumors that another officer had lost an eye in a fight with them. One Mexican-American man was so severely kicked in the head that he was rendered temporarily paralyzed. Others suffered punctured bladders and kidneys.[11] In the second verdict, the 1956 Hidalgo case, the CSO played an instrumental role convicting two L.A. County deputy sheriffs for the unprovoked beating of a thirteen-year-old boy. This marked the first such police brutality verdict in L.A. history.[12]

The CSO also carefully cultivated alliances among African Americans, Jewish Americans, Anglos, and others, to make political progress. In addition to Roybal's election, activists built upon cooperative momentum to try to elect Richard Ibañez, who had been on the Sleepy Lagoon Defense Committee, as a Superior Court judge. CSO activists also secured multiracial communities' votes for other Mexican-American politicians, including José Chávez, who won almost four times as many votes in his 1949 bid for the 51st assembly district than he did in 1946.[13] While fewer than 39 percent of one east side district's eligible voters had voted in 1945, in 1949 over 82 percent went to the polls.[14] Much of this turnout can be credited to the CSO, which made voter registration a top priority, registering 15,000 Spanish-speaking people in the ninth district alone for that election.[15] Mexican Americans, with the assistance of supporters from other ethnic and racial groups, mobilized city council members, congressional representatives, and judges to represent them and the issues important to them. These campaigns reflected what the *Los Angeles Daily News* characterized as a "great upsurge of inter-group cooperation."[16]

While the CSO is represented as a Mexican-American activist group in much Chicano scholarship, it was an interracial endeavor from its very beginning and its membership was diverse well into the 1950s.[17] The grassroots CSO drew its main support from a combination of older Mexican-American activists who had participated in the 1930s-era movements and newer ones who emerged out of the war as veterans.[18] It also received significant support from other Angelenos, most importantly Jewish Americans.[19] Its early organizers encouraged multiracial membership. "Although the great majority of CSO members are Mexican Americans, we have gradually had members of other groups come in," Ross reported of its 1948 meetings. "At the last meeting, for instance, we had 15 reps from the adjacent Jewish community, 4 Negroes and around

Figure 11: CSO Voter Registration, undated (late 1940s/early 1950s), Folder 2, Box 32, Fred Ross Papers, 1910–1992. Courtesy of Department of Special Collections and University Archives, Stanford University Libraries.

18 so called 'Protestant Anglos.' "[20] In 1949 Ross reported to the CRC that "Orientals, Negroes, Jews and Christians" composed the approximately 12 percent of membership that was not Spanish-speaking.[21] In the early to mid-1950s, the organization's chairman Tony Ríos reported that 15 percent of its more than 3,500 members (approximately 3,000 from three L.A. County branches and 500 from San Jose) were "from the Negro, Jewish, and the so-called Anglo-American communities."[22]

But the CSO was more significant in connecting its largely Mexican-origin membership with a coalitional community. Community activists frequently observed Mexican Americans' noticeable absence from previous interracial collaborative efforts. Fred Ross commented in 1946, the year before the CSO formed, that despite rampant discrimination against them as well, Mexican Americans were missing from a community meeting to protest a KKK attack on a black family's home. African Americans, Jews, Catholics, and Protestants all attended the meeting, where Ross reported that an "excited, white-haired little man from the Jewish community" urged collaboration against the KKK since otherwise "there'll be a lot more people hurt around here," including Jews and Catholics as well as blacks. But Ross' thoughts centered on the people he had visited in the barrio that morning, where residents had informed him that nearby skating rinks barred Mexican-origin children. Ross saw that fighting the KKK's anti-Catholic discrimination without the participation of Mexican Americans, who "undoubtedly made up the bulk of the Catholic population in the city [and] were nowhere to be found in that room," made no sense.[23]

The American Council on Race Relations (ACRR) reported in the same year that Los Angeles's Mexican-origin population "had practically no organizations whatever" representing them, while other West Coast groups had the NAACP, Urban League, JACL, and Filipino and Chinese organizations.[24] The ACRR's observation overlooked important community organizing attempts and even short-lived successes that included unions, labor strikes, and *mutualistas* (mutual aid societies), as well as organizations like El Congreso, the Citizens Committee for Latin American Youth, and the Coordinating Council for Latin American Youth. But the ACRR emphasized the common perception that the Mexican-origin community's difficulties were extreme and that it had less cooperative infrastructure than other minorities. Mexican-American activists like Manuel Ruíz, a prominent participant in the two Latin American youth organizations, also remarked upon the relatively unorganized character of Southern California's Mexican-American community. Ruíz attributed the organizational problems to the fact that Mexican Americans did not have a history as a "pressure group," unlike other minority groups.[25] African Americans and Jews who came to Los Angeles, for instance, brought the strength of their national organizations with them. These other groups used their experience and connections elsewhere to help themselves, as well as to help relatively less networked groups like Mexican Americans. The organized local Jewish community in particular also benefited from a history of sustained investment from a population with more financial resources than most other minorities. Its extremely organized and expansive structure (the Jewish Community Council umbrella encompassed more than 300 organizations at one point) provided a foundation that positioned it to maintain high involvement in its own and interracial initiatives.

The infrastructure and support from new political allies helped the CSO gain access to channels of power and enabled its success. "For the first time in the history of Los Angeles," explained Henry Nava, the chairman of the East Los Angeles branch in the 1950s, in a letter to supporters, Spanish-speaking neighborhoods now had "a genuine, mass-based, civic-action organization designed to improve living conditions, protect group and individual interests, protest, remedy and prevent violations of human rights, and provide a medium for social expression, leadership development, and *inter-group co-operation* [emphasis added]."[26] According to CSO president Ríos, the CSO was the first group through which Los Angeles's Spanish-speaking communities could "cooperate with...organized labor, the Church, and the highly organized Negro, Japanese American, Jewish and Anglo-American communities...on the solution of problems common to or affecting all."[27] CSO leaders realized that collaboration was essential to the Mexican community's progress in the postwar period, and that the CSO would help Mexican Americans change conditions that "precluded assistance and cooperation [from] other groups," they explained, by creating an "organized channel through which such groups could work."[28]

While these comments overlook earlier initiatives like the Sleepy Lagoon Defense Committee and El Congreso, it is true that other postwar Mexican-American groups, like Asociación Nacionál México-Americana (ANMA), collapsed by the mid-1950s in the face of anticommunism, and other groups that were strong elsewhere in the Southwest, like the League of United Latin American Citizens (LULAC), were much less active in Los Angeles.[29] "It is the first time the Mexican-American Community can be reached in an organized fashion," Jewish community organizations like the Community Relations Committee (CRC), the local Jewish community's most prominent civil rights and interethnic focused organization, explained to their members.[30] The CSO helped Mexican Americans tap into these other reform communities.

As a result, Mexican Americans' participation in collaborative Los Angeles civil rights efforts rose visibly after the CSO's creation. By the late 1940s, other community activists whose awareness of Mexican Americans' dire conditions had been heightened during World War II, and were increasingly concerned as postwar tensions mounted, more often discussed integrating Mexican Americans into their campaigns. Leaders of the California Federation for Civic Unity (CFCU) first began to mention Mexican Americans and to seek their participation around 1949. The CFCU's executive director Richard Dettering asked Ross in 1949 to persuade Roybal to serve on CFCU's southern board because "it is very important that CFCU establish some official tie-in with the Spanish-speaking people and here is a first step."[31] Dettering also asked L.A. CSO chairman Henry Nava to suggest two members to serve on the statewide organization's board of directors in order to "increase the participation of the Spanish speaking peoples in our state-wide civic unity program, following the pattern set so successfully by the CSO and capitalizing on the new state-wide Latin-American organization."[32] Tony Ríos and Henry Nava subsequently joined the board, where they worked with Frederick A. Schreiber, the director of the L.A. American Jewish Committee, and Milton Senn, of the L.A. (Jewish) Anti-Defamation League, among others. The CSO officially joined the CFCU as a member organization in October 1949.[33]

The CSO encouraged and relied upon cooperation with Japanese, African, Jewish, and Anglo Americans. It appointed leaders of African-American organizations to its own committees. The NAACP's West Coast Legal Committee chairman Loren Miller, for instance, soon chaired the CSO's Legal Aid Committee too.[34] The CSO highlighted the NAACP's field secretary Lester Bailey's comments at the CSO's national board meeting, where he spoke out on joint Mexican- and African-American voter registration projects and about the importance of cross-ethnic ties to the Mexican-American community. The CSO noted Bailey's comment that these ties were particularly significant in the West where, unlike the South, the African American was not "alone in his battle against discrimination" because of the large presence of groups like Mexican Americans in the region.[35]

In the case of the CSO, ties between the Mexican-American and Jewish communities were especially important. The CSO's initial success especially depended on collaboration with the Jewish community. Mexican Americans asked Fred Herzberg, the World War II veteran who became executive director of the Jewish community's CRC in 1947, to become the only non-Mexican-American member of its seven-person advisory committee, in part because he was "a real guy." But they also chose Herzberg because he could be "quite an asset," as Ross explained to Alinsky, since some east side neighborhoods important to Mexican Americans were as much as half Jewish.[36] The CSO invited Jewish groups to attend its community civil rights meetings, where they discussed housing, police brutality, and other pressing civil rights issues.[37] Ralph Guzman, a CSO vice president, asked Jewish community representatives

Figure 12: CSO Advertisement, "Help Build This Bridge!" March 1, 1952, *Los Angeles Daily News*, Folder 12, Box 10, Fred Ross Papers, 1910–1992. Courtesy of Department of Special Collections and University Archives, Stanford University Libraries.

to help his organization gain tax exempt status too.[38] Furthermore, from 1947 to 1950, Jewish community financial support was critical to the CSO's survival.[39]

Los Angeles Jews' interest developed largely through the efforts of Alinsky, whose savvy and charisma, according to Ross, "just charmed the pants right off of" Jewish groups.[40] In turn, they declared that cooperation with Mexican Americans in the form of the CSO "carried the greatest impact...of any project submitted to the CRC."[41] This statement is particularly impressive given the broad range of activities in which the CRC engaged. Herzberg similarly emphasized to CRC members the importance of their support for the CSO, which exemplified "grass roots democracy at its best."[42] The CRC further urged Jewish community members to value this "extremely important operation [the CSO]...which receives almost its sole support through the CRC" in no small part because it promoted democracy by "furnishing the means whereby Mexican Americans' civic consciousness may be expressed."[43] CRC members strongly supported the CSO in part because they believed it would, by helping break down the Mexican-American community's "suspicion of outsiders," allow the two communities to work more closely together.[44]

Such comments reveal that Jewish community members did not understand the Mexican-origin community very well. More likely explanations for this isolation included language barriers, constant immigration, and trauma from the 1930s deportations, not to mention power imbalances between the Jewish and Mexican communities. But whatever the reasons, until the CSO, the two communities had not had a significant vehicle for political collaboration. Thereafter, when Jewish community leaders like Isaac Pacht, the chairman of the Los Angeles branch of the Council for Equality in Employment—an interracial organization fighting employment discrimination—wanted to forge alliances with Mexican Americans, he could contact CSO leaders. He did so in 1949 to request their participation on the council's steering committee.[45]

Although the CSO was the first significant vehicle for political collaboration between Jews and Mexican Americans, their postwar cooperation emerged out of wartime and earlier connections, which exposes direct continuity between Cold War initiatives and earlier activism. The well-connected social justice activist Carey McWilliams plugged Alinsky into the local Jewish network by tapping into alliances he developed during the war through initiatives like the Sleepy Lagoon Defense Committee (SLDC). McWilliams introduced Alinsky to Isaac Pacht, the prominent Jewish community leader who became one of the CSO's key allies. Pacht soon became the local Industrial Area Foundation's initial chairman and assisted in persuading the Jewish community to support the CSO. He also held the initial CSO organizing meetings in his office. McWilliams knew Pacht, at least in part, because he had worked with one of Pacht's two law partners, Clore Warne, on the Sleepy Lagoon Defense Committee and Los Angeles Committee for American Unity.[46] McWilliams' long-time friend and CRC member Harry Braverman also joined the CSO effort just a few years after the two men had worked together on the

Sleepy Lagoon Defense Committee and shortly after Braverman had chaired the Los Angeles Committee for American Unity. Braverman's efforts raised $9,000 in seed money to help start the CSO; he also headed the CRC's CSO subcommittee.[47]

CSO advisory board members like Richard Ibañez and other Mexican- and Anglo-Americans involved in the CSO also illustrate the ongoing legacy of collaborative wartime activism. Ibañez had been active in war-time initiatives like the Sleepy Lagoon Defense Committee. Fred Ross's interest in the region's minority populations developed out of wartime work too. During the war Ross had worked for the War Relocation Authority assisting interned Japanese Americans who left the camps to find jobs and housing. Soon after the war ended, the American Council on Race Relations (ACRR), the Chicago-based but nationally active interracial organization, hired him to help organize Latinos through Councils for Civic Unity and Hispanic Unity Leagues. Ross came to the CSO from the ACRR.

Some of the CSO's interracial roots reached into an era even earlier than World War II. Two CSO members who eventually served as presi-dents of the organization, Tony Ríos and Gilbert Anaya, both began their political careers in the 1930s in the Congress of Industrial Organization's (CIO) United Steelworkers of America.[48] CSO treasurer María Durán had been an ILGWU leader, and executive board member Hope Mendoza Schechter had also been active in that organization.[49] Incidentally, Mendoza Schechter's personal life also illustrates the overlap between the CSO and the CRC. In 1955 she married Harvey Schechter, a Jewish community activist prominent in the Anti-Defamation League and tied to CRC activism.[50]

The CSO was only one of many cooperative initiatives among multi-racial Angelenos in the late 1940s and early 1950s. African-, Mexican-, and Jewish-American community members frequently collaborated. The NAACP, CSO, and Jewish organizations joined in 1952 to protest the destruction of African-American homes and Jewish institutions and racially motivated bombings in Florida that killed an NAACP official and his wife. When the NAACP sponsored a protest rally at the Shrine Auditorium, Jews circulated fund-raising petitions and provided organi-zational assistance, including recruiting Hollywood figures to speak at the rally. CRC member and influential Universal Studios leader Bill Gordon helped recruit actor Jeff Chandler.[51] CSO members joined the protest through a letter-writing campaign to the Department of Justice, which used language like "we protest with all the sincerity and furvor [sic] we possess the recent bombing and murder of Harry and Harriet Moore in Mims [sic] Florida."[52] In 1955 the president of the Los Angeles NAACP spoke at a CSO meeting to ask it to support the NAACP's push to more effectively integrate African Americans into the Los Angeles Fire Department. The CSO already had gathered 500 signatures to support the NAACP campaign, and after this meeting it sent letters urging integration to the mayor and fire commissioners.[53]

CRC leaders in 1953 welcomed the NAACP's national head Walter White to Los Angeles, where they introduced him to influential leaders. They wanted to be sure White knew that they were "in complete sympathy with the aims and purposes of the NAACP," and believed that "complete success in the race relations and human relations field can be achieved only if there is complete harmony and cooperation among all groups working in the field."[54] White appreciated that CRC chairman Mendel Silberberg, whom "they tell me [is] the most powerful guy in Los Angeles," used his influence to introduce White to powerful Californians in Hollywood and elsewhere.[55] In turn, influential African Americans frequently invited CRC members to participate in NAACP events. In 1954, for instance, Franklin Williams invited them to send delegates to observe and participate in the NAACP's West Coast Regional Conference. Williams explained that CRC delegates' attendance would help advance the NAACP's "major effort...to strengthen our bonds of mutual concern."[56]

Once Japanese Americans returned to Los Angeles, they too cooperated with other groups. In 1946 the JACL requested and received the support of other racial groups for its opposition to Proposition 15, which would have made the discriminatory Alien Land Law—which prevented Japanese immigrants from owning land—part of California's constitution (it failed). Other groups also supported their less successful attempts to gain naturalization privileges for Japanese immigrants through various bills in the House of Representatives from the mid to late 1940s.[57] In 1954, the Los Angeles Regional Director of the JACL, Tats Kushida, asked the CRC's executive director Joe Roos for help persuading MGM Studio president and CRC member Dore Schary to give the keynote at the JACL's 13th Biennial National Convention in Los Angeles. Kushida praised Schary as "a distinguished defender of civil rights and a champion of minority groups."[58]

Despite their failure to protest the violation of Japanese Americans' rights when internment began, Jewish Angelenos attempted to ease the readjustment process for returning evacuees. The JACL thanked the CRC for its assistance in Japanese Americans' attempts to gain compensation for the internment, including for a 1950 compensation bill Congresswoman Helen Gahagan Douglas sponsored.[59] Reversing their earlier position, the CRC concluded that justice now mandated compensation since "in a period of hysteria in the name of military defense, our country had participated in racist activities and had, without consideration of the individual loyalties of its members, put a minority group in detention camps."[60]

African Americans also cooperated with Japanese Americans to help ease their postwar return to the West Coast. In 1945 the NAACP's regional West Coast office actively campaigned alongside the JACL and local Councils for Civic Unity on behalf of Japanese Americans seeking employment. The JACL's Joe Grant Masaoka praised Noah Griffin, the NAACP's West Coast director: "Your forthright stand in upholding the right of a man to work, irrespective of his race or color, merits the commendation of all democratic-minded citizens."[61]

Japanese-American organizations were less prominent in these postwar racial justice initiatives than other groups, however. They may have wanted to avoid making waves after their return from the internment camps.[62] In some cases, Japanese-American organizations like the JACL did not agree with the strategies, or even goals, of other minority organizations. This became particularly apparent during disputes over the 1952 McCarran Walter Act, which perpetuated the discriminatory national origins quota system and integrated Cold War anticommunist policies into immigration law, making deportation easier. Most Jewish, African-American, Mexican-American, and other groups interested in civil rights opposed the act. The JACL, on the other hand, supported the act because of its progressive elements concerning the Japanese-origin community; it lifted long-term bans on Japanese naturalization and ended previous Japanese exclusion provisions.[63] Historian Scott Kurashige argues, too, that Japanese Americans' very different wartime experiences from groups like African Americans made the two groups misunderstand each other after the war. Moreover, they had different ideas of the role the state should play in remedying social ills.[64]

Overall, though, interracial cooperation among diverse groups was widespread in Los Angeles. That communities like Jews and Mexican Americans prioritized interracial cooperation in early Cold War Los Angeles, and that this collaboration was key to the early success of the CSO, is clear. What is less clear, though, is how Jewish and Mexican-American cooperation developed out of community connections and circumstances rooted in World War II and reinforced by the Cold War.

RESOLVING CONFLICT, PREVENTING VIOLENCE

The Zoot Suit Riots' legacy factored prominently into postwar calculations about the value of cooperating across community divides, especially as the mounting housing crunch and employment discrimination escalated racial tensions in minority areas. As tensions threatened Angelenos' safety, they stirred Jews' and Mexicans'—along with the rest of Los Angeles's—fears that violence would once again erupt in their city. The American Council on Race Relations' 1945 study titled *The Problem of Violence: Observations on Race Conflict in Los Angeles* explained: "There was general apprehension on the part of many who had seen the evidences of friction increasing and apparently cumulating, who had lived through the 'zoot-suit' riots." These people, the study reported, "feared that post-war Los Angeles with its restricted employment opportunities for Negroes and Mexicans, its wretchedly inadequate housing facilities and its greatly increased population would become a battle ground on which Americans battled each other."[65] The threat of violence forced Angelenos to realize that wartime attempts to improve race relations in the city had fallen short.

Sometimes the tensions and competition for resources did result in violence, both between whites and minorities and among minority groups. Much of the violence was perpetrated against minorities, especially African and Mexican Americans, by whites. In 1946, California daily newspapers reported eighteen incidents in a mere two-month period that were KKK-related. "There has been a resurgence of acts of racial violence in California," the CFCU lamented.[66] Minorities confronted rising police brutality and repression, such as the infamous 1951 "Bloody Christmas" incident.[67] Another case brought to trial in 1952 by CSO president Tony Ríos and Alfred Ulloa, who were beaten by allegedly drunk policemen when they tried to stop a beating, also highlights the ongoing violence.[68] Several years later the *CSO Reporter* told its readers about continuing police violence against Mexican Americans, reporting that two Mexican Americans, Roy Escarcega (age 42) and Mario Hidalgo (age 29), had died in the Lincoln Heights jail after brutal police beatings. Mexican Americans and African Americans faced similarly unjust, violent treatment from the police, the *CSO Reporter* commented. "From reports appearing constantly in the Los Angeles Negro press, Negroes and Mexican-Americans are being made the special target of a certain brutal, sadistic element in the Los Angeles Police Department," it wrote. "Regardless of the offense, any Mexican-American or Negro sent to jail in Los Angeles is in danger of being subjected to physical violence."[69]

Jews, too, confronted institutional discrimination, though anti-Semitism generally did not express itself violently the same way anti-Mexican and antiblack racism did. The police department frequently investigated and prosecuted anti-Semitic crimes lackadaisically. It dismissed anti-Semitic vandalism against a middle-aged Jewish couple—in which vandals painted swastikas on their home and destroyed their property—as "malicious mischief."[70]

Violence often erupted among minority communities competing for limited space and jobs in the postwar city. A series of holdups by

African Americans against elderly Japanese shook the Bronzeville/Little Tokyo neighborhood in 1947. When the Japanese business community responded by hiring two Nisei ex-G.I.s to patrol the streets, blacks angrily protested what they viewed as vigilantism, and rumors circulated that Japanese were trying to run blacks out of the district, which had been a primarily Japanese area before the war.[71] Workers at the Pilgrim House, a neighborhood community service center formed by cooperation among diverse local residents from 1945 to 1948, hoped to soothe these tensions. A Pilgrim House newsletter explained the situation it hoped to resolve in blunt terms: the "Negroes want to keep the Japanese from returning and the Japanese want to 'kick the niggers out.' "[72] The American Council on Race Relations reported that tensions were especially high among Jews, Mexican Americans, and African Americans of working-class and middle-class backgrounds.[73]

Problems in Los Angeles were more intense than they were elsewhere in the country, observers believed, due to the city's increased diversity. The NAACP's West Coast regional director Franklin Williams, who arrived from the East Coast in 1950, called his new region a "melting-pot" and a "barely half cooked potpourri whose various racial ingredients are more diversified than anywhere else in the country—and whose proportions have changed radically during the last few years," resulting in special "human relations problems." "Nowhere within the bounds of our country are there as many different types of 'hyphenated Americans' " as in California, Williams pronounced. There, unlike in other regions the "'race problem' may include the Negro, but, depending on the locality, will just as often include descendants of almost any so-called colored nation, or even the 'original American' himself."[74] The American Council on Race Relations concurred with this assessment of the unique problems stemming from the West's diversity. *Race Relations on the West Coast* reported that on the Pacific Coast, "in addition to problems of Negro-white relations and of anti-Semitism, which are found throughout the country, there are," it explained, "very specific issues affecting Japanese, Chinese, Armenians, Filipinos, native Indians, and Mexicans."[75] *A Study of Police Training Programs in Minority Relations*, conducted by Milton Senn of the Los Angeles Jewish community's Anti-Defamation League, discussed issues arising from the fact that "Approximately 40% of [Los Angeles's] population is composed of minority peoples—Negroes, Mexican-Americans, Japanese-Americans, and Jews."[76]

While these observers acknowledged that the diversity posed a challenge to West Coast residents, they also recognized it as an opportunity to create collaborative solutions. NAACP representative Lester Bailey emphasized this when he told CSO members that the West's diversity presented a collaborative opportunity for African Americans and Mexican Americans.[77] The ACRR also noted that such diversity necessitated new, creative responses. "We [working on the West Coast] feel that we cannot depend on New York or Chicago stimuli for social action," the ACRR's Lawrence Hewes explained in *Race Relations on the West Coast*. "We have to generate our own impulses."[78] Diverse communities in Los Angeles especially needed each other in the absence of a majority minority.

East Los Angeles Jewish and Mexican communities, among whom relations were particularly strained as the two groups' financial, social, and geographic distance increased, viewed potential violence as an especially salient issue. As Jews in Los Angeles, as elsewhere, confronted housing restrictions and employment discrimination, they, unlike Mexican Americans, also made economic strides, became increasingly integrated, and gradually moved toward the more affluent west side.[79] The Mexican-origin population, on the other hand, was "Southern California's largest and, in many ways, most disadvantaged minority," according to a 1949 report by Alinsky's Industrial Areas Foundation. The group's poverty, lack of networks to other communities, low voter turnout, and high percentage of noncitizens, according to reports like these, impeded attempts at securing financial backing to pressure politicians to improve their conditions.[80] A 1946 investigation of racial minorities' conditions by the ACRR concluded that the Mexican-American community was in even more dire straits than other poor Los Angeles minorities.[81]

Increasingly different class status distanced Jewish and Mexican Americans from one another. In the schools, the ACRR's report *The Problem of Violence* observed, "The great barrier to the acceptance of Mexican children by Jewish children is the middle-class bias of the Jewish parents expressed in excessive concern over dirt and disease." Divergent police action toward the two groups also, it explained, served to "contribute to the increase of community tension between middle-class Jews and lower-class Mexicans."[82] This "class bias" was intertwined with a racial bias, too, as Jewish Americans were becoming increasingly integrated into American society and accepted as white, while Mexicans increasingly faced categorization as brown "others."

Mexican Americans saw their Jewish neighbors moving to nicer neighborhoods while their own conditions stagnated or deteriorated, breeding "frustration and bitterness." Alinsky's Industrial Areas Foundation reported, "These, in turn, found expression in intergroup hostility and scape-goating with particular reference on the Eastside to the adjacent Jewish Community."[83] Jews who moved west frequently kept east side businesses and rental properties, which sometimes provoked charges of exploitation from their former neighbors.[84] Associating Jews with exploitation stemmed in some cases from anti-Semitic assumptions, since many non-Jews also became absentee landlords.[85]

This growing divide between two communities that seemingly had little in common after the war counterintuitively helps explain their interest in collaboration. Because Mexican Americans' daily struggle for survival left little money to fund organizations such as the CSO, they sought support from other Los Angeles ethnic communities, including Jews. The Jewish community's motives for assisting a group increasingly distant from its own population seem less apparent. CRC leaders, discussing the Mexican-American community, justified support for the CSO by explaining that it "deflects the hostility which exists in that community against the Jews, to constructive social issues of benefit to the Mexican-American and the Jew alike." The CSO could "by its very existence…prevent race riots such as have happened before in this city." CRC leaders claimed it already had "no doubt prevented serious repercussions which might have otherwise happened on the East Side."[86] CRC executive director Herzberg countered a member's protest that the CRC should stop funding the CSO, since it was not "closely related enough to the activities of the Jewish community," by explaining that its "prophylactic value" was "a relatively cheap investment" for the Jewish community.[87] Herzberg's comment that the CSO would help prevent 'gang fights and similar anti-social acts' also reveals underlying assumptions about Mexican Americans' violent potential. Fears of violence also shaped Jewish community interest in the African-American community. The CRC reported Jewish concern about the implications of demographic transformations in the Watts neighborhood, specifically the increasing African-American and Mexican-American populations. Mounting unemployment created a situation of "increasing problems of social relations" that "could be explosive as far as the Jewish community is concerned." Many of the retail stores on the main street of Watts were owned and run by Jews, it reported, explaining that the year before, "a vigorous anti-Semitic campaign" arose as unemployed residents demonstrated their frustration about limited job opportunities. The report also identified mounting tensions between the African-American and Mexican-American communities in the neighborhood. In response to such tensions, the CRC expressed to the director of planning of the City Planning Commission that it was "deeply concerned about some of the conditions of living in the Watts area of our city."[88]

Amidst these complex attitudes, which reflect some degree of prejudice and misunderstanding of each other, both Mexican-American and Jewish-American communities viewed bridge-building projects as critical for their mutual survival. The CSO particularly hoped to secure Jews' participation since, as Ross explained, "this is the other large group on the East Side and Jewish-Mexican American relations have left a good deal to be desired for some time."[89] Ross attempted to obtain Jewish community support by emphasizing to the CRC how the CSO's work improved "deplorable" East Los Angeles neighborhood conditions that "had been reflected in a history of hostility between Spanish speaking colonies and the Jewish Community surrounding Temple Street."[90] The CSO reported in 1949 that two years of efforts had redirected the "scape-goating" of nearby "disadvantaged groups" (specifically the "adjacent" Jews) and had "pav[ed the way] for cooperation with other groups particularly with those in the Jewish Community."[91]

In short, memories of World War II–era violence and fears of its recurrence helped inspire postwar collaboration. In cases like the CSO, such fears even resulted in important new postwar civil rights initiatives which continued the earlier thrust of reform and demonstrate the continuity between 1930s and World War II era collaboration and its later Cold War incarnation.

ANTICOMMUNISM DRIVES COALITIONS

Conditions new in the postwar era also motivated Jewish and Mexicans Americans to work together through organizations like the CSO. Cold War red-baiting encouraged activists who recognized that in order to maintain any effectiveness, they needed to reinforce their reputations as "acceptable" anticommunist activists. They did so in part by asserting that they were not communist and in part by seeking and strengthening alliances with seemingly "safe" civil rights proponents, those with established anticommunist credentials. In this way, interracial cooperation continued to be a pragmatic strategy for success, as it had during wartime, but it took on new urgency as it became crucial for self-protection.

The CSO's anticommunism resembled the anticommunism of its allies like the NAACP and the CRC. As with the NAACP and the CRC, CSO members also drew from strategies they and their predecessors had developed during World War II to justify their ongoing activism, protect themselves and their allies, and change civil rights activism from a disadvantage to an advantage. In this way, the country's Cold War preoccupation with fighting global communism kept the wedge in the window of opportunity first cracked open by World War II antifascism. Activists like those in the CSO articulated their work in terms suitable to the new global conditions, now justifying their work as a tool against communism.

Establishing legitimacy meant emphasizing that the CSO was not communist and, moreover, that its fight against discrimination helped combat communism by foiling communists' attempts to gain a foothold in marginalized communities. The CSO negated accusations that it was a communist organization and sometimes even claimed anticommunism. Bert Corona, a prominent Mexican-American civil rights and labor activist who joined the CSO in Northern California, where he lived for a time, recollected Alinsky insisting, "We're not a Communist organization. We know all about the commies, and we're not in agreement with them. They don't fool us a bit." Alinsky would say, "Don't for one minute think that we sympathize with the reds in any way, shape, or form. We're accused of being reds, but we're not. We're against the reds."[92] Corona illustrates disagreement with anticommunist approaches like the CSO's, as he expressed reservations about the organization's anticommunist stance.[93]

During CSO president Tony Ríos's 1952 police brutality case, the CSO emphatically repeated that neither Ríos nor other CSO members were communist. The CSO claimed in its news publication the *Reporter* that, to the contrary, they were anti-Communist: "We do not believe that before criticizing bad civic conditions a citizen must first prove his firm anti-Communist stand." But events forced the CSO to discuss the issue of Communism, it explained. The prosecuting attorney had "successfully injected the issue of communism into the trial" when questioning a prospective juror, and a member of the jury who was released from service stated that the panel of jurors was told that they were going to deal with a Communist group. The CSO's article explained: "We who belong to the CSO know that we are not Communists. The Communists know that we are not Communists. And Mr. Marshall Morgan, the prosecutor, is too astute and intelligent a lawyer not to know that we are not Communists." The article then emphasized the community's respect for Tony Ríos, as well as the fact that he was "a life-long devout Catholic, a delegate to the Democratic County Central committee, a deputy-registrar of voters, and one of the staunchest anti-Communists of the community."[94]

Ríos again emphasized the CSO's mainstream orientation when he reported to the United Steelworkers of America in a 1952 application for funding. Ríos explained that it had "developed to the point where it could and did seize the leadership in the Los Angeles fight against police brutality and remove it from the left-wing context which ha[d] stifled it in the past."[95] CSO pamphlets claimed the agency distanced itself from "the enveloping tactics of certain extremist 'Committees' beginning to operate among the Mexican-American community."[96] In some cases, this meant not joining protests, since joining a picket line against housing restrictions might lead to the CSO being labeled "Red" or to violence.[97]

CSO members' own anticommunism, however, did not mean that they kept silent when they believed other anticommunists were too extreme. For example, in a declaration critiquing the Loyalty Review Board's policies for finding communists, the CSO explained, "We are opposed to all forms of totalitarianism [meaning Communism]....We believe that the government should protect itself against totalitarianism." But the CSO also made sure to clarify, "For our part we do not believe in using totalitarian methods (i.e., thought control, curbing of speech, press, and assembly, and determination of guilt by association) to fight totalitarianism." The CSO argued that the board violated "the fundamental principles of our democratic faith" that it professed to protect. The CSO urged that to purge communist influences in such a time of crisis, the government instead must adhere to the same democratic process as it would in normal times. This included enacting laws that punish those found guilty "by a fair trial" and protecting rights "guaranteed by our Constitution."[98] At a September 1949 meeting, members concluded that "the Community Service Organization is opposed to the abuses enumerated above and urges the adoption, by the President, of procedures which will protect the security of the United States and at the same time avoid infringement upon the traditional constitutional and democratic rights of the individual."[99] They opposed the communist control ordinance for similar reasons. Roybal, for example, partially justified his opposition by explaining that the ordinance threatened to stifle the attempts of multiracial G.I.s who had crossed racial divides in Korea to fight together against the communists.[100]

For the CSO, negating communist influences meant marginalizing former allies, as it did for the NAACP, CRC, and anticommunist labor organizations. Carey McWilliams, a former SLDC member who had been integral to earlier coalitions but who the Tenney Committee in 1948 called a "notorious Communist fellow-traveler," was sidelined by fellow activists who believed the Cold War mandated more cautious associations.[101] Soon after the CSO's formation, leaders decided not to give McWilliams a role as an advisory committee member despite his initial assistance and their personal respect for him. McWilliams's associations might taint the organization red, they feared. The "Mexican American situation here is just so damned touchy and tender a thing that [his] presence on the Committee … might upset the apple-cart," Ross explained. "McWilliams is definitely 'labeled,' and even a *vague* label is more than enough to send the M.A.'s scurrying for cover and send the quasi-liberals and conservative Angl-Americans [*sic*] in the field out on a crusade to discredit the Committee."[102] The CSO also refused to affiliate with the more radically situated Associación Nacionál Mexicana-American (ANMA), agreeing only to send an observer—not an official representative—to the meetings.[103] Not everyone in the CSO agreed with the decision to distance radicals, but some internal disagreement did not change the organization's approach.[104]

Though the CSO experienced less internal turmoil than the NAACP and the Jewish Community Council, evidence suggests that forces interested in practicing less exclusionary politics tried to take over the organization in 1950. An internal CSO memo from 1957 reported, "In 1950 two different factions with leftist philosophies became interested in 'capturing' the organization." The CSO allegedly responded by shutting down the involved individuals' participation at meetings. When the "distructors [*sic*]" attempted to speak, the meeting chair would recognize "other (loyal) members who were prepared with items of business pertinent to the pruposes [*sic*] of the organization. It soon became difficult for the infiltrators to secure recognition." CSO leaders prevented this group from electing a president by conducting a "member by member, house to house" drive to gain support for a different (acceptable) candidate, the memo explained. "The leftists were defeated and the new officers continued the smothering techniques so effectively that many of the obstructers dropped out," it concluded.[105] Although there is no further evidence to confirm it, this episode parallels what happened in the Jewish- and African-American communities during the same period. Regardless of the episode's veracity, serious disagreement about CSO stances did consume members of Los Angeles's Mexican-American community, even if criticisms of the CSO did not undermine its influence as the representative organization of that community.

Even more than being noncommunist, the CSO asserted that its anti-discrimination activities would save the country from communism. "To drive out Communism we must strike at conditions which foster its growth," its publicity pamphlet explained.[106] Limiting communist influence on the eastside, particularly from the "red" Mexican-American members of organizations like the Communist Party or the ANMA, partly motivated the CSO's creation, activist Bert Corona confirmed. Keeping the "'reds' from establishing a base in the communities," he explained, was "one of its stated reasons for organizing," something Corona found objectionable.[107]

The CSO's mission resembled the increasingly anticommunist stance adopted by other ethnic communities' organizations. CSO members sometimes adopted anticommunist policies for ideological reasons, fearing Soviet domination. They sometimes resented communist and fellow traveler organizations' attempts to co-opt their efforts and undermine their causes, as when the CSO's president Tony Ríos simmered in frustration at communist methods. Ríos attacked communists for using his police beating to further their own goals, and for keeping money they raised supposedly for his defense.[108]

But the CSO's anticommunist arguments often were pragmatic. Its anticommunism likely stemmed more from fear that communist associations would jeopardize its efficacy than from ideological motivations. Corona later speculated that its anticommunist position reflected a "fund-raising gimmick." CSO leaders "gave you the impression that, more than anything else, they used their red-baiting to scare funders into" donating. Corona suggested they did this by arguing: "'Give us the money, or else the reds are very capable of organizing these people, and then the establishment will have problems with the *mexicanos*. If they're totally abandoned by the churches and social organizations, then it's logical that they will turn to the Communists.'"[109]

The CSO's decision to reject using red-baiting tactics that would have solidified its own legitimacy underscores the strategic element of its anticommunism. Members balked at the idea of stooping to Tenney and HUAC's level and decided against adopting an "anti-red clause." They realized that their decision mattered little, since the CSO "will be labeled whether the tag fits or not; it has been already." As Ross reported to Alinsky, hopefully the "'Boys on the Left' will keep their hot little hands out of the CSO...until a strong, liberal foundation is built."[110]

Jewish and African Americans' anticommunism seems to have been more ideological than Mexican Americans.' Jewish- and African-American organizations' language was more convincingly anticommunist, while Mexican-American CSO members' was more strategic. Internal NAACP documents exchanged among the West Coast offices, national offices, and anticommunist allies in Los Angeles during the purge crisis expose an anti-communism not intended for public exposure, which suggests its authen-ticity.[111] Private discussions among Jewish community members suggest a similar authenticity. On the other hand, the largely Mexican-American CSO's decision not to red-bait, and instead to pursue the strategy that "the only 'anti' is anti-discrimination," indicates a more pragmatic anticommu-nism.[112] In addition, Mexican Americans' relative political invisibility and largely regional population meant that the American public had weaker associations of them with communism than it did of African Americans and Jewish Americans, perhaps affording Mexican Americans greater pro-tection. It also may be that Mexican Americans' relatively weak organizing history meant that they needed as much assistance as possible and were less willing to totally marginalize communists and other leftists. Whether strategy or ideology motivated activists, though, the red scare drove building new alliances with "safe" individuals and organizations.

CSO members actively sought cooperation from allies whom they believed would shore up their legitimacy. Those articulating similar anti-communist civil rights positions looked to each other for reinforcement. For instance, Fred Ross decided to respond proactively rather than defen-sively to rumors that the CSO was a "Communist outfit" by pursuing alliances with other well-reputed interracial groups. He eagerly accepted an invitation from the Council for Civic Unity to attend a conference of agencies working in the "minorities field."[113] When Roybal first inquired how Ross expected, as a white person assisting Mexican Americans, to "escape the red label," Ross replied that he would seek backing from "legitimate," noncommunist organizations like the Catholic Church and "a number of respected, prominent Mexican-American business and professional men."[114] Alinsky also hoped to establish the CSO's legiti-macy by emphasizing its connection to the Church. "We're out here to organize the Spanish-speaking," he explained, "in conjunction with the Catholic Church."[115]

Ross's commitment to establishing his anticommunist reputation by forging safe alliances emerged from his own experience. A year earlier,

Ross had worked as an American Council for Race Relations representative helping Mexican Americans in Orange County fight school segregation as part of the initiatives that culminated in the landmark *Mendez v. Westminster* case. But accusations that Ross was communist undermined his effectiveness and even forced him out of Orange County. Hector Tarango, a Mexican American who worked with Ross in earlier years to fight segregation in education, as well as to register voters and improve farm workers' housing, explained that the Orange County Farm Bureau feared that such efforts would undermine the availability of cheap labor and used red-baiting and intimidation to try to dissuade Mexican Americans from working with Ross. The bureau filed a complaint against Tarango and three other Mexican Americans that resulted in their summons to the Orange County D.A. The D.A. cautioned them that they were getting involved with the wrong people, specifically Ross, whom the Farm Bureau labeled a communist. The D.A. told them that Ross would get them "down the wrong road and get you involved against our government and all that," Tarango recalled. The Farm Bureau also took the communist accusation against Ross to the Catholic Church, which used its influence in the Mexican-American community to persuade many activists to stop working with him. This episode helped convince Ross to leave Orange County for Los Angeles, where he resumed his activism but made sure to first establish his anticommunist credentials with the Church, businesses, and other institutions.[116]

When organizations in Los Angeles started rumors that Ross and the CSO were communist, Ross immediately sought the support of Bishop McGucken. The bishop agreed to write him letters of introduction to the priests in the various Mexican-American parishes.[117] Ross pursued the help of Monsignor O'Dwyer, too, with whom he had difficulty securing an audience. He succeeded only with the assistance of "relatively conservative sources," including the L.A. Council for Civic Unity (CCU). Even after a successful visit, Ross reported, O'Dwyer was still "a little suspicious of me and the I.A.F." This episode, and the CCU's help, again indicates that such alliances with other ethnic and racial communities were crucial to the CSO's survival during the early Cold War.[118]

Herman Gallegos, the vice president of the San Jose, California, CSO branch during this period, in later years remembered how much the CSO relied on the Catholic Church's reputation as a bulwark against anticommunism. Gallegos wrote to Father Ralph Duggan, a Catholic priest who had assisted in Cold War CSO struggles, that during the McCarthyite 1950s, "The presence of a few Roman collars helped immensely."[119] Clergy even offered invocation at the annual CSO meeting, which helped to reinforce the organization's anticommunist claims.[120]

The NAACP also explained the importance of Cold War alliances with the Catholic Church. Help from the Catholic Church was crucial, a

Long Beach NAACP official explained to the organization's West Coast Director Franklin Williams, since a recent meeting had made apparent that "the Communists…[who composed] over half of the audience…are attempting to move back into our branch." The Long Beach official explained that the assistance of a Father Berry, who pledged to support the NAACP, "will prove very worth while in the near future."[121] Religious institutions—Catholic, Protestant, and Jewish—had been involved in previous intercommunity efforts, but during the Cold War they especially bolstered civil rights coalitions.[122]

In the case of at least one prominent member in particular, the Church's support for the organization convinced her to join the CSO. Dolores Huerta, who became a key organizer in the farm workers' struggle alongside César Chávez, explained that the Church's involvement substantiated the CSO's claims that it was not a communist organization. Huerta joined the Fresno CSO (in central California) in 1955 only after conducting an FBI check on Fred Ross to ensure he did not have "unsafe affiliations."[123] In later years Huerta credited Alinsky for helping secure religious leaders' support and explained that church involvement—Catholic as well as Protestant and Jewish—helped combat the Communist label among CSO organizers in Stockton in the 1950s. She explained that when people told other Mexican-American community members that they should not join the CSO because "we were a bunch of communists," the label "didn't stick because we had the, you know, Daughters of the American Revolution, you had the Catholic Church, you had the Protestant churches, you had the Jewish churches, everybody."[124]

The CSO and their civil rights associates also looked to recently reorganized anticommunist labor organizations for legitimacy. Affiliates of the Los Angeles CIO, which had purged many members to restructure itself as an anticommunist organization, eventually became strong CSO allies. The AFL's International Brotherhood of Electrical Workers (IBEW) joined the CSO's Labor Advisory Committee.[125] In another example of Cold War labor/civil rights cooperation, the CSO, the Catholic Church, and the newly reorganized AFL and CIO supported the new anticommunist CIO-chartered International Union of Electrical, Radio and Machine Employees (IUE) in its bid for influence over the United Electrical, Radio, and Machine Workers (UE) in the Standard Coil factory. The CIO had expelled the UE in 1949 for supporting the Communist Party. CSO support of the IUE helped it achieve victory. The CSO became involved in this battle at the urging of the Catholic Church and the CIO, and to some degree the AFL, in no small part out of obligation to help these institutions whose support had helped legitimate its own reputation.[126]

Postpurge labor organizations reciprocated support for the CSO and other anticommunist groups' civil rights initiatives. The AFL's CLC

(Central Labor Council) worked to pass a fair employment ordinance Roybal authored. It also pressed the city council in early 1952 to investigate the police beating of CSO president Tony Ríos and the victims of the Bloody Christmas beatings.[127] Interracial activism continued to be union-based but now organized labor's anticommunism was key to such alliances' ability to maintain public legitimacy. Some observers believed labor's support of civil rights was greater in Los Angeles than elsewhere in the country. Lester Bailey, a national NAACP official, commented, "The response here [of organized labor to the NAACP] is even more gratifying than Chicago." Bailey explained that labor unions were making financial contributions of $100, $50, and $25 to the NAACP, helping conduct NAACP membership drives, and formally endorsing the organization.[128]

The same urgency to protect themselves from accusations of communism that motivated the CSO's collaboration with churches and with recently purged labor organizations inspired, and reinforced, the Jewish community's interest in collaborating with the CSO. Longtime activist Leonard Bloom, for instance, stated his admiration for the CSO's efforts to "protect itself from being captured or exploited by Stalinist and Trotskyite elements" and urged the CRC's executive director to support an even "larger and more expensive [CSO] enterprise" in the future.[129] (Bloom's anticommunism illustrates the Cold War realignment of civil rights coalitions. In the 1930s he had participated in popular front activities with activists like Carey McWilliams and the Filipino radical Carlos Bulosan, who by the Cold War were deemed too closely, and unacceptably, connected to communist activism.)[130] Jews did not always explicitly connect their interest in assisting other minority groups' civil rights struggles to the anticommunist climate, but their organizations' archival records reveal such a connection. The CRC filed a Jewish newsletter discussing Jews' interest in Mexican- and African-American struggles, for instance, in its "Committee on Communism" folder. An agency affiliated with the CRC published the newsletter, which explained to Jews why they should be concerned by the condition of Mexican Americans, who were forced into low-paying jobs, subjected to police brutality, "roundup for deportation without due process of law," and housing discrimination, and were "virtually without representation in government." In short, the newsletter urged, "It is in the interest of Jewish people to support the various Negro and Mexican-American candidates in the Los Angeles area."[131] While the newsletter's stated reasons for civil rights cooperation had nothing to do with communism, the CRC's choice to file the newsletter with "communism" issues belies the connection.

Other civil rights reformers who emphasized the importance of cooperation during this difficult time did not always articulate the connection to Cold War self-defense either. In 1949 California Federation for Civic Unity's director Richard Dettering urged more CFCU cooperation with the NAACP and other minority organizations: "Today our pressing need is to bring all organizations standing for religious and racial democracy into a stronger working relationship."[132] But these very words are a veiled reference to such organizations shoring up their strength through cooperation.

Joining forces decreased organizations' susceptibility to red-baiters. Ross reported that when some people attending an interracial activist meeting on youth issues voiced that the CSO's "pressure tactics" indicated it was too far left, Jewish community agency representatives rushed to the CSO's defense. The CSO's Jewish defenders fortified the agency, Ross wrote, by "promptly point[ing] out that such tacts [CSO tactics] rather than being a 'neighborhood liability' ... were definitely wholesome and indispensable."[133]

Fighting communism had the effect of bringing together anticommunist social justice groups in places around the country, not just in Los Angeles. A letter from John M. Mecartney of the Garrett Biblical Institute in Evanston, Illinois, to the NAACP's Roy Wilkins hints at how widespread this phenomenon may have been. Mecartney contacted Wilkins for support in his quest first to educate noncommunist groups about the communist influence, and then to bring together "social actionists who are not Communists but who are not aware of Communist front groups." The NAACP's anticommunism attracted Mecartney, who praised Wilkins and the NAACP "on the fine stand in excluding the pro-Communist elements from the Civil Rights mobilization which you sponsored."[134] Mecartney's inquiry indicates that civil rights activists in other parts of the country also hoped to fortify noncommunist civil rights groups by building coalitions among them. Though the extent of such interracial coalition building beyond Los Angeles cannot be fully explored here, civil rights activists who framed their activities as an all-American antidote to both radical and conservative extremes during the Cold War clearly looked to each other for support against red-baiting accusations.

STRENGTH IN NUMBERS, AND IN CAMOUFLAGE

In addition to fears of neighborhood violence and fortification against red-baiting, a third but related factor inspired Jewish, Mexican, and African Americans who collaborated through postwar interracial endeavors to find common ground. Each group found that because of the threats of violence, persecution, and red-baiting from mainstream society, they were not powerful enough on their own to achieve their civil rights goals.

Jewish activists who recognized that anti-Semites targeting their initiatives might easily derail them, for instance, strategically framed Cold War civil rights campaigns as collaborative efforts, and in universal terms, rather than as attempts originating in Jewish communities. They hoped to lend their efforts credibility, broaden their appeal, and help them succeed, since showcasing efforts' diverse collaboration, including white support and official city or county sponsorship, seemed likely to draw more widespread respect. In this way, pursuing civil rights in tandem with other minorities and willing whites and presenting them as an American concern served, in part, to mask civil rights efforts' ethnic and racial "specificity" and helped buffer them from public criticism. Such thinking inspired Jews' particularly heavy support for the CSO and other interracial initiatives in Los Angeles and elsewhere.[135]

Other minorities also recognized the importance of framing their efforts with universal appeal, and supporting institutions that camouflaged their activism. But none pursued this strategy more than Jews, whose status as an "in-between people" helps explain their particularly active role in interracial civil rights initiatives like the CSO. Jews found themselves between two poles of Los Angeles society. On the one hand, mainstream Americans increasingly accepted Jewish Americans, whose political and economic status gained them more access to avenues of power than African or Mexican Americans. The status of many CRC members who were judges or other prominent citizens like Mendel Silberberg and Isaac Pacht illustrates this access, as does many Jews' move toward the city's affluent Westside. Yet on the other hand, the anti-Semitism that marked the era also left them feeling uneasy. Many whites still considered Jews to be racially and culturally hated outsiders, and many Jews themselves persisted in thinking of themselves as an outsider minority group.[136] Jews' physical whiteness and ability to change their names to sound less Jewish if they wished—as many Jewish Americans did especially in the wake of the Holocaust—provided a cover, allowing them to conceal their activism by instigating interracial efforts.[137] As they moved between minority and white majority, L.A. Jews' in-between status placed them in a unique position to negotiate between the mainstream polity and minorities. They used their in-between status behind the scenes by serving in a way as civil rights brokers, as with the CSO.

Other groups sometimes recognized the utility of Jews' in-between status for their own goals. The L.A. NAACP's president Thomas Griffith, for instance, explained at a 1945 city council meeting that Jews could help blacks reach non-Jewish whites because "You Jewish people are white people and you are a bridge across which we can reach the other white people in the community."[138] Like their Mexican and Jewish counterparts who cooperated through the CSO, African Americans valued coalitional efforts partly because of their own relatively weak status. The West Coast

NAACP's field secretary Tarea Hall Pittman explained: "It is important that we carry to minority and majority groups our campaign [to fight restrictive covenants]." Pittman reported to the membership after the organization's 1948 West Coast conference, "There are a few things that can be done to carry out the democratic processes and if people of different races work in a membership campaign that would be a contribution they could make."[139] The NAACP's Franklin Williams and C. L. Dellums echoed six years later in a letter to the CRC's executive director Joe Roos, "As you know, a major effort has been put forth by the NAACP to strengthen our bonds of mutual concern and to develop greater cooperation and coordination among the labor unions, church groups, civic and fraternal organizations with which we either affiliate or associate." They then invited the CRC to send delegates to participate in the NAACP's next West Coast Conference, since they would "contribute immeasurably to these objectives."[140]

Jewish community organizations like the CRC pursued collaborative approaches instead of publicly opposing civil rights and civil liberties violations, committing to activism through a camouflaged path. Many shunned public activism *as Jews* and instead strategized about opposing injustice as invisibly as possible, through organizations like the CSO, the NAACP and others. "Jews should not be in the forefront of agitation for civil liberties," CRC members declared in 1951, because it was too dangerous.[141] CRC member I. B. Benjamin articulated this approach, too, when he wrote to the president of the local American Jewish Congress. Benjamin explained, "Even though we are unanimously agreed that the legislation [the anticommunist Mundt-Ferguson Bill] is most undesirable…I am not convinced of the wisdom of Jewish agencies assuming the primary responsibility and initiative in a matter of this character."[142] Instead of bringing attention to themselves through more specifically Jewish efforts, Benjamin recommended that local Jews express their opposition through local intergroup attempts. Downplaying Jews' involvement sometimes meant seeking non-Jewish organizations or individuals to serve as spokespeople on civil rights issues, as when a Beverly Hills high school principal contacted the American Jewish Committee in 1951 for help responding to a parent angry about a drama class singing a jingle about a "little nigger boy." The CRC's Roos argued that Jewish organizations would be prudent to "lessen potential friction for Jews by having other [non-Jewish] agencies intervene whenever possible," including the NAACP and the Los Angeles County Conference for Community Relations (LACCCR).[143]

Positioning activism as less Jewish-specific also often meant bringing multiple minority groups together under umbrella organizations that had official and/or white public support, which helps explain Jews' heavy involvement in such organizations and initiatives. Postwar Jews concentrated on building intergroup organizations, including the LACCCR, the L.A. County Committee on Human Relations, and others that would provide a cover for important items on their agenda. "We have created the County Conference on Community Relations," Isaac Pacht explained, in order "to have an outside organization serve in our behalf rather than to have a 'Jewish Society for the Prevention of Cruelty to Jews' do so consistently." Pacht's comment may have overestimated the Jewish community's influence on or involvement in the LACCCR, but it nevertheless revealed that Jews strongly promoted such intergroup initiatives which they hoped would advance their agendas by presenting a diverse, unified front. When Jews had to appear before the city council or some other agency to support or oppose a proposed ordinance, Pacht detailed, "we alert all member-organizations of the County Conference and thus we are not alone." Such efforts were also more effective "because of the weight of the memberships behind the 36 organizations affiliated with the Conference."[144] The CRC's executive director Fred Herzberg explained the CRC's support for the LACCCR in these terms too. This organization, which also drew substantial support from the Congregational Church, "will always be useful as the medium through which our interests can secure broad community support." The LACCCR also enabled Jews to "cooperate...in such constructive projects as other agencies may develop."[145] The CRC remained committed to the LACCCR's survival for reasons like these, and justified its financial support for the agency by explaining, "We can't afford to let the County Conference die, for we would immediately have to build a new one."[146]

Other interracial organizations and initiatives reflected disproportionate Jewish involvement too. By the late 1940s, Isaac Pacht, the past president of the Los Angeles Jewish Community Council, had become the president of the statewide California Federation for Civic Unity, and approximately a fourth of its directors were Jewish.[147] The Jewish community also at times heavily subsidized the Los Angeles Council for Civic Unity.[148] Together with the African-American labor leader and NAACP representative C. L. Dellums, Isaac Pacht cochaired the statewide California Fair Practices Committee, an interracial statewide organization that formed to fight employment discrimination and worked, in part, to enact a fair employment practices ordinance. Max Mont of the Southern California Jewish Labor Committee and Bill Becker of the San Francisco branch became the organization's two secretaries.[149] Much of these agencies' financial and other sustenance came from Jewish organizations. The LACCCR was, in fact, "one of the few agencies which we help support which is largely supported by non-Jewish groups," according to the CRC's executive director Herzberg.[150]

Collaborating with other groups was more than a way of hiding Jewish activism. Jewish community leaders also recognized that improving the status of other minority groups would also help Jews. In later years the CRC's postwar executive director Joe Roos reflected upon his organization's postwar policy of supporting organizations like the CSO, which he had encouraged by emphasizing that other peoples' problem was "our problem." Roos recalled his explanation that if Jews helped others yesterday, others would help them today. "I think we would have defeated ourselves," he continued, "if we would only have screamed for the poor Jews who were being discriminated against." Roos believed that fighting intolerance more generally, and making Americans judge individuals on a merit basis, would gradually eliminate prejudice against Jews.[151] Fred Herzberg, the CRC's executive director before Roos, articulated this same philosophy in 1948. He wrote in a letter to a CIO representative, "We [the organized Jewish community] realize that those things which are good for the greatest number of people would also be good for us."[152]

Helping Jews in the long run by helping Mexican Americans, African Americans, and others in the short run often meant supporting specific issues that did not directly relate to Jews, through the CSO and otherwise. The CRC "feels strongly that although the existing segregation in the State Militia does not discriminate against persons of the Jewish faith," Herzberg explained, "we are unalterably opposed to such discrimination among all those who have fought to preserve the faith and security of our country."[153] CRC leaders Joe Roos, Isaac Pacht, and Mendel Silberberg planned to explain to NAACP director Walter White when he visited Los Angeles and the CRC in 1953 that Jews collaborated because "complete success in the race relations and human relations fields can be achieved only if there is complete harmony and cooperation among all groups working in the field." They also planned to tell White that it had "always been the policy of the CRC to work in close cooperation with all race relations and human relations agencies excepting those whose motivations were not sincere [code for communists]." This collaborative policy, Roos elaborated, was based upon their conviction that discrimination and inequality against anyone was harmful to "us as Jews as well as American democracy in toto." CRC members wanted White to know that this conviction helped motivate their "constant cooperation" with the local NAACP, their assistance in creating the Los Angeles Council for Civic Unity and the County Conference on Community Relations, and their involvement in "the creation and financing of the CSO."[154]

Not surprisingly perhaps, Jews' decision to serve as civil rights brokers through organizations like the CSO was by no means a foregone conclusion, despite Jews' pervasive fear for their safety and status. Unlike more unambiguously racialized groups like African Americans, whose status generally left them no choice but to fight for more equality, Jews' ambiguous social, economic, and racial status between mainstream and minority confronted them with a dilemma. They wondered whether they should join forces with other minorities to address discrimination, or shun civil rights activism for fear that such collaboration would "lower" their status even further by association. Many postwar Jews did not agree with their community's ultimate decision to pursue collaboration with other minorities to fight common discrimination. "Some of my super-white Jews [were] not happy" with the policy the CRC adopted, the CRC's then-executive director Joe Roos later noted.[155] But other Jewish community members, and especially the influential ones whose opinions prevailed, agreed that Jews must develop a pro–civil rights policy and reject claiming whiteness, highlighting the danger that Jews still faced. They criticized other Jews who rejected their duty to fight discrimination and who refused to join forces with other oppressed peoples to save their own skin as "trying, in fact, to appear to society as 'white Jews'" and as contributing to the racial oppression that affected them too. These Jews should "never forget that the fate of our people is inseparably linked with that of all racial and religious minorities and with the future of progressive democracy," and they must uphold their responsibility to oppose injustice.[156] Coalition-minded Jews sometimes even protested when non-Jews classified them as "Anglo," as when Herzberg responded to the ACRR's report about L.A. Mexican Americans' conditions, which Fred Ross had written and the ACRR hoped to publish. Herzberg loved the report and thought it was spot-on, he wrote, but qualified his enthusiasm by saying that he wished Ross "could get a term other than 'Anglo.' Most of us [Jews] ain't Anglos."[157]

Jews were not the only Los Angeles minority group to find they occupied an in-between position that presented them with a choice about which civil rights avenue to pursue. Their in-betweenness also influenced Mexican Americans' decision to create and sustain organizations like the CSO, and the policies such organizations pursued. While Jews navigated between white and minority, Mexican Americans, particularly those with light skin, navigated between white and black. Mexican-American actors like Rita Hayworth and Anthony Quinn found success in Hollywood, attracting a wide following in the American public, by downplaying their Mexican heritage and embellishing their whiteness.[158] Societal power structures sometimes deemed Mexican-descent people white, as legal decisions and categories revealed. The decision rendered in California's 1946 *Mendez v. Westminster* case is one example. A U.S. district court judge ruled that segregating Mexican children was unconstitutional because they were "white," rather than because the principle of segregation itself was unconstitutional. Mexican Americans' census categorization as white throughout the twentieth century, except in 1930, also underscores their ambiguous status.[159]

This ambiguous status drove Mexican Americans to take different approaches. Some, like some Jews, sought to claim whiteness as a way to deflect discrimination and shunned cooperation with other minority groups. Such Mexican Americans distanced themselves, for instance, from African Americans for fear of lowering their status by association, as the American Council for Race Relations (ACRR) observed in its postwar report, *The Problem of Violence*. The ACRR reported that some of these Mexican Americans, who were especially likely to be middle class, "opposed cooperation with Negro groups, believing that the Mexican caste advantage would be compromised by any identification with Negroes."[160]

But other times Mexican Americans' attempts to claim whiteness, like some Jews' attempts, reflected an assertive claim to equality with other Americans more than a desire to separate from other more "tainted" groups, as certain CSO decisions reveal. This quest manifested itself particularly clearly through the CSO's struggle during the late 1940s to force the military to classify them as white rather than Mexican. CSO members supported the brother of CSO vice president Ralph Guzman when he walked off the Air Force's voluntary enlistment line after the recruiter refused to accept a claim by the Spanish-speaking man in front of Guzman that he was "white." The recruiter instead crossed out "white," which the man had marked as his racial category on the applications, and replaced it with "Mexican." This incident reveals that Mexican Americans often did not have a choice of how to identify, as dominant society ascribed them an identity regardless of their own self-perception. Southern California Air Force officials responded to protests by the CSO, which argued that Mexicans were white, by explaining that appropriate racial categories included "Negro, Mexican, Puerto Rican, Cuban, East Indian, Hawaiian, etc.," and that Mexicans needed to mark "Mexican."[161] The CSO emerged victorious in 1950, with the help of politicians Helen Gahagan Douglas and Chet Holifield. The secretary of defense conceded that the Army, Navy, and Air Force would begin using the racial categories of "Caucasian, Negroid, Mongolian, Indian (American), Malayan." Mexican, Puerto Rican, Cuban, and others were conspicuously absent from these new categories. The secretary of defense conceded, moreover, that selection would be left to the applicant.[162]

Actions like these show that postwar Mexican-American civil rights groups like the CSO argued that their community deserved rights not because they were Latin Americans or Mexican Americans.[163] Rather, they argued that they were part of an American population that deserved equality. But their claim to whiteness left intact the categories of blackness, "yellowness," and "redness," suggesting either that they did not always view their own quest for equality as part of a broader trans-minority struggle, or that they did not want to join the fight for other minorities if that might jeopardize their own.[164]

Mexican Americans, though, had a harder time blending in—when they wanted to—than Jews, despite these limited victories in their quest to gain acceptance, and generally faced more extreme discrimination. Socially, most Mexican Americans lived the experience of "otherness" despite their legal whiteness. This, combined with their less organized and less financially secure community structure, meant that they, like African Americans, could not claim the same role as "race brokers" that Jews could. It also meant that they, even more than Jews, relied upon external support from other communities to achieve their goals. Ultimately for both Jews and Mexican Americans their nebulous in-between status in Los Angeles society, somewhere between white and black, heightened both groups' commitment to building bridges across communities.

Recognizing Jews' previously obscured and disproportionate role in cooperative mid-century civil rights campaigns, particularly those with official city and county sponsorship, helps illustrate these campaigns' heavily pragmatic tendencies and complicates interpretations of growing racial liberalism in postwar American society. While many whites were becoming more racially liberal in this era, uncoupling Jewish and white activism unmasks the protective self-interest, alongside the universalism and humanitarianism, which also characterized postwar liberalism. The increasing interest in civil rights among government agencies and white communities, visible through mayor's committees, the board of supervisors, the CFCU, the Catholic Church, and others, did not merely reflect progressive whites' liberalized race thinking. Such institutions also served a utilitarian function for minority groups who hoped to downplay the racial specificity of their initiatives. The interracial and "official" agencies often created a cover for their activities, shielding them from public view to make them more effective. Racial liberalism in mid-century Los Angeles combined pragmatism and universalistic idealism, and much of it rested on a foundation of interracial collaboration. Moreover, racial liberalism had many incarnations, and racial liberals did not all share the same motivations, perspectives, and experiences. In places like Los Angeles, Cold War racial liberals—those who used anticommunism to advance racial equality—were Mexican-American, Jewish-American, African-American, as well as Anglo-American.[165]

TENSIONS SURFACE

Differing agendas and racial status meant that not all constituent groups were as enthusiastic about interracial initiatives, especially those with official city or county sponsorship, as members of the Jewish community were. Tensions frequently surfaced between the various coalition members. At times, Mexican Americans and African Americans expressed frustration that some cooperative official "intergroup relations" organizations' efforts lacked substance. In February 1952, the CSO *Reporter* critiqued one such effort initiated by President Truman and supported across the country by "intergroup relations committees." The *Reporter* stated that such efforts, like celebrations of "Brotherhood Month," which promoted understanding and tolerance about Americans' various cultures, were overly idealistic at the expense of recognition about the terrible conditions minorities faced. They also enabled "preaching brotherhood and living a lie" for whites who lived in restricted housing developments and supported discriminatory unions. Rather than celebrating "negro spirituals, Spanish dances, and kimonos," the CSO recommended attacking the second-rate conditions in minority communities.[166]

Franklin Williams, the NAACP's West Coast regional director, articulated similar criticisms during a speech before the LACCCR. While Williams knew and had "a deep regard for the personnel and executive membership of" the LACCCR, he also expressed the need for more action from such groups. Organizations like the JACL, NAACP, and CSO, along with the Southern California Jewish community that he saw as "aware and willing to wholeheartedly cooperate," had done much to advance equality in the Los Angeles area. But of the groups whose often sole "raison d'être is the improvement of inter-group relations," he said, the "appearance [was] deceiving…that our common goal" was being advanced. "A deep desire to raise community standards of human decency" stimulated the formation of groups like the CFCU and others, Williams acknowledged, but cautioned that they worked too much "for" disadvantaged people—specifically Mexican, Japanese, and African Americans—and not enough "with" them.[167]

To be fair, such groups did reach out—at least to some degree—to procure Mexican, Japanese, and African Americans' participation. A year earlier, LACCCR representatives had written to Williams and asked for his help securing greater NAACP cooperation. The LACCCR was unsure whether E. I. Robinson, the L.A. NAACP's president, had been unresponsive to their attempts from lack of interest or from overwork.[168] The CFCU's solicitation of CSO members to join its committee also indicated its attempts to take seriously minority organizations and their needs. But Williams's and the *Reporter*'s frustration reveals that collaboration was no easy exercise, and that non-Jewish minority communities at times would have liked to see more action from interracial agencies, even though they remained committed to working together through intergroup organizations.

Tensions also surfaced regularly among individual minority communities working together outside the sponsorship of official agencies. Conflict was as common as collaboration among Cold War activists, as the CSO's efforts to smooth neighborhood tensions between Mexicans and Jews illustrated. Despite Williams's praise for Jewish organizations' cooperative inclinations, African Americans complained that Jews did not take strong enough stands on the discrimination African Americans faced. Jewish organizations were unwilling to more strongly oppose restrictive covenants, blacks fumed. Further confirming such frustrations, the CRC decided in 1947 to "leave the matter up to the individual's choice" rather than take an official stance against restrictive covenants.[169] Although Los Angeles Jews did mobilize a coherent campaign against covenants not long afterward, the CRC's delay on this matter underscored African Americans' critique.[170]

Hollywood's role creating and projecting images of minorities became another source of black/Jewish tension. African Americans criticized Hollywood's lack of commitment to advancing racial equality and its continued reliance upon using African-American stereotypes. They hoped Jewish organizations would use their influence in Hollywood to pressure filmmakers to more aggressively eliminate these stereotypes. But in 1951, the CRC protested what it characterized as unfair criticism of certain Jewish filmmakers including Dore Schary, the head of MGM as well as a prominent CRC member, in the black newspaper the *California Eagle*. The CRC explained how much Schary had done to promote a fairer image of blacks and to advance better race relations, and called the *Eagle*'s characterizations of his films undeserved. Schary "has done more…than any other motion picture person to make people conscious of the dignity of each human being irrespective of race or creed," Roos countered. "It's another instance of 'kicking our friends.'"[171]

The CRC similarly defended Bill Gordon, a Universal Studio producer and CRC member—as well as a member of the CSO subcommittee— from the *Eagle*'s criticism. *Eagle* writers objected that Gordon planned to make the film *Red Ball Express* without adequately portraying "the valiant role the Negro soldier had in the success" of this massive World War II operation against the German army in France in 1944. The *Eagle* wanted the film to give more coverage to the critical role of the truck drivers who were heavily African American, due to the military's relegation of segregated African Americans to largely noncombat duties. Although the film starred Sidney Poitier as Corporal Andrew Robinson, one of the drivers who expressed resentment at his second-class status, African Americans criticized that it downplayed their role, and that it focused too much on interracial cooperation rather than the extensive segregation. The CRC's Roos defended Gordon by explaining that he had worked hard to help further African Americans' status. Gordon had, for example, secured Hollywood's participation in the NAACP's 1952 Shrine Auditorium protest rally against the race bombings in Florida, including persuading one of the film's white stars, Jeff Chandler, to make an appearance.[172] But African Americans remained frustrated with the film.

For their part, Jews sometimes believed that African Americans were unjustifiably hostile to their race relations efforts. Roos, Silberberg, and Pacht even discussed the possibility that the NAACP's West Coast branch head, Franklin Williams, might be anti-Semitic, which they suspected because he was "a nationalist," and "some of the nationalists are anti-Semitic."[173] These Jewish community leaders explained away African-American hostility in terms they could understand, given what they perceived as their own well-meaning efforts to help African Americans. "The local [NAACP] professionals are jealous of the success the Jewish organizations have achieved in the race relations field," Roos wrote to Pacht and Silberberg. "They are sniping at the Jewish defense agencies and are trying to undermine the County Conference on Community Relations."[174] Roos's comments underscored the tensions among frequent allies, and also show that such civil rights activism was less collaborative than it might appear, or as Jewish activists may have hoped.

Such tensions often concerned the types of approaches the various ethnic and racial communities were willing to pursue and the distances they were willing to go. Roos miscalculated African-American frustration, which more likely stemmed from dissatisfaction at Jewish agencies' limits concerning how far they were willing to stick their necks out for others, or even for themselves, than from what Roos labeled jealousy. Fred Schreiber, the director of the Los Angeles American Jewish Committee (AJC), exposed the limits of the Jewish community when he discussed the AJC's and the NAACP's mutual support for creating a California Fair Employment Practices Commission. The American Jewish Committee, Schreiber explained to the NAACP's Tarea Hall Pittman, would support the pending Hawkins Bill, but it would do so only through educational campaigns rather than through the picketing or other forms of "mass pressure" that the NAACP proposed.[175]

This difference of opinion over acceptable protest strategies exposes another divergence among constituent members of interracial efforts. Jewish groups were often less willing to pursue confrontational tactics than African Americans or Mexican Americans were. Still, even African Americans active in the NAACP and Mexican Americans in the CSO came under fire from other black, Mexicano, and white activists who viewed their approach as temperate. For instance, the NAACP pursued strategies that frustrated other activists who sought even more direct confrontation with members of the white establishment.[176]

To some degree, these differences reflected class issues. Organizations like the NAACP and the CRC heavily represented a middle-class community that did not necessarily pursue equality in the same ways as working-class community members. In one example, the Civil Rights Congress was willing to use more extreme tactics in the pursuit of equality than the NAACP, for instance, defending strikers at U.S. Motors in 1946 when they were beaten and arrested while the NAACP would not.[177] But class cannot completely explain such disagreements over tactics, as the CSO's heavily working class membership generally did not pursue more confrontational tactics than the CRC and NAACP.[178]

Despite these ongoing conflicts, Asian, Mexican, and African Americans involved in organizations like the JACL, CSO, and NAACP supported cooperative endeavors like fair employment and fair housing, as well as interracial organizations like the LACCCR. Representatives from their communities served as executive directors, executive secretaries, members of boards of directors, and in other capacities. The JACL's Tats Kushida cochaired an LACCCR committee and African American George Thomas was its executive secretary, while the JACL's Saburo Kido was Secretary of the CFCU and the NAACP's Miller sat on its board of directors. Such organizations strengthened individual minority groups' activism by lending them numeric strength and legitimacy for various endeavors.

The contact among the groups also strengthened the various communities' institutions. For instance, other groups sometimes patterned their civil rights organizations and activities on Jewish models, which they viewed as successful. The NAACP recommended at its 1948 West Coast regional conference that its member organizations follow in the footsteps of Jewish organizations, which secured large union contributions for their activities. If they followed this path and made "the proper approach and sell their program to the unions," they similarly could secure both money and members.[179] The Japanese American Citizens' League also sought Jewish advice and assistance. Tats Kushida asked the CRC's director Joe Roos in 1951 for his advice about the organization's public relations brochure and in return offered JACL assistance "if there is any way in which we, too, can be of service to you."[180] Kushida explained the influence of the Jewish community's organizational structure on Japanese groups in a letter to Roos three years later, explicitly citing its model of B'nai B'rith.[181] The JACL also developed an antidiscrimination committee it called the ADC, for which it drew on the Jewish community's Anti-Discrimination League (ADL) as a model.[182]

Despite common and significant tensions, the cooperation that formed the CSO and motivated ongoing collaboration among other moderately positioned interracial reformers was a hallmark of early Cold War Los Angeles. Such collaboration signaled an ongoing strategy for minority groups struggling to effect change.

ASSESSING CONTINUITY

The CSO and other collaborative anticommunist Cold War civil rights organizations clearly drew on past alliances, but they also departed from their predecessors and from their more radically situated contemporaries in certain ways. Anticommunism led postwar groups such as the CSO, the NAACP, and the CRC to shift course on certain issues, namely over the acceptability of forming alliances across the political left and critiquing U.S. foreign policy. Such coalitional fissures in the Mexican-American community, as in the African-American, Jewish-American, and labor communities, were serious and caused much bad blood. But on issues of domestic racial equality, Cold War activists often split from the past more over appearances than agendas: much of the CSO's agenda on civil rights carried Popular Front and World War II era activism into the Cold War.

The CSO's deviation from some other Mexican Americans over political campaigns like Henry Wallace's 1948 Progressive Party ticket presidential run exposes how postwar civil rights "liberals" and "radicals" disagreed more over anticommunism than equality agendas. The CSO did not support Wallace, while many Mexicanos joined his campaign. The ANMA, the other main postwar Mexicano civil rights group in Los Angeles, backed Wallace, and over 10,000 Mexicanos attended his May 1948 rally.[183] Among Wallace's supporters were two participants in cross-left alliances during the 1930s and World War II eras. Josefina Fierro de Bright helped organize the Independent Progressive Party and Wallace's Southern California campaigns before she went into Cold War exile, and Bert Corona campaigned for him in Northern California.[184] The United Mine, Mill, and Smelter Workers union organized Wallace supporters in many of the major mining and smelting regions of the Southwest, namely in New Mexico, Arizona, and parts of Texas, which were almost exclusively Mexican-origin. The union and other southwestern people of Mexican origin formed the Amigos de Wallace to support the third-party presidential candidate.[185]

On domestic equality issues, Wallace represented the positions of the CSO and its allied organizations such as the NAACP and CRC better than Democratic candidate Harry Truman. Wallace campaigned for racial equality more actively than his counterparts and identified with many of the same civil rights goals as the CSO. Fear of losing the support of the white Democratic South made Truman reluctant to advocate ending segregation and to support other racial equality agenda items. Wallace, however, spoke boldly about integrated housing and education, full voting rights for blacks, and universal health insurance. He also endorsed the FEPC. Moreover, when Wallace toured the South he refused to appear before segregated audiences or to eat or stay in segregated establishments.[186] His Southern campaign appearances before integrated audiences generated so much opposition that he was pelted with eggs and tomatoes when he spoke in North Carolina.[187] Wallace had better positions on combating racism, and Mexican Americans like Corona believed that his Progressive Party was the only one to speak out against racism, for integrated housing, and for better education.[188]

But concern over Wallace's cooperation with communists and fellow travelers in large part prevented the CSO and its supporting organizations from embracing his campaign.[189] The CSO eschewed overtures from the Progressive Party, in part because its tax-exempt status depended on not explicitly supporting any political candidate or party. CSO leaders also feared, though, that associating with a campaign visibly supported by communists and other "tainted" groups would undermine their Cold War credibility. Ross wrote to Alinsky in 1947 that the CSO resisted attempts by members of the Boyle Heights Progressive Citizens of America (PCA) to persuade the CSO and Roybal to take a stand on "labeled issues such as Wallace, the Third Party, etc." CSO officials tried to dissuade Wallace's advocates in part, Ross reported, by asking Carey McWilliams (the year before the CSO sidelined him too) to arrange a meeting with PCA officials. At these meetings Roybal and Ross explained to PCA officials that supporting their organization would endanger the CSO.[190] Still, the Eastside PCA continued to press the CSO for support. PCA members were "pretty resentful because CSO has not come out for the third party (or any other, of course) and attempt to belittle the organization's accomplishment and in 2 housing projects have tried to turn some of our members against CSO," Ross explained to Alinsky.[191]

In contrast, Mexican-American organizations like the ANMA supported the Progressive Party in 1948 both for its domestic civil rights platform and for Wallace's willingness to work with communists for common goals abroad and at home. Mexican-American members of the ANMA, which criticized the Korean War along with U.S. policy in Latin America, supported Wallace in no small part because he backed the peace movement and opposed the Marshall Plan.[192] Wallace's reluctance to marginalize the Soviet Union globally and to red-bait domestically drew a good deal of his support from the general population as well.[193]

This Wallace episode, together with the CSO's decision to marginalize McWilliams and embrace anticommunism as a civil rights tool, indicates that the ANMA rather than the CSO inherited El Congreso's international legacy and its tradition of Popular Front–style cooperation. The CSO's rise instead encapsulates the shift from cooperation across the left of the political spectrum to an emphasis upon mainstream legitimacy. Its unwillingness to critique the international policies of the United States and its allies, furthermore, reflects a departure from former organizations' international legacy.

In terms of domestic civil rights agendas, however, the CSO picked up where El Congreso, the SLDC, and earlier organizations that mobilized diverse Los Angeles residents to fight discrimination left off. CSO activists continued to work for many of the same domestic civil rights goals their predecessors had pursued. Both El Congreso and the CSO made voter registration a top priority. Both incorporated women into leadership positions, as officers and organizers as well as door-to-door voter registrars. The CSO's membership, furthermore, was half female, which was an even higher percentage than El Congreso could boast.[194] Like El Congreso, other CSO goals included improving health conditions for east side residents. The CSO focused on tuberculosis, providing free chest X-rays for thousands of residents. It also immunized school children against diphtheria.[195] Among other health initiatives, it opposed the privatization of ambulances. The CSO's victories against police brutality and discrimination in the Bloody Christmas and Hidalgo cases show continuities with El Congreso's protests against the police and military's role in the Zoot Suit Riots and the Sleepy Lagoon case. The CSO fought for other goals shared by the earlier organization, including job equality, integrating public venues, neighborhood improvement, and fighting housing discrimination.[196]

Figure 13: CSO Pledge of Allegiance, Citizenship Class, undated (late 1940s/early 1950s), Folder 3, Box 32, Fred Ross Papers, 1910–1992. Courtesy of Department of Special Collections and University Archives, Stanford University Libraries.

Also like El Congreso, the CSO worked with both immigrants and citizens. It taught citizenship classes to immigrants, helped them register to vote, and worked with the INS in order to increase the speed of citizenship processing. The CSO protested when the INS attempted to close regional offices, for fear it would jeopardize the immigrants' ability to gain citizenship.[197] This commitment to immigrant rights emerged partly from some of its members' World War II CIO union organizing experience, when Ríos, Anaya, and others fought for resident aliens' right to work in defense industries.[198] The CSO's work to secure old-age pensions that were not contingent upon citizenship continued another El Congreso tradition and resulted in a victory in 1961 when Governor "Pat" Brown signed this into law.[199] CSO collaborators like the NAACP also publicly committed themselves to some of the same measures Popular Front–era organizations like Congreso had supported. In a 1948 radio broadcast of the West Coast Regional convention in Los Angeles, NAACP officials expressed their support for minimum wages, social security increases, and national health insurance.[200]

African-American and Jewish-American community differences also concerned anticommunism more than specific civil rights disagreements. African-American leftists' criticisms of the NAACP indicate the focus on anticommunism rather than specific agendas. In a newspaper article titled "Anti-Communism Proves Poor Shield for NAACP," Abner Berry, an editor of the Communist newspaper the *Daily Worker* and an organizer for the CP in Harlem, argued that the NAACP made a "fundamental error of policy" and would be haunted by its failure to help preserve freedoms for communists.[201] The Jewish community's turmoil, too, stemmed more from Cold War organizations' commitment to anticommunism than from disagreements over domestic civil rights. In their discussion about expelling the JPFO, the CRC and other Jewish community members focused on the danger of maintaining ties with the group because of its communist affiliations. Similarly, criticism from the JPFO and from other groups angry with the Jewish community's policies focused on its domestic and international anticommunism and what they called its "hush hush" policy of stifling political dissent. Philip Connelly, a prominent "radical" formerly associated with the Los Angeles CIO, accused the Jewish community of trying to "establish beyond question that they are not Communist or Communist influenced."[202] CSO discussions of the PCA as a "labeled" organization, the domestic and international anticommunism that undergirded the CSO's reluctance to support Wallace and the ANMA's embrace of his candidacy, and Berry's argument, juxtaposed with Connelly's statement also reveal how divergence between civil rights "liberals" and "radicals" stemmed primarily from anticommunism, rather than domestic civil rights policy disagreements.

The difference between radicals and liberals has seemed greater in part because Cold Warrior reformers worked hard to protect themselves by emphasizing their differences from their "radical" counterparts, including using words like *liberal* and *radical*. And activists who hoped to collaborate across left-leaning political boundaries and who were critical of Cold War anticommunism used these words to criticize "liberals" for abandoning this approach. But scratching the surface of these disagreements reveals underlying similarities and shows that the terms are not useful for distinguishing between groups in terms of their domestic civil rights reform goals. The CSO and its allies, for instance, tried to distinguish their efforts from their "radical" counterparts by downplaying interracial collaboration and interracial unity, despite their interracial work. Local Cold War activists shifted to using language less threatening in the anticommunist climate, which meant framing initiatives in universal terms to garner more support. This new approach also keenly highlighted the concrete community and neighborhood improvements that would accompany cooperative civil rights efforts. Strategic activists framed their struggles for building better neighborhoods, better communities, and

Figure 14: John Carmona and Fred Ross Inspect Chávez Ravine for the CSO, ca. 1951, Los Angeles Daily News Collection, Department of Special Collections, Charles E. Young Research Library, UCLA.

stronger families as steps toward creating a better America and a happier and more democratic citizenry, rather than emphasizing race.

The CSO's main goals—community improvement and increasing residents' participation in American democracy through concrete strategies like voter registration—underscore this shift in emphasis.[203] Articles in Los Angeles newspapers with titles like "CSO Launches Slum Betterment Fund Drive for 1951" and "'Help Your Neighbor' Fund Will Be of Wide Benefits" were typical.[204] One CSO pamphlet from 1955 proclaimed that the organization's "New England town hall democracy" helped "integrate the Spanish-speaking people into our overall community life."[205] The Fresno County CSO billed itself as a "civic-educational group" that represented "the interests of the Spanish-speaking people...[and] is designed to assist them in bringing about appropriate improvements in their neighborhoods and full participation in all phases of community life."[206]

The new emphasis attracted pragmatic allies. Monsignor O'Grady urged the bishop of San Diego to support this worthy organization by

Figure 15: CSO Efforts Result in Eastside Sidewalks, undated (late 1940s/early 1950s), Folder 3, Box 32, Fred Ross Papers, 1910–1992. Courtesy of Department of Special Collections and University Archives, Stanford University Libraries.

granting Fred Ross an audience to discuss extending the CSO into the Imperial Valley east of San Diego. O'Grady based the CSO's worthiness on its "neighborhood" emphasis and its attempts to encourage Catholicism and Americanism. "What has impressed me about the entire program of the Foundation is the emphasis on neighborhood self-help," O'Grady wrote. "While the Industrial Areas Foundation is trying to develop Mexicans as part of a program for the American community, I believe that their workers are very sensitive to their religious traditions. From a practical angle it is the best approach that I have seen for the development of real Catholic leadership among Mexicans in our country."[207] Jewish supporters of the CSO used the new language to defend the organization at a youth issues meeting. By arguing that CSO tactics were "wholesome" and "indispensable," these CSO supporters emphasized that such civil rights activism was crucial for protection against communism in the Cold War era.[208]

Some groups decided to change their names to reflect this shift. In 1946, the L.A. County Committee for Inter-Racial Progress (previously the County Committee for Church and Community Co-Operation) became the well-known and still-functioning Los Angeles County Committee on Human Relations (LACCHR). While terms like "inter-racial progress" might sound dangerously close to communism, "human relations" seemed safer to Cold War Americans. Cold War pragmatists created a space that allowed for civil rights to survive in an environment that threatened to halt all social justice activism.

Another difference from their "radical" counterparts that anticommunists emphasized was that they worked *within* what they viewed to be the American political system. The NAACP made sure it sounded like a decidedly nonradical organization, as Roy Wilkins's description of his organization's policy indicates. Wilkins articulated in a memo to nationwide NAACP branches that the organization's anticommunist policy was rooted in "the Association's consistent policy of working within the American constitutional system in pursuit of its goal—an America of justice, equality, freedom and security for every citizen regardless of race, color, religious faith or national origin."[209] Wilkins's statement implies a difference from "radicals," who challenge the American constitutional system, but does not elaborate on what this meant. It also suggests that the NAACP's "moderation," or anticommunism, stemmed from a definition of the alliances it rejected. The CSO described itself in similar terms. Its stated goals—expanding Mexican-American and east side civic participation within the established sociopolitical system—were palatable to a worried populace. Bert Corona described the organization as attempting to "correct malformations in the system, not to demand a change in the system itself," often focusing on relatively uncontroversial issues like education and social services.[210]

The CSO's reformist rather than revolutionary focus reflects a certain consistency across time within the ethnic Mexican and collaborative civil rights community, as comparing the CSO with its predecessor El Congreso makes clear. The earlier Popular Front–era organization had also been a reform-oriented agency, even though its tactics were often more militant than the CSO's. For example, the CSO never organized immigration protest marches down Broadway or called for workers to strike as El Congreso did. Shying away from high-profile or confrontational stances, the CSO instead pursued legislative approaches, working quietly behind the scenes to mobilize voters and build support for new policies. Still, as historian Mario García explains in his examination of El Congreso and other Popular Front–era organizations, the Mexican-American Left that emerged out of the 1930s "was one centered on reform not revolution" and "the achievement of the mythical American dream."[211] According to historian George Sánchez, Congreso was "anxious to fight for American democracy" and viewed the United States as a place "where social activism had the potential for creating equality," and during the 1930s and 1940s its variety of political and labor activity was "the greatest 'Americanizing agent'" for the Mexican-origin population.[212] This comparison between the CSO and El Congreso indicates that while anticommunist rhetoric became a new method for establishing an acceptable, reformist reputation, the CSO's larger reformist outlook itself was less new than it might appear.

Moreover, anticommunist civil rights advocates' disagreement with "radicals" was less substantive than it seemed. Anticommunists misunderstood L.A. communism, believing it adhered to the Soviet line more closely than it did. But American Communists viewed their party as a means to gain social equality rather than to violently overthrow the current government. Since the mid-1930s, when it supported New Deal policies, the American Communist Party emphasized that it too worked within the American system. Evidence from leaders like Dorothy Healey active in the 1940s and 1950s suggests that the L.A. party's policies and agendas were even more distant from Moscow headquarters than other American CP offices, including the party's national headquarters in New York.[213]

CONCLUSION

The story of the CSO's creation and its early years indicates that anticommunism did not stifle civil rights activism as has often been assumed. In some ways, the Cold War even facilitated ongoing interracial collaboration among certain civil rights reformers. The agendas of these interracial civil rights activists substantially resembled the goals of earlier reformers, who were often the same people.

But the Cold War did force a shift in civil rights rhetoric, tactics, coalitions, and international stances as activists who hoped to survive in the new, harsh political climate regrouped and realigned. Local activists like those forming the CSO subjugated their racial emphasis to "safer," less debatable issues of citizenry and democracy and couched their participation in broader coalitional support. Anticommunism also led them to shy away from former allies deemed too radical, and from expressing international solidarity, especially if it seemed to undermine U.S. foreign policy. Cold War activists who gave in to the prevailing postwar "vital center" did step back from radical language, marginalize "radicals" (communists in particular), and become complicit with anticommunist U.S. foreign policy and frequent civil liberties violations. But in terms of their domestic civil rights goals, their visions resembled the past in significant ways.

Moreover, this interracial version of civil rights activism incubated in Los Angeles from the 1930s through the Cold War reached beyond the city and state. Strategies, alliances, and policies developed among diverse Los Angeles populations shaped national civil rights transformations, ethnic community movements, and politics in the 1940s, 1950s, and beyond, as the next chapter will explore.

CHAPTER 6

Los Angeles to the Nation

Los Angeles's diverse racial and ethnic populations incubated an inter-racial civil rights agenda that influenced civil rights activists nation-wide in ways that remain largely unrecognized. Sara Boynoff's 1957 article in *Look* magazine hints at the city's model for cooperative activism. She remarked that "this American city...is showing the country what people of different races can do to live side by side in harmony," suggesting to readers that they might benefit from following Angelenos' lead.[1] Davis McIntyre of the Chicago-based American Council of Race Relations (ACRR) explained the national significance of Los Angeles's 1945 Institute on Community Relations. Over 500 Los Angeles County public employees from fifty-one departments attended this mandatory race relations training program cosponsored by the local Committee for Inter-racial Progress and the national ACRR. The institute set "an important precedent," McIntyre explained, because it represented the first effort by any local government in the United States to "consciously set about educating its employees for an understanding of intergroup problems."[2] The committee's executive director George Gleason also explained that the institute's organizers hoped their cooperative work would become "a precedent for other sections of the country."[3] Indeed it did, as activists in places like Phoenix modeled their cooperative efforts on Los Angeles organizations like the Council for Civic Unity.[4]

But even beyond serving as a model for interracial cooperation else-where, Los Angeles served as an incubator and training ground for activists who later passed civil rights initiatives at the national level and who shaped emerging ethnic-specific reform movements. Campaigns during the 1940s and 1950s against housing discrimination and school segrega-tion are two examples of Los Angeles–area initiatives with national influence. Loren Miller's Los Angeles activism, which was rooted both in local interracial civil rights efforts and in the African-American community, launched him in the decade after World War II to argue before the Supreme Court against restrictive housing covenants and to assist the national campaign against school segregation. *Mendez v. Westminster*

(1946), a California Supreme Court case against school segregation brought to court by Mexican-American families and supported by inter-racial activists, became a training ground for national civil rights reformers. Among the California figures who served on a national level, perhaps the most influential was Earl Warren, whose experience with California civil rights activists while serving as governor shaped his tenure as chief justice of the U.S. Supreme Court. The work of interracial reformers in places like Los Angeles culminated in the Supreme Court decisions against school segregation in *Brown v. Board of Education* and against housing restrictions in *Shelley v. Kraemer* and *Barrows v. Jackson*. It also helped foster various ethnic-specific efforts of the 1960s, and the election or appointment of individuals who influenced local, state, and national policy in later decades.

RESTRICTIVE HOUSING COVENANTS: LOS ANGELES GOES NATIONAL

Rampant housing shortages and the intensity of overcrowding in Los Angeles, whose conditions were the worst in the West, generated wide-spread protest and motivated Los Angeles African Americans like Loren Miller to lead the national campaign to eliminate restrictive covenants.[5] The Los Angeles NAACP alone filed more suits against restrictive cove-nants between 1945 and 1948—the latter being the year of *Shelley v. Kraemer*, the Supreme Court decision that ruled that restrictive cove-nants were unenforceable—than were filed in any other part of the country.[6]

A letter from Los Angeles NAACP president Thomas Griffith to the national NAACP office in 1945 indicates Los Angelenos' lead in advocacy. Griffith alerted national NAACP officials about protests among white Compton residents, the Compton Chamber of Commerce, and the Compton City Council after local housing authorities announced plans to build 1,200 private housing units for minority groups in their area. The L.A. NAACP urged local, regional, and national housing authorities to challenge these "discriminatory attitudes" by going forward with the plans, Griffith reported. The branch appointed a special subcommittee, which included Miller among other local members, to pursue this agenda. And Griffith urged the national NAACP to press the Federal Housing Authority to oppose restrictive covenants.[7]

In a 1946 case, Miller defended white homeowners in L.A.'s Sugar Hill neighborhood against a lawsuit the West Adams Heights Improvement Association filed in California Superior Court. The lawsuit accused the white homeowners of violating racially restrictive covenants by selling their houses to blacks. Miller's dynamic defense helped score a victory against the covenants. This became one of many cases that helped persuade the U.S. Supreme Court to review the earlier decision that upheld racial restrictive covenants as judicially enforceable. Soon after the Superior Court agreed to review these cases, Miller traveled to Michigan to defend a black couple whose defense against a neighborhood association's accusations that their home purchase violated restrictive covenants became one of three cases that collectively became *Shelley v. Kraemer* (the other two were in D.C. and Missouri).[8] Three years later, such efforts resulted in victory when the Supreme Court ruled in *Shelley v. Kraemer* that restrictive covenants were unenforceable.[9]

Los Angeles NAACP members like Miller continued to fight after the inadequacy of the *Shelley v. Kraemer* decision became clear. Whites continued to evade the restraints the court had placed on them. Groups like the Los Angeles Realty Board and the California Real Estate Association even proposed a constitutional amendment to restore the old order. Many whites filed damage suits against other whites who violated their original commitment to restrictive covenants by later selling to African Americans and some state and local courts upheld such suits.[10] Miller and other Los Angeles NAACP members led teams lobbying the Supreme Court to close these last loopholes in restrictive covenant legislation. Miller helped Thurgood Marshall defend a white woman named Leola Jackson who lived in a neighborhood with a covenant and sold to a black family anyway. Ms. Jackson's neighbor Olive Barrows sued her for breaking the neighborhood covenant. Marshall and Miller hoped the Court would make such damage suits illegal, which it did with the 1953 *Barrows v. Jackson* decision. The closing of this last loophole in restrictive covenant legislation represented the culmination of a decades-long struggle among African Americans in Los Angeles and nationwide.[11]

Despite the importance of such legal victories, they did not ensure equality. The geographic boundaries of neighborhoods where blacks lived remained largely the same after the war, and most African Americans lived in increasingly concentrated black neighborhoods.[12] Nevertheless, they did represent an important breakthrough by delegitimating aspects of segregation's legal basis. Stanley Mosk, the CRC member who became California attorney general (in 1958) and whom Governor "Pat" Brown later appointed California Supreme Court justice (in 1964), commended Loren Miller, whose "courageous perseverance over the years has resulted in the recent United States Supreme Court decision against judicial enforcement of race restrictive covenants, and who, more than any other single person, is responsible for this milestone on the path toward true democracy and greater understanding among all people."[13] Even Dorothy Healey, a prominent civil rights contemporary of Miller's and a L.A. Communist Party leader who came from a different political perspective from Mosk, and from Miller in these years, went so far as to claim, "If anyone made the law in the United States as far as the fight against discrimination, it was Loren, who both initiated the cases and the research and the pleading before the courts, as well as participated in the mass movement for some forty years here."[14] Though such statements may have exaggerated Miller's importance, they nonetheless underscored the crucial influence of West Coast actors rooted in collaborative World War II and Cold War work in bringing about national change.

This spotlight on Miller also reinforces how his shift in the postwar era, when Miller worked to distance himself from the pro-communist past that threatened his Cold War efficacy and to establish his reputation as an acceptable civil rights leader, paved the way for him to argue before the Supreme Court. Moreover, Miller's continuing activism reveals the ongoing thrust of reform agendas between the 1930s and 1950s—and even 1960s, when Miller became a member of the California Advisory Committee to the U.S. Commission on Civil Rights and a member of the Civil Rights Committee of the State Bar.[15]

MEXICAN AMERICANS, INTERRACIAL ACTIVISM, *MENDEZ V. WESTMINSTER*, AND *BROWN V. BOARD OF EDUCATION*

During a 1955 appearance at the CSO, the NAACP's Lester Bailey observed that unlike in the South, African Americans in California had multiracial support. Bailey also asserted that CSO efforts to eliminate inequality for all people "regardless of race, color, creed or national origin" had been part of a larger movement culminating in the national desegregation victory in *Brown v. the Board of Education*. "It has been through the combined efforts of these types of organizations that have made this history-making decision possible," Bailey emphasized.[16] Mexican Americans' struggles, though, helped contribute to the outcome in *Brown v. the Board of Education* in an even more concrete way.

In 1946 Gonzalo and Felicitas Méndez initiated a lawsuit after Westminster Elementary School in Orange County, California, denied admission to their children, Sylvia, Gerónimo, and Gonzalo Jr., because of their dark skin and Spanish surname. Four other Mexican-American fathers joined Gonzalo in filing suit against four school districts in the area on behalf of children of "Mexican and Latin descent." While California schools were not segregated as entirely or as clearly as southern schools, they were segregated in ways unique to California's multiracial environment, targeting Japanese, Chinese, and Mexican children to different degrees.[17] Mexican-American groups supported the legal efforts in the *Mendez v. Westminster* case, including the Coordinating Council for Latin-American Youth, led by longtime activist attorney Manuel

Ruíz. A judge ruled in favor of the plaintiffs, and a federal court of appeals held that segregating Mexican Americans violated California's Constitution. The appeals court affirmed that California law, which permitted the segregation of people of Asian descent (Chinese, Japanese, and "Mongolian"), forbade the segregation of Mexican Americans. Unlike *Brown*, this decision did not rule against segregation per se. It sidestepped the issue of race by ruling that the California Constitution prohibited the segregation of Mexican-origin children, not any racial group.[18]

Mendez was unlike earlier desegregation cases because it was filed in federal court rather than in state or local courts. Because of this, supporters hoped that it might become the test case to overrule *Plessy v. Ferguson*, the 1896 Supreme Court case that had established the legal precedent for "separate but equal" facilities. They hoped the school districts would appeal the decision to the Supreme Court, which might then rule against the constitutionality of segregation itself and not just whether the California constitution allowed for Mexican Americans' segregation. But because the process stopped at the federal appeals court, *Mendez* did not become the high court's test case for segregation.[19] But the decision set an important precedent for similar cases involving Mexican Americans elsewhere, particularly Arizona and Texas, and shaped legal and political understandings of segregation in California and nationwide.[20]

While Mexican-American initiative lay at the heart of the case, interracial cooperation was crucial to its success. A Jewish-American civil rights attorney from Los Angeles, David C. Marcus, represented the plaintiffs.[21] Fred Ross, at the time a field-worker for the American Council of Race Relations, joined representatives from the League of United Latin American Citizens (LULAC) and other Mexican Americans in late 1946 to protest the Santa Ana Board of Education's failure to comply with Judge McCormick's initial ruling against segregation. The board insisted that the decision was unenforceable due to its pending appeal. Ross informed the board that "he had instructed the Mexican children to go to the school of their choice on the opening day of school and if they were not admitted, the Board of Education would be cited for contempt."[22]

But even more significant than Marcus's and Ross's involvement is the support *Mendez* received from the multiracial organizations that filed supporting *amici curiae* briefs when the school board appealed the initial decision. *Mendez* attracted national attention from many groups who hoped that a challenge to California's Ninth Circuit Court of Appeals' decision would bring the case to the Supreme Court. Organizations and individuals who supported the plaintiffs by articulating various antidiscrimination arguments included the ACLU, National Lawyers Guild, and California Attorney General Robert Kenny. The American Jewish Congress, the NAACP, and the JACL also became vocal advocates. Homegrown activist Carey McWilliams wrote on behalf of the American Jewish Congress, together with representatives Will Maslow, a Jewish-American attorney who was the organization's general counsel and the director of its Commission on Law and Social Action, and Pauli Murray, a prominent female African-American attorney and racial and gender equality activist, from the organization's national office. The American Jewish Congress also worked to fire up nationwide interest in the case. It financed the distribution of reprints of McWilliams's article about it in the *Nation*. Saburo Kido, a Japanese-American activist from the local JACL and one of the national organization's founders, and the local lawyer and ACLU representative A. L. Wirin cowrote the ACLU's brief. Loren Miller coauthored the NAACP's amicus curia brief with national NAACP representatives Robert Carter and Thurgood Marshall. Different *amici* briefs emphasized various antidiscrimination arguments, but as a whole they argued that separate was not equal and that the court should overrule *Plessy*.[23]

The American Jewish Congress, NAACP, and others honed their strategies in *Mendez* and seven years later argued on behalf of the *Brown* plaintiffs. Individuals who argued both cases included Carter and Marshall, who became two of the most prominent attorneys in the *Brown* case. Loren Miller, too, assisted in filing the amicus curiae briefs in the *Brown* case, as did the JACL's Saburo Kido and the American Jewish Congress's Will Maslow.[24] Evidence suggests that even *Brown* lawyers who had not been involved in *Mendez* relied upon tactics developed in the earlier California case to advance their national case. *Mendez* was the first federal court decision and the first use of the Fourteenth Amendment to overturn the widespread segregation of a minority group, according to legal scholars.[25] *Mendez* also set a precedent in terms of using social scientists to offer "expert" testimony against segregation as *Brown* lawyers did. Ralph Beals, the chair of UC Berkeley's Sociology and Anthropology department, and Marie Hughes, a former principal who at the time worked for the Los Angeles County Public Schools, gave evidence on the stand that segregation retards rather than helps the assimilation process and fosters feelings of inferiority among Mexican-American children, consequently breeding their hostility toward the majority group.[26] Robert Carter was so impressed by how social science knowledge had been used to criticize segregation in the *Mendez* case that he suggested to Marshall that the "social science approach would be the only way to overturn segregation in the United States."[27] He called the amicus curiae brief he and Marshall filed a "dry run for the future." David Marcus, the attorney for the *Mendez* plaintiffs, provided Marshall with all the briefs and notes he had compiled during the case.[28]

Legal scholars around the country recognized *Mendez*'s historical significance. Such venerable legal journals as the *Columbia Law Review* and the *Yale Law Journal* in 1947 reported on its significance. The *Columbia Law Review* discussed the case as "break[ing] sharply with" the past approach that authorized separate and equal facilities as "not in itself indicative of discrimination." In *Mendez*, the journal argued, the court instead "finds that the 14th Amendment requires 'social equality' rather than equal facilities."[29] The *Yale Law Journal* also reported that *Mendez* "has questioned the basic assumption of the *Plessy* case and may portend a complete reversal of the doctrine."[30] The *Yale Law Journal* article concluded by predicting, "There is little doubt that the Supreme Court will be presented with a case involving segregation in the schools within the next year or two."[31]

Yet some of the Mexican-American activists involved in the case were frustrated that the national significance of their painful struggles has been overlooked. Hector Tarango, one of the few LULAC members who stuck with the case in the face of local intimidation, spoke emotionally of this neglect. Tarango explained that Thurgood Marshall congratulated them in their victory, but then "didn't give us enough credit" when he went to D.C. for *Brown*. Tarango said with resignation, "we were too little down here, too insignificant. But it helped the Negroes' organizations to fight it because we had set a precedent...right here in Orange County."[32]

This still largely unrecognized connection between Mexican-American and African-American struggles highlights how local incidents on the multiracial West Coast influenced the shape of national reforms. Miller's involvement in postwar struggles against school desegregation and restrictive housing covenants illustrates the significance of interracial cooperation to what generally have seemed to be largely African-American struggles rooted in an eastern context. While African Americans from other parts of the nation deserve significant credit for these struggles, westerners like Loren Miller gained important civil rights experience by cooperating with a multiracial spectrum of Los Angeles's population. Southern California Mexican Americans' struggles to fight segregation in the 1946 *Mendez v. Westminster* case provided an important training ground for activists who later took the desegregation fight to the Supreme Court, where it culminated in the 1954 *Brown* decision.

Los Angeles–based cases concerning other civil rights issues also illustrate the national influence of western activism rooted in multiracial issues and coalitions, including the battle against various states' antimiscegenation laws, which prohibited racial intermarriage and which persisted especially in western and southern states since the nineteenth century. Historian Peggy Pascoe shows, for instance, how California became the first state to outlaw such prohibitions in its 1948 Supreme Court decision *Perez v. Lippold*. *Perez*, in which a Mexican-origin woman challenged the law that stated she, as a "white" woman, could not marry a "Negro" man, marked the first time since Reconstruction that a state court declared state miscegenation law unconstitutional. It set a national precedent, predating the 1967 Supreme Court *Loving v. Virginia* decision against antimiscegenation law by two decades. Pascoe shows how some of the same issues emerging out of the California case shaped later national discussions and decisions and makes clear that California set a precedent on the issue. She also highlights how a Los Angeleno who emerged out of interracial activism, Dan Marshall of the Los Angeles Catholic Interracial Council, was prominent in the California case.[33]

David Marcus's and the *Mendez* amici curiae briefs' connections between World War II and the segregation case, furthermore, highlight continuities between wartime and Cold War activism, specifically using the U.S. international agenda as a civil rights justification. Marcus asked, "Of what avail is our theory of democracy if the principles of equal rights, of equal protection and equal obligations are not practiced? Of what avail is our good neighbor policy if the good neighbor does not permit of honest neighborliness?" He further pointed out, "Of what use are the four freedoms if freedom is not allowed? Of what avail are the thousands upon thousands of lives of Mexican-Americans who sacrificed their all for their country in this 'War of Freedom' if the freedom of education is denied them?"[34] Supporting arguments in *Mendez* referred as well to the international imperative. Thurgood Marshall's brief for the NAACP asked the court to consider the country's new international commitments, which he argued together with the Constitution "demand that this court invalidate" school segregation for Mexican-descent children.[35] Though this argument was not what ultimately persuaded the court, it did consider it. Most important, perhaps, the strategy reveals Marshall's attempt to force the court to consider this kind of international thinking upon which he and others involved in *Brown* also later relied.[36] The American Jewish Congress also reinforced the World War II internationalist argument by appealing to popular fears of Nazi Germany's atrocities against the Jews, making what legal scholar Christopher Arriola calls an "ominous warning" to the court.[37] United States foreign policy interests played a key role in school reforms for Mexican Americans, including desegregation, making them "desirable, even necessary," according to Gilbert G. González, a scholar of Mexican-American education.[38] Marcus, Marshall, the AJ Congress, and others argued *Mendez* by focusing on U.S. hypocrisy in the international arena. In the emerging "American century," this argument was potent both during World War II and the developing Cold War.

EARL WARREN BRINGS CALIFORNIA TO THE NATION

Another California figure also sheds light on the earlier western, interracial roots of national civil rights struggles and outcomes specifically through the case of *Brown v. Board of Education*. Earl Warren, who

President Eisenhower tapped as chief justice of the U.S. Supreme Court in 1953 when the former chief justice suddenly died, proved a more progressive judge than Eisenhower had expected. The president later called Warren's appointment "the biggest damn fool thing I ever did."[39] Many other contemporaries and scholars, too, assessed Warren's transition as a drastic one. They believe that Warren, who was infamous for his role as California's wartime attorney general who helped orchestrate the World War II internment of 110,000 West Coast Japanese-descent people, shifted completely from a conservative to a liberal when he became chief justice.[40] Carey McWilliams's admiration for Chief Justice Warren did not extend back to the 1930s and 1940s when both men made names for themselves in California politics.[41] In those years, as attorney general (1938–42) and governor (1943–53), Warren frustrated Californians across the left political spectrum with his unwillingness to embrace the reforms they advocated.

However, while Warren's vehement support for internment was tragic, and he later expressed regret for what he had done, it is problematic to take internment as proof of how Warren reversed his stance on racial issues after he left California. Warren did indeed represent an extreme position on internment. As attorney general, he actively encouraged the federal government to intern Japanese-origin West Coast residents. And racism motivated him even more than others who may have only tacitly supported internment. But internment itself is not a good gauge of political liberalism or conservatism during World War II, as even the most otherwise progressive civil rights activists supported it, with a few brave exceptions. Nor did African-American, Jewish, or other ethnic community organizations, as chapter 3 explained, oppose internment. Though evaluations like those by legal scholar Sumi Cho are correct in arguing that Warren's culpability is not lessened by the fact that many Californians also did not oppose—and even supported—internment, Warren's role in the process does not adequately represent his views of civil rights and "minority issues" more generally.[42] Nor does internment represent a disjuncture between his experience in California and his tenure as chief justice of the U.S. Supreme Court.

A closer examination of Warren's gubernatorial career reveals a certain consistency between his California experiences and his Supreme Court persona. Warren carried more of his thinking, policies, and experiences with him to the Supreme Court than is readily apparent, and the seeds of his court positions on discrimination issues had been planted in California. Perhaps the clearest indicator that California shaped Warren's consciousness on race is Governor Warren's June 14, 1947, signature on a bill repealing the law that allowed the segregation of Native American and Asian students. Seven years before *Brown*, and only two months after the ruling in the *Mendez* appeal confirmed the initial ruling that segregating Mexican Americans was unlawful, Warren eliminated legal school segregation entirely in the Golden State.[43]

While Warren had been slow to act—Mexican-American activists including Manuel Ruíz of the Coordinating Council for Latin American Youth had been asking him to push such legislation since at least 1945—Warren instead could have changed the law to include Mexicans in the groups that could be legally segregated.[44] Incidentally, Ruíz and other proponents of a repeal emphasized that "segregation was a seed which if permitted to develop produced un-American tendencies." Ruíz even appealed to red-baiting congressman Jack Tenney to put the bill forward in the California Legislature for its second attempt. Ruíz and California assemblymen like Bill Rosenthal, who in 1945 proposed the original measure, believed that Tenney's anticommunist background and reputation made him "the ideal person to start the ball rolling."[45] This episode once again makes clear how mounting concerns about anticommunism played into such antidiscrimination proposals. But instead of adding Mexicans to the list of groups to be segregated, Warren followed advice he received from Ruíz, California's progressive attorney General Kenny, and others and signed this antisegregation legislation.

This California law making school segregation illegal no doubt shaped Warren's thinking when he faced similar issues on the Supreme Court, where he wrote the Court's opinion in *Brown* and in another important antidiscrimination case that preceded it by two weeks, *Hernandez v. Texas*. *Hernandez* ruled that systematically excluding Mexican Americans from juries in Jackson County, Texas, violated the Constitution. It represented an important step in the process of extending the Equal Protection Clause of the Fourteenth Amendment to Mexican Americans, which judicial experts previously had considered applicable only to African Americans. Warren's experience in the diverse state of California during a time when Mexican-American issues attracted more attention than during almost any other time in the twentieth century "undoubtedly contributed to the timing of the Court's decision in *Hernandez v. Texas*," according to legal scholar Kevin Johnson.[46] Warren himself reinforced his understanding about the multiracial context of discrimination by explaining in his memoirs that his court's ruling applied to "all racial groups that were discriminated against."[47]

In later years Warren reflected on the continuity between his experiences, philosophies, and politics in California and Washington D.C. He could not understand the surprise of either conservatives or liberals at his orientation as a Supreme Court justice. Warren responded in his memoir to people like Eisenhower who felt betrayed by his decision in *Brown*, claiming that these critics should have looked at his California roots before asking him to join the Supreme Court. "I know of no reason why they should have thought me ever to have been in favor of segregation in the first place. As far as I am aware, there is nothing in my career that would convey such an impression," Warren wrote. "I had been born and reared in California where there was no accepted policy of school segregation. I attended public schools and the University of California, and had sat in classrooms with blacks and members of almost every minority group. I never gave it a second thought."[48] Interestingly, time seems to have erased Warren's memory of California's history of segregation, including his role *undoing* it by signing the desegregation bill. It is impossible to explain why Warren glossed over these facts, which actually would reinforce his own interpretation of his California/Supreme Court consistency by showing that his stance against segregation originated in California. Warren nonetheless concluded, "I feel that my views and actions in later years are but an outgrowth of the earlier ones."[49]

Warren attributed any difference between his official stances as governor—where he exhibited what he saw as more restraint concerning racial equality—and as chief justice to constraints faced by an elected official. Warren believed that an elected official must compromise his or her own moral values in the interest of the constituents. Judges, on the other hand, had the liberty to follow concerns about morality and justice. "The basic ingredient of decision [on the Supreme Court]," he wrote, "is principle."[50] Warren explained, "I had not changed my spots."[51]

Much of Warren's record in California politics reinforces his claim that California trained him to hold the views that influenced him as chief justice more than both many liberal and conservative opponents had realized. Under the state's system that allowed cross-filing in primary elections until 1959—which facilitated nonpartisan politics by de-emphasizing party affiliation—both Democrats and Republicans elected the Republican Warren, whose policies were neither purely conservative nor liberal. Kurt Schuparra, historian of California conservatism, defines Warren as, in some ways, a liberal.[52]

In California Warren advocated a state law preventing prejudicial treatment of minorities. He first supported such a bill, which proposed creating a commission on political and economic equality, in 1945. If this bill had passed, it would have been the first such legislation in the country. After the 1945 bill failed, Warren crossed party lines in 1946 join the California Democratic Party in proposing a fuller Fair Employment Practices Commission law. The governor articulated his support of this bill to lawmakers in a speech using strong antidiscrimination language. "California is a cosmopolitan state. Here the United Nations Charter was born," Warren explained. "The Charter is based upon the protection of human rights, the most fundamental of which is the opportunity to earn a living. . . . I recommend that you enact legislation which will guarantee economic opportunity through a fair employment practices act."[53] Two months after this bill, too, died, Warren expressed his disappointment in his inaugural address, when he spoke to Californians about "minority problems" and the FEPC—albeit as the third-to-last item in the speech, or number eighteen of twenty issues he mentioned. "I feel certain that in rejecting Proposition 11 [the proposal for Fair Employment Practice Legislation] at the recent election, our people intended only to withhold their approval from a measure they considered unworkable," Warren explained optimistically. "I believe they would like to eliminate discrimination so far as is humanly possible."[54] In 1947, Warren again returned to the more moderate version he had sponsored in 1945, and continued to advocate similar versions of statewide fair employment practices legislation through 1953, when he left for Washington. Warren explained to the Governor's Council that "everything should be done to urge employers, both private and public, to see to it that applicants from minority groups are given fair, objective consideration in filling all job openings."[55] The legislature turned down all Warren and his allies' proposals, which only finally succeeded in 1959, during Governor Edmund "Pat" Brown's administration.[56]

During his time in California, Warren frustrated some racial equality activists but gained the admiration of others, some of whom benefited from aspects of his policies. "Warren represented the best strain of California Republicanism," assessed Roy Wilkins, who later became executive director of the national NAACP. "In 1942, when he was running for governor, he had come to an NAACP convention in Los Angeles and made a strong impression on me."[57] Warren appointed many minority activists to state commissions and positions, including Thomas L. Griffith, the former embattled head of the Los Angeles NAACP, to the position of Los Angeles municipal judge, only the second African American judge west of Chicago.[58] In 1945 Warren appointed the influential African-American businessman and local activist Norman Houston to the State Athletic Commission. In 1950, shortly after the Tenney Committee report had labeled Judge Isaac Pacht—then president of the Jewish Community Council—as in the "Stalin orbit," Governor Warren showed his support for Pacht by appointing him to the State Board of Corrections. Warren and Mendel Silberberg, the chairman of the Jewish community's CRC, remained close throughout the latter's governorship.[59] These California connections and experiences undoubtedly shaped Warren's thinking in ways that influenced him later on the Court.

Labels cannot adequately summarize Warren's racial politics in California. Clearly he was not as racially liberal as many of the subjects of this study. But neither was he as conservative as many California voters, particularly his Republican constituents, would have liked, on racial or other issues. While McWilliams and others on the left assessed Warren as too racially conservative, conservatives like Tenney accused him of falling prey to the "Jewish interests" that had been trying to get him to support civil rights. "The so-called Jewish bloc vote, manipulated by Silberberg through the Jewish Anti-Defamation League of B'nai B'rith and the Jewish Community Councils, was capable of influencing politicians everywhere, even the Governor of the State of California," Tenney fumed.[60] Warren implemented much social justice legislation that upset his Republican base, including raising unemployment benefits, boosting workmen's compensation, and increasing health and welfare services.[61] Warren's experience in such a racially mixed state like California made him recognize the necessity of affirmative governmental action.[62]

Through the careers of Warren and Miller, who carried their understanding of race and civil rights with them to the national stage, and the trajectory of the *Mendez* case's influence, California interracial activism's impact upon national housing and educational desegregation policies is clear.[63]

CALIFORNIA INTERRACIAL CIVIL RIGHTS AND NATIONAL POLITICS

Other Angelenos who had been involved in or influenced by mid-century civil rights collaboration also later became active at the national and state level and revealed the larger influence of the interracial Los Angeles political arena. Representatives of the Jewish community joined Loren Miller and Earl Warren to achieve such influence. Governor Warren's 1950 appointment of Isaac Pacht to the State Board of Corrections illustrates this influence. Even more prominent was Community Relations Council member Stanley Mosk, whom Warren's predecessor Governor Culbert Olson appointed to a Los Angeles County Superior Court judgeship. Mosk ruled racially restrictive covenants unconstitutional in 1946, two years before *Shelley v. Kraemer*, by upholding the transfer of a Hancock Park home to a black man. In 1958, Mosk became attorney general, and the first Jew elected by Californians statewide—albeit in a campaign marked by controversy over his Jewish background. Mosk used the position to help create a civil rights section to investigate complaints of discrimination in housing and public facilities, to integrate the Los Angeles Open Golf tournament, and to change PGA rules to allow black golfers to compete, among other initiatives. In 1964 Governor Pat Brown appointed him to the California Supreme Court.[64]

California African Americans and Mexican Americans achieved national prominence too. After leaving the position in the California state assembly to which multiracial cooperation initially had catapulted him almost thirty years earlier (in 1934), Augustus Hawkins in 1962 became a U.S. congressman. He launched from Los Angeles's interracial arena, where he fought to enact fair employment legislation and other multiracial

Los Angeles residents' agendas, to use his position to wage the national battle for civil rights legislation.[65] Roybal joined him in the U.S. Congress that same year, revealing Mexican Americans' increased national political representation.

INTERRACIAL ROOTS OF ETHNIC POLITICS

Southern California interracial cooperation also helped solidify a generation of ethnic protest in the Mexican-American community. The careers of people like Aileen Hernández, Henrietta Villaescusa, Tony Ríos, and most prominently Edward Roybal illustrate how the CSO became a training ground for many Mexican Americans' political careers. Edward Roybal in 1962 left the city council, a position that CSO activism had secured for him, to launch a long national career as a member of the U.S. House of Representatives. Mexican American Political Association (MAPA), a civil rights organization still active today—for which Edward Roybal was the first chair—also emerged out of the CSO. Aileen Hernández, an ILGW organizer and CSO member, received an appointment in the early 1960s to the Fair Employment Practices Commission, and Henrietta Villaescusa was appointed to the International Development Bureau for Latin America and later served at the Department of Health, Education, and Welfare.[66] Tony Ríos built upon connections and skills he developed through the CSO to become a delegate to the Los Angeles Central Committee of the Democratic Party. CSO member Hope Mendoza Schechter redirected her activism after the 1950s into the Head Start program. She also became a member of the National Advisory Council for the Peace Corps and a member of the Presidential Democratic Women's Forum.[67]

The CSO also launched the civil rights careers of future activists César Chávez and Dolores Huerta, whose influence extended later into the Chicano movement. The experiences of Chávez and Huerta make evident the CSO's influence on Chicano community organizing and activism. Chávez received his activist training as Ross's assistant in the Los Angeles CSO. "He thought I had what it took to be an organizer. He gave me a chance. And that led to a lot of things."[68] Ties between the two men remained strong after Chávez left the CSO, and Chávez's former mentor soon rejoined him at the United Farm Workers (UFW), where he spent fifteen years training organizers.

Dolores Huerta gained experience in the Los Angeles CSO before helping Chávez form the Farm Workers Association—later the United Farm Workers—in 1962. Huerta joined the CSO in 1955 and eventually became a paid legislative advocate for the CSO in Sacramento.[69] Huerta believes that the day she met Ross in 1955 was one of the most important events in her life, since he convinced her to become an activist.[70] She also reflected on the CSO's legacy, which she believed was twofold: it led to the creation of the United Farm Workers and created a generation of leaders.[71]

While Chicano movement leaders like Chávez and Huerta developed from this Cold War activism, many others developed in opposition to it. In either case, the CSO helped launch a later generation of "ethnic-specific activism."[72] The CSO's history also exposes the interracial foundations of this later activism, which illustrates that the continuity between World War II and the early Cold War extended even further into the twentieth century. In this way, interracial mid-century cooperation provided an important base for later ethnic-group-specific movements.

CONCLUSION

Interracial civil rights activism in Los Angeles and California more generally influenced "national" struggles, revealing that the trajectory of civil rights activism is more complex than eastern and southern black and white struggles later trickling to the west and catalyzing struggles there. Activism did sometimes move east to west, as other parts of this study demonstrate. Some western organizations that influenced Los Angeles interracial struggles, like the Los Angeles NAACP and various Los Angeles Jewish organizations, were transplants from the East. But the relationship was more reciprocal, often moving west to east as well. Others grew organically out of their Los Angeles environment, including the Jewish Community Relations Committee and Mexican Americans' Community Service Organization, which both established models for other activist communities nationwide.

Struggles rooted in interracial collaboration in Los Angeles provided a foundation for later activism on the U.S. stage, making visible the city's imprint on national programs and policies. Moreover, certain national struggles and policy changes that seemed to originate in African-American efforts, like those against housing and school segregation, actually originated—at least in part—in collaboration among various racial and ethnic communities.

Conclusion: A Lasting Legacy

Civil rights collaboration among racially diverse Los Angeles groups declined as the 1950s and 1960s passed, in part challenged by the increasing physical distances between them. As Jews' and Japanese Americans' social, economic, and political status improved, their relocation to the city's more affluent neighborhoods like the Westside and to surrounding areas like the San Fernando Valley, San Gabriel Valley, and the South Bay accelerated. By the 1960s and 1970s, few Japanese Americans and even fewer Jews remained in Los Angeles's east side neighborhoods, which became increasingly composed of those of Mexican origin, while the city's south side and its adjacent poor suburbs like Compton became more exclusively African-American.[1] Mounting differences about which agendas to prioritize also helped erode such cooperative initiatives. For instance, while Mexican Americans in the CSO focused on issues like obtaining old age pensions for long-term resident noncitizens during the 1950s and 1960s, African Americans in the NAACP made fair housing a main goal.[2] Of course differences in their primary social reform agendas characterized these groups' efforts in the 1930s, 1940s, and early 1950s, but they became more pronounced over time, exposing an underlying impermanence in mid-century coalitions that coalesced around a shared, or enough of a perception of a shared, agenda for a couple of decades.

But interracial cooperation continued to be an important component of the CSO and other organizations well into the 1950s and even early 1960s. For example, the CSO depended upon funding and organizational assistance from Alinsky's Industrial Area Foundation into the late 1950s. CRC financial support decreased from 1950 to 1951 and largely stopped in subsequent years, to the point where its involvement in the foundation of the CSO has nearly been forgotten.[3] But the CRC diminished its funding for the CSO in the early 1950s because its members believed the CSO should be more independent and able to sustain itself for the long term, not because they believed the organization's work was no longer important.[4] Even as it stopped directly providing funding to the CSO, the CRC continued to encourage the "citizenry at large" to support it, including helping search for other funds to sustain it and soliciting help from the

201

national ACLU in 1953. Roos asked the head of the national ACLU to assist the CSO "because we [the Los Angeles organized Jewish community] sincerely believe in the urgent need of an organization like the C.S.O."[5] Jewish-American community leaders helped Mexican Americans create a Community Service Foundation for fund-raising purposes. Working alongside Mexican Americans doing the same, CRC and other Los Angeles Jewish community leaders used their contacts locally and nationally to help connect the foundation to possible donors.[6] The CRC encouraged the Jewish community to support the CSO, both because it helped the Mexican-American community and "cemented" good relations between them and other Los Angeles minority groups. Jewish community support continued to help sustain the CSO even into the early 1960s.[7]

Although these coalitions, which focused on fighting police brutality and implementing fair housing and fair employment among other long-time goals, did deteriorate over time, they left a lasting legacy. Los Angeles's civil rights coalitions culminated in political and legal successes. They increased minorities' representation in local and national politics, as Edward Roybal, Augustus Hawkins, Stanley Mosk, and eventually Tom Bradley, indicate. Interracial coalition politics, particularly among Jewish and African Americans, helped elect Bradley first to the city council (1963) and later as mayor (1973).[8] Such interracial activism also culminated in "on the ground" change, as CSO activism reveals. Previously disenfranchised residents of poor, minority neighborhoods increased their political participation. CSO efforts helped Mexican Americans and other marginalized eastside residents attain unprecedented enfranchisement.[9] Moreover, Mexican Americans, previously alienated from even minority coalitions and activism, increasingly made their voices heard, winning victories in court against police brutality and in their neighborhoods for community improvement. Although police brutality continued, and continues, to terrorize minority communities, activists' efforts succeeded in making it an object of public attention and critique.[10]

Almost two decades of pressure also led to other political and legal victories that reflected central aspects of these interracial activists' agenda. In addition to the previously discussed successes against school segregation and restrictive covenants, legislation passed for fair employment practices in 1959 and for fair housing in 1963 (the Rumford Fair Housing Act).[11] National legislation like the 1964 Civil Rights Act, which outlawed racial segregation in schools, public places, and employment further reveals how many of the longtime goals pursued by Los Angeles's interracial activists and their colleagues nationwide came to fruition.[12]

At the same time that the 1960s witnessed ongoing cooperation in Los Angeles and brought some victories to those whose moderately framed activism carried through the early Cold War era, the decade also brought to a head long-simmering, unresolved tension among certain ethno-racial communities, as well as between minorities and white society. The legislation, increased political representation, and even the limited on-the-ground victories did not address the core dissatisfaction of many still-excluded minorities, whose smoldering frustration at their poor housing conditions and dismal job opportunities soon exploded in the 1965 Watts Riots and Black Power, Chicano, and other protest movements by communities of color in the 1960s and 1970s. The Watts Riots—which killed thirty-four people, injured more than a thousand, and resulted in 3,952 arrests—shocked the nation, which had witnessed President Lyndon Johnson signing the Voting Rights Act just five days earlier. The Watts Riots and other incidents of urban violence, along with the rise of Black Power and other ethnic protest movements, which in Los Angeles often struggled to find lasting common ground with each other while addressing the persisting inequalities they each faced, made evident these victories' incomplete promise.[13] For all its accomplishments, the interracial activism of groups like the CRC, the NAACP, and the CSO did not address some festering community needs. In fact, shortcomings inherent in some of these mid-century activists' agendas ironically even seem to have contributed to such violence by reinforcing inequities that the activists believed they were challenging. For instance, coalitions that came together in California to fight for fair employment and fair housing, which approached integration as an issue of changing individual attitudes rather than challenging economic and political power structures that created and maintained inequality, ultimately contributed to the ongoing inequality that fed poor communities' frustrations.[14]

To some extent, clashes in the 1960s revealed class conflicts. The success of pragmatic interracial activism reflected the triumph of a largely middle-class community. This was true especially for the NAACP and the CRC, whose leaders and many of whose active participants were influential middle-class community members. By the early Cold War, these organizations pursued agendas without significant working-class representation, even though many of their goals were consistent with those of the earlier, more inclusive 1930s and World War II–era activism.

Even in groups like the CSO, which experienced no such dramatic class divisions, activists struggled with conflicting class needs and ideologies. The CSO was unlike the CRC and the NAACP in that it put greater emphasis upon a wider variety of working-class needs, including health care and neighborhood improvement. It was a largely working-class organization, perhaps because of the relatively small size of the Mexican-American middle class, or perhaps because Mexican Americans' nascent history of political involvement meant they could not afford class divisions. A combination of factors likely helps explain why the CSO was more working-class in orientation than the other ethnic and racial organizations with which it frequently collaborated. It nonetheless portrayed itself as an organization that was consonant with values the middle class held dear during the Cold War, namely Americanism and anticommunism, even if it refused to purge its membership and to red-bait to its collaborators' extremes.

The radical resurgence of the late 1960s revealed that the approaches of these pragmatic, Cold War organizations did not achieve change fast enough or deeply enough for many members of the ethnic and racial communities they claimed to represent. In reaction there emerged a new set of ethnic power movements, which were more, if not entirely, working-class based. A generational component also shaped such movements as younger activists who had come of age after World War II pursued strategies which often involved more direct confrontation.[15] The earlier activists provided a vision and agenda against which these later movements defined and asserted themselves.

The latter part of the twentieth century continued to reveal ongoing fissures among ethno-racial communities in Los Angeles and California more generally. Jewish and Japanese-origin Angelenos became increasingly accepted and integrated at the same time that increasing Mexican immigration and immigration of new Asian groups in the wake of the 1965 Immigration Act brought to the surface new racial tensions. Disagreements in the 1970s between African Americans on the one hand, and Mexican and Chinese Americans on the other over California desegregation initiatives, for instance, highlight such fissures: while the NAACP and other African-American agencies fought especially hard for school desegregation and busing, some Mexican-American organizations feared that it would undermine their quest for bilingual education.[16] The riots following the 1992 acquittal of the police officers who beat Rodney King made clear, too, mounting tensions between Korean immigrants and African Americans.[17] Such ongoing tensions and inequalities reveal the failure of the subjects of this study to change on-the-ground conditions.

These two parallel, but very different, stories of interracial cooperation and interracial tension that developed, and intensified previous threads of both, during the mid-1960s, 1970s, and beyond raise questions about which one better explains the significance of L.A. interracial activists' legacies. Yet both stories, one of cooperation and victory and the other of tensions, disillusionment, and unfulfilled hopes, equally reflect their legacy. Scholars are correct to mourn the shortcomings of the accomplishments of those mid-century civil rights activists who caved in to anticommunism. Yet such activists also succeeded in a difficult political climate in bringing about at least a measure of greater equality to their city, state, and nation.

Understanding the achievements and shortcomings of cooperative civil rights campaigns like those in Los Angeles might provide insights to contemporary activists in Los Angeles and elsewhere attempting to bridge racial and ethnic divides in pursuit of common goals. Los Angeles's racial and ethnic heterogeneity was a bellwether for the nation's future. Early twenty-first-century communities nationwide face complexities associated with a multiracial society that these Angelenos first encountered in the 1930s, 1940s, and 1950s.[18] Fissures among seemingly like-minded activists in the 1940s and 1950s foreshadowed contemporary tensions. In California locations activists confronted what historian Mark Brilliant has called the multiple "axes of discrimination" facing racial and ethnic minorities. While these communities shared similar experiences of discrimination and hostility—though to different degrees—their interests also diverged, and their coalitions often were fragile and superficial. But activists from an earlier era found ways to transcend sometimes different interests and agendas, and their story suggests how and why groups come together in tense times to achieve shared goals. Their Cold War–era collaboration also sheds light on the relationship between conservative environments and social reform.

Contemporary activists continue to highlight the relationship between the international and the domestic arenas to advance their goals. Today, the United States' global "war on terror" continues to reveal the relationship between domestic race relations and the international agendas of the world's only remaining superpower. Just as earlier discrimination against Latin American, Asian, and African-origin people affected the United States' international reputation and risked threatening its international agenda, the treatment of minorities today has potentially disastrous repercussions for American attempts to promote democracy around the globe, provoking comments about U.S. hypocrisy for promoting democracy abroad but not adequately fighting racism at home. Contemporary domestic activists too might maneuver to use this international agenda to their advantage.

Both political expediency and the relationship between domestic and international affairs played roles determining when struggles succeeded, facilitating activists' own persistent efforts. Civil rights reforms gained strength during World War II in part because the United States needed to maintain a unified home front, and failing to enact civil rights changes threatened to disunite the population and disrupt the domestic war effort. The United States' growing involvement in the international arena and concern for its reputation as a beacon of democracy during the war further opened the door for civil rights groups to articulate a cooperative reform agenda. These groups together reminded officials that civil rights violations imperiled the international war effort by undermining the United States' attempts to promote itself abroad as a crusader for democracy at home. As the potential negative impact of discordant race relations on American diplomatic efforts became clear, officials' willingness to sanction certain civil rights efforts increased. The international imperative to promote civil rights persisted well into the postwar years as Americans challenged the Soviets to a battle for hearts and minds, although this same attention to international political developments also constrained many social critics' approach to reform. The story of Los Angeles in an earlier era testifies to how the perception of first a fascist and later a communist threat against the nation helped incubate a persistent, if reframed, civil rights agenda.

Racial minorities' conditions and stances today, though, present even more obstacles to collaboration than the earlier era. The meaning of "equality" in the early twenty-first century seems even more contested than it did at mid-century. In the earlier era, most reformers in this study, who of course were not the only activists with views on the matter, agreed that equality meant at the very least access to good jobs, housing, integrated schools, and protection from police brutality, if they sometimes prioritized different goals and pursued different methods for attaining them. In recent decades, marginalized Mexican Americans and African Americans resemble their 1940s and 1950s counterparts in that they too struggle over limited political, social, and economic resources.[19] Moreover, like their predecessors, minority populations today also face the threat of internal fracture over the issue of political conservatism. Internal dissent has mounted as some members seemingly "betray" their ethnic community by affiliating with the Republican Party. Obama's 2008 election reflects a departure, if perhaps only temporary, from that trend among elements of the Latino population.[20] In recent years, increasingly extreme inner-city poverty intensifies this competition over resources, and conflicts over party affiliation make clearer than ever the tenuousness of even the idea of a "minority group" interest—which, of course, always has been a nebulous concept. Furthermore, fissures around certain issues like immigration have deepened. Congressional debates and White House proposals over immigration legislation expose tensions among diverse communities. For instance, conflicts over this issue pit many African Americans and white Americans against more recently immigrant-descent populations like Latinos and Asians, who are often less likely to favor stringent immigration policies.[21] Tensions between African Americans and Jewish Americans also have mounted since the 1960s, as blacks have expressed frustration about what they call Jews' abandonment of many liberal causes for which they fought earlier in the century.[22] Asian-origin groups like Japanese Americans and Chinese Americans often find themselves on opposing sides of debates from other minority groups, including more recently arrived Southeast Asian groups, over affirmative action and school diversity.[23]

Nonetheless, the possibility of achieving reform through interracial coalitions remains real. In recent years, Latino and African-American cooperative efforts to elect Los Angeles Mayor Antonio Villaraigosa, and the support of multiracial communities nationwide for what became the victory of the first African-American president, Barack Obama, again reveal the ongoing salience of interracial collaboration, even if these politicians' rhetoric is often more real than their policy achievements. Collaboration becomes particularly significant in a country whose "majority" population composition has in recent decades become noticeably less white. Moreover, international coverage of the political campaigns of Latino and African-American candidates reveals that, once again, eyes abroad are searching for signs of American hypocrisy and finding comfort in such successes. These recent episodes, in Los Angeles and nationwide, focus Americans' attention on the importance of interracial coalitions. Where they may lead remains to be seen.

Notes

INTRODUCTION

1. On national impressions of Villaraigosa's coalition-based election, see, for instance, John M. Broder, "Latino Victor in Los Angeles Overcomes Division,' *New YorkTimes*, May 19,2005,http://www.nytimes.com/2005/05/19/national/19angeles. html?_r=1&n=Top/Reference/Times%20Topics/People/V/Villaraigosa,%20 Antonio&oref=slogin (accessed December 14, 2009); John M. Broder, "A Black-Latino Coalition Emerges in Los Angeles," *New York Times*, April 24, 2005, http:// query.nytimes.com/gst/fullpage.html?res=9E0DE2DA1231F937A15757C0A963 9C8B63&sec=&spon=&pagewanted=print (accessed December 14, 2009); Harold Meyerson, "A City Hesitates at Political Change," *New York Times*, June 8, 2001, http://www.nytimes.com/2001/06/08/opinion/a-city-hesitates-at-political-change.html (accessed December 14, 2009). For more on Bradley, Villaraigosa, and coalition politics see Gottlieb, Vallianatos, Freer, and Dreier, *The Next Los Angeles*; Kurashige, *The Shifting Grounds of Race*, 277–85; Sonenshein, "Coalition Building in Los Angeles," in de Graaf, Taylor, and Mulroy, *Seeking El Dorado*, 450–73; and Sonenshein, *Politics in Black and White*.

Roybal's election suggests we rethink a claim by historian Raphael Sonenshein that minorities in Los Angeles were not seen and heard until the 1960s. Sonenshein concludes that it was this exclusion that forced them to collaborate in the 1960s more than minorities in other eastern and Midwestern cities (where they had more power earlier) did. This study's conclusions suggest that this case for exclusion is overstated. See Sonenshein, *Politics in Black and White*, xvi–xvii, 33–35.

Interracial refers throughout to collaboration, communities, and relationships across racial and ethnic divides—including across white/nonwhite, or among Jewish-, African-, Mexican-, and Asian-descent minorities. *Multiracial* indicates the presence of multiple racial groups.

The term *civil rights* is used the way activists themselves used it in the 1930s, 1940s, and 1950s, to refer to their quest for political, social, legal, and economic opportunities and equality.

2. New York was largest, with 7,891,957 people, Chicago second at 3,620,962, Philadelphia third at 2,071,605, while Los Angeles had a population of 1,970,358. See Bureau of the Census, *Seventeenth Census of the Population*, 1–46.

Though Chinese Americans were important in California, Los Angeles's population was relatively small in this period. There were also small numbers of Koreans, and many other ethnic groups resided in Los Angeles, including Italians, Poles, and other European immigrant groups. But they were not as actively involved in civil rights issues, nor were they identified by contemporaries as key targets of discrimination, unlike the four groups that are the focus of this study.

The difficulty of defining race, ethnicity, identity, and membership in any "group" makes using such terminology problematic. *Bridges of Reform* uses terms that the study's subjects generally would have chosen, rather than contemporary labels. *Ethnic Mexican community, ethnic Mexicans, ethnic Mexican people, Mexican-descent, Mexican-origin, Mexicano,* and *Spanish-speaking* refer to the group of people whose ancestry came, at least in part, from Mexico—or from the part of the United States that before 1848 had been Mexico. *Mexican* refers to a U.S. resident of Mexican nationality, while *Mexican American* refers to an American citizen. This same terminology structure applies to the categorization of Japanese and Chinese communities in Los Angeles. Terms like *Japanese-descent* or *ethnic Chinese* refer to all residents with Chinese or Japanese ancestry, while *Japanese* or *Chinese* refer only to immigrants from Asian countries. *Black* and *African American* are used somewhat anachronistically, since the subjects of this study usually referred to themselves as *Negro*, but this latter term is avoided because of its negative historical connotation and association with the Jim Crow era of segregation. *Jews* refers to the population, American- and foreign-born, that identified with Jewish culture or religion, while *Jewish Americans* refers to U.S. citizens of Jewish background. For some Jews, Judaism was a religious affiliation, while for others it was racial or cultural, but for all, this identification meant some degree of exclusion, if less severe than what other L.A. minority groups faced. The Jews I refer to were Euro-American, though of course there were (and are) other Jewish communities. But in Los Angeles, as in the United States generally, the majority of Jews were of European descent.

The terms *Anglo* and *white* are perhaps most problematic of all, masking even greater internal differences than categories pertaining to other ethno-racial groups. I use them to refer to the native-born Christian population whose society and culture during the period of this study marked the dominant "American" way of life. This group was by no means monolithic, and included Catholics as well as Protestants. But because its general characteristics gave it relative social and political power, I view it as the mainstream. Admittedly, these terms neglect Angelenos of southern or eastern European descent, particularly recent arrivals like Italians, Russians, and others, who found themselves situated socially, economically, and politically far beneath native white Protestant Americans. But the general absence of such groups on the civil rights political scene means they do not merit a separate category of analysis in this study. At times this study does identify Protestant, and especially Catholic, civil rights initiatives, both of which were fairly common. Catholics were still somewhat excluded from West Coast society—though less than they were in eastern locations. See, for instance, Issel, "Jews and Catholics against Prejudice."

The terms *minority* and *minorities* are troublesome, too, especially since in some contexts these groups were numerical majorities. However, this study uses these terms for lack of better alternatives to refer to ethno-racial groups who faced social, economic, and/or political exclusion.

Los Angeles is also a term that begs definition. This project studies the city of Los Angeles, though occasionally it encompasses events in other areas of Southern California, especially greater Los Angeles County. The exact parameters are not particularly important, though, to the study's goal of understanding how politics and events in the area produced an interracial version of persistent civil rights with national influence.

Even the terms *race* and *ethnicity* are slippery. For the purposes of this book, which focuses on communities deemed outsiders because of their minority status, the term *ethno-racial* is applied, since it encompasses both race and ethnicity and calls attention to the constructedness of these categories. My use of the terms *racial* and *ethnic* is informed by the work of sociologists Michael Omi and Howard Winant and historian David Hollinger, who understand them as sociohistorically determined. Omi and Winant refer to race as the outcome of a process they call racial formation, through which social, economic, and political forces determine the content and importance of racial categories, which change over time, rather than as a fixed concept with biological boundaries. See Omi and Winant, *Racial Formation in the United States*. David Hollinger's term "ethno-racial" also understands race and ethnicity as socially and historically determined, changing concepts. Hollinger uses the term to refer to the ways racial and ethnic identities are not fixed or indefinitely determined. For instance, some groups categorized as "racial minorities" at points in time have become "ethnic minorities," and vice versa. See Hollinger, *Postethnic America*. For an interesting overview of the historical formation of *race*, see Fields, "Ideology and Race in American History."

3. Lester P. Bailey, Letter to Gloster B. Current, April 29, 1950, "Los Angeles, Calif, 1950" Folder, Box C15, Group II, NAACP LOC.

4. Oyama had been in Heart Mountain internment camp in Wyoming, then Denver, and finally Chicago before returning to Los Angeles in 1945. Mary Oyama, "A Nisei Report from Home," *Common Ground* (Winter 1946), 26–28, 28. See too "The Race War That Flopped," July 1946, *Ebony*, 3–9, and Ted LeBerthon, "Council of All Races," *Interracial Review*, Oct. 1945, 150–52. I thank Charlotte Brooks for pointing out these sources.

5. Sara Boynoff, "Los Angeles: A Race Relations Success Story," *Look*, March 19, 1957, LACCCR scrapbook, Box 76, Ford.

6. Ibid.

7. Scholarship, which since the various ethnic movements of the 1960s has tended to focus on individual groups, seldom has explored these forgotten coalitions in detail. For a discussion of how 1960s ethnic nationalisms shaped scholars' tendency to focus on single ethno-racial groups, see Sánchez, "'What's Good for Boyle Heights is Good for the Jews,'" 656.

In recent years, some scholars have started to answer calls to integrate racial and ethnic minority groups, particularly in the West, where racial diversity was characteristic. For such calls see Faragher, "The Social Fabric of the American West," 448; Kurashige, "The Many Facets of Brown"; Lotchin, "The Impending Western Urban Past," 63; West, "Expanding the Racial Frontier," 556; White, "Race Relations in the American West," 397; and Widener, "Perhaps the Japanese Are to Be Thanked?" For examples of recent studies in comparative racial and ethnic history, see Álvarez and Widener, "A History of Black and Brown"; Foley, *Quest for Equality*; Foley, *The White Scourge*; Greenberg, *Troubling the Waters*; Jacobsen,

Special Sorrows; Johnson, "Constellations of Struggle"; Kurashige, *The Shifting Grounds of Race*; Leonard, *Making Ethnic Choices*; and Varzally, *Making a Non-White America*. Forthcoming work includes Brilliant, *The Color of America Has Changed*. Some very early studies also recognized the importance of integrative racial and ethnic studies, including Bodnar, Simon, and Weber, *Lives of Their Own*, and Kessner, *The Golden Door*.

Scholarship on interracial relations and collaboration during the 1930s and 1940s in particular has increased in the last decade, though most civil rights studies of the Popular Front and WWII eras continue to focus on single communities. Many of the studies that do focus on interracialism are centered in Los Angeles, which is not surprising given the city's unusual diversity, particularly since the World War II years. The interracial cultural and social character of wartime Los Angeles both reflected and shaped its interracial political organizing tradition. See, for instance, Álvarez, *The Power of the Zoot*; Álvarez, "Zoot Violence on the Home Front"; Barajas, "Resistance, Radicalism and Repression on the Oxnard Plain"; Escobar, *Race, Police, and the Making of a Political Identity*, 281–84; Geary, "Carey McWilliams and Antifascism"; Pagán, *Murder at the Sleepy Lagoon*; and Wild, *Street Meeting*. Some scholars also have begun to examine interracial relations in Los Angeles during the 1960s and 1970s. See Pulido, *Black, Brown, Yellow and Left*.

Interracial activism in the early Cold War era remains relatively unappreciated, with a few recent exceptions. See Freer, "L.A. Race Woman"; Sánchez, "What's Good for Boyle Heights Is Good for the Jews"; and Widener, "Perhaps the Japanese Are to Be Thanked?" For interesting studies of interracial relations in postwar Los Angeles's cultural arena, specifically dance and music, see García, "Memories of El Monte"; Macias, "Bringing Music to the People"; and Macias, *Mexican American Mojo*.

8. Los Angeles offers an extremely rich set of sources from which this study draws. Students in its multiple universities documented the city's transformations from as early as the first decades of the twentieth century, beginning in the classes of USC scholars like sociologist Emory Bogardus and historian Rockwell Hunt, where students explored L.A. neighborhoods studying poverty and social problems. They collected oral histories, wrote sociological and historical theses, and helped archive source collections from individuals and organizations prominent in L.A. civil rights stories in local and not-so-local depositories. Multiracial Los Angeles continues to be the subject of scholarly and media inquiries by sociologists, historians, legal scholars, journalists and others. See for instance Baldassare, ed., *The Los Angeles Riots*; Bobo, Oliver, Johnson Jr., and Valenzuela Jr., eds., *Prismatic Metropolis*; Camarillo, "Black and Brown in Compton"; Chang and Leong, eds., *Los Angeles*; Davis, *City of Quartz*; various essays in de Genova, ed., *Racial Transformations*; Kurashige, *The Shifting Grounds of Race*; Leonard, "'The Little Fuehrer Invades Los Angeles'"; Macias, "Bringing Music to the People"; Macias, *Mexican American Mojo*; Pulido, *Black, Brown, Yellow, and Left*; Sánchez, "'What's Good for Boyle Heights Is Good for the Jews'"; Sonenshein, *Politics in Black and White*; Allen and Turner, *Changing Faces, Changing Places*; and Waldinger and Bozorgmehr, eds., *Ethnic Los Angeles*.

9. By recognizing that U.S. history is fundamentally entwined with global developments, this study builds on work by scholars such as Thomas Borstelmann,

Mary Dudziak, Kevin Gaines, James Meriwether, Brenda Gayle Plummer, Renee Romano, Jonathan Rosenberg, and Penny von Eschen, whose work represents only a slice of this rich field of study. See Borstelmann, *The Cold War and the Color Line*; Dudziak, *Cold War Civil Rights*; Gaines, *American Africans*; Meriwether, *Proudly We Can Be Africans*; Plummer, *Rising Wind*; Romano, "No Diplomatic Immunity"; Rosenberg, *How Far the Promised Land?*; and Eschen, *Race against Empire*.

10. See Dias, "Cold War Cities in the American West," 71. Richard White also discusses how the federal government invested in the West throughout the nineteenth century and the early twentieth century, and especially in the World War II and Cold War eras when national money made the West the center of what would become the aerospace industry. See White, "It's Your Misfortune and None of My Own," particularly chapter 18 passim. See too McGirr, *Suburban Warriors*.

11. Throughout this study, the term *communism* lowercased indicates a political orientation that did not necessarily stem from a Soviet directive. In Los Angeles, *communism* and *communists* more accurately described the political affiliation of those who generally only loosely identified with a Communist Party oriented toward Moscow. Members in Los Angeles often embraced the label only insofar as it represented domestic equality issues rather than an international revolution to overthrow capitalism. *Anticommunism* indicates a comparable perspective. Proponents targeted more than members of the Communist Party, seeking to stifle any idea, approach, or group they viewed as too critical of American society and thereby "dangerous" to democracy.

12. On fascism in Los Angeles, see interview with local Jewish community leader Joe Roos, in Pitt, *Joe Roos Oral History Interview*, CRC. See also Scobie, "Jack B. Tenney," and Stephan, "*Communazis.*" On communism, see Furmanovsky, "Communism as Jewish Radical Subculture" and Healey and Isserman, *California Red*.

13. On Los Angeles and communist registration ordinances, see Barrett, *The Tenney Committee*; Long, "Loyalty Oaths in California, 1947–1952," chapter 4 passim. For a larger discussion of the strength of Tenney Committee activities and this repressive movement in California, see Long, "Loyalty Oaths in California" as well as Scobie, "Jack B. Tenney."

14. For more on the interracial and interethnic neighborhood ties that flourished in parts of Los Angeles before World War II, see, for instance, Moore, *To the Golden Cities*; Sánchez, *Becoming Mexican American*; Sides, *L.A. City Limits*; and Wild, *Street Meeting*. On workplace interaction and coalitions, particularly among Mexican, Jewish, and other women, see Ruiz, *Cannery Women, Cannery Lives*. On the decreasing neighborhood ties and increasing segregation in the postwar era, see Sánchez, "What's Good for Boyle Heights Is Good for the Jews."

15. In the context of Los Angeles, most people associate "CRC" with the Civil Rights Congress, another more radically situated civil rights group. But in this study, CRC refers to Jewish Americans' Community Relations Committee, which in later years became the Jewish Community Relations Committee (JCRC), which is still in existence.

16. On this point, I thank Mark Brilliant and Robert Self for their comments on conference papers.

17. Los Angeles was different from elsewhere in the Southwest, especially Texas, where the League of United Latin American Citizens (LULAC) was Mexican Americans' main civil rights organization. LULAC was much less active in Los Angeles, where the CSO instead was dominant.

18. Historians who have examined the organization generally debate whether it represents a form of accommodation to the surrounding culture or resistance among the "Mexican-American generation." For scholarship that places the CSO in a Chicano history framework, see Apodaca, "They Kept the Home Fires Burning" and *Mexican American Women and Social Change*; Camarillo, *Chicanos in a Changing Society*, 80–82; Chávez, *Mi Raza Primero!*; Lozano, "The Struggle for Inclusion"; Pitti, *The Devil in Silicon Valley*; Rose, "Gender and Civic Activism in Mexican American Barrios in California"; Scott, "The Mexican-American in the Los Angeles Area," 294–99; and Vargas, *Labor Rights Are Civil Rights*, which calls CSO a "newly formed all-Mexican American organization," 15.

Some of these studies acknowledge the CSO's multiracial roots in Roybal election efforts and hint at its early dependence on a multiracial community for funding. But because most discussions of such multiracial activism are merely side-bars to studies of specific ethnic groups or individuals, they have not explored the ongoing collaboration in its early years that ensured the CSO's later success as a Mexican-American organization. See Pitti, *The Devil in Silicon Valley*, 242 n. 5; Pitti, "Quicksilver Community," 438, 439–41; and Underwood, "Process and Politics," 18, 99–100. One recent exception to this scholarship which recognizes the CSO's multiracial roots as central to the organization is Burt, *The Search for a Civic Voice*.

19. The JPFO is spelled differently in different places, sometimes as Jewish People's Fraternal Order, others as Jewish Peoples' Fraternal Order, and other times without the apostrophe at all.

20. Scholars of ethnic studies examining this period often impose contemporary understandings of inclusion and identity onto the past and exclude Jews from their analysis. I agree with Roger Lotchin, who argues that we need to change the way we look at "white" in the history of the American West, though I apply this critique to a larger national history. Lotchin asserts that we need to redefine the idea of "Anglo" or "Caucasian" in western history because it ignores the complexity of the ethnic origins of the supposedly Anglo founders of western cities. I recognize that by neglecting Irish, Italians, and other "undesirable" European-descent westerners besides Jews, I replicate this problem to some degree. Nevertheless, Jewish involvement in civil rights was far more substantial than these others groups, thereby justifying a focus on them exclusively among "less desirable" European-origin groups. See Lotchin, "The Impending Western Urban Past," 61. I draw upon Thomas Guglielmo's argument about the difference between race and color concerning another European-descent minority group, Italians, in Chicago. Guglielmo, *White on Arrival*. Mai Ngai's discussion of the connection between the privileges of whiteness and immigration law is also useful. Ngai, *Impossible Subjects*.

21. Historians often miss or underestimate Jews' involvement, characterizing it simply as white participation. For instance, Zaragosa Vargas discusses black, Mexican, and "Anglo" involvement in civil rights and labor activism, but with a few exceptions overlooks Jews' role. See, for example, his discussion of FEPC,

which does not mention that Jews were among the most active FEPC advocates in California. Vargas, *Labor Rights*, 258. Other scholarship acknowledges Jews' active role in civil rights initiatives at the same time they downplay it. Toni and Greg Robinson, for example, portray *Mendez v. Westminster* as "a golden moment of intergroup unity among Latinos, Asian Americans, and African Americans," overlooking Jews' role at the same time they also highlight the American Jewish Congress's heavy involvement in the case. See Robinson and Robinson, "The Limits of Interracial Coalitions," 94, 106–7.

22. For a wonderful study of the ways pragmatism shaped Jewish-American (as well as African-American) communities' civil rights involvement during this time, see Greenberg, *Troubling the Waters*, especially 8 and chap. 4. While Greenberg focuses on African Americans and Jews, *Bridges of Reform* makes clear that in multiracial places like Los Angeles, other diverse groups like Mexican Americans exhibited similar characteristics.

A partial explanation for why Jewish Americans' role in struggles for equality in the mid-twentieth century has been neglected or equated with Anglo in much civil rights literature, especially on the West Coast, is that literature on Jews in the West is relatively sparse in the first place. For a discussion of this absence, see Livingston, "Introduction," in Rischin and Livingston, *Jews of the American West*. In the late 1960s and early 1970s, books like Vorspan and Gartner's pioneering *History of the Jews of Los Angeles* began to explore the subject and, by the late 1970s, the field was beginning to attract more professional interest, with books like Moses Rischin's edited collection, *The Jews of the West*. In recent years scholars have increased our knowledge of western Jewish history, including Eisenberg, *The First to Cry Down Injustice?*; Kahn and Dollinger, eds., *California Jews*; Moore, *To the Golden Cities*; Raphael, Dollinger, and Kahn, eds. *Jewish Life in the American West*; and Toll, *The Making of an Ethnic Middle Class*.

There is, however, much literature on Jewish involvement in civil rights struggles in World War II and the postwar period at the national level (which in practice means in the Midwest and the East), as well as on the traditional southern civil rights movement in the 1950s and 1960s. See Greenberg, *Troubling the Waters*; Lerner, *Jews and Blacks*; various essays in Salzman and West, *Struggles in the Promised Land*; Schultz, *Going South*; Svonkin, *Jews against Prejudice*; and Webb, *Fight against Fear*.

23. My book responds to calls from scholars to bring the West into a national narrative, in the process revealing its significance to national stories—civil rights and otherwise. For a sample of such calls, see Limerick, "The Case of the Premature Departure"; Taylor, *In Search of the Racial Frontier*, 278; and West, "Reconstructing Race."

24. Brilliant. *The Color of America Has Changed*. Other scholars have argued that western cities like Los Angeles shaped twentieth-century national developments in respects besides civil rights. See, for instance, Abbott, *The Metropolitan Frontier*. Exploring multiracial Los Angeles also highlights the importance of distinguishing western urban civil rights movements from northern ones, where the struggles were more exclusively African American. In this way, this study speaks to scholarship that generally aggregates all nonsouthern movements as northern. See, for instance, Hall, "The Long Civil Rights Movement and the Political Uses of the Past"; Sugrue, *Sweet Land of Liberty*, xxvii; and Theoharis, "Black Freedom Studies," 363 n. 24.

25. While scholarship has made great advances in the field of civil rights in the last few decades, we still do not fully grasp the relationship between civil rights struggles before and after World War II or whether (and how) events in the global arena outside Africa and Europe shaped U.S. struggles.

On developments in civil rights scholarship, it has become clear that civil rights struggles, and even the Black Power movement, began before the 1950s, 1960s, and 1970s. See Korstad and Lichtenstein, "Opportunities Found and Lost," 786; Singh, *Black Is a Country*; and Tyson, *Radio Free Dixie*.

Scholars also have recognized how international affairs shaped domestic struggles. African Americans, especially in the North and West, fought for their rights before the popularly understood mass civil rights movements, particularly during the 1930s and World War II. By engaging the international arena, particularly anti-colonial struggles in Africa and fascism in Europe, they shaped and justified their cause. See Dalfiume, *Desegregation of the U.S. Armed Forces*, 138–39; Horne, *Black and Red*; Meriwether, *Proudly We Can Be Africans*; and von Eschen, *Race against Empire*.

It is also now apparent that activism grew out of multiple communities—African American as well as Mexican, Asian, and other Americans—in the North and West from as early as the 1930s and did not result from a "trickle-west/north" effect from the southern civil rights movement. African Americans in the North and West were actively fighting for increased opportunities well before the large-scale southern movement began. See Biondi, *To Stand and Fight*; Robinson and Sullivan, eds., *New Directions in Civil Rights Studies*; Self, *American Babylon*; and Sides, *L.A. City Limits*. See too Vargas, *Labor Rights*, and Svonkin, *Jews against Prejudice*, among many others that examine Mexican and Jewish Americans' pre-1960s activism. On Asian Americans see Brooks, *Alien Neighbors, Foreign Friends*; Chung, "Fighting for Their American Rights"; and Yu, *To Save China, To Save Ourselves*.

26. For an excellent study of anticommunism's destructive impact, see Schrecker, *Many Are the Crimes*.

27. Hurewitz, *Bohemian Los Angeles and the Making of Modern Politics*, 225–27.

28. Taft-Hartley greatly restricted the activities and power of labor unions. The Internal Security Act required communists to register and made deporting noncitizens much easier. The loyalty oaths were widespread, especially in California, and required public employees to swear loyalty to the United States.

29. The Marshall Plan was the United States' postwar plan for rebuilding Western Europe and repelling communism, while containment was the general U.S. policy for limiting the spread of global communism. For more on the split on international issues between Cold War liberals and their former allies, see, for instance, Kleinman, *A World of Hope, a World of Fear*; Walton, *Henry Wallace, Harry Truman, and the Cold War*.

30. The dominant previous interpretation of Cold War civil rights is that many racial justice groups supposedly abandoned economic justice goals in favor of "less radical" legal and political goals, which undercut the possibility for any significant socioeconomic change and deprived future generations of radical role models. In this view, anticommunism watered down postwar reform agendas as what became known as the "vital center" prevailed, and radical change initiatives did not resurface again until the 1960s. Arthur Schlesinger coined this term, which came to

represent a politically moderate group of thinkers who criticized extremism on both sides of the political spectrum. Schlesinger, *The Vital Center*. This perspective assumes that in this anticommunist "consensus" era, civil rights groups hoping to survive sold out to Cold War liberalism and abandoned their commitment to real equality. It tends to assess postwar civil rights organizations like the NAACP, CSO, CRC, JACL, and their members as too moderate and ineffective, and implicitly or explicitly contrasts them with the supposedly more substantive social justice campaigns of the 1930s and late 1960s and 1970s.

Scholars who are critical of this postwar generation of activists and organizations for supposedly abandoning radical causes like anticolonialism and economic justice, and who adopt the declensionist line that the Cold War derailed civil rights include Acuña, *Anything but Mexican*, 44; Anderson, "Bleached Souls and Red Negroes"; Cha-Jua and Lang, "The 'Long Movement' as Vampire," esp. 272; Ceplair and Englund, *The Inquisition in Hollywood*, 152–53; Dowd Hall, "The Long Civil Rights Movement and the Political Uses of the Past," 1249; Fraser and Gerstle, eds., *The Rise and Fall of the New Deal Order, 1930–1980*; Honey, "Operation Dixie, the Red Scare, and the Defeat of Southern Labor Organizing," esp. 237; Horne, *Black and Red*; Janken, "From Colonial Liberation to Cold War Liberalism"; Korstad and Lichtenstein, "Opportunities Found and Lost," 811; Lawson and Payne, *Debating the Civil Rights Movement*, 9; Marable, *Race, Reform, and Rebellion*, esp. 31; Schrecker, *Many Are the Crimes*; Self, *American Babylon*, 6, 12; Sitkoff, *The Struggle for Black Equality, 1954–1992*; Sullivan, *Days of Hope*; and von Eschen, *Race against Empire*.

While this view is important because it acknowledges the unfulfilled civil rights legacies of mid-century, and also draws important attention to a "long civil rights movement" which began a decade or two before *Brown v. Board of Education*, examining events on the ground in Los Angeles across the 1940s and 1950s illustrates that it overestimates the foreclosing of domestic civil rights by anticommunism. It both overestimates the radicalism of many earlier activists and their domestic goals and underestimates the persistence of much of "liberal" activists' agendas from earlier. In this way, *Bridges of Reform* critiques the "long civil rights movement" literature's overstatement of domestic civil rights' Cold War rupture. (Interestingly, scholarship on the "long civil rights movement," which views the movement as beginning in the 1940s and even 1930s rather than the 1950s, tends to subsume the West into the North, generally assuming that anything outside the South was similar enough to be lumped together—though some do briefly acknowledge how the presence of Latinos and Asians make the West somewhat different. See Hall, "The Long Civil Rights Movement and the Political Uses of the Past"; Sugrue, *Sweet Land of Liberty*, xxvii; and Theoharis, "Black Freedom Studies," 363 n. 24. Even articles critical of this "long movement" literature tend to focus on the North/South Mason-Dixon line divide. See Cha-Jua and Lang, The 'Long Movement' as Vampire," esp. 280.)

While scholars have increasingly come to acknowledge this mid-century generation of activists, most of their studies emphasize the way the Cold War limited their ongoing activism. See for instance Biondi, *To Stand and Fight*; García, *Mexican Americans*; Pitti, *The Devil in Silicon Valley*; Vargas, "In the Years of Darkness and Torment; Vargas, *Labor Rights Are Civil Rights*; and Whitaker, *Race Work*. Some very recent scholarship, however, also has emphasized the ways the Cold War enabled aspects of their activism. See Brooks, *Alien Neighbors, Foreign Friends,* and "Sing Sheng vs. Southwood; and Chen, "'The Hitlerian Rule of Quotas.'"

For more on racial liberalism, see Brilliant, *The Color of America Has Changed.* I use Brilliant's definition of racial liberalism as the wide-ranging set of initiatives for fighting racial discrimination pursued by a wide-ranging group of reformers who hoped to extend the social safety net from the New Deal to nonwhite minorities who had been excluded from 1930s policies.

31. This study builds the case for the Cold War as an era signifying continuity rather than discontinuity with the past in another way as well, specifically the international arena's ongoing impact on domestic civil rights. Recent scholarship has argued that the United States' Cold War international imperatives facilitated certain domestic civil rights accomplishments, specifically that the U.S. struggle during the 1950s and 1960s to convince African hearts and minds that democracy was more appealing than communism helped facilitate the abolition of segregation in schools and public accommodations. According to this argument, such discrimination, if permitted to remain on the books, would continue to highlight U.S. hypocrisy. See Borstelmann, *The Cold War and the Color Line*; Dudziak, *Cold War Civil Rights*; and Romano, "No Diplomatic Immunity."

But because such scholarship generally concentrates on the period either before or after 1945, it largely overlooks the continuity that characterized the relationship between the international arena and such campaigns. Examining L.A. activist communities across the 1945 divide reveals that a significant international influence on civil rights transformations emerged even earlier, especially during World War II. Wartime events in Los Angeles such as the Zoot Suit Riots and the Sleepy Lagoon case make clear that the United States' burgeoning international agenda was not a significantly new influence on civil rights in the Cold War era. Local and national officials scrambled to implement reforms in the city in the wake of the global embarrassment over these incidents.

Moreover, focusing on a Western U.S. location also reveals how relationships among residents and governments of the Western Hemisphere and Pacific Rim fundamentally shaped domestic civil rights trajectories. Scholars of Asian American and Latino history have illuminated such connections, but such studies generally are not directly in conversation with civil rights scholarship and are still largely peripheral to the larger literature on twentieth-century U.S. history, unlike those scholars who focus on African-American civil rights developments and the relationship with Africa and Europe. Studies of Latino and Asian American civil rights still generally remain within the framework of studies of that particular ethnic group. See, for instance, Brooks, *Alien Neighbors, Foreign Friends,* and "Sing Sheng vs. Southwood"; Guglielmo, "Fighting for Caucasian Rights"; Gutiérrez, *Walls and Mirrors*; Takaki, *Strangers from a Different Shore*; and Yung, *Unbound Feet.* One exception is Hart, "Making Democracy Safe for the World."

By recognizing that the international realm significantly influenced domestic civil rights before the Cold War, *Bridges of Reform* applies some of the long civil rights movement literature's insights—that civil rights movements began earlier than previous understandings allowed—to the "Cold War civil rights" historiography, namely by pushing its chronological reach back a decade or two.

32. Lillian Faderman and Stuart Timmons argue that the Mattachine Society was a foundational organization for gay rights, specifically that it "marked the

beginning of the national homophile movement."They also argue that Los Angeles was a nationally and internationally influential capital of gay rights movement, since "more lesbian and gay institutions started in Los Angeles than anywhere else on the planet." Faderman and Timmons, *Gay L.A.*, 3, 11. Historian Daniel Hurewitz argues that the city's gay activists built their movement in part upon their earlier involvement in racial equality struggles, and by modeling their struggles on racial minority groups' struggles for full citizenship. According to Hurewitz, the Mattachine Society activists had experience in particular with more radically situated organizations than those discussed in this study, namely the Communist Party and the Civil Rights Congress. Such campaigns for racial equality in the city opened the door for gay rights activists to also lay claim to full citizenship and protection as oppressed social minorities. Hurewitz, *Bohemian Los Angeles*, 191, 228, 231–32, 237, 249, 255, 272–73, 277–79.

On the way that studies in gay history—and in women's history—recognize the origins and persistence of gay and women's struggles for equal rights during the early Cold War, see D'Emilio, *Sexual Politics, Sexual Communities*, 249; Horowitz, *Betty Friedan and the Making of the Feminine Mystique*; Hurewitz, *Bohemian Los Angeles*; Faderman and Timmons, *Gay L.A.*; and Meyerowitz, ed., *Not June Cleaver*.

33. John Morton Blum emphasizes that CORE was biracial (black and white) from its founding in 1942 Chicago. See Blum, *V was for Victory*, 215–16.

34. On the American Council on Race Relations, and its work in Washington D.C. specifically, see Pritchett, "A Local and National Story."

35. Interracial organizations also appeared elsewhere in California, including the Bay Area Council against Discrimination, which formed in 1942. See Broussard, *Black San Francisco*, 193–97. For more on cooperative interracial origins of fair employment legislation and other civil rights initiatives in New York, see Biondi, *To Stand and Fight*; Chen, "'The Hitlerian Rule of Quotas'"; and Svonkin, *Jews against Prejudice*. On Denver, see Romero, Jr., "Of Race and Rights." On San José, see Pitti, *The Devil in Silicon Valley*, and on the San Francisco's East Bay Area, see Self, *American Babylon*. On Miami see Mohl, *South of the South*.

36. This idea first materialized during a panel discussion with Nancy MacLean and Tom Romero at the Western History Association conference in St. Louis in October 2006. I thank them for their ideas and insights on this topic.

37. Japanese Americans are of course an exception here, as *Bridges of Reform* will explore, since they arguably had no leverage in the years following Pearl Harbor.

CHAPTER 1

1. See Rawls and Bean, *California*, 277; Fogelson, *The Fragmented Metropolis*, 43–62; Gregory, *American Exodus*, 8; and McWilliams, *Southern California Country*, 125–27. Numbers are from Fogelson, *The Fragmented Metropolis*, 64–78.

2. According to Max Bond, the adults in the original Los Angeles settlement of twenty-two people were of the following backgrounds: two Spaniards, nine

Indians, one "half-breed," two Negroes, seven mulattoes, and one Chino [Chinese]. Bond, "The Negro in Los Angeles," 44. For a first-hand observation about the Mexican-origin population's continued influence in Los Angeles in the 1850s, see Bell, *Reminiscences of a Ranger, or Early Times in Southern California*, introduction. See also Camarillo, *Chicanos in a Changing Society*.

3. For a discussion of the changes in the mid to late nineteenth century see del Castillo, *The Los Angeles Barrio, 1850–1890*, 33–34.

4. For more information on the declining status of these Mexicanos, or Californios, in Southern California see Albert Camarillo's seminal study, *Chicanos in a Changing Society*. For a discussion on the loss of power among Spanish-speaking people see Romo, *East Los Angeles*, specifically p. 5 and chapter 2 passim.

5. For a discussion of Jews' declining status, see Vorspan and Gartner, *History of the Jews of Los Angeles*, particularly 91–94, 135–38, 143–45.

6. Vorspan and Gartner, *History of the Jews of Los Angeles*, 91.

7. In contrast, New York had about 35 percent foreign-born population in the same period. Romo, *East Los Angeles*, 10–11.

8. In 1910 only 45 percent of New York's population was native-born white, 62 percent of Chicago's, and 65 percent of San Francisco's. By 1930, Los Angeles was 71 percent native-born white, New York was 49 percent, Chicago was 67 percent, and San Francisco 70 percent. See Fogelson, *Fragmented Metropolis*, 80–82. For further discussion of the midwestern roots, values, and cultures of most Los Angeles migrants in the early twentieth century, see Fogelson, *Fragmented Metropolis*; see also Thernstrom, *The Other Bostonians*.

9. The overall population grew twelve times, from 102,479 in 1900 to 1,238,048 in 1930, while nonwhites and foreign-born whites increased from 22,314 to 346,312. While the Mexican-origin population seems to have been included in the nonwhite population for 1930 (when "Mexican" was a separate census category), in 1900 this population is not clearly accounted for—many may have been classified as "native-born white." See United States Bureau of the Census, *Twelfth Census of the United States Taken in the Year 1900*, cxix, and United States Bureau of the Census, *Fifteenth Census of the United States*, 260.

10. Mark Wild, *Street Meeting*, 13–14, and chapter 1 generally, especially 19–34. For more on Asian immigrants, see Chan, *Asian Americans*, chapter 3 passim and Takaki, *Strangers from a Different Shore*.

11. Mark Wild, *Street Meeting*, 28.

12. The city's early twentieth-century Italian population was only 1,000 to 2,000. Ibid., 28.

13. The birthrate among the Chinese-origin community was low because of the combination of difficulties of Chinese female migration (in part because of restrictions on Chinese women's immigration) and antimiscegenation laws. See Wild, "A Rumored Congregation," 38–39. For more on the Chinese community, see Wild, *Street Meeting*, 16–18, 23–24.

14. For a discussion of the Mexican-origin community in Los Angeles at this time, see Romo, *East Los Angeles*, particularly 31–33, 148–55, and Sánchez, *Becoming Mexican American*.

15. It is not clear why the earthquake and fire did not have the same effect upon San Francisco's Chinese population, which largely remained in San Francisco

after 1906. For a discussion of Japanese migration to Los Angeles, see Wild, *Street Meeting*, 24. See also Kurashige, *The Shifting Grounds of Race*, chapter 1 passim, and Kurashige, "Transforming Los Angeles," chapter 2 passim.

16. Vorspan and Gartner, *History of the Jews of Los Angeles*, 103.

17. For a discussion of Jewish influx to Los Angeles during the war, see Vorspan and Gartner, *History of the Jews of Los Angeles*, 116.

18. While the black population grew to only 2,000, from 1880 to 1900 the city's overall population grew from 11,183 to 102,479. De Graaf, Mulroy, and Taylor, eds., *Seeking El Dorado*, 6, 15, 18, 19.

19. Taylor, *In Search of the Racial Frontier*, 206.

20. Fogelson, *Fragmented Metropolis*, 76.

21. Ibid., 83.

22. In the early part of the twentieth century these diverse working-class migrants and immigrants lived in mixed neighborhoods, largely in the city center, from northwest of downtown through both sides of the L.A. river, as far south along Central Avenue as Watts. Though groups often clustered, few areas were mono-ethnic and most had a lot of residential integration. In this way they were different from New York and Chicago's more segregated ghettoes at this time, as well as postwar mono-racial ghettoes of the "inner city." For more discussion of early twentieth-century neighborhood integration and residential patterns in Los Angeles, see Wild, *Street Meeting*, 18–34.

23. For a study that discusses the *relative* freedoms and liberties of the West, see, for instance, Sides, *L.A. City Limits*, 11–13. Mark Wild argues that West Coast cities were relatively more racially and ethnically integrated than other American cities; see Wild, *Street Meeting*, 2. See also Broussard, *Black San Francisco*; Rischin, ed., *The Jews of the West*, 10; and Rischin and Livingston, *Jews of the American West*, 21–23. See too Flamming, *Bound for Freedom*.

24. Sides, "Working Away," 33, and *L.A. City Limits*, chapter 1.

25. Sides, "Working Away," 29. For further discussion of this topic, see Flamming, *Bound for Freedom*, esp. 2–3, and 13–14.

26. De Graaf, "Negro Migration to Los Angeles, 1930 to 1950," 87. For a discussion of integration in Los Angeles schools see Wild, *Street Meeting*, chapter 4 passim.

27. Sides, "Working Away," 35. Los Angeles schools tended to be somewhat racially integrated as well. This level of diversity and integration with other immigrant and African-American communities was markedly different from schools in nearby Orange County, in which Mexican children were in utterly segregated schools, separate from the white inhabitants of the County. Romo, *East Los Angeles*, 138–39, and Munroy, *Rebirth*, 197–99.

28. Sides, *L.A. CityLimits*, 16. For another study of African-American Los Angeles in the first decades of the twentieth century, see Flamming, *Bound for Freedom*.

29. Camarillo, *Chicanos in a Changing Society*, 166–74, 211; Munroy, *Rebirth*, 99, 158; and Romo, *East Los Angeles*, 118, 128.

30. Sides, *L.A. CityLimits*, 24–26.

31. De Graaf, Mulroy, and Taylor, *Seeking El Dorado*, 18–19, 23. See too Flamming, *Bound for Freedom*.

32. By 1930 African Americans had attained membership in only 20 percent of local unions. De Graaf, "Negro Migration to Los Angeles," 81. See also Taylor, *In Search of the Racial Frontier*, 206. Also see Flamming, *Bound for Freedom*, esp. 248–52.

33. Louis, *A Study of American-Born and American-Reared Chinese in Los Angeles*, 21–22.

34. Fukuoka, *Mutual Life and Aid among the Japanese in Southern California with Special Reference to Los Angeles*, 11. See also Kurashige, *The Shifting Grounds*, 80–81, and Kurashige, "Transforming Los Angeles," 97–113.

35. Vorspan and Gartner, *A History of the Jews of Los Angeles*, 91–94, 135, 143–45. See too Rischin, ed., *The Jews of the West*.

36. Interestingly, at the same time white residents romanticized the city's Mexican past. See Deverell, *Whitewashed Adobe*, and Kropp, *California Vieja*.

37. Perry and Perry, *A History of the Los Angeles Labor Movement, 1911–1941*, vii.

38. See Stimson, *Rise of the Labor Movement in Los Angeles*, 104–22, and McWilliams, *Southern California Country*, 276–77 (page citations are to the reprint edition), cited in Munroy, *Rebirth*, 116 n. 5.

39. On the picketers see McDougal, *Privileged Son*, 48. See Perry and Perry, *A History of the Los Angeles Labor Movement*; Deverell, "My America or Yours?"; Davis, "Sunshine and the Open Shop"; and Pintar, "Behind the Scenes." For more on Los Angeles in the 1920s, see Tygiel, *The Great Los Angeles Swindle*. On the BAF, see Deverell, "My America or Yours?" On the meaning of the "white spot" see Wild, *Street Meeting*, 38–39.

40. McDougal, *Privileged Son*, 48–63.

41. Fogelson, *The Fragmented Metropolis*, 130–32.

42. Taylor, *In Search of the Racial Frontier*, 235. For a wonderful discussion of housing, discrimination, and restrictive covenants facing African Americans, see Flamming, *Bound for Freedom*, especially 65–69, 152–56, 218–25.

43. Romo, *East Los Angeles*, 84–85.

44. *Linking Our Lives*, 18. For a discussion of residential segregation and other issues in the Chinese-origin community, see Chen, "Chinese Socio-Cultural Patterns of the Chinese Community in Los Angeles." For a discussion of the general anti-Chinese movement, see Saxton, *The Indispensable Enemy*.

45. Hayashi, *"For the Sake of Our Japanese Brethren,"* 128–29. For more information on anti-Japanese sentiment and activity in California and Los Angeles specifically, see Modell, *The Economics and Politics of Racial Accommodation*, 30–66.

46. For a further discussion of this act, see Kitano and Daniels, eds., *Asian Americans*, 12.

47. The barred zone included immigrants from China, South and Southeast Asia, the Asian part of Russia, Afghanistan, Iran, part of Arabia, Pacific and Southeast Asian Islands not owned by the United States. Quotas for northern and western Europe were large (1931 numbers for Great Britain and Northern Ireland was 65,000, Ireland almost 18,000, and Germany almost 26,000) while eastern and southern Europe's were small (the 1931 numbers for Poland and Italy were 6,000 each). Kitano and Daniels, *Asian Americans*, 12. For an excellent overview of immigration restriction in twentieth century America, see Ngai, *Impossible Subjects*.

Asian immigrants had been denied citizenship since 1790, when the Naturalization Law specified that naturalized citizenship applied only to whites. Takaki, *Strangers from a Different Shore*, 203–5. See too Gardner, *The Qualities of a Citizen*.

48. The head tax was not enforced systematically until the late 1920s. See Hoffman, *Unwanted Mexican Americans in the Great Depression*, 30–33. And, at the request of southwestern employers who needed their labor during World War I, this rule was suspended concerning Mexican immigration (but only for work in agriculture, the railroads, or coal mining). Munroy, *Rebirth*, 98. For an excellent discussion of immigration laws affecting a broad spectrum of America's minority populations, see Ngai, *Impossible Subjects*.

49. For a discussion of nativism in American history, see Higham, *Strangers in the Land*. For discussions of the Sacco and Vanzetti trial, see, for instance, Avrich, *Sacco and Vanzetti*; Somkin, "How Vanzetti Said Goodbye;" and Young and Kaiser, *Postmortem*.

50. Romo, *East Los Angeles*, 90, and Wild, *Street Meeting*, 160–61, 167.

51. Romo, *East Los Angeles*, 90–111.

52. Wild, *Street Meeting*, 185. Also see Perry and Perry, *A History of the Los Angeles Labor Movement, 1911–1941*, vii, 269–70, 440, and Scobie, "Jack B. Tenney," 29–30.

53. See Furmanovsky, "Communism as Jewish Radical Subculture;" Perry and Perry, *A History of the Los Angeles Labor Movement*, vii, 269–70, 440; and Sides, *L.A. City Limits*, 23–24. Also see Scobie, "Jack B. Tenney," 29–30. For a discussion of red squads in American history more generally, see Donner, *Protectors of Privilege*. See also Escobar, *Race, Police, and the Making of a Political Identity*.

54. Modell, *The Economics and Politics*, 40–41.

55. For a discussion of the activities of the KKK in Los Angeles in this period, see Bass, *Forty Years*, 53–60.

56. The organization disintegrated in 1942. De Graaf, Mulroy, and Taylor, *Seeking El Dorado*, 20.

57. The organization did not survive the Depression. Taylor, *In Search of the Racial Frontier*, 242. See also Tolbert, *The UNIA and Black Los Angeles*.

58. De Graaf, Mulroy, and Taylor, *Seeking El Dorado*, 20; and Sides, "Working Away," 71–72. The national organization had been formed shortly after riots in Atlanta in 1906 and in Springfield, Illinois in 1908. Black leaders and white liberals met in New York in 1908 and eventually formed the national NAACP in 1910. See Kellogg, *NAACP*.

59. Other groups in the West, like the Chinese, established similar societies— for instance, the Chinese Six Companies, which focused on the exclusion laws. See Chan, *Asian Americans*, 69. For information on Asian resistance to oppression as early as the nineteenth century, see Chan, *Asian Americans*, chapter 5 passim. On other Los Angeles-area Japanese associations, see Fukuoka, "Mutual Life and Aid among the Japanese in Southern California with Special Reference to Los Angeles," 26. For information on the merger and the L.A. Chamber of Commerce's role, see Japanese Chamber of Commerce of Southern California, *Japanese in Southern California*, 3. Also see Modell, *The Economics and Politics*, 79–83, 88.

60. Romo, *East Los Angeles*, 149. For a wonderful discussion of mutualistas, particularly women's involvement, see Ruíz, *From Out of the Shadows*, particularly

chapter 4, "With Pickets, Baskets, and Ballots," esp. 86–89. For a discussion of religion and churches—both Protestant and Catholic—in Mexican Los Angeles, see Sánchez, *Becoming Mexican American*, 151–70.

61. Romo, *East Los Angeles*, 148–55. Quote from 155. For more discussion on Mexican immigration into Los Angeles and the development of a Mexican-American community there, see Sánchez, *Becoming Mexican American*.

62. Vorspan and Gartner, *History of the Jews of Los Angeles*, 141, 146–47, 150, 171–80. The American Jewish Committee, a prominent national defense organization formed in 1906 which focused on Jews in the U.S. and abroad, did not come to Los Angeles until 1945. See AJC Los Angeles website, http://www.ajclosangeles.org/site/c.mlI0IfN1JyE/b.2026491/k.246B/Who_We_Are.htm (accessed December 14, 2009). Another crucial antidiscrimination organization, the American Jewish Congress, did not even organize at the national level until 1934. See Dollinger, *Quest for Inclusion*, 13.

CHAPTER 2

1. The organizations collectively represented 874,000 members.

2. Davis, *Company Men*, 198–99. For further discussions of the depression in Los Angeles and on the West Coast, see Leader, *Los Angeles and the Great Depression*, and Mullins, *Depression and the Urban West Coast, 1929–1933*.

3. Gordon, *Employment Expansion and Population Growth*, 121–27.

4. See Kuznets and Thomas, *Population Redistribution and Economic Growth*, 114. See appendix F for net migrations to other parts of the United States, 1910–1950. Cited in de Graaf, "Negro Migration to Los Angeles, 1930 to 1950," 72, 73. For more information on the Dust Bowl, the resulting migrations, and the impact on California, see Gregory, *American Exodus*; Hurt, *The Dust Bowl*; Stein, *California and the Dust Bowl Migration*; Wunder, Kaye, and Carstensen, eds., *Americans View Their Dust Bowl Experience*; and Worster, *Dust Bowl*.

5. California's population increased by 22 percent between 1930 and 1940, from 5,677,251 to 6,907,387. Though California may have attracted more migrants, a couple of other states' populations grew by a higher percentage from 1930 to 1940. Florida's grew by 29 percent and New Mexico's by 26 percent. United States Bureau of the Census, *Sixteenth Census of the United States: 1940 Population, Vol. I*, 16. As with California, Los Angeles's growth was slower than in previous years— Los Angeles County had its smallest proportionate increase ever during the 1930s. The county's population only rose from 2,208,000 in 1930 to 2,785,000 in 1940. Vorspan and Gartner, *History of the Jews of Los Angeles*, 193. For a discussion of the number of immigrants attracted to Los Angeles, see de Graaf, "Negro Migration to Los Angeles," 72.

6. From 1930 to 1940 Los Angeles's population increased from 1,238,048 to 1,504,277 people. See United States Bureau of the Census, *Fifteenth Census of the United States 1930*, 260; United States Bureau of the Census, *Sixteenth Census of the United States 1940. Population, Vol. II*, 132.

7. From 1930 to 1940, the African-American population grew from 38,894 to 63,774. The Jewish population rose from about 70,000 in 1930 to

130,000 in 1941. See United States Bureau of the Census, *Fifteenth Census of the United States*, 61–63; United States Bureau of the Census, *Sixteenth Census of the United States: 1940 Population, Vol. II*, 114; and de Graaf, "Negro Migration to Los Angeles," 78. Forty thousand of the 60,000 Jewish arrivals came from within the United States. Vorspan and Gartner reach this number for the Jewish population by applying the local ratio between natural increase and migration increase to the Jewish population. While there were German and Jewish refugees evacuating to Los Angeles during the decade (about 2,500 in 1939, for example), the post–World War I movement of European immigrants to Southern California was overshadowed by an even bigger westward trend of American Jews. See Vorspan and Gartner, *History of the Jews of Los Angeles*, 115, 196, 197. For a brief discussion of the ways this made Los Angeles unusual in terms of African-American migration, see Sides, "Working Away," 36.

8. The Japanese population grew from 21,081 to 23,321, while the Chinese population increased from 3,009 to 4,736. See United States Bureau of the Census, *Fifteenth Census of the United States*, 61–63, and United States Bureau of the Census, *Sixteenth Census of the United States: 1940 Population, Vol. II*, 114.

9. Hoffman, *Unwanted Mexican Americans in the Great Depression*, 2. For more on anti-Asian and anti-Mexican sentiment in Southern California, particularly on the relationship between such sentiment and views about public health, see Molina, *Fit to Be Citizens?* On this topic see also Abel, "From Exclusion to Expulsion" and *Tuberculosis and the Politics of Exclusion*.

10. McWilliams, *Southern California Country*, 317.

11. Hoffman, *Unwanted Mexican Americans*, 38, and Romo, *East Los Angeles*, 162. For a detailed discussion of the deportation campaign in Los Angeles, see Hoffman, *Unwanted Mexican Americans in the Great Depression*, chapter 4 passim. See also Balderrama and Rodriguez, *Decade of Betrayal*. Estimates of the number that left vary. Government reports estimated that 13,332 Mexican-origin people from Los Angeles County were forcibly removed on sixteen trains to Mexico between March 1931 and April 1934. See Balderrama, *In Defense of la Raza*, 20. Other reports estimated, however, that up to one-third of the Mexican population in Los Angeles (which some place at approximately 50,000 and others place at approximately 35,000) repatriated in the early years of the Depression. The first estimate comes from Munroy, *Rebirth*, 65, and the second from Sánchez, *Becoming Mexican American*, 123. Others reported that as many as 75,000 had left the region. McWilliams, *Factories in the Field*, 125.

12. The relief figures for minorities and whites were obtained by comparing the unemployment record for 1933 with the total population as cited in the 1930 census. See Federal Emergency Relief Administration, *Unemployment Relief Census*, 94, and United States Bureau of the Census, *Fifteenth Census of the United States*, 61–63. For information on Mexican American relief, see Scott, "The Mexican-American in the Los Angeles Area," 123.

13. For the discussion of conditions for Mexican-origin people still in Los Angeles, see Cardoso, *Mexican Emigration to the United States*, 145, cited in Romo, *East Los Angeles*, 164 n. 5.

14. In 1931, 30 percent of L.A. blacks were unemployed, and this figure grew to 34 percent in 1937. This figure was higher than some cities and lower than others. For instance, this figure went in the same period from 18 percent to 27 percent in San Francisco, and from 40 percent to 16 percent in Houston. Taylor, *In Search of the Racial Frontier*, 229. For information on Japanese unemployment, see Modell, *The Economics and Politics of Racial Accommodation*, 133. For a similar discussion of the relatively low unemployment among the San Francisco Chinese population, see Yung, *Unbound Feet*, 178–222. For a very interesting discussion of the internal dynamics of the Japanese and Japanese-American community in the 1930s, as well as its relationship with larger Los Angeles, see Kurashige, *Japanese American Celebration and Conflict*. See too Yoo, *Growing Up Nisei*.

15. Vorspan and Gartner, *History of the Jews of Los Angeles*, 205–6. For more general discussions of the history of the Jews in America, see the following: Diner, *A Time for Gathering*; Mayo, *The Ambivalent Image*; Moore, *At Home in America*; and Sachar, *A History of the Jews in America*.

16. De Graaf, "Negro Migration to Los Angeles," 84, 88.

17. Ibid., 81, 82, 87. For an excellent discussion of all of these issues confronting African American Los Angeles, see Douglas Flamming, *Bound for Freedom*.

18. Examples of capitalists who supported the program include A. P. Giannini (of Bank of America) and Henry J. Kaiser. Other states like Texas and Washington similarly supported the administration and received rewards as well. Munroy, *Rebirth*, 124. For a discussion of the New Deal on the West Coast, see Lowitt, *The New Deal and the West*. For a sampling of the extensive literature on the New Deal, see Brinkley, *The End of Reform*; Chafe, ed., *The Achievement of American Liberalism*; Mink, *The Wages of Motherhood*; and Leuchtenburg, *Franklin D. Roosevelt and the New Deal*.

19. Flamming, "Becoming Democrats," 290; Munroy, *Rebirth*, 125.

20. Flamming, "Becoming Democrats," 290–91. For other discussions of African Americans in the New Deal era, see Cash, *African American Women and Social Action*; Ferguson, *Black Politics in New Deal Atlanta*; Flamming, *Bound for Freedom*; Sitkoff, *A New Deal for Blacks*; and Sullivan, *Days of Hope*. For discussions of the New Deal's effects on Mexican Americans, see Weber, *Dark Sweat, White Gold*, and Vargas, *Labor Rights Are Civil Rights*.

21. Larkin was listed in 1933. Bass, *Forty Years*, 64–65.

22. Sánchez, *Becoming Mexican American*, 261; Weber, *Dark Sweat, White Gold*, 127. For more on the ways the New Deal aided (and did not aid) Mexican Americans in Los Angeles and elsewhere, see Vargas, *Labor Rights Are Civil Rights*.

23. Wenger, *New York Jews and the Great Depression*, 123–24. For a discussion of the New Deal's impact on white ethnic workers in cities like Chicago, see Cohen, *Making a New Deal*. For a discussion of its impact on Jews in New York, see also Moore, *At Home in America*, and Wenger, *New York Jews and the Great Depression*.

24. Vorspan and Gartner, *History of the Jews of Los Angeles*, 216–17.

25. Registered Republicans dropped from 1,638,575 to 1,458,373 while Democrats rose from 456,096 to 2,419,629. Some Los Angeles blacks had shifted to supporting the Democratic Party ahead even of other urban California blacks, beginning as early as the 1920s. Flamming, "Becoming Democrats," 283. For a

firsthand discussion of this shift, see de Graaf, Interview with Judge Loren Miller, 11–12.

26. De Graaf, "Negro Migration to Los Angeles," 73, 79. Los Angeles County's population rose only from 2,208,000 in 1930 to 2,785,000 in 1940. See footnote 5.

27. Vorspan and Gartner, *History of the Jews of Los Angeles*, 201. Others who became influential in the CRC and other Jewish community organizations included Harry A. Hollzer, David L. Coleman, Lester W. Roth, Benjamin Scheinman, and Ben Rosenthal.

28. Ibid., 201. See also Moore, *To the Golden Cities*, 193.

29. Gabler, *An Empire of Their Own*, 6, 395, and Vorspan and Gartner, *History of the Jews of Los Angeles*, 201. For more on Hollywood in the 1930s, see Buhle and Wagner, *Radical Hollywood*; May, *The Big Tomorrow*; and Rogin, *Blackface, White Noise*. Silberberg was quite influential in Los Angeles. Before becoming an attorney, he worked briefly for the *Los Angeles Times*, where he made connections with the powerful Chandler family. He later cofounded one of the most powerful law firms in Los Angeles and became what Neal Gabler calls the most important entertainment lawyer in the country. Soon after meeting Louis B. Mayer, Silberberg went to work for MGM and his firm became general counsel for Columbia and RKO. Such ties helped Silberberg gain funds from Hollywood executives for the CRC. Gabler, *An Empire of Their Own*, 294–97; Navasky, *Naming Names*, 110; and Pitt, *Joseph Roos Oral History*, 9–10. On the meeting at Pacht's house, see Leon Lewis to Richard Gutstadt (national ADL in Chicago), August 25, 1933, Folder 19, "Anti-Defamation League/B'nai B'rith—National: correspondence, Aug 1933," Box 22, Series I, CRC.

30. Modell, *The Economics and Politics*, 170–71. Members of the Young Democrats were predominantly working class and student based, in contrast to more middle class/professional/small business background of members in organizations like the Japanese American Citizens' League (JACL), which adopted a nonpartisan stance. For a discussion of the Young Democrats, see Takahashi, *Nisei/Sansei*, 68. For a further discussion of Nisei political affiliation in the 1930s, see Yoo, *Growing Up Nisei*, and Takahashi, *Nisei/Sansei*, esp. 60–74.

31. Munroy, "Mexicanos in Los Angeles, 1930–1941," 156. For a discussion of the Mexican-origin population's tendency in the prewar period to orient itself toward Mexico, see also Sánchez, *Becoming Mexican American*.

32. The Mexican community had been involved in "formal politics" before the New Deal as well, to a limited extent. For instance, Mexicans in Los Angeles gave much support to Upton Sinclair's run for the governorship in 1934. See Scott, "The Mexican-American in the Los Angeles Area," 125; Munroy, "Mexicanos in Los Angeles," 156; and Nash, *The American West in the Twentieth Century*, 171.

33. Sánchez, *Becoming Mexican American*, 222, 260–62. For a discussion of Mexican American support for the New Deal at the national level, see García, *Mexican Americans*, 42.

34. Sánchez, *Becoming Mexican American*, 250–51. For more on Roybal and Quevedo, see Burt, "The Power of a Mobilized Citizenry," 8, 416.

35. Flamming, "Becoming Democrats," 279, 289; Flamming, *Bound for Freedom*, 315; and Taylor, *In Search of the Racial Frontier*, 231–32. For another discussion on the realignment of African Americans in Los Angeles and California more

generally, see Fisher, "A History of the Political and Social Development of the Black Community in California," 223–35.

36. Munroy, *Rebirth*, 225–27. For an in-depth discussion of the development of business and a business culture in Los Angeles, see Davis, *Company Men*.

37. Vorspan and Gartner, *History of the Jews of Los Angeles*, 197–98.

38. For a good summary discussion of Mexican-American labor activity and strikes in this period, see Gutiérrez, *Walls and Mirrors*, 100–107.

39. Sánchez, *Becoming Mexican American*, 229 and chapter 11 passim, which nicely summarizes the rise of organized American labor union activity among the Mexican and Mexican American population. For a discussion of the development of a Mexican-American identity in Los Angeles from 1900 to 1945, see Sánchez.

40. Munroy, *Rebirth*, 234, 239. Although the ILGWU's membership was multiracial, its leaders were mostly Russian/Jewish. Out of nineteen officers on the board of Local No. 96, only six were Mexicans. However, despite this inequitable distribution of power among the minority groups within labor organizations like this one, the attitudes of groups like the ILGWU toward the largely Mexican-origin membership, especially by the early 1930s, and the increasing involvement of women like Rose Pesotta—a Russian immigrant—were more progressive than the majority of American society's. Munroy, *Rebirth*, 240–41, and Sanchez, *Becoming Mexican American*, 232–35. UCAPAWA worked in places like Texas and across California, not only in Los Angeles. For an excellent discussion of UCAPAWA's activities, see Ruiz, *From Out of the Shadows*, esp. 77–82. On Pesotta's involvement and impressions, see Pesotta, *Bread upon the Waters*.

41. Munroy, *Rebirth*, 248–49, and Ruiz, *From Out of the Shadows*, 80–82. George Sánchez explains that strikes and American-oriented labor activity became an important part of the Los Angeles Mexican community in the 1930s and 1940s, as opposed to earlier politics, which had focused more on Mexico. This was part of community's transformation from one dominated by the Mexican-born to one centering around the American-born. Sánchez, *Becoming Mexican American*, 228. For an excellent summary of Mexican strike and union activity in Los Angeles in the 1930s, see Sánchez, *Becoming Mexican American*, 227–52. For a discussion of an interesting precursor to the interethnic labor activity of the 1930s, see Tomás Almaguer's discussion of the first example of successful agricultural strikes among California's minority populations—the 1903 Japanese and Mexican Oxnard beet workers' strike—in *Racial Fault Lines*, 183–204. For an excellent study of the ILGWU in Los Angeles, see Ruíz, *Cannery Women, Cannery Lives*.

42. Bass, *Forty Years*, 77–79; Sides, "Working Away," 45, 53–63; and Sides, *L.A. City Limits*, 27–29. See too Flamming, *Bound for Freedom*, 316, 356–59. Nationally, African Americans' status in organized labor campaigns increased in the 1930s, as more unions needing their backing welcomed them. Sitkoff, *A New Deal for Blacks*, 169–89.

43. Bass, *Forty Years*, 77–79; Sides, "Working Away," 45, 53–63; and Sides, *LA City Limits*, 27–29.

44. Munroy, *Rebirth*, 249–52; Sánchez, *Becoming Mexican American*, 240–43; and Sides, *L.A. CityLimits*, 27–28.

45. Kurashige, "Transforming Los Angeles," 272. For more on the CIO in the Japanese community, see Kurashige, *The Shifting Grounds of Race*.

46. This discussion refers to the conclusion Lizabeth Cohen makes in her study of the Depression and New Deal's effects upon communities in Chicago. Cohen, *Making a New Deal*. Sides, "Working Away," 12.

47. Munroy, *Rebirth*, 249–52, and Sánchez, *Becoming Mexican American*, 240–43. For the fascinating story of Bert Corona, see García, *Memories of Chicano History*. For more information about María Durán, see Burt, *The Search for a Civic Voice*, 61, 63, 65.

48. See García, *Memories of Chicano History*, especially 105–6.

49. Wild, *Street Meeting*, chapter 7, 178–80.

50. Wild, *Street Meeting*, 182–83, 189.

51. Munroy, "Mexicanos in Los Angeles," 158, 160, and Sánchez, *Becoming Mexican American*, 230.

52. The director of the Los Angeles branch was the famous LaRue McCormick. The ILD also defended Sacco and Vanzetti and the Scottsboro boys, and worked to release labor activist Tom Mooney from jail. The CP was instrumental in the ILD's founding in 1925, though it claimed it was not a communist organization. Munroy, "Mexicanos in Los Angeles," 190–93.

53. Among these leaders were Guillermo Taylor and Lupe Mendoza. Munroy, "Mexicanos in Los Angeles," 195–96.

54. Wild, *Street Meeting*, 189–90.

55. On Yoneda, see Yoneda, *Ganbatte*. See too Raineri, *The Red Angel*. Katayama helped found, for instance, the Japanese Labor Association. Wild, *Street Meeting*, 179, 191.

56. On Pettis Perry, see Sides, *L.A. City Limits*, 32–33. See also Wild, *Street Meeting*, 190, 194. Other African-American CP leaders included Lou Rosser (the head of JCL), and Frank and Hursel Alexander. See Sides, *L.A. CityLimits*, 32.

57. Press Release, May 12, 1964, Mayor Bowron's office, Folder 14a, "Miller Congratulations (Judicial Appointment)," Carton 3, Miller. See too de Graaf, Interview with Judge Loren Miller, 5–6. Miller attended Washburn University Law School in Topeka.

58. For more on Miller's Soviet trip and its influence upon his thinking, see de Graaf, Interview with Judge Loren Miller, 7, and various news clippings and other documents in Binder, Carton 2, Miller. When the author saw this collection it was in process, so the filing system has undoubtedly changed; see Miller Collection for updated files. For more on Loren Miller in the 1930s, see Flamming, *Bound for Freedom*, 302–3, 305, 325, 368–69; and Wild, "A Rumored Congregation," 382–84.

59. De Graaf, Interview with Judge Loren Miller, 9.

60. Munroy, "Mexicanos in Los Angeles," 189, and Vargas, *Labor Rights Are Civil Rights*, 183.

61. Kurashige, *The Shifting Grounds of Race*, 79, and Kurashige, "Transforming Los Angeles," 273. For more on Japanese-origin community participation in communist activities, see Kurashige, "Transforming Los Angeles," 273–79, 285–91.

62. Wild, "A Rumored Congregation," 384.

63. See Healey and Isserman, *Dorothy Healey Remembers*, 59. Also see Furmanovsky, "Communism as Jewish Radical Subculture," footnote 14. Furmanovsky's estimates are based on several documents as well as interviews with party activists and extrapolations from reports on the party's membership a little earlier.

64. Wild, "A Rumored Congregation," 382.

65. For a discussion of Corona's relationship with the Communist Party throughout the decade, see his memoirs, García, *Memories of Chicano History*, 127–29, and on Bulosan's, see his memoirs throughout, Bulosan, *America Is in the Heart*.

66. See García, *Memories of Chicano History*, 127–29; García, *Mexican Americans*, 145; and Munroy, "Mexicanos in Los Angeles," esp. chapter 4 (165, 173, 198, specifically), 157–58. Munroy argues that the CP failed to appreciate or adequately integrate the Mexican-origin community's revolutionary anarcho-syndicalist tradition they had been influenced by from the Mexican Revolution, especially by the members of the Mexican liberation party (Partido Liberal Mexicano) who were exiled to Los Angeles beginning in 1904. García disagrees with Munroy about the importance of the revolutionary tradition to the Mexican community and rather argues that a reformist bent was more important to the community's growing activism.

67. Sides, *L.A. City Limits*, 32–33. On African Americans and the CP generally, see Kelley, *Hammer and Hoe*; Naison, *Communists in Harlem during the Depression*; Record, *The Negro and the Communist Party*; and Sitkoff, *A New Deal for Blacks*, 139–68.

68. Furmanovsky, "Communism as Jewish Radical Subculture;" Wild, "A Rumored Congregation," 391, 394; and Wild, *Street Meeting*, 195–97.

69. For a discussion of many of the reasons the party failed, see Wild, *Street Meeting*, 195–97.

70. Carey McWilliams, quoted in Scobie, "Jack B. Tenney," 29–30.

71. Wild, *Street Meeting*, 180–95.

72. See First National Congress of the Mexican and Spanish American People of the United States, Los Angeles, California, April 28, 29, 30, 1939, Folder 9, Box 13, Galarza. See also Camarillo, "Mexicans and Europeans in American Cities;" García, *Mexican Americans*, 146–50; and Vargas, *Labor Rights Are Civil Rights*, 186. For a firsthand discussion on El Congreso, see García, *Memories of Chicano History*, 111–16.

73. García, *Mexican Americans*, 161.

74. See García, *Memories of Chicano History*, 60, 112; García, *Mexican Americans*, 153; and Vargas, *Labor Rights Are Civil Rights*, 187–88.

75. LULAC included women, but usually in separate women's councils. García, *Mexican Americans*, 165, and Sánchez, *Becoming Mexican American*, 247. For a recent reinterpretation of LULAC, see Orozco, *No Mexicans, Women, or Dogs Allowed*.

76. García, *Mexican Americans*, 159–60, and Sánchez, *Becoming Mexican Americans*, 247–48.

77. See Ruiz, "Luisa Moreno and Latina Labor Activism," 178–84.

78. García, *Mexican Americans*, 147, 153, 155–58. Sánchez discusses the relationship between UCAPAWA, El Congreso de Pueblos que Hablan Espanol (the National Congress of Spanish Speaking Peoples), and the Communist Party. See Sánchez, *Becoming Mexican American*, 242–46. For more discussion of Fierro de Bright, Moreno, and on support from local and state politicians, see Vargas, *Labor Rights Are Civil Rights*, 181–82, 185–86.

79. I use terms like *inside and outside the formal political system* rather than *liberal* and *radical* to describe these El Congreso activists and their allies in the

1930s. Labels like liberal and radical, and the associations we give them, distract from understanding these activists' agenda. Scholars typically interpret that radicals and liberals had different goals, with the former being more substantive. Yet the description of those goals often remains amorphous, and terminology often obscures understanding. Evidence suggests that for groups like El Congreso, its allies, and similar organizations and individuals in the 1930s, their agenda was more reform-oriented than revolutionary. For scholars who characterize the organization as reform-oriented, not revolutionary, see García, *Mexican Americans*, 174; Sánchez, *Becoming Mexican American*, 249; and Vargas, *Labor Rights Are Civil Rights*, 184. Interestingly, García and Vargas use the terms *radical/left* and *liberal* to describe its members, but the terms seem to describe the members' political affiliation rather than the overarching goal of their activism—reforming American democracy to be more inclusive and fair to Mexican-origin people.

80. García, *Mexican Americans*, 163–64, and Sánchez, *Becoming Mexican American*, 247. See too Vargas, *Labor Rights Are Civil Rights*, 156–57.

81. See García, *Mexican Americans*, 146–50. See too Camarillo, "Mexicans and Europeans in American Cities." For a firsthand discussion on El Congreso and its significance, see García, *Memories of Chicano History*, 111–16.

82. Leonard, "In the Interest of All Races," 316.

83. García, *Memories of Chicano History*, 106.

84. García, *Mexican Americans*, 158.

85. De Graaf, "Negro Migration to Los Angeles," 81, 82, 87. For an excellent discussion of all of these issues confronting African American Los Angeles, see Flamming, *Bound for Freedom*.

86. The Federation of Spanish-Speaking Voters was one of the first groups to organize Mexican Americans in Los Angeles politically. Scott, "The Mexican-American in the Los Angeles Area," 148.

87. For this argument, see Sánchez, *Becoming Mexican American*, 228–29.

88. Takahashi, *Nisei/Sansei*, 55. For information on the JACL see Chan, *Asian Americans: An Interpretive History*, 117; Hosokawa, *JACL*; Takahashi, *Nisei/Sansei*, 54–65; and Japanese Chamber of Commerce of Southern California, *Japanese in Southern California*, 20–23. John Modell disagrees with the date of the JACL's formation, stating the L.A. chapter formed in 1929; Modell, *The Economics and Politics*, 168.

89. See Chan, *Asian Americans: An Interpretive History*. Also see discussion in Daniels, *Asian America*, 179–82. Historian John Modell has argued that the Los Angeles branch was less active than other JACL branches, but it was nevertheless an important local ethnic defense organization. Modell argues that because of both the relatively larger number of potential Nisei voters there and the loose nature of Southern California politics, Nisei in Los Angeles often worked more through New Deal–style coalition politics than through organizations like the JACL. Modell, *The Economics and Politics*, 182. In the late 1930s and early 1940s Los Angeles Japanese Americans also expressed their increased involvement in the public realm by emphasizing their Americanism through cultural events like Nisei Week. See Kurashige, *Japanese American Celebration and Conflict*.

90. De Graaf, Mulroy, and Taylor, *Seeking El Dorado*, 20; and Sides, "Working Away," 71–72.

91. Sides, *L.A. City Limits*, 27–30; Sides, "Working Away," 71–72; and Taylor, *In Search of the Racial Frontier*, 238.

92. The L.A. Urban League was created in 1930, and the National Urban League was founded in New York in 1911. The local and national branches of the National Negro Congress both began in 1936. Though scholars and contemporaries criticized the Urban League for being more of an "uplift" organization than a protest one, it nonetheless represented increasing efforts on the part of African Americans to improve their conditions. See Taylor, *In Search of the Racial Frontier*, 242. See also Sides, "Working Away," 72. According to Doug Flamming, founders hoped the National Negro Congress would unite labor and left-leaning groups with more middle class organizations like the NAACP and Urban League. Flamming, *Bound for Freedom*, 356.

93. See Vorspan and Gartner, *History of the Jews of Los Angeles*, 205.

94. Vorspan and Gartner, *History of the Jews of Los Angeles*, 205–6.

95. Vorspan and Gartner, *History of the Jews of Los Angeles*, 205. For a discussion of Nazi and Bund activities in Los Angeles, see Scobie, "Jack B. Tenney," especially 10.

96. During the same year the CRC formed, devoting its primary activities to monitoring rising anti-Semitism and anti-Semitic agitators, already established national Jewish organizations formed special units for this same purpose. While organizations including the American Jewish Congress (AJ Congress) and American Jewish Committee (AJC) had concentrated in previous decades on Jewry in Europe and elsewhere, they now increasingly turned toward domestic issues. Though the American Jewish Committee's (AJC) national subcommittee also formed in 1933 to deal with the same issues, it was a branch of another organization rather than a separate organization created specifically to address growing anti-Semitism. Only in 1936 did it become an independent organization that took on this project as its main task, as the CRC had done earlier in Los Angeles. It was called the Jewish Survey Committee. For more on this, see Wall, *Inventing the "American Way,"* 82–83, and Wall, "The Idea of America," 135–43. The Survey Committee later morphed into the still-existing national organization, the National Community Relations Advisory Council (NCRAC), formed in 1944. On NCRAC, see Svonkin, *Jews against Prejudice*, 3.

Later, branches of national defense-oriented agencies like the American Jewish Committee (AJC) and the American Jewish Congress (AJ Congress) were established in Los Angeles too. The Anti-Defamation League of B'nai B'rith, or ADL, was already established in Los Angeles, but its focus encompassed more than community defense activities. Pitt, *Joseph Roos Oral History*, 20, and Community Relations Committee, Minutes of the Meeting of the Special Subcommittee on Agencies Concerned with Intra Jewish Community Problems and Services, December 6, 1949, Subcomms: Special—Agencies; Intra-Jewish 1949–1950 Folder, Section AII, Series III, CRC.

97. For additional discussion of the Community Relations Committee, see Vorspan and Gartner, *History of the Jews of Los Angeles*, 221–24.

98. Pitt, *Joseph Roos Oral History*, December 18, 1979, 9–10. Hollywood funding helped get the agency off the ground. In 1933, Leon Lewis reported to Isaac Pacht, "Some of the M.G.M. executives clearly manifested a desire to cooperate, and I am satisfied that they will do their share." Warner Brothers secured

pledges of about $3,000, Warner and MGM promised $5,000, and Universal promised about $2,500. Leon Lewis letter to Isaac Pacht, November 2, 1933, Folder 31 Pacht [Judge] Isaac, 1933–1937, Box 1, Series I, CRC. For interesting discussions of Hollywood's ties to the CRC and other Jewish organizations in the 1930s, see Gabler, *An Empire of Their Own*; Herman, "Hollywood, Nazism and the Jews, 1933–41." See too Herman, "Jewish Leaders and the Motion Picture Industry." For a broader discussion of Warner Bros.'s involvement in anti-Nazi activity in the 1930s, specifically through several of the films it made in that decade, see Birdwell, *Celluloid Soldiers*.

99. Pitt, *Joseph Roos Oral History*, December 18, 1979, 9–10.

100. Gabler, *An Empire of Their Own*, 294-97; Navasky, *Naming Names*, 110; and Pitt, *Joseph Roos Oral History*, 18.

101. See introductory overview of the CRC files, in binder catalog, CRC.

102. Letter from Leon Lewis to Walter Hilborn, February 25, 1935, Folder 21—Hilborn, Walter 1935, Box 1, Series I, CRC.

103. Memorandum, 1934, Folder 15—Lewis, Leon L. [Executive Secretary]: reports, 1933–1934, Box 2, Series I, CRC.

104. The speaker was Ludwig Laithold, "Nazis Hold First Open Meet Here," July 27, 1933, Schwinn, Herman—Nazi Leader Folder, *Los Angeles Examiner* clippings. Los Angeles was a center for the German-American Bund and other suspected Nazi organizations, while San Francisco was a center for Italian fascist organizations. Scobie, "Jack B. Tenney," 10. Los Angeles, along with New York, was also a center of German exile activity in the late 1930s and 1940s. In the 1930s and 1940s the federal government suspected these exiles, who had left Germany for fear of persecution by Hitler, of Communism. According to Alexander Stephen, the two cities were also the centers of European exile activities in the 1920s. Consequently, J. Edgar Hoover established his two largest field offices of the FBI in New York and Los Angeles in the 1920s. Stephan, "*Communazis*," 19. For a discussion of the activities and experiences of German exiles alienated by Hitler's regime and seeking refuge in Los Angeles and elsewhere in the United States and Mexico, see the book. See too Bahr, *Weimar on the Pacific*.

105. Letter from Leon Lewis to Mrs. Mischel, January 6, 1944, Folder 20—Inter-Racial Relations Jan–June 1944, Box 111, Series II, CRC.

106. "Raids Nab Bund Leader, 4 Followers," January 16, 1939, Schwinn, Herman—Nazi Leader Folder, *Los Angeles Examiner* clippings.

107. Photo of Nazi flag outside downtown Los Angeles businesses, 1938 (?), Folder 8, Box 2, CRC Photo Collection.

108. *A Proclamation*, September 25, 1935, The American Nationalist Party for Nation-Wide Distribution (Los Angeles: General Headquarters), reproduced in McWilliams, *It Can Happen Here*. McWilliams claimed that *Los Angeles Times* officials had been unaware of the pamphlet's inclusion in the paper's home edition, and that at the time of his booklet's publication, were investigating the incident. See too discussion in Pitt, *Joseph Roos Oral History*, December 18, 1979, 8–9, 20, and Gardner *Honorable in All Things*, 86–87. Roos misremembers the timing of the incident—he placed it two years earlier, in 1933.

109. McWilliams, *It Can Happen Here*, 3. For more on McWilliams's concern about rising anti-Semitism in the 1930s, see Gardner, *Honorable in All Things*, 86–87, and Geary, "Carey McWilliams and Antifascism, 1934–1943."

110. "Coastwide Plot Charged to L.A. Bund," October 1938 (possibly 1939, date not clear), Schwinn, Herman—Nazi Leader Folder, *Los Angeles Examiner* clippings.

111. Wall, "The Idea of America," 136. See also Wall, *Inventing the "American Way,"* 29–31.

112. The article quoted testimony provided to Congress by Representative Dickstein (D) of New York. "116 on List as Leaders of Nazis Here," November 19, 1937, Schwinn, Herman—Nazi Leader Folder, *Los Angeles Examiner* clippings.

113. Some articles reported that Germany provided Mexico with agricultural machinery in exchange for $3 million worth of crude diesel and gas, but the Mexican ambassador to the United States denied this accusation. See various newspaper articles, including "Mexico Trades Oil for Nazi Machinery," June 1938; "Nazis Seeking Mexican Oil," September 19, 1938; "Mexico-Germany Make Oil Deal"; "Mexico Not Buying Planes in Germany," February 19, 1939; "Mexico Rejects Nazi Deal: Refuses to Trade Oil for Planes," February 24, 1939, all in Mexico, Germany Relations Folder, *Los Angeles Examiner* clippings.

114. Untitled article, July 3, 1940, Mexico, Germany Relations Folder, *Los Angeles Examiner* clippings. For another interesting article, see "Nazis Goad Mexico; U.S. Embassy Periled," June 9, 1939, Mexico, Germany Relations Folder, *Los Angeles Examiner* clippings.

115. Pitt, *Joseph Roos Oral History Interview*, December 18, 1979, 8.

116. Letter from Leon Lewis to Mrs. Mischel, January 6, 1944, Folder 20—Inter-Racial Relations Jan–June 1944, Box 111, Series II, CRC.

117. A reported drop in the Friends of New Germany's membership from its 1933 high point of about 350 to about 130 by mid-1934 is one example that hints at this shift, which the CRC attributed to its own activities. Leon Lewis, Summary of Operations from June 1933 to March 1934, Folder 15—Lewis, Leon L.: reports, 1933–1934, Box 2, Series I, CRC.

118. Leon Lewis (?), Memorandum on Conference held this morning with Mr. Armin Wittenberg and Chief of Police Davis, September 15, 1933, Folder 22—Los Angeles Police Department-Intelligence Division [the "Red Squad"], 1933–1937, Box 30, Series I, CRC.

119. While officials became more active against fascists and perceived fascists once the Japanese bombed Pearl Harbor and the United States entered the war, federal agencies did monitor such groups' activities before 1941, and were to some degree receptive to information from Jewish agencies. In one case, the FBI, HUAC, and Tenney Committee all used information it received from the News Research Service, a camouflaged agency secretly run by Joe Roos and the Community Relations Committee, to monitor fascist activity in Los Angeles, including from German and Japanese descent residents. See Eisenberg, *The First to Cry Down Injustice?* chapter 4.

120. "6 Southland Folk Indicted as Seditious," January 4, 1944, Schwinn, Herman—Nazi Leader Folder, *Los Angeles Examiner* clippings, and "More Sedition Cases Seen," October 5, 1943, Schwinn, Herman—Nazi Leader Folder, *Los Angeles Examiner* clippings.

121. "'Baby Bunds' Shown Still in Existence," September 2 1942, Schwinn, Herman—Nazi Leader Folder, *Los Angeles Examiner* clippings.

122. Yung, *Unbound Feet*, 224–26. For more on Chinese Americans in California during this period, see Brooks, *Alien Neighbors, Foreign Friends*.

123. Zheng, "Chinese-Americans in San Francis co and New York City during the Anti-Japanese War," esp. 75–94. For more on the relationship between Chinese Americans and events in Asia, see Chen, *Chinese San Francisco, 1850–1943*.

124. For discussions of Chinese exclusion and anti-Chinese discrimination, see, for instance, Daniels, *Asian America*; Hing, *Making and Remaking Asian America through Immigration Policy, 1850–1990*; and Takaki, *Strangers from a Different Shore*.

125. Takaki, *Strangers from a Different Shore*, 113–15.

126. Zheng, *Chinese-Americans in San Francisco and New York City*, 94. For further discussion of some of these reasons Chinese and Chinese Americans felt allegiance to China, see Zheng, who discusses the links created by tradition and culture as well as discrimination, 75–94.

127. García, *Mexican Americans*, 147, 153, 155–58. See too the discussions in the following works about the ways the Mexican Revolution influenced Mexican-origin peoples' struggles for social justice in the United States: Munroy, "Mexicanos in Los Angeles," 161–73; Munroy, *Rebirth*, 223–48; and Sánchez, *Becoming Mexican American*, 246.

128. Loren Miller, "Goodbye to Isolation," March 31, 1933, Folder 2 "Negro Labor," Carton 1, Miller.

129. Ibid.

130. Ibid.

131. On African Americans' international involvement in the 1930s and its connection to their domestic equality struggles, see von Eschen, *Race against Empire*. See too Plummer, *Rising Wind*.

132. McWilliams, *The Education of Carey McWilliams*, 92–93.

133. Surprisingly, given national African Americans' involvement in the Ethiopian issue, and the prevalence of antifascist activity in Los Angeles more generally, I did not find much information on the subject in Los Angeles African-American community files.

134. Hollywood Anti-Nazi League for the Defense of American Democracy, letter to Ford, December 24, 1936, 46/B/III/11/d—Communism, Fascism, Nazism, Ford.

CHAPTER 3

1. For an interesting study of the war's impact upon various communities nationwide, see Daniels, *Prisoners without Trial*; Moore, *GI Jews*; Honey, ed., *Bitter Fruit*; Morehouse, *Fighting in the Jim Crow Army*; Rivas-Rodriguez, ed., *Mexican Americans and World War II*; and Takaki, *Double Victory*.

For more on the war's impact on civil rights activism both nationwide and in Los Angeles, see Acuña, *A Community Under Siege*; Dalfiume, *Desegregation of the U.S. Armed Forces*; Daniel, *Chicano Workers and the Politics of Fairness*; Kurashige, *The Shifting Grounds of Race*; Leonard, *The Battle for Los Angeles*; Leonard, "Years of Hope, Days of Fear"; Sides, *L.A. City Limits*; Takaki, *Double Victory*; Taylor, *In*

Search of the Racial Frontier; Yung, *Unbound Feet;* and Zamora, *Claiming Rights and Righting Wrongs in Texas.*

2. San Diego and Los Angeles had the worst wartime labor shortages in the nation. Sides, "Working Away," 80–81. Not all scholars agree that the war transformed the city, whether in terms of major changes in racial composition or otherwise. For this perspective, see Lotchin, *The Bad City in the Good War.*

3. Sides, "Working Away," 80–81, and Sides, *L.A. City Limits,* 37. The Los Angeles metropolitan area's population increased in the same time by almost 12 percent, from 2,904,596 to 3,250,000. The county's population of industrial workers had tripled from 1940 to 1943 (from 139,368 to 420,275), since 75 to 80 percent of newcomers worked in war-related plants and industries. From 1930 to 1940 the city of Los Angeles's population increased from 1,238,048 to 1,504,277. It grew to 1,718,000 in 1943, and to 1,970,358 by 1950. See Mayor Fletcher Bowron, Address before Sub-Committee of Military Affairs, U.S. Senate, April 27, 1943, Extra Copies of Letters 1943 Folder, Box 1, Bowron; United States Bureau of the Census, *Fifteenth Census of the United States 1930,* 260; United States Bureau of the Census, *Sixteenth Census of the United States 1940. Population, Vol. II,* 132; United States Bureau of the Census, *A Report of the Seventeenth Decennial Census of the United States Census of the Population 1950. Vol. II,* 5–51.

4. The black population increased by over 268 percent, from 63,774 to 171,209. United States Bureau of the Census, *Sixteenth Census of the United States 1940. Population, Vol. II,* 629, and United States Bureau of the Census, *A Report of the Seventeenth Decennial Census of the United States Census of the Population 1950. Vol. II,* 5–100.

5. Sides, "Working Away," 80, 84. He does not indicate if this is to the city or county of Los Angeles.

6. The Mexican-descent population grew from 107,680 to 157,067 from 1940 to 1950. Approximately 250,000 resided in Los Angeles County by 1945. "Los Angeles County Committee for Interracial Progress Origin and Functions," 1945, 3, Folder 9—Comm on Human Relations, LA County: Corresp Jan–Apr 1945, Box 218, Series II, CRC. The figures for the Mexican-origin population in 1940 and 1950 are estimates, as the census in these periods did not categorize this population separately. The only information we have is from the 1940 census, which counted the "Spanish-mother tongue population" in Los Angeles and the 1950 census, which counted the "Spanish-surnamed population" in the city. The census numbers are almost certainly undercounts. See United States Bureau of the Census, *Sixteenth Census of the United States, 1940, Population: Nativity and Percentage of the White Population, Mother Tongue,* 34, and United States Bureau of the Census, *U.S. Census of the Population: 1950—Special Reports: Persons of Spanish Surname,Vol. IV, Special Reports Part 3, Chapter C,* 3C-43.

7. In 1941 only about 130,000 Jews lived in the city of Los Angeles, and by 1945 there were about 150,000. By 1946 approximately 168,000 Jews lived in the city, which skyrocketed in the following two years to about 250,000 by 1948. Vorspan and Gartner, *History of the Jews of Los Angeles,* 225.

8. Vorspan and Gartner, *History of the Jews of Los Angeles,* 242; Milton A. Senn, "A Study of Police Training Programs in Minority Relations," August 7, 1950, Folder

1, Box 5, Ross. This 1946 number differs from census estimates for 1940 and 1950, cited in previous footnotes, revealing the difficulty of achieving accuracy. The figures for 1950 [171,209 African Americans; 25,502 Japanese-descent individuals; 157,067 Mexican-descent individuals, 250,000 Jewish Americans (this is a 1948 figure, but the best estimate available)] put the sum total of the largest minority groups' population at 603,778 of a total city population of 1,970,358, or 30%. On the 1950 population total see Bureau of the Census, *A Report of the Seventeenth Decennial Census of the United States Census of Population: 1950, Vol. II: Characteristics of the Population*, Part 5: California (Washington, D.C.: U.S. Government Printing Office, 1952), 10, 54. On Los Angeles County numbers and percentages, the census and other scholarly estimates place the total minority number at approximately 800,000 of a total population of 4,367,911, or 18 percent. See numbers cited in previous footnotes, with the addition of the Jewish-American population estimates.

9. Sides, "Working Away," 123.

10. LA County Committee on Human Relations Report, *Housing for Negroes in LA County*, July 9, 1945, Folder 11—Comm on Human Relations, LA County: Corresp Jul–Dec 1945, Box 218, Series II, CRC; and Sides, "Working Away," 108.

11. On the Menorah Center and its swimming pool, see Rabbi M. Siegelstein (Director Menorah Center) letter to John Anson Ford, July 8, 1954, 75/B/IV/5/i/ cc—Jewish, 1954 Folder, Ford. For more on ethnic mixing in Los Angeles and elsewhere in California in the World War II period, see Varzally, *Coloring Outside Ethnic Lines*. For an interesting discussion on this in the 1920s and 1930s, see Wild, *Street Meeting*.

12. For a discussion of police brutality and repression in the Mexican-American community in this period, see Escobar, *Race, Police, and the Making of a Political Identity*.

13. Sánchez, *Becoming Mexican American*, 267. The most serious injury was to an African-American victim who was blinded. See Pitt, *LA A to Z*, 571.

14. For a general discussion of the Zoot Suit Riots, see Mazón, *The Zoot-Suit Riots*. Mazón's discussion, however, does not mention the international implications of the Zoot Suit affair. For a discussion of Filipino men's involvement, too, see España-Maram, *Creating Masculinity in Los Angeles's Little Manila*. See also Escobar, *Race, Police, and the Making of a Political Identity*; Pagán, *Murder at the Sleepy Lagoon*; and Ramirez, *The Woman in the Zoot Suit*. For more on Mayor Bowron's reactions— namely, his support for the LAPD and blame for the servicemen and Mexican-American "gang members," see Sitton, *Los Angeles Transformed*, 68–69. For an interesting discussion of zoot suit culture, see Álvarez, *The Power of the Zoot*.

15. Ford, *Thirty Explosive Years in Los Angeles County*, 129–30. See too Milton Senn, "Preface," *A Study of Police Training Programs in Minority Relations*, August 7 1950, Folder 1, Box 5, Ross.

16. Americanism Defense Committee of the Seventeenth District American Legion, Dept. of California, *Report No. 2, "Since Dec. 7": Enemy Propaganda in Southern California*, February 20, 1942, Carton 6, Ford.

17. Ibid.

18. Ibid.

19. Stephan, "*Communazis*," 47. In the late 1930s and 1940s, Los Angeles, along with New York, was a center not only of Nazi activity but also of German exile

activity. See Stephan, *"Communazis,"* 47–55. For more on these émigrés and their impact, see Aschheim, *Beyond the Border*, and Starr, *The Dream Endures*, 342–96. The Tenney Committee formed in 1941, just three years after the national organization HUAC. Scobie, "Jack B. Tenney," 2.

20. Mazón, *The Zoot-Suit Riots*, 14.

21. Jack Smith, *Los Angeles Times*, undated, quoted in Jack Smith, "The Great Los Angeles Air Raid," in Caughey, ed., *Los Angeles*, 364.

22. *Los Angeles Times*, May 20, 1943, part 1, 1.

23. Ford, Letter to Francis Biddle, U.S. Attorney General, May 28, 1942, 74/B/IV/5/i/bb—Japanese, 1942 Folder, Ford.

24. Guy Endore, "Sleepy Lagoon Mystery," 1944, Folder 26, Box 28, Corona. The *Times* and the Hearst press featured many stories on alleged Mexican-American crime and juvenile delinquency, which greatly exaggerated the issue and whipped up other Angelenos fears of this population. See Escobar, *Race, Police, and the Making of a Political Identity*, and García, "Americans All," 285–86.

25. For a discussion of the Sleepy Lagoon situation, trial, and convictions, as well as the committee that fought to overturn the conviction (the Sleepy Lagoon Defense Committee), see Escobar, *Race, Police, and the Making of a Political Identity*, 207–29, 281–84. See also Pagán, *Murder at the Sleepy Lagoon*.

26. Quoted in McWilliams, *North from Mexico*, 237–38. For a wonderful collection of similar Latin American newspaper articles concerning American discrimination against Latin American-descent people, see articles like "Discriminación vs. Panamericanismo," *El Mundo* (Mexico), November 1943, and others in Folder 3, Box 58, Galarza.

27. "Report: Mexicans and the United States," April 10, 1944, Folder 6, Box 58, Galarza. For more on Texas discrimination and its relationship to international relations and increased U.S. government civil rights concerns see Zamora, *Claiming Rights and Righting Wrongs in Texas*.

28. Griswold Del Castillo, "The Los Angeles 'Zoot Suit Riots' Revisited," 373–74.

29. See Hensley C. Woodbridge, "Mexico and U.S. Racism: How Mexicans View Our Treatment of Minorities," *Commonweal*, June 22, 1945, 235, cited in Gutiérrez, *Walls and Mirrors*, 140.

30. Griswold Del Castillo, "The Los Angeles 'Zoot Suit Riots' Revisited," 390.

31. The United States had worked particularly hard to strengthen relations with Latin America through the Good Neighbor Policy, whose origins dated to Herbert Hoover's administration in the late 1920s, and which solidified during FDR's first term. For discussions of the Good Neighbor Policy, see, for instance, Ellis, *Republican Foreign Policy, 1921–1933*; Leuchtenburg, *Franklin D. Roosevelt and the New Deal, 1932–1940*; Marks, *Wind Over Sand*; Pike, *FDR's Good Neighbor Policy*; Williams, *The Tragedy of American Diplomacy*; and Wood, *The Making of the Good Neighbor Policy*.

The threat of collaboration between Mexico and Germany, which the Zimmerman Telegram highlighted in earlier decades, resurfaced with a new urgency in World War II. During World War I, the United States intercepted this German message to Mexico, which promised that Germany would assist Mexico regain land the United States had taken in 1848 in exchange for Mexico's wartime help. Memories of the Zimmerman Telegram motivated some of the concern among U.S. policymakers for strengthening the United States' influence in Mexico. See Niblo, *War, Diplomacy, and Development,* 65.

32. Griswold Del Castillo, "The Los Angeles 'Zoot Suit Riots' Revisited," 373–74.

33. Ibid., 382.

34. Niblo, *War, Diplomacy, and Development,* 63–64.

35. See Pike, *FDR's Good Neighbor Policy,* 229. For Fireside Chat, see Broadcast, December 19, 1940, in Buhite and Levy, eds., *FDR's Fireside Chats,* 167–68, 175.

36. Haglund, *Latin America and the Transformation of U.S. Strategic Thought, 1936–1940,* 184, 196, quoted in Pike, *FDR's Good Neighbor Policy,* 231.

37. Though historians later dismissed this evidence as overblown, concluding that in some cases Latin Americans overemphasized the Fascist influence in order to lure Americans back into intervening in Latin American affairs, North Americans feared Latin America's vulnerability. See discussion in Pike, *FDR's Good Neighbor Policy,* 233, and Niblo, *War, Diplomacy, and Development,* 66–68. Also, for discussion of pre-1941 U.S. concern with Axis advances in Latin America, see Niblo, *War, Diplomacy, and Development,* 63–64.

38. García, *Mexican Americans,* 168, and McWilliams, *North from Mexico,* 264–65. For an interesting discussion of sinarquista activities in Los Angeles and elsewhere in the United States and Mexico, as well as Mexican-American efforts to fight them, see Vargas, *Labor Rights Are Civil Rights,* 188–192.

39. This program began in August 1942 as an agreement between the United States and Mexican governments allowing Mexican workers into the United States on an emergency—and temporary—basis. By 1947 almost 220,000 braceros had worked under contract in the United States; almost 57 percent of them labored on large corporate California farms, harvesting crops crucial to maintaining the American war effort. From Wayne David Rasmussen, *Emergency Farm Labor Supply Program,* 199, 226, in Gutiérrez, *Walls and Mirrors,* 134. American employers routinely abused these workers, violating promises the U.S. government had made to Mexico that it would ensure that braceros' rights were respected.

40. Mexico produced fifteen of twenty metals critical to the U.S. war effort. Mexico agreed in 1943 to increase its cultivated lands by 3,300,000 acres to provide additional food and agricultural material for the Allied war effort. Niblo, *War, Diplomacy, and Development,* 91–94.

41. Ibid., 95–99.

42. Two days after Pearl Harbor, Mexico broke off relations with Japan and committed itself to a U.S. pact. By December 11 it severed diplomatic relations with Germany and Italy as well and froze German and Italian assets, forbade the sending of messages in languages besides Spanish or English, and ordered all Axis nationals to leave coastal and defense areas. It also forbade the exporting of strategic raw materials without governmental approval. Ibid., 77.

43. Ibid., 83.

44. For further discussion of the relationship between U.S. foreign policy and domestic race relations during World War II, see Hart, "Making Democracy Safe for

the World." See too Zamora, "Mexico's Wartime Intervention on Behalf of Mexicans in the United States." For a discussion of the relationship between international World War II affairs and Mexican Americans' civil rights struggles in Texas, see Guglielmo, "Fighting for Caucasian Rights." For more on how L.A. discrimination encouraged the federal government to intervene in Los Angeles and elsewhere, like Texas, see Zamora, *Claiming Rights and Righting Wrongs in Texas*, esp. 76–78.

45. Quoted in McWilliams, *North from Mexico*, 237–38.

46. Institute on Inter-American Relations and Post-War Planning, January 30, 1943, Carton 6, Ford.

47. For a discussion of officials' previous trivialization of the Mexican community's troubles, see Sánchez, *Becoming Mexican American*, 83.

48. Los Angeles County Public Library, *Republics of the Western Hemisphere*, 1942, Carton 6, Ford.

49. Mayor Bowron, Speech in Los Angeles, January 7, 1942, Remarks at Public Events Addresses by the Mayor, 1942 Folder, Box 34, Bowron.

50. Mayor Bowron, Speech at the Anniversary of the Celebration of Mexico's Independence Day, September 15, 1943, Remarks at Public Events Addresses by the Mayor, 1943 Folder, Box 34, Bowron.

51. Mayor Bowron, Speech in Los Angeles at the Cinco de Mayo Celebration, May 5, 1944, Remarks at Public Events Addresses by the Mayor, 1944 Folder, Box 34, Bowron.

52. Bowron, Letter to Vierling Kersey (Superintendent of Schools), February 1, 1943, Extra Copies of Letters 1943 Folder, Box 1, Bowron.

53. Bowron, Letter to Vierling Kersey (Superintendent of Schools), February 1, 1943, Extra Copies of Letters 1943 Folder, Box 1, Bowron.

54. Bowron, Letter to Elmer Davis, Office of War Information, Washington DC, June 28, 1943, Extra Copies 1943 Folder, Box 1, Bowron. For more on Bowron in general, and in terms of racial issues specifically, see Sitton, *Los Angeles Transformed*.

55. Ford, Letter to Nelson Rockefeller of Office of Coordinator of Inter American Affairs, June 9, 1943, 75/B/IV/5/i/dd—Mexican, 1943 Folder, Ford.

56. Ford, Letter to Nelson Rockefeller of Office of Coordinator of Inter American Affairs, 9 June 1943, 75/B/IV/5/i/dd—Mexican, 1943 Folder, Ford.

57. Southern California Council of Inter-American Affairs, *The Southern California Council of Inter-American Affairs*, 1944(?), Carton 6, Ford. This agency was officially designated by the Department of State, the Office of Inter-American Affairs, the Inter-American Development Commission, the Pan-American Union, and the Institute of International Education. Ford, Letter to Sheridan Downey, June 25, 1943, 75/B/IV/5/i/dd—Mexican, 1943 Folder, Ford.

58. Bowron, Letter to Elmer Davis, Office of War Information, Washington DC, June 28, 1943, Extra Copies 1943 Folder, Box 1, Bowron. For more on this aspect of Bowron, see Sitton, *Los Angeles Transformed*.

59. Bowron, Letter to C.B. Horrall, Chief of Police, July 19, 1943, Extra Copies 1943 Folder, Box 1, Bowron.

60. Bowron, Letter to C.B. Horrall, Chief of Police, July 19, 1943, Extra Copies 1943 Folder, Box 1, Bowron.

61. Bowron, Letter to State Department, August 3, 1943, Extra Copies 1943 Folder, Box 1, Bowron. For a thorough discussion of Mayor Fletcher Bowron's tenure in Los Angeles, see Sitton, *Los Angeles Transformed*.

Most investigators, including the State Department and the L.A. County Grand Jury, emphasized instead that antisocial "Pachucos" and a few "bad servicemen" caused the riots. Griswold Del Castillo, "The Los Angeles 'Zoot Suit Riots' Revisited," 377–78, 384–85. Ford was unusual among investigating authorities. Unlike the others, he placed the blame for provoking the clash largely on the servicemen. Ford, Letter to Nelson Rockefeller of Office of Coordinator of Inter American Affairs, June 9, 1943, 75/B/IV/5/i/dd—Mexican, 1943 Folder, Ford.

62. "How to Tell Your Friends from the Japs," *Time*, December 22, 1941, 33.

63. "How to Tell Japs from the Chinese," *Life*, December 22, 1941, 81–82.

64. Takaki, *Double Victory*, 112; *Time*, December 22, 1941, 33.

65. "G-Men Seize 4 Japanese in Little Tokyo," *Los Angeles Examiner* clippings, December 8, 1941.

66. "How to Tell Japs from the Chinese," *Life*, December 22, 1941, 81.

67. Congressman's quote from *Congressional Record*, 78th Congress, 1st Session, 1943, vol. 89, part 6, 8580, 8581, 8597, from Takaki, *Double Victory*, 120.

68. Yung, *Unbound Feet*, 251; Takaki, *Double Victory*, 112–20.

69. Yung, *Unbound Feet*, 250, 251. For more on the way the war transformed Chinese Americans' status, see Chen, *Chinese San Francisco*, and on the Cold War as well see Brooks, *Alien Neighbors, Foreign Friends*.

70. For a discussion of the role fear of Japanese propaganda played, see Takaki, *Double Victory*, 119; see also Dower, *War without Mercy*. For more on the way China's status as an ally forced the United States' hand repealing exclusion laws, as well as a discussion of Chinese-American activism pushing for these changes, see Leong, "Foreign Policy, National Identity, and Citizenship."

71. Zheng, "Chinese-Americans in San Francisco and New York City during the Anti-Japanese War: 1937–1945," esp. 75–94. For more on the role of Chinese American activism, see Takaki, *Double Victory*, 118–19.

72. For more information on the history of anti-Japanese policies, see Takaki, *Strangers from a Different Shore*.

73. See for instance literature by Daniels, *Concentration Camps USA*; Girdner and Loftis, *The Great Betrayal*; Grodzins, *Americans Betrayed*; Hayashi, *Democratizing the Enemy*; Robinson, *By Order of the President*; and tenBroek, Barnhart, and Matson, *Prejudice, War and the Constitution*. For other interesting illustrations of Japanese American internment, see Chang, *Morning Glory, Evening Shadow*, and Weglyn, *Years of Infamy*.

74. White, *Earl Warren a Public Life*, 75. There is disagreement as to the exact role Warren played in orchestrating internment. For viewpoints that see Warren's role as crucial and influential, see Chuman, *The Bamboo People*, and White, *Earl Warren a Public Life*, 74–75. For those who dispute the characterization, see Jacobus TenBroek et al., *Prejudice, War and the Constitution*, 200, and Daniels, *Concentration Camps, North America*, 51–52. Mayor Bowron later claimed he had played only a small role in internment, but evidence uncovered by Tom Sitton reveals that by early 1942 Bowron pressured the federal government to pursue internment. See Sitton, *Los Angeles Transformed*, 64–65.

75. See Blum, *V Was for Victory*, 147–55, 172, and Takaki, *Double Victory*, 131–36. See also D'Amelio, "A Season of Panic"; Fox, *America's Invisible Gulag*;

Hacker, "Aliens in Montana"; Krammer, *Undue Process*; Lothrop, "Unwelcome in Freedom's Land"; and Saunders and Daniels, eds., *Alien Justice*.

76. See Girdner and Loftis, *The Great Betrayal*; Grodzins, *Americans Betrayed*; Daniels, *Concentration Camps USA*. For a discussion of one particular group that opposed internment, see, for instance, Bernstein, "Against the Grain." See too Austin, *From Concentration Camp to Campus*.

77. Healey and Isserman, *Dorothy Healey Remembers*, 86. For an account of this from the perspective of Karl Yoneda, see Yoneda, *Ganbatte*.

78. C. L. Dellums (NAACP Alameda County), letter to Walter White (NY NAACP), April 7, 1942, "Japanese 1942–45" Folder, Box A325, Group II, NAACP LOC. For more on Dellums, see Self, *American Babylon*.

79. Walter White, Letter to Wendell Berge, July 27, 1942, "Japanese 1942–45" Folder, Box A325, Group II, NAACP LOC.

80. The *California Eagle* largely ignored internment until 1943, when it published an apology for not opposing it sooner. Only the *LA Tribune*, the smallest of Los Angeles's three black newspapers, opposed internment at the time. See Widener, "'Perhaps the Japanese Are to Be Thanked?'" 165–66.

81. Lewis, Letter to H. U. M. Higgins at the LA Hall of Justice, March 20, 1942, Folder 42—Los Angeles County Defense Council (Re: Japanese Americans) 1942, Box 223, Series II, CRC.

82. Widener, "'Perhaps the Japanese Are to Be Thanked?'" 165–66. See too Greenberg, "Black and Jewish Reponses to Japanese Internment," and Kurashige, *The Shifting Grounds of Race*, esp. 104–5. On this subject also see Balter, *Law and Social Conscience*, interview of Ben Margolis, 94; Leon Lewis, Letter to George Gleason (exec secretary LA County Committee for Church and Community Cooperation), 12 May 1942, Committee for Church and Community Cooperation: County of Los Angeles [Dr. George Gleason, exec sec] 1941–1942; 1944–1945 Folder 4, Box 218, Series II, CRC; and Pitt, *Joseph Roos Oral History Interview*, 21–22. Roos discusses later how at the time the Jewish community had been "bitterly anti-Japanese."

83. Eisenberg, *The First to Cry Down Injustice?* esp. 118–36. See too Eisenberg, "Civil Rights and Japanese American Incarceration," in Kahn and Dollinger, eds., *California Jews*.

84. Bowron, Letter to President Roosevelt's Administrative Assistant, January 26, 1945, Folder 1945, Box 1, Bowron. For more on Bowron and internment, see Sitton, *Los Angeles Transformed*, 64–65.

85. Ford did not go so far as opposing internment, but instead supported it as a temporary "quarantine." Ford, Letter to Francis Biddle, U.S. attorney general, May 28, 1942, 74/B/IV/5/i/bb—Japanese, 1942 Folder, Ford.

86. Takaki, *Double Victory*, 161–64. For a fascinating discussion of the experience of Los Angeles Japanese and Japanese Americans in the camps during the war, particularly how they expressed their ethnic identity in the face of the war, see Kurashige, *Japanese American Celebration and Conflict*.

87. "Rotarians Told America Plays Into Hands of Jap Propagandists by Attacks on Nisei," *LA Citizen News*, June 22, 1945.

88. Roy Wilkins (NY office NAACP), News Release, April 27, 1944, "Japanese 1942–45" Folder, Box A325, Group II, NAACP LOC.

89. Ford's assistant, Memo to Ford concerning Housing Conference in mayor's office, August 10, 1943, 76/B/IV/5/i/ee—Negro, 1943 Folder, Ford, and *Report from Meeting on War Housing for Negroes, Board of Public Works Session Room, August 10, 1943*, Extra Copies 1943 Folder, Box 1, Bowron.

Los Angeles's riots, in which nobody died, did not compare to the Detroit riots, which began on a hot summer day as a scuffle between a black man and a white man and quickly spread throughout the crowd and the city. They lasted from June 20 to 22, 1943, and resulted in death for twenty-five blacks and nine whites and injury to hundreds more, as well as in $2 million of property damage. Clive, *State of War*, 94, 133, 156–62, cited in Kennedy, *Freedom from Fear*, 770. For more on the Detroit riots, see Fine, *Violence in the Model City*; McHaney et al., "Detroit's 1943 Riot"; Shogan and Craig, *The Detroit Race Riot*; and Sitkoff, "The Detroit Race Riot of 1943." For a good discussion of all the 1943 riots, see Blum, *V Was for Victory*, 199–207.

Mayors in cities like Chicago reacted to the Detroit riots by appointing the first municipal committee on race relations in July 1943. See *Race Relations in Chicago, Report of the Mayor's Committee on Race Relations*, December 1944, Carton 6, Ford.

90. Ford's assistant, Memo to Ford concerning Housing Conference in mayor's office, August 10, 1943, 76/B/IV/5/i/ee—Negro, 1943 Folder, Ford.

91. Bowron, Letter to Frank Knox (Secretary of the Navy), September 24, 1943, Extra Copies 1943 Folder, Box 1, Bowron.

92. Bowron, Mayor's Remarks at Mass Meeting—Council for Civic Unity, April 24, 1944, Remarks, 1944 Folder, Box 34, Bowron. Hollywood director Orson Welles and actor Edward G. Robinson, who also spoke at the rally, echoed these justifications. Bowron, Speech at Council for Civic Unity Unity Rally, *United We Stand*, April 24, 1944, Carton 6, Ford.

93. Ford, *Thirty Explosive Years in Los Angeles County*, 135–36.

94. Ibid. On funding to Mexican Americans in the wake of the Zoot Suit Riots, and specifically the connection to the international war effort, see Coordinating Council of Latin American Youth, Report to the Governor of the State of California, Citizens Committee on Youth in Wartime, California State Council, undated (likely June or July 1943), Folder 2, Box 4, Ruíz.

For more on the ways the Zoot Suit Riots ensured Mexican-American activists' access to the workings of city government and civic organizations, see Pagan, *Murder at the Sleepy Lagoon*.

95. For instance, Mayor Bowron urged, "We know they [men on the battlefields using weapons built in Los Angeles] fight well—we must build well. This is the responsibility of all our people, all races, all colors, all creeds....Our freedoms are for all of the people and must be maintained on the home front to assure victory on the battlefront." Bowron, Speech at Council for Civic Unity Unity Rally, *United We Stand*, April 24, 1944, Carton 6, Ford. Frank Wilkinson of the L.A. City Housing Authority also underscored the connection between American freedoms on the home front and what was being achieved on the front lines. "While sending men and tanks abroad for fighting our war for democracy it is important that we get back to the home front, get down to the social problems of all minority groups, primarily the Mexican American, and see that democracy is not only properly

served but, in order that it may carry on, that it be extended," Wilkinson emphasized in an early 1943 speech. Institute on Inter-American Relations and Post-war
Planning, Institute on Inter-American Relations and Post-war Planning pamphlet,
January 30, 1943, Carton 6, Ford. Wilkinson's revelation that new housing developments included nursery schools to provide Mexican-American mothers with the
"opportunity" to "get into war production fields and feel [themselves] a part of war
production" further illuminates how officials linked Mexican Americans' well-being
and the success of the war effort.

96. John Anson Ford, Speech, May 22, 1947, 72/B/IV/5/a/cc—Los Angeles
County Committee on Human Relations, 1946 Folder, Ford. For more on Ford's
role in the committee, see Valenciana, *Mexican-American Repatriation during the
Depression*; Interview with John Anson Ford," 7–8.

97. Suggestions to Mr. John Anson Ford (Chairman of the Board of
Supervisors, Los Angeles County), Board of Supervisors, December 28, 1943,
72/B/IV/5/a/dd—LA County Committee for Interracial Progress, 1943 Folder,
Ford.

98. Ibid and LA County Committee for Interracial Progress, *Report on
Interracial Committees in Los Angeles County*, April 17, 1944, Folder 8—Council
for Civic Unity, LA Corr 1944, Box 12, Series II, CRC; Mayor's Committee for
Home Front Unity, *Digest of Activities of the Los Angeles Committee for Home Front
Unity*, January 10, 1945, Folder 10—Mayor's Committee for Home Front Unity:
Digest of Activities Jan 1944–Jan 1945, Box 13, Series II, CRC; George Gleason,
Letter to L.A. Board of Supervisors, July 23, 1943, 69/B/IV/2/c—LA County
Committee for Church and Community Cooperation Folder, Ford; and Unknown
author, Interracial Committees and Groups Functioning in Los Angeles County,
March 1944, 72/B/IV/5/a/dd—LA County Committee for Interracial Progress,
1944, Folder, Ford. George Gleason (for County Committee for Church and
Community Cooperation, calling conference of community leaders), Letter to
Manuel Ruíz (Chairman Citizens Committee for Latin American Youth), July
23, 1943, Folder 9, Box 4, Ruíz.

99. *Los Angeles County Committee for Interracial Progress Origin and Functions*,
1945, 3, Folder 9—Comm on Human Relations, LA County: Corresp Jan–Apr
1945, Box 218, Series II, CRC.

100. Earl Carpenter was vice president of the L.A. Chamber of Commerce
Committee. Other members included people like Mrs. Harvey Dye, the president
of the First District Parent-Teachers Association. Unknown author, "New Interracial
Plan Launched by Church Group," July 31, 1943, *Los Angeles Times*, in Folder
8—Comm on Human Relations, LA County: Corresp 1943–44, Box 218, Series II,
CRC. The difference between the Coordinating Council for Latin American Youth
(CCLAY) and the Citizens Committee for Latin American Youth is that the former
was appointed by the Los Angeles County Board of Supervisors while the latter
was citizen-initiated, by people like Ruíz and others; Ruíz was the chairman of the
former and the secretary of the latter.

101. Various documents and authors, 1941, 69/B/IV/2/c(1)—LA County
Committee for Church and Community Cooperation, 1941 Folder, Ford.

102. Leon Lewis, Memo to CRC members, April 9, 1945, Folder 12–Comm on
Human Relations, LA County: Corresp, Box 219, Series II, CRC. See also George
Gleason, Memo, February 19, 1945, Folder 9, Box 218, Series II, CRC and "Los

Angeles County Seeks Advice on Intergroup Cooperation," *NOW*, March 1945, in Folder 9, Box 218, Series II, CRC.

103. Floyd Covington (President of LA Urban League), Letter to Charles S. Johnson (Fisk University), September 9, 1943, Folder 28, Box 1, Los Angeles Urban League.

104. Executive Secretary of LA County Committee for Interracial Progress, April 17, 1944, 72/B/IV/5/a/dd—LA County Committee for Interracial Progress, 1944 Folder, Ford.

105. Furthermore, the participation of the Aircraft War Production Council's general manager John Lee reveals Bowron's awareness of the connection between interracial issues and wartime concerns. LA Committee for Home Front Unity, "Digest of Activities of the Los Angeles Committee for Home Front Unity," January 10, 1945, Folder 10—Mayor's Committee for Home Front Unity: Digest of Activities Jan 1944–Jan 1945, Box 13, Series II, CRC; Unknown author, "Interracial Committees and Groups Functioning in Los Angeles County," March 1944, 72/B/IV/5/a/dd—LA County Committee for Interracial Progress, 1944 Foder, Ford.

106. Other members included Judge Frank Ogden, John S. Carroll, E. W. Lester, James K. Lytle, Charlotte P. Elmott, Josephine Randall, Hyman Kaplan, Mrs. Paul Eliel, Rev. Joseph Mulkern, Mrs. Mildred Bevil, Walter Helms, Mrs. A. M. Drury, James Corson, and Judge L. N. Turrentine. Minutes of Meeting of Citizens Committee on Youth in Wartime, California State War Council, November 1, 1943, Folder 1, Box 4, Ruíz.

107. Laurence I. Hewes Jr. (ACRR), *Race Relations on the West Coast*, September 1946, Folder 6, Box 18, Civil Rights Congress.

108. Gardner, *Honorable in All Things: Carey McWilliams*, 158.

109. The Purpose of the Program of the Council for Civic Unity, undated, Carton 6, Ford.

110. George Pepper (executive secretary of Hollywood Democratic Committee), Letter to Judge Hollzer (President LA Jewish Community Council), December 10, 1943, Folder 18—Inter-Racial Relations Dec 1943, Box 111, Series II, CRC. For more on the Hollywood Democratic Committee, see Ceplair and Englund, *The Inquisition in Hollywood*, esp. 226–28.

111. Activists seized the opportunity provided by the changing intellectual climate concerning race. During and because of the war, ideas about race shifted from a belief that actual racial differences explained minorities' circumstances and conditions to a belief that discrimination was responsible for many of minorities' social problems, and therefore needed to be remedied. This shifted the blame from the communities themselves. Kevin Leonard explains how this shift happened in Los Angeles specifically, where he argues that the turning point was the Zoot Suit Riots. See Leonard, *The Battle for Los Angeles*.

112. For an excellent summary of this literature and movement, see Ronald Takaki, *Double Victory*. See also Skinner, "The Double 'V.'" For a fascinating discussion of how, through radio broadcasts, African Americans in the late 1930s and 1940s used U.S. international goals to articulate a critique of American race politics and advocate greater racial equality, see Savage, *Broadcasting Freedom*.

113. Reverend Clayton D. Russell, Interview, Los Angeles, California, February 18, 1975, quoted in Anderson, *The Development of Leadership and Organization*

Building in the Black Community of Los Angeles from 1900 through World War II,
85. Well-known members of the Negro Victory Committee included local politi-
cian Augustus Hawkins, George Anderson (AFL organizer), Dr. Price Cobbs
(American Medical Assoc), Walter Williamson (CIO Organizer), and Reverend
Clayton D. Russell (People's Independent Church of L.A.). For a further
discussion, see Kurashige, *The Shifting Grounds of Race,* and Unrau, "The Double
V Movement in Los Angeles during the Second World War: A Study in Negro
Protest."

114. Reverend Clayton D. Russell, Speech: *America! This Is Our Stand, Report
Delivered at Mass Rally of Negro Citizens,* April 12, 1942, Los Angeles, Carton 6,
Ford.

115. Ibid.

116. Ibid.

117. Ibid.

118. Bass, *Forty Years,* 71. This entry is undated, but specifies it occurred during
World War II. For more on the Boilermakers, see Kurashige, *The Shifting Grounds of
Race,* 132.

119. Ford, Letter to Noel Edwards, May 10, 1944, 76/B/IV/5/i/ee—Negro,
1944 Folder, Ford.

120. For discussion of Randolph's threat and demands, see Takaki *Double
Victory,* 40–41. Also see Bracey Jr. and Meier, "Allies or Adversaries?"; discussion in
Kennedy, *Freedom from Fear,* 763–68; and Martin, "March on Washington
Movement."

121. Sitkoff, *The Struggle for Black Equality,* 11–12. For information on FEPC's
ineffectiveness, see Takaki, *Double Victory,* 42–43. Scholars disagree about the effectiveness of this legislation, particularly for groups other than African Americans.
Clete Daniel, for instance, argues that FEPC was less than effective for Chicano
workers during World War II. See Daniel, *Chicano Workers and the Politics of Fairness.*
For an examination of FEPC and other wartime federal race policy reforms that
argues the government designed such reforms merely to advance the war effort and
to maintain the Democratic Party coalition, see Kryder, *Divided Arsenal.*

122. Bass, *Forty Years,* 86. No date specified, but it seems to have been in 1942.
Many white workers also resisted the integration, showing that not all, or neces-
sarily even most, celebrated the integration. See Kurashige, *The Shifting Grounds of
Race,* 154–56.

123. Sitkoff, *The Struggle for Black Equality,* 11. On the L.A. NAACP's membership, see Sides, *L.A. City Limits,* 140. Walter White, the head of the national
NAACP, explained in his 1945 book *A Rising Wind* that "World War II has immeasurably magnified the Negro's awareness of the disparity between the American
profession and practice of democracy." He predicted that black soldiers would
return "determined to…[improve] their lot." Walter White, *A Rising Wind,* 1945,
cited in Blum, *V Was for Victory,* 219.

124. Chicano scholars do not all agree that World War II marked an increase in
civil rights consciousness. Historian Rodolfo Acuña argues that it "crystallized [a]
new political consciousness [an interest in politics]," while George Sánchez argues
the 1930s were as important, if not more so, in increasing civil rights activism. See
Acuña, *A Community Under Siege,* 44, and Sánchez, *Becoming Mexican American,*
esp. 256.

125. Petition, November 24, 1942, Folder 11 (unclear), Box 4, Ruíz. Quevedo also implored the federal Office of War Information to intervene in local press coverage of the Zoot Suit Riots by arguing it not only inflamed the riots, it also drew negative international attention. Eduardo Quevedo, Letter to Elmer Davis at the Office of War Information, June 1943, Folder 4, Box 16, Ruíz. For more on Mexican Americans' Double V approach in Texas, see Zamora, *Claiming Rights and Righting Wrongs in Texas*.

126. They asked for $12,204, which they received. The County Board of Supervisors also soon responded to the council's concern. It hoped that appointing the committee to address both Mexican-American youth "delinquency" and discrimination against Mexican-origin people would limit enemies' ability to exploit these issues. Coordinating Council of Latin-American Youth, Resolution, August 1943, Folder 6, Box 4, Ruíz. On this international justification for helping Mexican Americans, see also Manuel J. Avila (Los Angeles Bar), "Constructive Approach to Youth Problem: Much of Information on Subject has Led to Axis Propaganda, But Abuses Are Now Being Corrected," March 15, 1943, *Los Angeles Daily Journal*, in Folder 6, Box 4, Ruíz. For a further discussion of this organization, see Garcia, "Americans All."

127. Minutes, Meeting December 2, 1942, Folder 6, Box 4, Ruiz. See too Gutiérrez, *Walls and Mirrors*, 129.

128. Minutes, Meeting January 4, 1943, Folder 6, Box 4, Ruiz.

129. Minutes, Meeting June 7, 1943, Folder 6, Box 4, Ruiz.

Mexican Americans nationwide, not just in Los Angeles, underlined the international urgency of remedying anti-Mexican discrimination. Dr. Joaquín Ortega of the University of New Mexico, Dr. George I. Sánchez of the University of Texas, and Arizona state senator C. J. Carreón joined white activists such as Carey McWilliams in encouraging Nelson Rockefeller, the head of the Office of the Coordinator of Inter-American Affairs, to recognize that fighting discrimination would strengthen the U.S.-Latin American solidarity that Rockefeller hoped to promote. McWilliams, *North from Mexico*, 245–46. In a letter to Rockefeller, Sánchez underscored that anti-Mexican discrimination affected "national defense and international goodwill." It affected both "our internal situation" and also "is highly significant in our relations with the Mexican Republic." Sánchez to Rockefeller, February 7, 1942, Box 42, Correspondence file "R," Sánchez Papers, cited in Gutiérrez, *Walls and Mirrors*, 131–32. Rockefeller eventually responded by creating a Spanish-speaking people's division to improve relations between whites and Mexican Americans in the Southwest. McWilliams, *North from Mexico*, 245–46. For more on how Mexican Americans fought job discrimination nationwide by using the federal government's interest in buttressing the Good Neighbor Policy, see Daniel, *Chicano Workers and the Politics of Fairness*, 16–17, and Zamora, *Claiming Rights and Righting Wrongs in Texas*. On the relationship between U.S. international imperative concerning Latin America and governmental concessions toward Mexican Americans' equality struggles, particularly concerning education, see González, *Chicano Education in the Era of Segregation*, and Zamora, *Claiming Rights and Righting Wrongs in Texas*.

130. Confidential Report "Spanish-Americans in the Southwest and the War Effort," [Office of War Information], August 18, 1942, Folder 4, Box 58, Galarza.

See also Daniel, *Chicano Workers and the Politics of Fairness*, 19–21. For various reports concerning the connection between international wartime unity and fighting anti-Mexican discrimination, involving American and Mexican officials as well as Mexican American activists, see various reports in Folders 4, 5, Box 58, Galarza.

131. See García, *Mexican Americans*, 165–74, and Sánchez, *Becoming Mexican American*, 249.

132. Eugene Davidson (Field Representative President's Commission on Fair Employment Practices), at Conference of Non-Sectarian Anti-Nazi League, March 1, 1942, Folder 9—Discrimination Employment 1942–43, Box 108, Series II, CRC.

133. Ibid.

134. Ibid.

135. CRC, *Resolution on Inter-Racial Democracy in the Schools*, Folder 18—Inter-Racial Relations, Dec. 1943, Box 111, Series II, CRC.

136. Ford, Letter to Noel Edwards, May 10, 1944, 76/B/IV/5/i/ee—Negro, 1944, Ford.

137. Gutiérrez, *Walls and Mirrors*, 127.

138. On Quevedo's involvement in the 1930s-era CIO movement, specifically in Local 300 of the Laborers Union, see García, *Memories of Chicano History*, 124. On Connelly, see Sides, *L.A. City Limits*, 63–64. Other prominent members included Al Waxman, the editor of the newspaper *Eastside Journal*, Leo Gallager of the Lawyers' Guild, Jerome Posner of the Amalgamated Clothing Workers' Union, Jess Armenta of the Laundry Workers Union, and Gray Bemis of the International Workers' Order. Gardner, *Honorable in All Things: Carey McWilliams*, 155; Sánchez, *Becoming Mexican American*, 249; and George E. Shibley (the lead Defense Committee attorney), "Sleepy Lagoon: The True Story," in *New West*, January 15, 1979, 88 in Folder 27, Box 3, McGrath. On El Congreso members' prominent involvement, see García, *Memories of Chicano History*, and García, *Mexican Americans*, 171–72. On Communist Party (including Guy Endore) and front organizations', as well as Hollywood's, involvement, see Ceplair and Englund, *Inquisition in Hollywood*, 134 and 195, and Pagan, *Murder at the Sleepy Lagoon*, 85–86. For a more extensive discussion of the Sleepy Lagoon case, see Acuña, *Anything but Mexican*; Pagan, *Murder at the Sleepy Lagoon*; and Sánchez, *Becoming Mexican American*. For further discussion of McWilliams's involvement, see Geary, "Carey McWilliams and Antifascism, 1934–1943," 930–31.

Scholars of Chicano history disagree whether Fierro de Bright was as involved as some accounts claim. For this discussion, see Pagan, *Murder at the Sleepy Lagoon*, 85–86.

139. On Braverman, see Richardson, *American Prophet*, 120.

140. Zaragosa Vargas, *Labor Rights Are Civil Rights*.

141. Sleepy Lagoon Defense Committee, *The Sleepy Lagoon* Case, (n.p.), ca. 1944, quoted Gutiérrez, *Walls and Mirrors*, 128.

142. Ibid.

143. Vicente Peralta (Consul General de Mexico), letter to Alice McGrath, January 25, 1945, Alice McGrath Folder, Box 24, McWilliams 1319.

144. Gardner, *Honorable in All Things: Carey McWilliams*, 156, and McWilliams, *The Education of Carey McWilliams*, 111.

145. Harry Braverman (Provisional Chairman, Los Angeles Committee for American Unity), Letter to State Attorney General Robert W. Kenny and Bishop Joseph T. McGucken (Chairman Governor's Special Committee on Los Angeles Emergency) June 11, 1943, Folder 4, Box 16, Ruíz.

146. Laurence I. Hewes Jr. (ACRR), *Race Relations on the West Coast*, September 1946, Folder 6, Box 18, Civil Rights Congress.

147. For a discussion of pre–World War II black leadership and efforts, see Sides, *L.A. City Limits*.

148. Floyd C. Covington, *Exploratory Survey Racial Tension Areas* to Charles S. Johnson (Fisk University), December 31, 1942, Folder 27, Box 1, Los Angeles Urban League.

149. Leon Lewis, various letters to heads of Jewish organizations in places including Seattle, Minneapolis, Pittsburgh, San Francisco, Florida, Summer 1942, Folder 22, Box 5, Series II, CRC.

150. CRC, Minutes of Public Relations Subcommittee Meeting, April 29, 1943, Folder 1–Subcomms: PR 1943, Box 6, Series II, CRC.

151. Leon Lewis, Letter to George Gleason, November 13, 1945, Folder 14—Comm on Human Relations, LA County: Corresp Jul–Dec 1945, Box 218, Series II, CRC.

152. LA Jewish Community Council, Letter to members, February 7, 1944 and Floyd C. Covington (Exec Director LA Urban League), Letter to Jewish Community Council, March 16, 1944, Folder 1—Negroes: National Urban League 1944; 1946, Box 113, Series II, CRC.

153. CRC Agenda, June 18, 1943, Folder 11, Box 1, Series II, CRC.

154. Ted LeBerthon, "Ted LeBerthon" (Column), *LA Daily News*, June 1, 1943. Incidentally, LeBerthon was also, together with Dan Marshall, a founder of the Catholic Interracial Council of Los Angeles. See Pascoe, *What Comes Naturally*, 209. Scholarship on other cities and regions suggests that Jews elsewhere also often were at the forefront of cooperative efforts. On events in San Francisco, see Issel, "Jews and Catholics against Prejudice." On New York, see Svonkin, *Jews against Prejudice*.

155. Letter from Silberberg to Edmund Cooke (the mayor's office), April 9, 1945 and 24 October 1945, Mayor's Committee for Home Front Unity, LA Apr–Jun 1945 Folder 6, Box 13, Series II, CRC.

156. For more on this, see chapter 6.

157. Memo of meeting, 18 February 1941, Folder 29—Legal and Legislative, Feb. 1941, Box 4, Series II, CRC. Among the proposed legislation were AB 63, which concerned questions of race in state employment, AB 704, concerning discrimination in state work, and another Senate bill that would set up a commission on race relations in California.

158. Pitt, *Joseph Roos Oral History Interview*, 53.

159. G. W. Sherman, "United They Stand: Another Minority's Fight against Discrimination," article in *Frontier*, Folder 9—Race: Anti-Mexican Americans, Box 27, ACLU.

160. On San Francisco Jews, see Issel, "Jews and Catholics against Prejudice," and a longer version of this essay, Issel, "Jews and Catholics against Prejudice: Interfaith Cooperation in the San Francisco Civil Rights Campaign, 1940–1960." On BACAD, see too de Graaf, Mulroy, Taylor, eds., *Seeking El Dorado*, 31–32, and

Broussard, *Black San Francisco*. For more on Jewish collaborative activism in New York, see Svonkin, *Jews against Prejudice*.

161. Historian Eric L. Goldstein has shown Jews' ongoing ambivalence throughout the first half of the twentieth century. See Goldstein, *The Price of Whiteness*.

For more on black/Jewish coalitions generally outside the West, see, for instance, Greenberg, "Negotiating Coalition," and Greenberg, *Troubling the Waters*. On an earlier period of black/Jewish relations, see Diner, *In the Almost Promised Land*.

162. George A. Beavers Jr., Delegate to the Annual NAACP Conference (and rep of Los Angeles Negro Business League), Memo to Thomas L. Griffith (LA branch president), September 3, 1942, concerning national conference 1942, Los Angeles, Calif, 1942–43 Folder, Box C14, Group II, NAACP LOC.

163. See for example discussion in Blum, *V Was for Victory*, 215–18.

164. Guglielmo, "Fighting for Caucasian Rights," and MacLean, *Freedom Is Not Enough*, esp. 156. Guglielmo makes an interesting and persuasive case that for Mexican Americans in Texas, World War II, particularly international concerns, facilitated their civil rights struggles. But in Texas, unlike in Los Angeles, Mexican Americans fought for what Guglielmo calls "Caucasian rights" rather than for the collaborative civil rights struggles that are evident in Los Angeles. This is not to say that L.A. Mexican-origin populations did not claim whiteness—they did. But such claims were not to the exclusion of frequent collaborations with African Americans and sometimes Japanese Americans, as well as "white" minorities like Jews. MacLean argues that Chicanos did not consistently depart from their "whiteness" strategy until the Civil Rights Act of 1964, and Title VII more specifically. This legislation in the 1960s enabled them to shift toward a new strategy of claiming "Mexicanness" rather than whiteness and joining together with other minority groups. In Los Angeles, Mexican Americans joined coalitions at the same time that they often claimed white racial status, revealing variation in regional national stories. For disagreement with this conclusion pertaining to Texas Mexicans, see Zamora, *Claiming Rights and Righting Wrongs in Texas*.

165. For an overview of the conditions of Mexican and Mexican American communities in Los Angeles and elsewhere during this era, see Gutiérrez, *Walls and Mirrors*.

166. For a discussion of Los Angeles Mexican Americans' ambivalence about their permanence in the United States, and how the 1930s shifted the population toward a sense of investment and a willingness to fight for their rights, as Americans, see Sánchez, *Becoming Mexican American*.

167. The American Council on Race Relations, *The Problem of Violence: Observations on Race Conflict in Los Angeles*, 1945, Carton 6, Ford.

168. Ibid., 13, 19–20.

169. Ibid., 14.

170. For more on Mexican-American "assimilationist," or whiteness strategies before the middle of the twentieth century, see, for instance, Foley, "Becoming Hispanic: Mexican Americans and the Faustian Pact with Whiteness"; Guglielmo, "Fighting for Caucasian Rights"; Gutiérrez, *Walls and Mirrors*; and MacLean, *Freedom Is Not Enough*. See too discussion in chapter 5 of this study.

171. The American Council on Race Relations, *The Problem of Violence*, 1945, 14, Carton 6, Ford.

172. Editorial, unidentified Los Angeles Japanese newspaper (probably *Rafu Shimpo*), February 15, 1942, Folder 24—Jewish Survey Committee, SF [Block] Jan–Mar 1942, Box 142, Series II, CRC. Interestingly, the Jewish Community Relations Committee's executive director Leon Lewis privately acknowledged, "There are of course a few instances of unscrupulous Jews who are trying to take advantage of the situation." But Lewis emphasized that "they are small fry compared to some of the others" which included farmers' associations and Chambers of Commerce. Letter from Lewis to Eugene Block, February 19, 1942, Folder 24—Jewish Survey Committee, SF [Block] Jan–Mar 1942, Box 142, Series II, CRC. Interestingly, Lewis did not mention the News Research Service's role in urging the internment, as discussed previously.

173. Lewis, Letter to H. U. M. Higgins at the LA Hall of Justice, March 20, 1942, Folder 42—Los Angeles County Defense Council (Re: Japanese Americans) 1942, Box 223, Series II, CRC.

174. Lucius W. Lomax Jr. (publisher *LA Tribune*), Letter to Rabbi Edgar F. Magnin, November 11, 1944, Folder 20—Inter-Racial Relations Jan–Jun 1944, Box 111, Series II, CRC.

175. Magnin, Letter to Lomax, January 17, 1944, Folder 20—Inter-Racial Relations Jan–Jun 1944, Box 111, Series II, CRC.

176. For a general discussion of the ways Jews at the national level felt insecure because of anti-Semitism in the Depression and World War II period, see Svonkin, *Jews against Prejudice*.

177. Minutes of Public Relations Committee Meeting, July 1, 1943, Folder 2—Subcomm: PR 1943, Box 6, Series II, CRC.

178. Pitt, *Joseph Roos Oral History Interview*. For more on the CRC's work monitoring 1930s-era Fascist activities, see Eisenberg, *The First to Cry Down Injustice?* chapter 4.

179. Judge Isaac Pacht, Text of speech made by Judge Pacht at luncheon meeting, November 6, 1951, County Conference on Community Relations (Corresp) 1951 Folder, Box 59, Series IV, CRC. For a discussion of this shift in national Jewish agencies, see Svonkin, *Jews against Prejudice*.

180. Leon Lewis, Letter to Mrs. Mischel, January 6, 1944, Folder 20—Inter-Racial Relations Jan–Jun 1944, Box 111, Series II, CRC.

CHAPTER 4

1. Lawrence I. Hewes Jr. (West Coast Regional Director, American Council on Race Relations), *Race Relations on the West Coast*, September 1946, 1–2, Carton 6, Ford.

2. Quoted from Robert E.G. Harris (chief editorial writer), editorial, *Los Angeles Daily News*, April 1, 1948.

3. On Moreno, see Ruiz, "Luisa Moreno and Latina Labor Activism," 189–190. See too Ruíz, "Una Mujer Sin Fronteras." On Fierro de Bright, see García, *Mexican Americans*, 173.

4. Los Angeles Council for Civic Unity, Pamphlet, 1947(?), Carton 6, Ford.

5. Ibid.

6. At the time it was called the California Council for Civic Unity; the name later changed to Federation. Ibid.

7. CRC, Press Release(?), 1947, Communism 1947 Folder, Section 3C, Series III, CRC.

8. I use the term *pragmatic* here as a way to designate these specific reformers but not to imply that other civil rights activists—communists and others deemed radical, for instance—were not pragmatic as well. They too were pragmatic, but I am using this term in this context to refer to those who negotiated a "middle ground" of civil rights.

9. For discussions of the conservative social climate in postwar America, see for instance May, *Homeward Bound*; May, ed., *Recasting America*; Schuparra, *Triumph of the Right*; and Whitfield, *The Culture of the Cold War*.

10. For a discussion of national-level red-baiters' tendency to target civil rights activists more than others due to the closeness of civil rights groups (like NAACP) and communist platforms, see Horne, *Black and Red*, chapters 16, 17, and 20 passim, particularly 205, 295.

11. Patterson, *Grand Expectations*, 157.

12. Ibid.

13. James Patterson argues that this Employment Act did represent a step in the direction of government taking responsibility for economic welfare, but it was much more cautious and noncommittal than reformers had hoped. Ibid., 142–43.

14. The Committee's October 1947 report was called *To Secure These Rights*. Ibid., 145.

The backlash against civil rights was part of a larger conservative trend in the nation. Conservatives triumphed in the elections of 1946; victorious Republicans swept into both houses of Congress, taking control of them for the first time since 1930. Republicans had a majority in the House (245 to 188) and Senate (51 to 45). Ibid., 145. Government agencies transferred surveillance techniques they had perfected during World War II primarily to monitor suspected fascists to suspected communists. See Stephan, "*Communazis*,"17. Congress passed the U.S. Internal Security Act, otherwise known as the McCarran Bill, in September 1950, forcing all members of "communistic" groups to register with the attorney general.

For a sampling of the literature on American anticommunism and conservatism in this era, see Caute, *The Great Fear*; Fried, *Nightmare in Red*; Haynes, *Red Scare or Red Menace?*; Heale, *American Anticommunism*; Kutler, *The American Inquisition*; and Theoharis, *Seeds of Repression*.

15. The University of California's Board of Regents also forced state and city employees to swear their loyalty to the United States by adopting a loyalty oath in September 1950. See Long, "Loyalty Oaths in California, 1947–1952," 28, and chapter 1 passim.

16. Nixon took Voorhis's position as representative of California's Twelfth Congressional District. See Chambless, "Pro-Defense, Pro-Growth, and Anti-Communism," 107–8.

17. Schuparra, *Triumph of the Right*, xxii, and Lotchin, *Fortress California, 1910–1961*, 202. For more on Southern California's strong anticommunism, see McGirr, Suburban Warriors. For a firsthand account of the difficulty the left faced in Los Angeles, see García, *Memories of Chicano History*, 159. On the influence of Southern California religious evangelicalism, see Dochuk, *From Bible Belt to Sunbelt*.

18. See California Legislature Joint Fact-Finding Committee on Un-American Activities in California, *Fourth Report of the Senate Fact-Finding Committee on Un-American Activities*, 79.

19. Ibid.

20. SB [Senate Bill] 129 articulated this definition in 1949. See Barrett, *The Tenney Committee*, 303.

21. Tenney's zealous anticommunism masked his own radical past. In the 1930s, he had been an active leftist, involved in musicians' and other unions. He was even the president of the American Federation of Musicians local in Los Angeles, and chaired Labor's Non-Partisan League for Southern California. Communist Party member Dorothy Healey remembered him as one of the two "Red [state] assemblymen," and one of the Party's "closest allies in the state legislature" during the 1930s. Healey and Isserman, *Dorothy Healey Remembers*, 70, 85.

Tenney's chance to display his anticommunism in the national arena as well as in California came when he accepted the nomination to run as the vice presidential candidate for the Christian Nationalist Party, alongside General MacArthur in 1952. He accepted the nomination, he said, to give the American people an "alternative to Tweedle-Dum Adlai and Tweedle-Dee Ike" and saw his party's campaign as a "crusade" to get the country out of the hands of what he called socialists, communists, and "welfare-staters" who had "captured, controlled, and directed the Democratic Party." He also accused some Republican candidates of "selling the same fraudulent New Deal tonic and Fair Deal snake oil." "Tenney Accepts Nomination for Vice-President," *LA Times*, September 15, 1952.

22. See Long, "Loyalty Oaths in California, 1947–1952," 28, and chapter 1 passim. Long explains that early loyalty oath activity in Los Angeles and California was due to a combination of factors including the heightened social tensions brought about by migration and race conflict, high unemployment in a peacetime economy, and an unusually high level of leftist activity in local politics and trade unions. From its inception, the committee occupied itself with both fascism and communism, though initially it focused more on monitoring suspected fascist activity. By the Cold War its focus was almost exclusively communism. For a complete discussion of the Tenney Committee and its activities, see Barrett, *The Tenney Committee*. On Tenney's role as a main instigator, see Scobie, "Jack B. Tenney," 2.

Despite newspaper announcements in late 1999 that the Senate Rules Committee of the California Legislature, which oversees the use of the Tenney Committee files, was allowing the California State Archives in Sacramento to open them to public review for the first time since the 1970s, the materials made available to researchers are quite limited. The Senate Rules Committee wrote in response to an inquiry that it limited access to the files in order to protect the privacy of thousands of citizens from "pernicious gossip and rumors…and even allegations of criminal conduct" and prevent causing "irreparable harm to the reputations and memories of many thousands of persons, living and dead." Gregory Schmidt (secretary of the Senate), letter to the author, February 29, 2000, in author's possession.

23. Ceplair and Englund, *The Inquisition in Hollywood*, generally and 68 specifically. For more discussion and critique of Tenney's methods, see Barrett, *The Tenney Committee*, particularly 44.

24. See United Press, "Reds Pouring into U.S.? Rep. McDowell Says They're Streaming in via Mexico," *Washington Daily News*, May 22, 1947, in Folder 1, Box 50, Galarza.

25. Ernest Brashear, "Red Spies Sneaking in from Mexico," *Daily News*, February 19, 1951, in Folder 1, Box 50, Galarza. This folder contains numerous similar articles, from newspapers in Los Angeles and nationwide, including the *New York Times*. The Los Angeles *Daily News*, for instance, reported in February 1951 that its investigation showed that Communists infiltrated the Mexican "wetbacks" who hated the "Yanquis and pledged to carry out the orders of Moscow wherever they are." See Garcilazo, "McCarthyism, Mexican Americans, and the Los Angeles Committee for Protection of the Foreign-Born, 1950–1954," 274–75.

26. For an interesting discussion of anticommunism's roots in a broad range of the local population, and especially white women's role in the movement, see Nickerson, *Mothers of Conservatism*.

27. Dudley Nichols, letter to Freda Kirchway, September 9, 1952, Folder 4, Box 13, McWilliams 1319.

28. Ibid.

29. From 1945 Tenney Committee Report, cited in Barrett, *The Tenney Committee*, 93, 95–96, 100.

30. Tenney's 1948 report listed the Sleepy Lagoon Defense Committee as "Communist created and controlled" and the Spanish Speaking Peoples Congress a Communist or Communist-front organization. California Legislature Joint Fact-Finding Committee on Un-American Activities in California, *Fourth Report of the Senate Fact-Finding Committee on Un-American Activities. 1948*, 34–35, 309, 375.

31. The AFL, CIO and other trade unions, as well as some other organizations, shared the NAACP's classification. California Legislature Joint Fact-Finding Committee on Un-American Activities in California, *Fourth Report of the Senate Fact-Finding Committee on Un-American Activities. 1948*, 43.

32. In its 1948 report, the Tenney Committee listed the National Lawyers' Guild as "the Communist front for attorneys," and cited Loren Miller along with California attorney general Robert Kenny, Carey McWilliams, Isaac Pacht, Clore Warne, A. L. Wirin, Ben Margolis, and others for their involvement in the organization. See California Legislature Joint Fact-Finding Committee on Un-American Activities in California, *Fourth Report of the Senate Fact-Finding Committee on Un-American Activities. 1948*, 331–32.

33. California Legislature Joint Fact-Finding Committee on Un-American Activities in California, *Report 1: 1943*, especially part III and part VI; California Legislature Joint Fact-Finding Committee on Un-American Activities in California, *Report 2: 1945*, especially part III and last part.

34. Milton Senn, Letter to Don Epstein, October 16, 1947, Civil Rights: Correspondence Sept–Oct 1947 Folder, Section 3C, Series III, CRC; Herzberg (CRC executive director), Letter to Pacht, June 14, 1949, Subcomm, Special: Tenney Comm Corr 1948–1949 Folder, Section AII, Series III, CRC.

35. Tenney[AU: Edit OK?] described Pacht as "a short man with a large head, strongly chiseled Jewish features and an amazingly loud and violent voice, [who] looked like the proverbial cat who had just swallowed a canary." See Schippers, *Jack B. Tenney*, 366. Tenney also welcomed support from infa-

mous anti-Semites like Gerald L. K. Smith. Unidentified News Research Service article, vol. 6, no. 176, December 10, 1941, Tenney Folder, Box 75, Series IV, CRC.

36. See Schippers, *Jack B. Tenney*.

37. Scobie, "Jack B. Tenney," 220–21.

38. Tenney, Letter to "Dear Member of Congress and Fellow Americans," 1953, Tenney, Jack B. (P.M.)—Folder, Box 82, Series IV, CRC, and untitled article, *B'nai B'rith Messenger*, April 10, 1953, in Tenney, Jack B. (P.M.)—Folder, Box 82, Series IV, CRC.

39. Tenney, Letter to "Dear Member of Congress and Fellow Americans," 1953, Tenney, Jack B. (P.M.)—Folder, Box 82, Series IV, CRC and untitled article, *B'nai B'rith Messenger*, April 10, 1953, in Tenney, Jack B. (P.M.)—Folder, Box 82, Series IV, CRC.

40. See Schippers, *Jack B. Tenney*. For more on historic associations (and assumptions about this association) between Jews, African Americans, and communism, see Furmanovsky, "Communism as Jewish Radical Subculture"; Greenberg, *Troubling the Waters*, esp. 172–76; Horne, *Black and Red*; Howe, *The World of Our Fathers*; Liebman, *Jews and the Left*; Navasky, *Naming Names*, esp. 110–21; Record, *The Negro and the Communist Party*; and Woods, *Black Struggle, Red Scare*. See too various works by Paul Buhle.

41. See numerous newspaper articles on this issue, including Sara Boynoff, "Tenney's Theme Song Hits Sour Note as He Brands Housing Council 'Red,'" *Los Angeles Daily News*, December 1, 1945, and "Housing Group to Meet as Red Charges Hurled," *Los Angeles* Herald, December 1, 1945.

42. Frank Wilkinson, letter to John Anson Ford, June 21, 1956, 46/B/III/11/d—Communism, Fascism, Nazism, 1956 Folder, Ford. Don Parson argues that the red scare was the main reason previously successful public housing campaigns in Los Angeles collapsed during the 1950s. See Parson, *Making a Better World*. Tom Sitton argues that the *LA Times*, the chamber of commerce, the realty board, and the Hearst Press were especially influential in the downfall of public housing in Los Angeles. See Sitton, *Los Angeles Transformed*, esp. 157–160, 165–90. See too de Graaf, Mulroy, and Taylor, eds., *Seeking El Dorado*, 34. For an interesting film treatment of Chavez Ravine, see Mechner, "Chavez Ravine."

43. Sides, "Working Away," 123.

44. Mr. Howard Holtsendorf, quoted in "Red Letter Dates for Unity," Council for Civic Unity, 1945, Folder 5—CCU: LA, Box 13, Series II, CRC.

45. For a general discussion of housing issues and minority populations in postwar Los Angeles, see Kurashige, "Transforming Los Angeles," 459–68. See too Kurashige, *The Shifting Grounds of Race*.

46. See Taylor, *In Search of the Racial Frontier*, 270.

47. Title unclear, January 22, 1949, *Los Angeles Daily Tribune*, Housing: Printed Matter 1949 Folder, Section 3C, Series III, CRC.

48. Milton A. Senn (Director, Southern California Anti-Defamation League), *Report on Efforts in the Los Angeles Area to Circumvent the United States Supreme Court Decisions on Restrictive Covenants*, December 31, 1948, Housing: Restrictive covenants, printed matter 1948–50 Folder, Section 3C, Series III, CRC, 3, 4–10; and Sides, "Working Away," 14.

49. García, *Memories of Chicano History*, 155–56. For a detailed discussion of the living and working conditions of Southern California's Mexican-origin community, see McWilliams, *North from Mexico*, 217–21.

50. For information on anti-Semitism and discrimination in Los Angeles in this period, see Moore, *To the Golden Cities*, 48, and Vorspan and Gartner, *History of the Jews of Los Angeles*, esp. 238–47.

51. County Supervisor John Anson Ford made this estimate in 1945. See John Anson Ford's office, letter to Dillon Myer (Director, War Relocation Authority), October 1, 1945, 74/B/IV/5/i/bb—Japanese, 1945 Folder, Ford. One estimate places the number of evacuees who returned to Los Angeles by the end of 1946 at over 25,000. See Murase, *Little Tokyo*, 18. For a discussion of tensions between returning Japanese and African Americans, see Japanese American Citizens' League, *Official Statement Pertaining to Pilgrim House and the Japanese Union Church Building at 120 North San Pedro Street, L.A.* Pamphlet, 1947, Intergroup Relations: Japanese American Citizens League 1947 Folder, Section 3C, Series III, CRC.

52. Mayor Fletcher Bowron, Letter to William H. McReynolds (Admin Assistant to President Roosevelt), January 26, 1945, Folder 1945, Box 1, Bowron. For a further discussion of the internment of Japanese Americans, see the following: Daniels, *Prisoners without Trial*; Daniels, Taylor, and Kitano, eds., *Japanese Americans*; Hayashi, *Democratizing the Enemy*; and Kurashige, *Japanese American Celebration and Conflict*.

53. Takaki, *Strangers from a Different Shore*, 405. For discussions at the time of the dangers faced by returning internees and the fears their return would exacerbate racial tensions, see correspondence in 1945, 74/B/IV/5/i/bb—Japanese, 1945 Folder, Ford; correspondence in 1947 and 1948, 76/B/IV/5/i/ee—Negro, 1942 Folder, Ford and Council for Civic Unity, Los Angeles, *Uni-Facts*, *Council for Civic Unity* Report, June 1946, Folder 7, Box 18, Civil Rights Congress. For more on the experience of Japanese and Japanese Americans returning to Los Angeles after the war, specifically in terms of the community's various stances concerning integration and ethnic identity, see Kurashige, *Japanese American Celebration and Conflict*.

54. Meeting on War Housing for Negroes, Board of Public Works meeting transcript, August 10, 1943, Extra Copies 1943 Folder, Box 1, Bowron; Samuel Ishikawa (Staff of Pilgrim House, a Bronzeville/Little Tokyo community institution), *Pilgrim House Newsletter*, September 10, 1945, 74/B/IV/5/i/bb—Japanese, 1945 Folder, Ford; and Letters, 1947–1948, 76/B/IV/5/i/ee—Negro, 1942 Folder, Ford. The figure on the evacuation from Little Tokyo is from Murase, *Little Tokyo*, 16. Though most Japanese evacuees who returned to Los Angeles after the war came back to their old neighborhood, some also started to build a new "Little Tokyo" in another area of the city (along Jefferson Bd.). See Murase, *Little Tokyo*, 16–18. The statistics on African American residents are from George Gleason (executive director, L.A. County Committee on Human Relations), Report, July 9, 1945, Folder 11—Comm on Human Relations, LA County: Corresp Jul–Dec 1945, Box 218, Series II, CRC.

55. Milton Senn, "Preface," *A Study of Police Training Programs in Minority Relations*, August 7, 1950, Folder 1, Box 5, Ross.

56. Four hundred thousand of 4,000,000 unemployed Americans in the country were in California, and 250,000 of those in California lived in Los Angeles. Governor Earl Warren, letter to Fred Herzberg (Executive Director CRC), November 10, 1949, Employment 1949 Folder, Section 3C, Series III, CRC; and Report issued by Reverend

Clayton D. Russell (chairman of Emergency Jobs Conferences), August and November 1949, Employment 1949 Folder, Section 3C, Series III, CRC.

57. Information from the U.S. Employment Service, in Lawrence B. de Graaf and Quintard Taylor, introduction, in de Graaf et al., *Seeking El Dorado*, 32, and Scott, "The Mexican-American in the Los Angeles Area, 1920–1950," 338.

58. The NAACP staged a protest against this in Los Angeles in November 1947. See Loren Miller (West Coast NAACP legal staff), Memo, May 1948, Civil Rights: Corresp May 1948 Folder, Section 3C, Series III, CRC.

59. Southern California Anti-Defamation League, Core Survey of Downtown Stores Memo, July 28, 1948, Discrimination—Corresp. 1948–49 Folder, Section 3C, Series III, CRC.

60. The *Los Angeles Times* contained the most discriminatory help wanted advertisements—25 of 400 ads. Just over 2 percent of the *Los Angeles Examiner*'s ads contained racially or religiously discriminatory language, while there were none in the more progressive papers such as the *Herald-Express* and the *Hollywood Citizen-News*. The *Daily News* did not have help wanted advertising in this period. Southern California Anti-Defamation League, Discriminating Advertising Survey, September 20, 1948, Discrim—Employment Corresp. 1947–48 Folder, Section 3C, Series III, CRC.

61. Ed Roybal, Letter to Southland Jewish Organization, July 20, 1956, Jewish Organizations Folder, Box 20, Roybal.

62. Edward W. Mehren (Chairman L.A. County Conference on Community Relations), *Accomplishments and Program of Los Angeles County Conference on Community Relations*, December 2, 1950, 4, L.A. County Conference on Community Relations Folder, Box 44, NAACP.

63. Marvin Jager (Bureau of Jewish Economic Problems), Letter, June 17, 1947, Discrim Employment Corresp 1947–1948 Folder, Section 3C, Series III, CRC.

64. Vorspan and Gartner, *History of the Jews of Los Angeles*, 245. Scholars of the Jews of Los Angeles argue that Jews there faced more limited opportunities than Jews in more established eastern cities. For information on anti-Semitism and discrimination in Los Angeles in this period, see Vorspan and Gartner, *History of the Jews of Los Angeles*, esp. 238–47. For a further discussion of Jewish life in postwar Los Angeles (specifically a comparison of Miami and Los Angeles Jewish life), including discussions of anti-Semitism, see Moore, *To the Golden Cities*.

65. For comparison, white unemployment dropped only from 11 percent to 9 percent; but still, the overall white unemployment levels were lower both in 1940 and 1950. Sides, "Working Away," 226.

66. For a discussion of the changing job status of Mexican-origin people in California in this period, see Camarillo, *Chicanos in a Changing Society*, 72–74, 79. For a detailed discussion of the living and working conditions of Southern California's Mexican-origin community, see McWilliams, *North from Mexico*, 217–21. For a general discussion of discrimination against Mexican-origin people in the western United States in this period, see Gutiérrez, *Walls and Mirrors*, esp. chapters 4 and 5 passim.

67. For discussion of the bracero program, see Gutiérrez, *Walls and Mirrors*.

68. See "Job Discrimination Has Soared in California Since V-J Day," editorial in *Action: Quarterly Bulletin of Los Angeles Branch NAACP*, October 1946, Vol. 2, No. 1, O.A.—Correspondence—Branch, Los Angeles, 1946 Folder, Box 15, NAACP,

and Reverend Clayton D. Russell (chairman of Emergency Jobs Conferences), Report, August and November 1949, Employment 1949 Folder, Section 3C, Series III, CRC. See also de Graaf and Taylor, introduction, in de Graaf, Mulroy, and Taylor, eds., *Seeking El Dorado*, 32; Sides, "Working Away," 226; and Smith, "Black Employment in the Los Angeles Area, 1938–1948."

69. Fred Herzberg, letter to Eugene Block (SF CRC), September 9, 1949, Discrim: Corresp. 1948–9 Folder, Section 3C, Series III, CRC, and N.Y. Anti-Defamation League Memo to ADL Regional Offices, June 13, 1950, Discrim: Corresp. 1950 Folder, Section 3C, Series III, CRC.

70. Los Angeles NAACP, News Release: Anti-Negro Demonstrations and Violence in Los Angeles Mount as Second Cross within Three Weeks Is Burned on Lawn," June 15, 1952, Los Angeles, Calif, 1952 Folder, Box C16, Group II, NAACP LOC.

71. Camarillo, *Chicanos in California*, 79–80, and Acuña, *Anything but Mexican*, 44.

72. See Vorspan and Gartner, *History of the Jews of Los Angeles*, particularly 238–47. For more on Fifield, on Smith's visits to Los Angeles, as well as support and opposition, see Sitton, *Los Angeles Transformed*, 82–92. See too Leonard, "The Little Fuehrer Invades Los Angeles.'"

73. Ruth Kingman (CFCU), Letter to the SF American Automobile Association, April 30, 1947, Outgoing Correspondence 1947 Folder, Box 1, CFCU.

74. The East Los Angeles area was City Terrace Drive. "Swastika Emblems Like Nazis' Painted on Walls," *Los Angeles Times*, July 16, 1952, Folder 8, Box 21, Civil Rights Congress; "Vandalism Spurs Call for Unity," unidentified L.A. newspaper, July 24, 1952, Folder 8, Box 21, Civil Rights Congress; and "Vandals Desecrate Synagogue in L.A.; Torah Destroyed," *Southwest Jewish Press*, August 6, 1954, Vandalism-Violence (Correspondence) 1954 Folder, Box 76A, Series IV, CRC.

75. The American Council on Race Relations, *The Problem of Violence: Observations on Race Conflict in Los Angeles*, (date?), 13, Carton 6, Ford.

76. Zane Meckler (Western Director of the Anti-Discrimination Department of the Jewish Labor Committee), Memo to L.A. CRC, May 12, 1947, Communism 1947 Folder, Section 3C, Series III, CRC.

77. See Furmanovsky, "Communism as Jewish Radical Subculture"; Gardner, *Tradition's Chains Have Bound Us*, 278, 281; and Healey and Isserman, *Dorothy Healey Remembers*, 104–5.

78. Historian Deborah Dash Moore argues that communism and anticommunism tore the Los Angeles Jewish community apart in the late 1940s and early 1950s, and that Jewish leaders chose anticommunism as their stance. Though she does not specifically address the number of communists or communist sympathizers in the Jewish community, her work acknowledges that a strong community presence persisted in the community, enough to drive a wedge into it. See Moore, *To the Golden Cities*, 196–201.

79. Sides, *LA City Limits*, 142; Sides, "Working Away," 200–202; and Gardner, *Tradition's Chains Have Bound Us*, 105, 205. For the national discussion, see Gerald Horne, *Black and Red*, 291, and Klehr, *Communist Cadre*, 60, 62, 67. For an excellent discussion of one case study of blacks' relationship with the Communist Party, see Kelley, *Hammer and Hoe*. For contemporary accounts of African Americans and the CP nationally, see Ford, *Communists in the Struggle for Negro Rights*, and Wilkerson, *Why Negroes Are Joining the Communist Party*.

80. Gardner, *Tradition's Chains Have Bound Us*, 278–82. On the role of the Communist Party in the Mexican American community in an earlier era, see Vargas, *Labor Rights*. According to Bert Corona, the CP's Rose Chernin told Josefina Fierro that at one point there were 435 Mexican-origin members in LA CP in the 1930s. Corona noted that "neither Josefina nor anyone else batted an eye about that number, because in fact the CP was very active in the barrios during the Depression." García, *Memories of Chicano History*, 126.

81. Yoneda, *Ganbatte*.

82. The director was Joe Esquith of the Soto-Michigan Jewish Center. For more information on the investigation and Tenney's interest in the Eastside Jewish community, see Barrett, *The Tenney Committee*, 37–38.

83. On the ANMA, see García, *Mexican Americans*, 203.

84. For more on this organization, see Garcilazo, "McCarthyism, Mexican, "Communism, Workshop On" Folder, Box 58, Series IV, CRC.

85. For an excellent study of anticommunism's destructive impact, see Schrecker, *Many are the Crimes*. See too the examples and citations provided in the introduction.

86. AJ Congress, Resolution on the Mundt Bill, May 6, 1948, Civil Rights: Corresp May 1948 Folder, Section 3C, Series III, CRC. See too E.I. Robinson (LA NAACP President), letter to Gloster B. Current (NY NAACP), May 15, 1950 Los Angeles, Calif, 1950 Folder, Box C15, Group II, NAACP LOC.

87. CRC Declaration, 1948, Tenney, Jack B.: Corr., 1948 Folder, Section 3C, Series III, CRC.

88. CRC, Memo, 1947, Memos from Exec Office Staff 1947 Folder, Section AII, Series III, CRC.

89. Herzberg to Pacht, June 14, 1949, Subcomm, Special: Tenney Comm 1948–1949, AII, Series III, CRC.

90. Jewish Information Service, *Facts for Action* Report, June 1954, Folder 10, Box 6, Jewish Secular Material.

91. Gloster B. Current (director of branches), speech, March 7, 1948—1949 Folder, Los Angeles, Calif, 1949 Folder, Box C15, Group II, NAACP LOC.

92. This was California Senate Constitutional Amendment 21 (SCA 21). CFCU, quoted in untitled, February 12, 1953, *SF News*, America Plus 1951–1953, Box 43, NAACP. The CSO too opposed Tenney's SCA 21. It was one of four issues on its civil rights agenda that year. See Anthony Ríos (CSO chairman), letter to George I. Sánchez (University of Texas professor and Mexican-American activist). The other three items were eliminating segregation in private and public housing; discriminatory IQ testing, zoning, and counseling practices in the L.A. public school system; and the mass search and seizure practices of the LAPD. Folder 1, Box 6, Ross.

93. Roybal, Speech before L.A. City Council on his opposition to the Communist Control Ordinance, September 13, 1950, Folder 13—Communism, Box 8, Roybal. For more on Roybal's election, see the subsequent chapter.

94. Ibid.

95. Roybal, Speech before L.A. City Council on his opposition to the Communist Control Ordinance, September 13, 1950, Folder 13—Communism, Box 8, Roybal.

96. "Scroll for Courage Heartening Example," editorial, *Daily News*, November 14, 1950, Communism Folder, Box 8, Roybal.

97. Roybal, letter to George E. Rundquist (Assistant Director ACLU, NY), October 17, 1950, Folder 13—Communism, Box 8, Roybal, and Esther Pasthoff (Director Emma Lazarus Division of JPFO), letter to Roybal, November 9, 1950, Folder 13—Communism, Box 8, Roybal.

98. "Scroll for Courage Heartening Example," editorial, *Daily News*, 14 November 1950, Communism Folder, Box 8, Roybal.

99. Executive Committee, American Jewish Congress, Resolution on the Mundt Bill, May 6, 1948, Civil Rights: Corresp. May 1948 Folder, Section 3C, Series III, CRC.

My argument that Cold Warriors argued fighting discrimination would help combat communism is not new. Ellen Schrecker, for instance, argues that anticommunists viewed civil rights as an avenue for eliminating communism, but I emphasize a different nuance: that civil rights reformers saw anticommunism as a civil rights avenue. For more on the first emphasis, see Schrecker, *Many Are the Crimes*.

100. Executive Committee, American Jewish Congress, Resolution on the Mundt Bill, May 6, 1948, Civil Rights: Corresp. May 1948 Folder, Section 3C, Series III, CRC.

101. John Slawson (American Jewish Committee) to American Legion, March 21, 1950, Communism: Jewish—Involvement and Response 1950 Folder, 3C, Series III, CRC.

102. H. H. Collins (President of Bakersfield NAACP and minister of St. Paul's Methodist Episcopal Church), Statement, [date?], Real Estate, Carton I, CFCU.

103. "Constitution: Seek Passage of Race Curb Amendment," *LA Herald Express*, August 11, 1948, Housing: Restrictive Covenants—printed matter 1948–50 Folder, 3C, Series III, CRC; Untitled, September 25, 1947, *California Eagle*, Housing: Corresp 1947–48 Folder, 3C, Series III, CRC.

104. Milton A. Senn, *Report on Efforts in the L.A. Area to Circumvent the U.S. Supreme Court Decisions on Restrictive Covenants*, December 31, 1948, Housing: restrictive covenants, printed matter 1948–50 Folder, AII, Series III, CRC.

105. Al Antczak, "'Homes for Veterans': But Not Just Any Vet," *The Tidings*, January 30, 1948, 1, 3.

106. Ibid.

107. Thomas L. Griffith, Membership campaign flyer, May 2, 1947, Los Angeles, Calif, 1947 Folder, Box C14, Group II, NAACP LOC.

108. "Argument in the Matter of the Citizens' Advisory Committee," August 1, 1948, Tenney, Jack B.: Corresp 1948 Folder, Section 3C, Series III, CRC.

109. Minutes of the CRC Legal and Legislative Committee Meeting, April 13, 1949, Subcomm: Legal and Legislative—Minutes 1947–1950 Folder, Section AII, Series III, CRC.

110. Senn, Letter to President of B'nai B'rith Women's Grand Lodge San Mateo [similar letters sent to many other California Jews], October 31, 1947, Civil Rights: Corresp Sept–Oct 1947 Folder, Section 3C, Series III, CRC.

111. American Jewish Congress (NY), Resolution on the President's Executive Order No. 9835 Prescribing Procedures for Administering an Employees' Loyalty Program, April 30–May 1, 1947. Will Maslow of the AJ

Congress shared this resolution with the Mexican-American Community Service Organization in a letter to Henry Nava and Ralph Guzman, August 24, 1949, Folder 12, Box 5, Ross.

112. Forster (NY ADL), Letter to Senn, October 22, 1947, Civil Rights: Correspondence Sept–Oct 1947 Folder, Section 3C, Series III, CRC; CRC, Minutes of Joint Staff Meeting, July 31, 1951, Joint Staff Comm. Minutes May–Jul 1951 Folder, Unnumbered Box, Series IV, CRC.

113. NAACP, President's Loyalty Order Adopted by the 40th Annual Convention NAACP Los Angeles, California, July 16, 1949. The NAACP shared this resolution with the CSO in a letter from Roy Wilkins to Henry Nava, August 23, 1949, Folder 12, Box 5, Ross.

114. Other named organizations included the National Negro Congress, the Civil Rights Congress, the Socialist Workers Party, the Committee on Racial Equality (CORE), the International Workers Order, and the American Veterans' Committee. Loren Miller (NAACP legal staff), Memo, May 1948, Civil Rights: Corresp May 1948 Folder, Section 3C, Series III, CRC. See too CRC, Memo, May 6, 1948, Civil Rights: Corresp. May 1948 Folder, Section 3C, Series III, CRC and John H. Dial, Jr. (Director Fair Practice and Anti-Discrimination Committee), letter to Milton Senn (ADL), May 19, 1948, Civil Rights: Corresp. May 1948 Folder, Section 3C, Series III, CRC.

115. E.I. Robinson (LA NAACP President), letter to Gloster B. Current (NY NAACP), May 15, 1950 Los Angeles, Calif, 1950 Folder, Box C15, Group II, NAACP LOC.

116. Eschen, *Race against Empire*, 149.

117. Editorial, *Daily News*, January 6, 1951, Communism, Box 8, Roybal.

118. "Goodbye to Isolation," March 31, 1933, Folder 2 Negro Labor, Folder, Carton 1, Miller.

119. For more, see chapters 2 and 3.

120. For scholarship on this issue, see, for instance, Horne, *Black and Red*; Meriwether, *Proudly We Can Be Africans*; Plummer, *Rising Wind*; and von Eschen, *Race against Empire*.

121. This is a simplification of complex arguments. For more on this, see, for instance, Horne, *Black and Red*; Meriwether, *Proudly We Can Be Africans*, 83, and von Eschen, *Race against Empire*, 116–17.

122. For a fuller discussion of Dubois and other African Americans' critiques of Cold War U.S. foreign policy, and of NAACP and other "liberal" African-American groups' abandonment of foreign policy critiques to fortify their support for domestic civil rights reform, see Horne, *Black and Red*; Janken, "From Colonial Liberation to Cold War Liberalism"; Meriwether, *Proudly We Can Be Africans*; Plummer, *Rising Wind*; and von Eschen, *Race against Empire*.

123. Gloster B. Current, roundtable radio discussion at Los Angeles NAACP West Coast Regional Conference, March 7, 1948, in NAACP West Coast Region Report, March 5–7, 1948, West Coast Conference—2nd Annual, 1948 Folder, Box 35, NAACP.

124. Wilkins, with Mathews, *Standing Fast*, 206.

125. "Roybal Raps Bias in LA Realty Deals," *Los Angeles Daily News*, September 18, 1950, p. 9, in Chávez, *Mi Raza Primero!* 19.

126. On the ANMA, see García, *Mexican Americans*, 208–11, and García, *Memories of Chicano History*, 186–87. On the CSO, see the subsequent chapter.

127. See G. Raymond Booth (executive secretary CCU), Memo, January 2, 1946, Folder 12—Comm on Human Relations, LA County: Corresp Jan–May 1946, Box 218, Series II, CRC; Raymond Booth, Letter to Leon Lewis (CRC), January 4, 1946, Folder 12—Comm on Human Relations, LA County: Corresp Jan–May 1946, Box 218, Series II, CRC; Ruth W. Kingman (CFCU), Memo to Laurence I. Hewes, Jr. (American Council on Race Relations) concerning Report on Los Angeles Community Attitudes Toward CCCU [California Council for Civic Unity], March 1, 1946, 4, Outgoing Correspondence 1946 Folder, Box 1, CFCU; and various documents in Folder 6—Special: Council for Civic Unity, 1946, Series II, CRC. For further discussion of the splits within the CCU, see various documents in Folders 12 and 13, Box 219(?), Series II, CRC.

128. Dale Gardner (exec secty. for LACCHR), Memo to Ford, November 5, 1947, 72/B/IV/5/1/cc—Los Angeles County Committee on Human Relations, 1947 Folder, Ford.

129. LA Central Labor Council, *Los Angeles Central Labor Council* Report, August 6, 1948, Folder 25—Jewish Labor Committee 1946, Box 141, Series II, CRC.

130. For a discussion of tensions in the CIO in the postwar period, see Burt, "The Battle for Standard Coil," and Zieger, *The CIO 1935–1955*.

131. García, *Mexican Americans*, 200.

132. The L.A. branch grew from 2,000 members in 1941 to 11,000 in 1945. For figures on wartime gain and postwar loss, see Sides, "Working Away," 197–200.

133. "NAACP branch officers not 'all-wise,' says doleful Roy Wilkins in interview," March 5, 1949, *LA Tribune*, Los Angeles, Calif, 1949 Folder, Box C15, Group II, NAACP LOC.
For a discussion of anticommunism and its impact on civil rights in the New York City NAACP branch, see Biondi, *To Stand and Fight*. See too Anderson, "Bleached Souls and Red Negroes."

134. N. W. Griffin (Regional Secretary), Letter to Walter White (Secretary N.Y. NAACP), September 13, 1946, Communism 1946–54 Folder, Box 43, NAACP. For a discussion of how the conflict also involved criticism that the NAACP was not radical enough, see Sides, "Working Away," 198–200. Sides recognizes the growing ties between African Americans and communism after the war, and the fact that the local NAACP was "racked with strife" in this period, but does not recognize the extent to which these issues were related. He attributes the organization's divisions to poor and ineffective leadership, crediting the community's dissatisfaction with the NAACP to its *lack* of militancy and its unwillingness to make ties to labor. Although this undoubtedly explained the more radical members' dissatisfaction, other less radical members criticized it because they felt it was too heavily influenced by radicals and even feared that the communists were running the organization.

135. "NAACP branch officers not 'all-wise,' says doleful Roy Wilkins in interview," March 5, 1949, *LA Tribune*, Los Angeles, Calif, 1949 Folder, Box C15, Group II, NAACP LOC. For a discussion of perceived communist involvement in the San Francisco NAACP, see various November 1946 correspondence between Noah

Griffin and Walter White, November 1946, Los Angeles, Calif, 1946 Folder, Box C14, Group II, NAACP LOC.

136. According to the national branch official Roy Wilkins, the drop in Los Angeles membership was so large it contributed considerably to the national membership decline. "NAACP branch officers not 'all-wise,' says doleful Roy Wilkins in interview," March 5, 1949, *LA Tribune*, Los Angeles, Calif, 1949 Folder, Box C15, Group II, NAACP LOC.

137. The NAACP had decided in 1947 and 1948 to oppose "infiltration" by the Communist Party. For a discussion on the national NAACP's official anti-communism, see Gerald Horne, *Black and Red*, 65 and chapter 7 passim. See also Blakely, *Russia and the Negro*, 105–27, and Record, *Race and Radicalism*, 132–41.

138. N. W. Griffith (West Coast Branch director), Letter to Roy Wilkins (Assistant Secretary of the N.Y. NAACP), December 23, 1948, O.A. Corresp—Branch, Los Angeles, Nov–Dec 1948 Folder, Box 15, NAACP.

139. Norma O. Houston, letter to Wilkins, December 20, 1948, Los Angeles Branch Controversy, 1948 Folder, Box C379, Group II, NAACP LOC.

140. Mary Alton Cutler letter to Roy Wilkins, December 11, 1948, Los Angeles Branch Controversy 1948 Folder, Box C379, Group II, NAACP LOC.

141. "Communist Threat to 'Take Over' Local NAACP Fought," *Los Angeles Tribune*, December 18, 1948, Los Angeles, Calif, 1948 Folder, Box C15, Group II, NAACP LOC, and Mary Alton Cutler (Executive Secretary LA Branch), letter to Gloster Current (NY Office), October 4, 1948, Los Angeles, Calif, 1948 Folder, Box C15,Group II, NAACP LOC.

142. Roy Wilkins (N.Y. NAACP Assistant Secretary), Letter to Norman Houston (prominent moderate L.A. NAACP member), December 29, 1948, O.A. Corresp—Branch, Los Angeles, Nov–Dec 1948 Folder, Box 15, NAACP.

143. Gloster B. Current (national head of branches), Letter to Noah Griffin (West Coast Office), December 30, 1948, O.A. Corresp—Branch, Los Angeles, Nov–Dec 1948 Folder, Box 15, NAACP.

144. Gloster B. Current, letter to Noah Griffin (West Coast Regional Office), December 30, 1948, O.A. Corresp—Branch, Los Angeles, Nov–Dec 1948 Folder, Box 15, NAACP.

145. Declaration (undersigned by Loren Miller, Herman Talley, Victor Nix, Eugene S. Pickett, and Robert H. Irwin), January 11, 1949, Los Angeles, Calif, 1949 Folder, Box C15, Group II, NAACP LOC.

146. George L. Thomas, letter to Roy Wilkins, January 11, 1949, Los Angeles, Calif, 1949 Folder, Box C15, Group II, NAACP LOC. For another discussion of the splits between moderates and radicals in the CIO and the NAACP, see Kurashige, "Transforming Los Angeles," 401, 422–44, and Kurashige, *The Shifting Grounds of Race*. Griffith won against Howard Kingsley, a black reverend who headed the Pilgrim House Community Center, which was a center in Little Tokyo organized to improve interracial relations.

147. Loren Miller, Memo, July 29, 1952, 76/B/IV/5/i/ee—Negro, 1952 Folder, Ford.

148. On Bass's increasing radicalism, and sympathy toward communism and the Soviet Union in the 1940s and 1950s, see discussion on her visits to Moscow and the Soviet Union, and other elements in her memoirs. Bass, *Forty Years*, esp.

165–71. On the *Eagle* and Bass's accusations in the 1930s that Miller was a communist, and for more on her political trajectory, see Flamming, *Bound for Freedom*,
325, 365–72. Also on Bass, see Freer, "L.A. Race Woman," and Gottlieb, Vallianatos,
Freer, and Dreier, *The Next Los Angeles*, 49–64.

149. Miller became disillusioned with the Communist Party after the 1939
Nazi-Soviet Pact revealed that the Communist Party prioritized the Soviet Union
more than anything else. De Graaf, Interview with Loren Miller, 5–6, 8–9.

150. Miller, Letter to Helen Gahagan Douglas, November 14, 1949, Folder
Miller Correspondence 1949 (third folder), Box 1, Carton 2, Miller.

151. Roy Wilkins (N.Y. NAACP Assistant Secretary), Letter to Norman
Houston (prominent L.A. NAACP member), December 29, 1948, O.A. Corresp—
Branch, Los Angeles, Nov–Dec 1948 Folder, Box 15, NAACP.

152. Walter White, Telegram to Franklin H. Williams (West Coast Regional
Office), February 16, 1952, Communism 1946–54 Folder, Box 43, NAACP. For
another discussion of the role anticommunism and radicalism played in fracturing
this organization, see Leonard, "Years of Hope, Days of Fear."

153. NAACP, "Keep Your Eyes Wide Open: Don't Get Sucked In!" Flyer,
undated (likely 1950s), Communism—Printed Matter and Newsclippings Folder,
Box 43, NAACP.

154. CRC Meeting minutes, April 18, 1947, Minutes 1947 Folder, Section AII,
Series III, CRC, and Minutes of Meeting of Subcommittee Re: Tenney Investigation,
June 30, 1948, Subcomm, Special: Tenney Comm—Minutes 1948 Folder, Section
AII, Series III, CRC.

155. Roth had been the judge in earlier years whom the Sleepy Lagoon Defense
Committee hoped would take over the trial because he was more sympathetic to
their causes than the judge who had been assigned to the case. See Pagán, *Murder
at the Sleepy Lagoon*.

156. CRC Meeting Minute Notes, March 18, 1949, Minutes 1948 Folder,
Section AII, Series III, CRC.

157. CRC meeting minutes, April 2, 1950, Minutes 1950 Folder, Section AII,
Series III, CRC. See also CRC, Meeting Minutes, March 3, 1949 and March 11,
1949, Minutes 1949 Folder, Section AII, Series III, CRC and Vorspan and Gartner,
History of the Jews of Los Angeles, 266.

158. CRC Meeting Agenda, September 14, 1945, Folder 17 Agendas, Apr–Dec,
1945, Box 1, Series II, CRC.

159. CRC Meeting Minutes, January 10, 1947, Minutes Jan–June 1947 Folder,
Section AII, Series III, CRC.

160. Los Angeles Chapter of the American Jewish Labor Council, *Achievements
and Perspectives*, Report of Third Annual Convention, Folder 8, Box 21, Civil
Rights Congress. For more discussion of the rise of anti-Semitism in America in
this period, see Dinnerstein, "Anti-Semitism Exposed and Attacked, 1945–1950."

161. JPFO, Letter to "Dear Friend," December 12, 1950, 4, 11, JPFO (Printed
Matter) 1951 Folder, Box 53, Series IV, CRC.

162. JPFO, Report, undated (probably 1951 or 1952), Untitled [all JPFO
material] Folder, Box 77, Series IV, CRC.

163. "Jews in California ought to be told they are playing with fire, says a
prominent lawyer concerning Jewish Communist activities and leftists activities
within the Community Council," *Jewish Daily Forward*, September 1950, 6, quoted

in memo, "Los Angeles Jewish Community Council Still Harbors Pro-Communist Jewish Peoples Fraternal Order. American Jewish Congress in California Continues to Demonstrate Sympathy for Communist Groups. Statement by Ten National Jewish Organizations Denouncing Stockholm Petition Not Publicized in Los Angeles. Like Playing With Fire," September 18, 1950, Communism: Jewish 1950 Folder, Section 3C, Series III, CRC.

164. Mendel Silberberg, Letter to all CRC members, October 17, 1950, meeting Notices 1950 Folder, Section AII, Series III, CRC.

165. CRC, Press release(?), 1947, Communism 1947 Folder, Section 3C, Series III, CRC.

166. Zane Meckler (Western Director of the Anti-Discrimination Department of the Jewish Labor Committee), Memo to L.A. CRC, May 12, 1947, Communism 1947 Folder, Section 3C, Series III, CRC; LA Central Labor Council, *Los Angeles Central Labor Council* Report, August 6, 1948, Folder 25—Jewish Labor Committee 1946, Box 141, Series II, CRC.

167. Judge Isaac Pacht, Speech at opening of Workshop on the Problem of Communism, March 13, 1951, "Communism, Workshop On" Folder, Box 58, Series IV, CRC.

168. CRC, Press release(?), 1947, Communism 1947 Folder, Section 3C, Series III, CRC. For a further discussion of Jews' and African Americans' anticommunism, both their commitments to it and American democracy, and also their pragmatism, see Greenberg, *Troubling the Waters*, especially 169–76.

169. Gabler, *An Empire of Their Own*, 373–74. See too Schary, *Heydey*, 164–67. Schary had been reluctant to sign the Waldorf Statement, but when Silberberg encouraged him to help draft it in order to incorporate some of his concerns, he reluctantly acquiesced. Other Hollywood figures who signed included Louis B. Mayer of Metro-Goldwyn-Mayer, Harry Cohn of Columbia Pictures, Samuel Goldwyn of Samuel Goldwyn Company, Albert Warner of Warner Bros., and many others (Spyros Skouras of 20th Century Fox, Nicholas Schenck of Loews Theatres, Barney Balaban of Paramount Pictures, William Goetz of Universal-International, Eric Johnston of the Motion Picture Association of America, and James F. Byrnes, the former U.S. secretary of state).

170. Gabler, *An Empire of Their Own*, 376.

171. CRC Meeting Minutes, March 18, 1949, Minutes 1949 Folder, Section AII, Series III, CRC.

172. Ibid.

173. CRC, Press Release, April 21, 1952, Communists—Jews (Corresp) 1952 Folder, Box 59, Series IV, CRC.

174. Ibid. For a discussion of the Jewish community's response to the Rosenberg case at the national level, see Cheryl Greenberg, *Troubling the Waters*, 191–93.

175. Fineberg (AJ Committee N.Y. Office), Letter to Herzberg (L.A. CRC), December 3, 1947, Civil Rights: Corresp Dec 1947 Folder, Section 3C, Series III, CRC.

176. CRC Meeting Minutes, May 3, 1948, Minutes 1948 Folder, Section AII, Series III, CRC.

177. Philip M. Connelly, "'Hush-Hush' Revival Faces L.A. Jews," *Daily People's World*, March 12, 1951.

178. Joe Roos, Letter to Eddie Albert, February 19, 1952, NAACP Shrine Affair 1952 Folder, Box 61, Series IV, CRC.

179. Meckler reported on a meeting in Milwaukee attended by CRCs of every local Jewish community in America where they talked for five hours specifically about communism. Zane Meckler (Western Director of the Anti-Discrimination Department of the Jewish Labor Committee), Memo to L.A. CRC, May 12, 1947, Communism 1947 Folder, Section 3C, Series III, CRC.

180. Henry Lee Moon, memo to Walter White, July 6, 1950, Communism— General Jan–Sept 1950 Folder, Box C329, Group II, NAACP LOC.

181. The article observed the issue of Communism forced Americans to take a stand—hard-line against civil rights or to become civil rights advocates. The author wrote about the formation of one prominent civil rights group, the Council for Civic Unity. Mary Hornaday, untitled article, *Christian Science Moitor*, July 19, 1947, 69/B/IV/3/b—Federation for Civic Unity, Ford.

182. Ibid.

183. Albert T. Lunceford (CIO), "Labor's Role in the Community" (Speech before the Democratic Luncheon Club), September 1949, Labor: Corresp 1948–1950 Folder, Section 3C, Series III, CRC.

CHAPTER 5

1. "The Latin One-Eighth," *LA Daily News*, July 1, 1949. For more on Roybal's election coalition, see Burt, "The Power of a Mobilized Citizenry and Coalition Politics"; Scott, "The Mexican-American in the Los Angeles Area, 1920–1950"; Underwood, "Pioneering Minority Representation"; and Underwood, "Process and Politics." On the local population's composition, see Acuña, *Anything but Mexican*, 45. On the Eastside's multiracial diversity through 1945, see Sánchez, *Becoming*, and on the postwar era, see "What's Good for Boyle Heights."

2. Burt, *The Search for a Civic Voice*, 79–82, 86, 88.

3. ibid., 85–87. For a nice discussion of Roybal's significance to the Mexican-American community, and some of his achievements, see Chávez, *Mi Raza Primero!*, 18–21.

4. Other committee members included Charles Brown, Judge John C. Clark, Dr. E. C. Farnham, John Anson Ford, James Roosevelt, and Judge Thomas P White. CSO, Publicity Pamphlet, undated (approx 1948),"CSO" Folder 12, Box 10, Ross. On Alinsky, see Finks, *The Radical Vision of Saul Alinsky*, 34–45, and Horwitt, *Let Them Call Me Rebel*, 127–29 and 222–35. On Ross, see *The Devil in Silicon Valley*, 149–50.

5. Ross, letter to Alinsky, September 27, 1947, Folder 1, Box 2, Ross.

6. On Ross, see Pitti, *The Devil in Silicon Valley*, 149–50.

7. Anthony P. Ríos, Application for Funds to United Steelworkers of America, approx 1953, CSO Folder, Box 9, Roybal, and Scott, "The Mexican-American," 299. On women's significant role in the CSO, see, for instance, Apodaca, "They Kept the Home Fires Burning" and Rose, "Gender and Civic Activism in Mexican American Barrios in California," 180. A note on sources: the CSO papers are

scattered and sparse, and had to be pieced together from other collections and oral histories.

8. For more on this, see previous chapter and Rose, "Gender and Civic Activism in Mexican American Barrios in California," 193.

9. Ibid., 194.

10. Ibid., 192. See too CSO, publicity pamphlet, undated, CSO Folder 12, Box 10, Ross.

11. Anthony P. Ríos, Application for Funds to United Steelworkers of America from Community Service Organization Los Angeles, California, undated, Community Service Organization Folder, Box 9, Roybal; CSO, CSO *Reporter*, 1958, Community Service Organization, Inc., 1955–1960 Folder, Box 10, NAACP. For more on Bloody Christmas, see Escobar, "Bloody Christmas and the Irony of Police Professionalism," 171–72.

12. Camarillo, *Chicanos in California*, 81–82.

13. They mobilized 138, 132 votes for Ibañez, though they did not succeed in electing him. "The Latin One-Eighth," *LA Daily News*, July 1, 1949.

14. See Gutiérrez, *Walls and Mirrors*, 169.

15. On the CSO's success registering voters, see Danny Feingold, "Common Threads," *L.A. Times*, October 21, 1998.

16. "The Latin One-Eighth," *LA Daily News*, July 1, 1949.

17. Scholars who discuss the CSO in a Chicano history framework include the following: Apodaca, *Mexican American Women and Social Change*; Apodaca, "They Kept the Home Fires Burning"; Burt, *The Search for a Civic Voice*; Camarillo, *Chicanos in California*, 80–82; Chávez, *Mi Raza Primero!*; Lozano, "The Struggle for Inclusion"; Pitti, *The Devil in Silicon Valley*, chapter 7 passim; Rose, "Gender and Civic Activism in Mexican American Barrios in California"; and Scott, "The Mexican-American in the Los Angeles Area, 1920–1950," 294–99.

18. García, *Memories of Chicano History*, 164. Roybal is one example. He worked for the New Deal's Civilian Conservation Corps in the 1930s, and served in the military during World War II. Burt, "The Power of a Mobilized Citizenry," 416.

19. Some of the above scholars acknowledge CSO's multiracial roots in Roybal election efforts, and hint at its early dependence for funding on a multiracial community. But with the exception of Burt's study, they have not explored the ongoing collaboration in its early years that ensured CSO's later success as a Mexican-American organization. See, for example, Lozano, "The Struggle for Inclusion"; Pitti, *The Devil in Silicon Valley*, 242 n. 5; Pitti, "Quicksilver Community," 438, 439–41; and Underwood, "Process and Politics," 18, 99–100.

20. Ross, Report, February 20, 1948, Folder 1, Box 2, Ross.

21. Fred Ross speaking with Saul Alinsky at the CRC's Meeting of the Subcommittee on Agencies, Minutes of the Meeting of the Subcommittee on Agencies, February 14, 1949, Subcommittees Agencies—Minutes 1947–1950 Folder, Section AII, Series III, CRC.

22. Anthony P. Ríos, Application for Funds to United Steelworkers of America, 1953(?), CSO Folder, Box 9, Roybal.

23. Ross Manuscript, undated, Folder 22 San Bernardino: Ruth and Ignacio, Box 22, Ross.

24. The report acknowledged certain attempts at representation by and for the Mexican-American community, including the Southern California Council on Inter-American Affairs, and the Mexican American Movement. Lawrence I. Hewes, Jr. (West Coast Regional Director, American Council on Race Relations), *Race Relations on the West Coast*, September 1946, 3, Carton 6, Ford.

The most convincing explanation for why Mexican Americans were slower to develop politically effective organizations than other Los Angeles minority communities is developed by George Sánchez. Sánchez argues that until the postwar period, the Mexican-origin community had only one eye on the United States, with the other on Mexico, and that this split focus and uncertainty of future location prevented a deeper investment in developing the American community until the postwar period. See Sánchez, *Becoming Mexican American*. For a discussion of groups outside of California as well, see Gómez-Quiñones, *Chicano Politics*.

25. Quotation from Daniel, *Chicano Workers and the Politics of Fairness*, 9. For descriptions of the Los Angeles Mexican-origin population's history and circumstances through 1945, see Sánchez, *Becoming Mexican American*, esp. 37–38, 52–64; and Romo *East Los Angeles*.

26. Henry Nava, Letter to "Dear Reader," undated (probably early 1950s), Community Service Organization, Inc., 1955–1960 Folder, Box 10, NAACP.

27. Anthony P. Ríos, Application for Funds to United Steelworkers of America, approx. 1953, CSO Folder, Box 9, Roybal. For more discussion on labor's role in CSO, see Burt, "The Battle For Standard Coil."

28. CSO/Industrial Areas Foundation, Southern California Division, Program, 1949, 2, Folder 11, Box 5, Ross.

29. On the ANMA, see García, *Mexican Americans*, 199–230. Other organizations, like the American GI Forum, did not come to Los Angeles until 1957, while LULAC was not very strong there. See Vargas, "In the Years of Darkness and Torment," 384. I agree with Vargas's assessment that Mexican-American activism continued in important ways after World War II, but disagree with his conclusion that McCarthyism eventually stifled it, with the CSO's continuing activism as a case in point. For more on the CSO's Cold War influence, see Burt, "Latino Empowerment in Los Angeles," 23, and Lozano, "The Struggle for Inclusion," 12. On the significance of the San José area's CSO activism in the 1950s see Pitti, *The Devil in Silicon Valley*, 149 and 152–53.

30. CRC, Memo, September 6, 1949, Memos from Exec Office Staff Nov–Dec 1949 Folder, Section AII, Series III, CRC.

31. Richard Dettering (Exec Director CFCU), Letter to Fred Ross, May 24, 1949, Outgoing Corresp 1949, Apr–May Folder, Box 2, CFCU.

32. Dettering, Letter to Henry Nava (Chairman LA CSO), July 26, 1949, Outgoing Corresp 1949, June–Aug Folder, Box 2, CFCU.

33. Dettering, letter to Henry Nava, October 25, 1949, Outgoing Correspondence 1949 Sept–Oct Folder, Box 2, CFCU and various documents in Outgoing Correspondence 1949 Nov–Dec Folder, Box 3, CFCU.

34. CSO, Minutes, October 29–30, 1955, 28, Folder 4, Box 5, Ross.

35. CSO, Memo, 1955, Folder 10, Box 11, Ross; CSO, National CSO Executive Board Meeting Minutes, July 17, 1955, CSO Folder, Box 9, Roybal.

36. Herzberg joined, among others, Richard Ibañez, the Superior Court judge whose election the CSO helped secure, and Gilbert Anaya, who later became a CSO officer. Ross, to Alinsky, September 26, 1947, Folder 1, Box 2, Ross. See also Lozano, "Struggle," 25. The Jewish community's Seniel Ostrow also was an honorary CSO president; see CSO Executive Board Minutes 1955, Folder 4, Box 5, Ross. On the Eastside's postwar multiraciality, see Sánchez, "'What's Good for Boyle Heights Is Good for the Jews.'"

37. Carmen Medina (CSO), to Ida A. Siegel, August 19, 1949, Folder 12, Box 5, Ross.

38. Ralph Guzman, to Rabbi Magnin, February 25, 1950, Subcommittee: CSO, 1949–1950, Section AII, Series III, CRC.

39. The CRC provided $7,500 of CSO's $10,500 1948 funding. CSO, Memo, April 18, 1951, Folder 6, Box 5, Ross; CRC, Meeting Minutes, August 30, 1948, Subcommittees: Agencies—Minutes 1947–1950 Folder, Section AII, Series III, CRC; CRC, Meeting Minutes, July 14, 1949, Subcommittee: CSO 1949–1950 Folder, Section AII, Series III, CRC. Jewish financial support continued for several more years.

40. Horwitt, *Let Them Call Me Rebel*, 227, and Finks, *The Radical Vision of Saul Alinsky*, 34–45. Mr. Miley, Memo to Ford, September 29, 1948, B/IV/5/i/dd-Mexican, 1948 Folder, Box 75, Ford.

41. Memo, August 13, 1948, Minutes Jul–Dec 1948 Folder, Section AII, Series III, CRC.

42. Herzberg, Letter to CRC members, February 17, 1949, Meeting Notices 1949 Folder, Section AII, Series III, CRC.

43. CRC, Memo, September 6, 1949, Memos from Exec Office Staff Nov–Dec 1949 Folder, Section AII, Series III, CRC.

44. Ibid.

45. Pacht (Chairman of Council for Equality in Employment in L.A.), Letter to Henry Nava (CSO Chair), 1949(?), Folder 12, Box 5, Ross.

46. On McWilliams's connection to Pacht, see Carey McWilliams, May 18, 1948, *Diary 1943–1949*, Diary 1943–49 (various) Folder, Box 52, McWilliams 1319. On Warne's connection to Pacht, see Balter, *Law and Social Conscience:* Interview with Ben Margolis (another Sleepy Lagoon attorney), 138. See too Mr. Miley, memo to John Anson Ford, September 29, 1948, Mexican, 1948 Folder, B/IV/5/i/dd, Box 75, Ford.

47. Harry Braverman (Provisional Chairman, Los Angeles Committee for American Unity), Letter to State Attorney General Robert W. Kenny and Bishop Joseph T. McGucken (Chairman Governor's Special Committee on Los Angeles Emergency) June 11, 1943, Folder 4, Box 16, Ruíz; Richardson, *American Prophet*.

48. For more on CSO members' past involvement and relation to labor organizations, see Burt, "Latino Empowerment in Los Angeles." Specifically on Ríos and Anaya's past, see Gutiérrez, *Walls and Mirrors*, 169. On the connection between 1930s labor struggles and later "civil rights" initiatives, see Vargas, *Labor Rights Are Civil Rights*. Vargas convincingly argues that labor rights and civil rights are inseparable.

49. Burt, *The Search for a Civic Voice*, 61.

50. Chall, *Hope Mendoza Schechter*.

51. Roos, Memo to Silberberg and Pacht, January 16, 1953, NAACP (Corresp) 1953 Folder, Box 73, Series IV, CRC.

52. Anthony Ríos, Letter to J. Howard McGrath (Department of Justice), February 21, 1952, Folder 1, Box 5, Ross.

53. Thomas G. Neusom became the L.A. NAACP president during this campaign, and spoke about it at an October 1955 CSO meeting. See CSO 1955 fall quarterly report of the CSOs, Folder 4—Exhibit CR-7, Box 5, Ross. For more on these efforts, see Sides, *L.A. City Limits*, 148–49.

54. Roos, Memo to Silberberg and Pacht, January 16, 1953, NAACP (Corresp) 1953 Folder, Box 73, Series IV, CRC.

55. Walter White, letter to Mendel Silberberg, January 28, 1953, NAACP (Corresp) 1953 Folder, Box 73, Series IV, CRC.

56. Franklin Williams and C. L. Dellums, letter to Joe Roos, September 2, 1954, Legal and Legislative Committee 1954 Folder, Box 68, Series IV, CRC.

57. Bills to gain naturalization privileges included (including HR 2933 in 1947, the Judd Bill in 1948, HR 199 in 1949, and the House Joint Resolution 238 in 1949). See various files in Japanese American Citizens League 1946 Folder 14, Box 223, Series II, CRC and in Intergroup Relations: Japanese American Citizens League, 1948–49 Folder, Section 3C, Series III, CRC. These attempts eventually succeeded a few years later, when the McCarran Walter Bill passed this as part of a larger—and generally more conservative—immigration package.

58. Tats Kushida, Letter to Joe Roos, April 7, 1954, "Schary, Dore (Correspondence) 1954" Folder, Box 74, Series IV, CRC.

59. Minutes of Legal and Legislative subcommittee, CRC, February 16, 1950, Subcomm: Legal and Legislative—Minutes 1947–1950 Folder, Section AII, Series II, CRC. See also various files in Japanese American Citizens League 1946 Folder 14, Box 223, Series II, CRC.

60. Minutes of the Meeting of the Legal and Legislative Subcommittee, February 16, 1950, Subcomm: Legal and Legislative—Minutes 1947–1950 Folder, Section AII, Series III, CRC.

61. Joe Grant Masaoka (Regional JACL representative), Letter to Noah Griffin, August 30, 1945, West Coast Regional Office Reports, 1945–49 Folder, Box C239, Group II, NAACP LOC. NAACP West Coast Regional Office, Monthly Report for September 1945, October 1945, West Coast Regional Office Reports, 1945–49 Folder, Box C239, Group II, NAACP LOC.

62. For discussions of Los Angeles' postwar Japanese-American community, particularly tensions over how much to "assimilate," see Kurashige, *Japanese Celebration and Conflict*, esp. 119–50.

63. For a further discussion of these tensions, see Bernstein, "Building Bridges at Home in a Time of Global Conflict," chapter 6.

64. See Kurashige, *The Shifting Grounds of Race*, chapter 7 passim, esp. 173–74.

65. The American Council on Race Relations, *The Problem of Violence: Observations on Race Conflict in Los Angeles*, undated, 1, Carton 6, Ford.

66. California Federation for Civic Unity, Report, July 1, 1946, Federation for Civic Unity Folder, B/ IV 3b, Box 69, Ford.

67. For a discussion of Bloody Christmas and its larger significance, especially in terms of police repression and brutality, see Escobar, "Bloody Christmas and the

Irony of Police Professionalism," 171–72. Particularly compelling, but not directly related to the subject of this enquiry is Escobar's argument about how the incident ironically consolidated the LAPD's reputation as the least corrupt, best paid, best trained police department in the country, 197.

68. The Ríos/Ulloa trial ran from February 26 to March 10, 1952.

69. CSO *Reporter*, 1958 (month unclear), Community Service Organization, Inc., 1955–1960 Folder, Box 10, NAACP.

70. This incident was in the heavily Jewish neighborhood of the Fairfax district. Untitled article, *People's World*, March 27, 1951, Folder 8, Box 21, Civil Rights Congress.

71. R. Benajah Potter (Past President Rotary Club of Northeast L.A.), Memo concerning Pilgrim House's prevention of race tensions, July 9, 1947, Negro 1947 Folder, B/IV/5/i/ee Box 76, Ford.

72. Samuel Ishikawa (staff of Pilgrim House), *Common Ground* newsletter, September 10, 1945, Japanese, 1945 Folder, B/IV/5/i/bb, Box 74, Ford. The City Health Department, the Los Angeles Chamber of Commerce, and several religious bodies jointly sponsored this center housed in a former Japanese church. Its board members included African-American and Japanese-American clergy and John Anson Ford, and it operated in the area to integrate migrants, improve health, and ameliorate race relations. For more on the Pilgrim House, see Widener, "'Perhaps the Japanese Are to Be Thanked?,'" 166–67. See too Sides, *L.A. City Limits*, 53.

73. American Council on Race Relations, *The Problem of Violence: Observations on Race Conflict in Los Angeles*, Carton 6, Ford.

74. Franklin H. Williams, Speech "Our Unfinished Task: Text of Address made by Franklin H. Williams (regional director of NAACP) to 6th annual meeting of LACCCR," October 11, 1952, Los Angeles County Conference on Community Relations Folder, Box 44, NAACP.

75. Lawrence I. Hewes, Jr. (West Coast Regional Director, American Council on Race Relations), *Race Relations on the West Coast*, September 1946, 1, Carton 6, Ford. See also Mary Hornaday, untitled article, *Christian Science Monitor*, July 19, 1947, 69/B/IV/3/b—Federation for Civic Unity Folder, Ford.

76. Milton A. Senn, *A Study of Police Training Programs in Minority Relations*, August 7, 1950, Folder 1, Box 5, Ross. This number is too high. See information in note 8, chapter 3.

77. CSO, Memo, 1955, Folder 10, Box 11, Ross; CSO, National CSO Executive Board Meeting Minutes, July 17, 1955, CSO Folder, Box 9, Roybal.

78. Lawrence I. Hewes, Jr. (West Coast Regional Director, American Council on Race Relations), *Race Relations on the West Coast*, September 1946, 1, Carton 6, Ford. See also Mary Hornaday, untitled article, *Christian Science Monitor*, July 19, 1947, 69/B/IV/3/b—Federation for Civic Unity Folder, Ford.

79. In 1940, Jews lived in both the poor and wealthy areas of the city. As time passed they lived increasingly in the wealthier areas. In 1940 25 percent were in poorest areas, 22 percent in wealthiest. By 1960 they were in an even wider range of areas, but on the whole more prosperous than before the war. See Moore, *To the Golden Cities*, 58, and 56, 58–60; Sánchez, *Becoming Mexican American*; and Vorspan and Gartner, *History of the Jews of Los Angeles*.

80. CSO/Industrial Areas Foundation, Southern California Division, Program, 1949, 2, Folder 11, Box 5, Ross.

81. Lawrence I. Hewes, Jr. (West Coast Regional Director, American Council on Race Relations), *Race Relations on the West Coast*, September 1946, 3, Carton 6, Ford.

82. The American Council on Race Relations, *The Problem of Violence: Observations on Race Conflict in Los Angeles* (date?), Carton 6, Ford.

83. CSO/Industrial Areas Foundation, Southern California Division, Program, 1949, 2, Folder 11, Box 5, Ross.

84. Conference re the Watts Community Situation, Tues, Feb. 15, 1949, Housing: Watts Community Program (1947–1949) Folder, Section 3C, Series III, CRC. On this phenomenon nationwide, see Diner, "Between Words and Deeds: Jews and Blacks in America, 1880–1935," and Kaufman, "Blacks and Jews."

85. On Mexican American anti-Semitism, see the American Council on Race Relations, *The Problem of Violence: Observations on Race Conflict in Los Angeles*, undated, 14, Carton 6, Ford.

86. CRC, Memo, September 6, 1949, Memos from Exec Office Staff Nov–Dec 1949 Folder, Section AII, Series III, CRC. See too CRC, Meeting Minutes, February 3, 1950, Minutes 1950 Folder, Section AII, Series III, CRC.

87. CRC, Meeting Minutes, July 14, 1949, Subcommittee: CSO 1949–1950 Folder, Section AII, Series III, CRC.

88. The document reported that the minority population of Watts increased 100 percent in the last eight years: in 1940 about 60 percent were Mexican, 20 percent Negro, 20 percent white, and in 1949 about 24 percent were Mexican, 75 percent were Negro, and 1 percent were all others. Author unknown, "Conference Re the Watts Community Situation, held Tues, Feb 15, 1949," Housing: Watts Community Program (1947–1949) Folder, Section 3C, Series III, CRC. Spitzer (CRC), Letter to Charles B Bennett, Director of Planning, City Planning Commission of LA, March 7, 1949, Housing: Watts Community Program (1947–1949) Folder, Section 3C, Series III, CRC.

89. Ross, Report, February 20, 1948, Folder 1, Box 2, Ross.

90. CRC, Meeting Minutes, February 14, 1949, Subcommittees: Agencies—Minutes 1947–1950 Folder, Section AII, Series III, CRC.

91. CSO/Industrial Areas Foundation, Southern California Division, Program, 1949, 4, Folder 11, Box 5, Ross.

92. García, *Memories of Chicano History*, 164. Dorothy Healey mentioned that communists, specifically Henry Steinberg, "one of the better-known Communist community leaders in East Los Angeles," helped organize the CSO. But whether or not communists were involved, the CSO publicly repudiated communists and camouflaged whatever involvement they may have had in the organization. See Healey, *Dorothy Healey Remembers*, 135.

93. García, *Memories of Chicano History*, 164. For more on Corona's involvement with and thoughts about the CSO, see 163–68.

94. "Rios-Ulloa Trial Opens," in *CSO Reporter*, February 28, 1952, 1, Folder 12, Box 10, Ross.

95. Anthony P. Ríos, CSO LA Application of Funds to United Steelworkers of America, 1953(?), CSO Folder, Box 9, Roybal.

96. CSO, *Across the River* pamphlet, 1950(?), Folder 8, Box 13, Galarza.

97. Margarita Duran, CSO Secretary, Program Planning Committee Minutes, September 5, 1950, CSO Folder 12, Box 10, Ross.

98. Declaration, Civil Rights Committee papers, September 7, 1949, Folder 1, Box 5, Ross.

99. CSO, Minutes from CSO program planning committee meeting, September 12, 1949, Folder 5, Box 5 Ross.

100. Roybal, Speech at LA City Council, September 13, 1950, Folder 13, Box 8, Roybal.

101. California Legislature Joint Fact-Finding Committee on Un-American Activities in California, *Fourth Report of the Senate Fact-Finding Committee on Un-American Activities. 1948*, 146. McWilliams described himself to the Tenney Committee, when called to testify on June 22, 1943, as a "liberal New Deal Democrat. I subscribe to all the reforms of the New Deal Administration." The committee did not accept his characterization and instead claimed he embraced Communist Party ideology. For the next two decades the committee listed 161 entries for McWilliams. See Richardson, *American Prophet*, 128–29.

102. Ross to Alinsky, September 26, 1947, Folder 1, Box 2, Ross.

103. CSO Secretary, Minutes, Program Planning Committee, October 10, 1949, Executive Committee, Minutes, 1949–50 Folder 5, Box 5, Ross.

104. On internal disagreement see Fred Ross, Report, February 20, 1948, Folder 1, Box 2, Ross.

105. Glad Burgeni, CSO Training Program Memo, 1957, CSO Folder 15, Box 10, Ross. The memo never mentions who these "leftist agitators" were, nor any specifics, and I have been unable to locate any other information about this episode.

106. CSO, *Across the River* Pamphlet, 1950 (likely), Folder 8, Box 13, Galarza.

107. García, *Memories of Chicano History*, 164.

108. Burt, "The Battle for Standard Coil."

109. García, *Memories of Chicano History*, 166.

110. Ross, to Alinsky, November 3, 1947, Folder 1, Box 2, Ross.

111. See for instance Roy Wilkins (N.Y. NAACP Assistant Secretary), Letter to Normal Houston (prominent L.A. NAACP member), December 29, 1948, O.A. Corresp—Branch, Los Angeles, Nov–Dec 1948 Folder, Box 15, NAACP.

112. Ross, to Alinsky, November 3, 1947, Folder 1, Box 2, Ross.

113. Ross to Alinsky, November 16, 1947, Folder 1, Box 2, Ross.

114. Ross to Alinsky, September 26, 1947, Folder 1, Box 2, Ross.

115. García, *Memories of Chicano History*, 164.

116. In addition to Tarango, Manuel Vega (the president of the local LULAC), Cruz Barrios (Varios?), and Isidor Gonzales went before the D.A. to defend themselves. Eric Kutner and Gilbert Padilla Interview with Hector Tarango, November 15, 2005, CSO Project, University of California San Diego, http://csoproject.org/ (accessed December 13, 2009). Citation from pages 12–14 written transcript, in author's possession. Tarango, who was a Baptist, did not heed the Church's advice and was angry at the other Mexican Americans who did. Ross defended himself when the American Council for Race Relations asked him about this episode and his anticommunist accusations. He explained to Laurence Hewes, the head of the ACRR, "I think you know me well enough to realize I don't go in for 'rabble rousing.'" Ross, letter to Laurence I. Hewes (ACRR), January 12, 1947, Incoming Correspondence R: Ross, Fred Folder, Box V, CFCU. See too Ross, letter and enclosure to Laurence I. Hewes, October 13, 1946,

"Incoming Correspondence R: Ross, Fred" Folder, Box V, CFCU. For more on the *Mendez* case, see the following chapter.

117. Letter from Ross to Alinsky, November 16, 1947, Folder 1, Box 2, Ross.

118. At the time Ross still spoke as an IAF spokesperson, rather than the CSO. Letter from Ross to Alinsky, date unclear, Folder 1, Box 2, Ross.

119. Herman Gallegos to Rev. John [Ralph] Duggan, August 5, 1982, Unfiled material, Box 14, Gallegos. I thank Gina Marie Pitti for sharing this source.

120. For more on Duggan and the Catholic Church's role in California civil rights struggles, see Pitti, "To 'Hear about God in Spanish.'" For more discussion of the relationship between the Catholic Church and the CSO, specifically how the Church legitimized the CSO, see Burt, "The Battle for Standard Coil."

121. Unknown Long Beach NAACP official to Franklin Williams (West Coast Director NAACP), April 5, 1952, Southern California Area Council (2nd Annual Conference) May 2–4 1952 Folder, Box 35, NAACP.

122. For an intriguing discussion of the Catholic Church's increasing role in civil rights activism, see Burt, "The Battle for Inclusion."

123. Rose, "Gender and Civic Activism," 183.

124. Gallegos, interview with Dolores Huerta, page 5, written transcript, in author's possession.

125. Burt, "The Battle for Standard Coil," 121.

126. For a detailed discussion of the Los Angeles CSO's support of and cooperation with anticommunist union organizations during the late 1940s and early 1950s, see Burt, "The Battle for Standard Coil." For more on CSO members' work in labor organizations as well, specifically on the female CSO members, see Rose, "Gender and Civic Activism," 185–87.

127. Burt, "The Battle for Standard Coil," 121.

128. Lester P. Bailey, Letter to Gloster B. Current, April 29, 1950, Los Angeles, Calif, 1950 Folder, Group II, Box C15, NAACP LOC.

129. Leonard Bloom, Memo to Herzberg attached to Minutes of the Committee on Agencies, July 14, 1949, Subcommittee: CSO 1949–50 Folder, Section AII, Series III, CRC.

130. In 1943, for instance, Bloom had participated in a roundtable discussion titled "Minority Groups" with those later deemed radicals like Bulosan, Charlotta Bass, McWilliams, the to-be-blacklisted Hollywood director Dalton Trumbo, as well as activists later deemed moderates like the NAACP's Walter White. See Walter White, Letter to Bette Davis, September 18, 1943, Film, Hollywood Writers Mobilization, Writers Congress, 1943 Folder, Box 277, Group II, NAACP LOC. See too Bulosan, *America Is in the Heart.*

131. Jewish Information Service, *Facts for Action* Newsletter, October 1954, Communism, Committee On—1954 Folder, Box 68, Series IV, CRC.

132. Richard W. Dettering, Memo to member organizations and Board of Directors concerning NAACP, April 14, 1949, Los Angeles, Calif, 1949 Folder, Box C15, Group II, NAACP LOC.

133. Ross, Report, February 20, 1948, Folder 1, Box 2, Ross.

134. John M. Mecartney (Garrett Biblical Institute Evanston, IL), letter to Roy Wilkins, June 17, 1950, Communism—General, Jan–Sept 1950 Folder, Box C329, Group II, NAACP LOC.

135. Jewish community individuals and organizations especially became a central force behind many collaborative initiatives in Los Angeles and elsewhere including places like San Francisco and New York, often alongside Catholic and African-American leaders. See Greenberg, *Troubling the Waters*; Issel, "'Jews and Catholics against Prejudice"; and Svonkin, *Jews against Prejudice*.

136. For a sample of this literature on the postwar decrease of racism against groups like Jewish Americans, Italian Americans, Irish Americans, and other groups previously viewed as racially other, and the hardening of color lines against African Americans, Mexican Americans, and others, see Barrett and Roediger, "In Between Peoples"; Brodkin, *How Jews Became White Folks and What That Says about Race in America*; Ignatiev, *How the Irish Became White*; Jacobson, *Whiteness of a Different Color*; Ngai, *Impossible Subjects*; Roediger, *The Wages of Whiteness*; Self, *American Babylon*; Thomas Sugrue, *The Origins of the Urban Crisis*; and Svonkin, *Jews against Prejudice*.

Tom Guglielmo's argument is particularly worth noting here. He argues that even in the prewar period, groups like Italians and, by extension, other similarly situated European immigrants, were not in the same outsider category as African Americans, for instance, were. Though Italians were not accepted in the first half of the century as northern and western Europeans were, they were never totally nonwhite since they always had the privileges that accompanied whiteness, even if they faced racial discrimination, categorization, and so forth. Guglielmo, *White on Arrival*.

Eric L. Goldstein shows how Jews' sense of being outsiders persisted well beyond the World War II period, in large part because of their investment in an identity rooted at least in part in marginality. See Goldstein, *The Price of Whiteness*. I believe that this persistent identification as and with outsiders partly explains Jews' ongoing interests in working with other minorities, as does the ongoing anti-Semitism they faced in the postwar era.

137. For more on postwar Jewish interests in integrating themselves and not calling attention to themselves as Jewish, see Novick, *The Holocaust in American Life*.

138. Report on First Hearing of Bennett Ordinance at City Council, October 31, 1945, Mayor's Committee for Home Front Unity, LA Nov 1945 Folder 8, Box 13, Series II, CRC.

139. Tarea Hall Pittman, Report on NAACP Second West Coast Conference, Region One, March 5–7, 1948, 16, West Coast Conference—2nd Annual, 1948 Folder, Box 35, NAACP.

140. Franklin Williams and C.L. Dellums, Letter to Roos, September 2, 1954, Legal and Legislative Committee 1954 Folder, Box 68, Series IV, CRC.

141. CRC, Minutes of Meeting of Legal and Legislative Committee, October 11, 1951, Subcomm: Legal and Legislative 1951–1952 Folder, Unnumbered Box, Series IV, CRC.

142. I. B. Benjamin, Letter to Alfred Buckman, President of L.A. AJ Congress, April 18, 1950, Communism: Jewish Involvement and Response 1950 Folder, Section 3C, Series III, CRC.

143. Minutes of Joint Staff Meeting, July 31, 1951, Joint Staff Comm Minutes Mar–Jul 1951 Folder, Unnumbered box, Series IV, CRC.

144. Isaac Pacht, Speech, November 6, 1951, County Conference on Community Relations (Corresp) 1951 Folder, Box 59, Series IV, CRC.

145. Fred Herzberg, Memo on CRC History and Purpose, September 6, 1949, Subcomms: Special—Agencies; Agency Reports, CRC 1949 Folder, Section AII, Series III, CRC.

146. CRC, Agenda: Community Relations Committee Meeting, Friday, May 28, 1954, CRC—Agenda and Minutes, 1954 Folder, Box 68, Series I, CRC.

147. Federation for Unity: The C.F.C.U. Story, undated (approximately 1948 or 1949), Carton 6, Ford. On Jewish involvement in the national intergroup movement, see Svonkin, *Jews against Prejudice*.

148. G. Raymond Booth (LA CCU Executive Secretary), January 2, 1945, Comm on Human Relations, LA County: Corresp Jan–May 1946 Folder 12, Box 218, Series II, CRC.

149. Pitt, *Joseph Roos Oral History*, 53. On Dellums, see Self, *American Babylon*, 76–86.

150. Fred Herzberg, Memo to the chairman of committee on agencies, November 9, 1949, Subcommittees: Agencies—Corr 1949 Folder, Section AII, Series III, CRC. Only $1,700 of the LACCCR's $7,250 budget for 1949 was from the Jewish community. Minutes of the Meeting of the Subcommittee on agencies, November 16, 1949, Subcommittees: Agencies—Minutes 1947–1950 Folder, Section AII, Series III, CRC.

151. Pitt, *Joseph Roos Oral History Interview*, 55–58, CRC.

152. Fred Herzberg, Letter to Philip Lerman (UAW/CIO) concerning Displaced Persons legislation, February 5, 1948, Displaced Persons: Corr Jan–Apr 1948 Folder, Section 3C, Series III, CRC.

153. CRC Executive Director (Herzberg), letter to Tenney, May 25, 1949, Subcomm: Legal and Legislative: Corr 1947–1949 Folder, Section AII, Series III, CRC.

154. Roos, Memo to Silberberg and Pacht, January 16, 1953, NAACP (Corresp) 1953 Folder, Box 73, Series IV, CRC. Such efforts to camouflage Jewish involvement were not new. During World War II, Jews who feared that focusing on Jewish issues would fuel religious intolerance also sometimes concealed their influence in their campaign against Nazism, emphasizing the dichotomy between Nazis and democracy rather than Nazi anti-Semitism. But this emphasis on inter-racial efforts as a key strategy became most important in the years following World War II.

155. Pitt, *Joseph Roos Oral History Interview*, 55, CRC.

156. "Argument in the Matter of the Citizens' Advisory Committee," August 1, 1948, Tenney, Jack B.: Corresp 1948 Folder, Section 3C, Series III, CRC. See also CRC, Minutes of Meeting of Legal and Legislative Committee, October 11, 1951, Subcomm: Legal and Legislative 1951–1952 Folder, Unnumbered Box, Series IV, CRC.

157. See Fred Herzberg, Letter to Davis McEntire, August 25, 1947, and Davis McEntire, Letter to Herzberg, August 8, 1947, in Inter-group Relations: American Council on Race Relations Corresp. May–Oct 1947 Folder, Section 3C, Series IV, CRC.

158. See, for instance, Beltrán, "Bronze Seduction"; McLean, *Being Rita Hayworth*; and Rodríguez, *Heroes, Lovers, and Others*.

159. See Arriola, "Knocking on the Schoolhouse Door," and González, *Chicano Education in the Era of Segregation*. For mention of the 1930 census's uniqueness in

terms of its classifying "Mexicans" separately, see Camarillo, *Chicanos in a Changing Society*, 201. For more on *Mendez*, see the subsequent chapter.

160. The American Council on Race Relations, *The Problem of Violence: Observations on Race Conflict in Los Angeles*, undated, 14, Carton 6, Ford.

161. Tony Serrato (CSO LA Civil Rights Committee), inter-office memo, June 29, 1949, Folder 1, Box 5, Ross.

162. In cases in which there was "reason to doubt" applicants' decision, however, "sufficient justification may be required by the service concerned." Personnel Policy Board of the Secretary of Defense, "Policy Regarding 'Race' Entries on Enlistment Contracts and Shipping Articles (M-63(a))" Memo to Secty of Army, Navy, Air Force, April 15, 1950, Folder 1, Box 5, Ross. For more on this matter, see also various files in Folder 26, Box 4, Ross.

163. García, *Mexican Americans*, 74.

164. While Mexican Americans elsewhere, particularly in Texas, most often seemed to pursue this "whiteness strategy" during this time period, my research reveals that their approach in Los Angeles was more mixed. Sometimes they worked and identified with African Americans, whereas other times they shunned such cooperation. For more on national and especially Texas strategies, see MacLean, *Freedom Is Not Enough*, chap. 5. MacLean argues that Mexican Americans nationwide only embraced "brownness" as a strategy in the 1960s, when new federal legislation made it practical and they could benefit from protection and civil rights aimed at helping "black" people. See too Arredondo, *Mexican Chicago*; Arredondo, "Navigating Ethno-Racial Currents, Mexicans in Chicago, 1919–1939"; Foley, "Becoming Hispanic"; Foley, "Over the Rainbow"; Guglielmo, "Fighting for Caucasian Rights"; and Kaplowitz, *LULAC, Mexican Americans, and National Policy*. Emilio Zamora's recent study disagrees with the conclusion that Texas Mexicans' whiteness strategy prevented alliances with African Americans. See Zamora, *Claiming Rights and Righting Wrongs in Texas*.

165. Historians have argued that in the postwar era, progressive white Americans, horrified by a new understanding of the Holocaust as the logical outgrowth of racism, increasingly recognized the common humanity of diverse peoples. Their intensified universalistic vision of humanity and justice led them to work to remedy domestic racism through increased civil rights and international inequality through initiatives like the United Nations. For a discussion of the development of the idea of universalism in the World War II and postwar period, see Wall, *Inventing the "American Way,"* 79, and Wall, "The Idea of America," 131–65. In recent years studies have questioned the prevalence of this white liberalism, specifically whether there really was a northern white liberal consensus on the issue. See, for instance, Sugrue, *Origins of the Urban Crisis*. For an interesting overview of universalism and its place in American history, see Higham, "Multiculturalism and Universalism."

Most scholarship on racial liberalism focuses on whites and, to some degree, on Jews and African Americans. On the ways pragmatism and universalism shaped African-American and Jewish-American communities' liberalism during the mid-twentieth century, see Greenberg, *Troubling the Waters*. Greenberg argues that Jews and blacks were typical American liberals because of their deeply held values like cultural pluralism, individual equality (individuals, not groups, get rights), the state's obligation to protect and extend both, and their emphasis on reform rather than revolution and compromise rather than confrontation. Greenberg, *Troubling the Waters*, 8 and chap. 4. See too Carson, "Black-Jewish Universalism in the Era of Identity Politics," esp. 177–79. Los Angeles shows how in multiracial places groups like Mexican Americans also were a part of this story. For more on this see too Brilliant, *The Color of America Has Changed*.

166. CSO *Reporter*, 28 Feb 1952, Folder 12, Box 10, 4, Ross.

167. Franklin Williams, speech to LACCCR 6th Annual Meeting, October 11, 1952, Los Angeles County Conference on Community Relations Folder, Box 44, NAACP.

168. Unidentified LACCCR representative, letter to Franklin Williams, December 28, 1951, Los Angeles County Conference on Community Relations Folder, Box 44, NAACP.

169. CRC, notes on Legal and Legislative Subcommittee Meeting, April 2, 1947, Subcomm: Legal and Legislative—Minutes 1947–1950 Folder, Section AII, Series III, CRC. For national blacks' frustration concerning this policy, see Walter White, unsent letter to George Mintz, December 2, 1948, Jews 1945–49 Folder, Box A325, Group II, NAACP LOC.

170. Fred Herzberg, letter to Judge Stanley Mosk, November 3, 1947, Subcomm: Legal and Legislative: Corr 1947–1949 Folder, Section AII, Series III, CRC.

171. Joe Roos, letter to Loren Miller (*California Eagle* publisher), August 3, 1951, Newspapers (Correspondence) 1951 Folder, Box 62, Series IV, CRC. The CRC's criticisms of the *Eagle* directly challenged one of its frequent allies, since the *Eagle* was published at the time by the NAACP's Loren Miller, one of the CRC's civil rights partners.

172. Joe Roos, Letter to Loren Miller (*California Eagle* publisher), February 28, 1952, Newspapers (correspondence) 1952 Folder, Box 62, Series IV, CRC.

173. Roos, Memo to Silberberg and Pacht concerning Walter White's LA visit, January 16, 1953; NAACP (Corresp) 1953 Folder, Box 73, Series IV, CRC.

174. Ibid.

175. Frederick A Schreiber (Area Director in LA of AJ Committee), Letter to Tarea H. Pittman (Exec Secty of California Committee for Fair Employment Practices [and NAACP]), March 13, 1953, Incoming Correspondence A: American Jewish Committee Folder, Box 4, CFCU.

176. See, for instance, the Civil Rights Congress's critique of the NAACP for not pursuing more confrontational tactics, in Sides, "You Understand My Condition."

177. Ibid., 241.

178. For more on class differences among various Los Angeles activist populations, see the American Council on Race Relations, *The Problem of Violence: Observations on Race Conflict in Los Angeles*, 1945, Carton 6, Ford, esp. 16.

In some cases differences reflected how different historical trajectories shaped groups' concerns, as Peggy Pascoe illustrates through her discussion of the NAACP's early reluctance to support ACLU and JACL efforts against anti-miscegenation laws. Because of factors like the historical violence interracial romantic relationships had long sparked against them, African Americans were highly sensitive and cautious about supporting cases like *Perez v. Lippold* and shied away from such cases until the 1950s. See Pascoe, *What Comes Naturally*, 205–45.

179. NAACP 2nd West Coast Conference, Report, March 5–7, 1948, West Coast Conference—2nd Annual, 1948 Folder, Box 35, NAACP.

180. Kushida, Letter to Roos, July 7, 1951, Japanese (printed matter) 1950–1951 Folder, Box 53, Series IV, CRC.

181. Kushida, Letter to Roos, April 7, 1954, Schary, Dore (Correspondence) 1954 Folder, Box 74, Series IV, CRC.

182. Ishikawa (JACL), Letter, September 7, 1948, Intergroup Relations: Japanese American Citizens League 1948–49 Folder, Section 3C, Series III, CRC.

183. García, *Mexican Americans*, 341 n. 2.

184. García, *Mexican Americans*, 173; García, *Memories of Chicano History*, 161–63. On Mexican-American support for Wallace, see too Vargas, *Labor Rights Are Civil Rights*, 275–76.

185. García, *Mexican Americans*, 200.

186. Vargas, *Labor Rights Are Civil Rights*, 276. For more on Wallace's platform and approach, see MacDougall, *Gideon's Army*.

187. Sullivan, *Days of Hope*, 261.

188. García, *Mexican Americans*, 161–62.

189. Truman's strategic move to advocate certain civil rights policies also played a role in luring NAACP members and other African Americans away from Wallace. For instance, Truman became the first U.S. president to address the NAACP's national convention. He also recommended establishing a permanent Commission on Civil Rights, a Joint Congressional Committee on Civil Rights, and a Civil Rights Division in the Justice Department. Truman also advocated strengthening existing civil rights statutes, providing federal protection against lynching, better protecting the right to vote, and prohibiting discrimination in interstate transportation—though some of these measures did not materialize. At its 1948 national convention the Democratic Party adopted the strongest civil rights plank in its history, and soon after Truman issued an executive order forbidding racial discrimination in federal hiring, and signed an order that eventually desegregated the military. For more on African Americans and Wallace/Truman, see, for instance, Meriwether, *Proudly We Can Be Africans*, 79–87; Plummer, *Rising Wind*, 188–89; and von Eschen, *Race against Empire*, esp. 107–14.

190. Ross, Letter to Alinsky November 16, 1947, Folder 1, Box 2, Ross.

191. Ross, Report to Alinsky, February 20, 1948, Folder 1, Box 2, Ross.

192. Vargas, "In the Years of Darkness and Torment," 399, 401, and Vargas, *Labor Rights Are Civil Rights*, 276–77. On the ANMA see too García, *Mexican Americans*, 199–227.

193. Kleinman, *A World of Hope, a World of Fear*; Walton, *Henry Wallace, Harry Truman, and the Cold War*.

194. El Congreso had approximately thirty percent female membership. On women's involvement, especially in leadership roles, see García, *Memories of Chicano History*, 166. On El Congreso, see García, *Mexican Americans*, 165, and Sánchez, *Becoming Mexican American*, 247.

195. CSO, Untitled publicity document, undated (approximately 1948), CSO Folder 12, Box 10, Ross. El Congreso health programs included instructing Spanish-speaking mothers at meetings about health problems, including treating children's tuberculosis. García, *Mexican Americans*, 164.

196. For a discussion of other CSO activities, see Carmen Medina (CSO), to Ida A. Siegel, August 19, 1949, Folder 12, Box 5, Ross.

197. For evidence on CSO protests of INS attempts to close regional offices, see letter to Senator Knowland, February 11, 1955, Folder 10, Box 11, Ross. For information on CSO immigration-related activities, which focused on citizenship classes and aiding the INS in processing applications, see CSO Report, *The C.S.O. Story: American Democracy Is Not a Fake. C.S.O. Program…Its Future*, 1965, Folder 8, Box 13, Galarza.

198. Others included Balt Yanez and Arnoldo Torres. See Gutiérrez, *Walls and Mirrors*, 170.

199. Scott, "The Mexican-American in the Los Angeles Area," 299, and Gutiérrez, *Walls and Mirrors*, 172. For more on the CSO's work with Mexican immigrants, see Gutiérrez, *Walls and Mirrors*, esp. 168–72.

200. See, for instance, Gloster B. Current, roundtable radio discussion at Los Angeles NAACP West Coast Regional Conference, March 7, 1948, in NAACP West Coast Region Report, March 5–7, 1948, West Coast Conference—2nd Annual, 1948 Folder, Box 35, NAACP.

201. Abner Berry, "Anti-communism Proves Poor Shield for NAACP," unidentified newspaper, undated (probably 1952 or 1953), Communism—Printed Matter and Newsclippings Folder, Box 43, NAACP. For an article that implicitly reinforces the idea that "liberals" and "radicals" disagreed more over approach than over concrete civil rights agendas and goals, see Sides, "You Understand My Condition." Sides discusses disagreements between the Civil Rights Congress and the Los Angeles NAACP. For an interesting discussion of tensions between civil rights liberals and radicals over communism itself, see Arnesen, "No Graver Danger." See too responses to Arnesen's article in the same volume of *Labor* by John Earl Haynes, Martha Biondi, Carol Anderson, and Kenneth R. Janken.

202. Philip M. Connelly, "'Hush-Hush' Revival Faces L.A. Jews," March 12, 1951, *Daily People's World*.

203. I thank Gina Marie Pitti for her insight on this issue. For a discussion of this community improvement emphasis, see Pitti, *The Devil in Silicon Valley*, 155–56.

204. See Vern Paltrow, "CSO Launches Slum Betterment Fund Drive for 1951," undated, Folder 12, Box 10, Ross and unknown author, "'Help Your Neighbor' Fund Will Be of Wide Benefits," March 12, 1952, Folder 12, Box 10, Ross.

205. *What Is the CSO?* (pamphlet, Monterey County, 1957), Box A-13, Gallegos. I thank Gina Marie Pitti for sharing this source.

206. Paul O. Solis to Mr. Stanton M. Levy, May 19, 1954, Folder 2, Box 11, Ross. Thanks to Gina Marie Pitti for pointing out this source.

207. Rt. Rev. Msgr. John O'Grady, Letter to Rev. Charles F. Buddy, S.T.D. Ph.D., July 27, 1954, Folder 8, Box 7, Ross.

208. Ross, Report, February 20, 1948, Folder 1, Box 2, Ross.

209. Roy Wilkins (Acting Secretary NAACP), Memo to NAACP Branches: "The Communists vs. the NAACP's Civil Rights Front," March 22, 1950, Communism, Attacks on NAACP 1950–54 Folder, Box C329, Group II, NAACP LOC.

210. García, *Memories*, 164. Historian Steve Pitti characterizes the CSO as an organization that represented itself as "politically moderate and dedicated to mainstream activities" and argues that it gained support because of such language. Pitti, *The Devil in Silicon Valley*, 153.

211. García, *Mexican Americans*, 174.

212. Sánchez, *Becoming Mexican American*, 249.

213. See Healey and Isserman, *Dorothy Healey Remembers*. For more on the U.S. CP as reform rather than revolutionary minded, see García, *Mexican Americans*, 203. See too Waltzer, "The New History of American Communism."

CHAPTER 6

1. Sara Boynoff, "Los Angeles: A Race Relations Success Story," *Look* magazine, March 19, 1957, LACCCR scrapbook, Box 76, Ford.

2. Leon Lewis, Memo to CRC members, April 9, 1945, Folder 12—Comm on Human Relations, LA County: Corresp, Box 219, Series II, CRC. See also George Gleason, Memo, February 19, 1945, Folder 9, Box 218, Series II, CRC, and "Los Angeles County Seeks Advice on Intergroup Cooperation," *NOW*, March 1945, Folder 9, Box 218, Series II, CRC.

3. George Gleason, Memo, February 19, 1945, Folder 9, Box 218, Series II, CRC. For a discussion of national increases in interracialism, see, for instance, Stuart Svonkin, *Jews against Prejudice*.

4. For more discussion of how Phoenix activists used Los Angeles multiracial organizations as models, see Whitaker, *Race Work*, 84, 93.

5. Taylor, *In Search of the Racial Frontier*, 270.

6. African Americans also were busy on this issue in the period before the end of World War II: between 1917 and 1945 they filed over 100 cases in Los Angeles courts. Loren Miller and the determination of Los Angeles African Americans to pursue these cases helped win *Shelley vs. Kramer*. See de Graaf, Mulroy, Taylor, eds., *Seeking El Dorado*, 32–37; Sides, *L.A. City Limits*, 99–100; and Sides, "Working Away," 237.

7. Thomas L. Griffith, letter to Roy Wilkins (Acting Secretary NAACP), March 14, 1945, Los Angeles, Calif, 1945 Folder, Box C14, Group II, NAACP LOC.

8. Sides, *L.A. City Limits*, 99–100.

9. For more on Miller's involvement, see de Graaf, Interview with Judge Loren Miller, 23.

10. Miller, *The Petitioners*, 326–7.

11. For a discussion of Miller's role in 1952 litigation ruling the enforcement of restrictive covenants illegal in California, see Los Angeles Branch NAACP, News Release "NAACP Sponsored Case Strikes Death-Blow to Race Restrictive Covenants; District Court of Appeals Here Upholds Property Rights," August 14, 1952, Los Angeles, Calif, 1952 Folder, Box C16, Group II, NAACP LOC. See too de Graaf, Interview with Judge Loren Miller, 23; Flamming, *Bound for Freedom*, 369; and Sides, *L.A. City Limits*, 100–101. Incidentally, A. L. Wirin, who at the time was JACL counsel, joined Miller in these efforts. See Robinson and Robinson, "The Limits of Interracial Coalitions," 99, 113.

12. De Graaf and Taylor, introduction, in de Graaf et al., *Seeking El Dorado*, 32–37; Kurashige, *The Shifting Grounds of Race*, chapter 10 passim; and Sides, *L.A. City Limits*, 97–98. Scholars debate the limits of ending restrictive covenants and other 1940s and 1950s civil rights "landmarks," though they were nonetheless achievements and the outcome of long struggles. For instance, while he does not dispute that the 1954 *Brown* decision led to civil rights change, Michael Klarman argues that it led to school desegregation and other reforms more indirectly than directly. When the backlash it provoked among extremely conservative white southerners brought negative national and international attention to southern white society, previously apathetic whites subsequently mobilized to support the civil rights campaigns. See Klarman, "How *Brown* Changed Race Relations." For further discussion of the limits, as well as the accomplishments, of *Brown* see various essays in Lau, ed., *From Grassroots to the Supreme Court*, and Goluboff, *The Lost Promise of Civil Rights*.

13. Letter from Judge Stanley Mosk (at the time on the California Superior Court), May 10, 1948, Miller Correspondence 1948 Folder, Carton 2, Miller.

14. Healey and Isserman, *Dorothy Healey Remembers*, 209–10. Miller's story also shows how difficult—if not impossible—it was to totally distance oneself from the past. As Healey praised Miller for his activism, she indicated that likely had been his closeness to the CP in the 1930s that prevented Governor Brown in the 1960s from appointing him to be a Superior Court judge, a position many people thought Miller deserved. Brown appointed Miller only to a Los Angeles municipal court judgeship. Healey and Isserman, *Dorothy Healey Remembers*, 209–10. Douglas Flamming also argues that Miller's earlier radicalism prevented him from receiving a federal judgeship. See Flamming, *Bound for Freedom*, 369. On Miller's judgeship, see various correspondence in Miller congratulations (Judicial Appointment) Folder 14a, Carton 30, Miller.

15. Press Release, Governor "Pat" Brown's office, May 12, 1964, Miller congratulations (Judicial Appointment) Folder 14a, Carton 3, Miller.

16. CSO, Memo, 1955, Folder 10, Box 11, Ross. For same, see too CSO, Minutes National Community Service Organization Executive Board Meeting, July 17, 1955, Community Service Organization Folder, Box 9, Roybal.

17. On California school segregation, see for instance Brilliant, "Color Lines," 73–94, and Wollenberg, *All Deliberate Speed*.

18. For more on Ruíz and the Coordinating Council, see García, "Americans All," esp. 281–83. See too discussion in chapter 3.

19. For insightful studies of *Mendez* and its significance statewide and nationally, see Arriola, "Knocking on the Schoolhouse Door"; González, *Chicano Education in the Era of Segregation*; Johnson, "*Hernández v. Texas*: Legacies of Justice and Injustice"; and Valencia, "The Mexican American Struggle for Equal Educational Opportunity in *Mendez v. Westminster*."

20. *Mendez* built on a long history of Mexican and Asian-origin parents' desegregation challenges in the Golden State. The Lemon Grove case of 1931, which scholars label "the nation's first successful desegregation court case." Though the Lemon Grove case applied only to the local schools, and did not overturn the principle of separate but equal—it ruled only that Mexican children could not be segregated—it was the first successful case. See Alvarez, "The Lemon

Grove Incident"; González, *Chicano Education in the Era of Segregation*, 28. For a fuller discussion of the history of Mexican Americans' segregation and challenges, see González, *Chicano Education in the Era of Segregation*.

21. Scholars have mistakenly identified attorney David Marcus as African American. He was actually descended from Russian Jewish immigrants. I thank Mark Brilliant for this insight, and for sharing the following source that documents Marcus's origins: Sheet 24B, Block A 27/Assembly District 27, Los Angeles, Population Schedule, Fifteenth Census of the United States: 1930, microfilm, Record Group No. 29, Publication No. T626, Roll No. 136, National Archives and Record Administration, Pacific Region (Laguna Niguel).

22. Santa Ana Board of Education, Minutes, September 12, 1946, cited in González, *Chicano Education in the Era of Segregation*, 154. See too untitled document, Fred Ross, date unclear (late 1946), Folder 1, Box 8, Ross.

23. Arriola, "Knocking on the Schoolhouse Door," 194–96. According to Toni Robinson and Greg Robinson, the AJ Congress's amicus curiae brief was the most powerful since it asked the appellate court to overturn segregated schools as a violation of the Fourteenth Amendment equal protection guarantees as well as federal government treaty obligations under the UN Charter. It asked the court to reject the *Plessy* "separate but equal" standard. Robinson and Robinson, "The Limits of Interracial Coalitions," 106–7. The Robinsons present another viewpoint on *Mendez*, one that focuses on the limits of interracial collaboration in *Mendez*. McWilliams's article was called "Is Your Name Gonzales?" *Nation*, March 15, 1947.

24. For a discussion of these people and their activities in both cases, see Arriola, "Knocking Down the Schoolhouse Door," 194–96; Brilliant, "Color Lines," 88–89; The Brown Foundation for Educational Equity website, http://brownvboard.org/research/opinions/347us483.htm (accessed December 14, 2009); and Valencia, "The Mexican American Struggle for Equal Educational Opportunity," 407.

25. González, *Chicano Education in the Era of Segregation*, 28. See also Valencia, "The Mexican American Struggle for Equal Educational Opportunity," and Johnson, "Hernández v. Texas."

26. González, *Chicano Education in the Era of Segregation*, 28, and Valencia, "The Mexican American Struggle for Equal Educational Opportunity," 402.

27. Stan Oftelie, "Murder Trial Obscured 1946 O.C. Integration Landmark," *Santa Ana Register*, August 22, 1976, quoted in González, *Chicano Education in the Era of Segregation*, 28. For more on these arguments' influence on the *Brown* attorneys, see too Valencia, "The Mexican American Struggle for Equal Educational Opportunity," 417.

28. González, *Chicano Education in the Era of Segregation*, 28. For another study that argues that NAACP strategy arguing against school desegregation shifted after *Mendez*, see Flores, "Social Science in the Southwestern Courtroom," 105–16, 116. For another discussion of the ties between Mendez and Brown, see Ruiz, "Tapestries of Resistance."

29. "Segregation in Schools as a Violation of the XIVth Amendment," *Columbia Law Review* 47 (March 1947): 325–327, 326–27.

30. "Segregation in Public Schools—a Violation of 'Equal Protection of the Laws,'" 1060.

31. Ibid., 1066–67.

32. Kutner and Padilla, Interview with Hector Tarango, citation from pages 9–10, 12, written transcript, in author's possession.

33. See Pascoe, *What Comes Naturally*, 205–24, 227, 293, 300, and Pascoe, "Miscegenation Law, Court Cases, and Ideologies of 'Race' in Twentieth-Century America," 61–63. See too Pascoe, "Race, Gender, and the Privileges of Property." For other discussions of California antimiscegenation law and its larger influence, see Lubin, "What's Love Got to Do with It?" and Orenstein, "Void for Vagueness."

34. Arriola, "Knocking Down the Schoolhouse Door," 193.

35. Ibid., 195.

36. Ibid. On *Brown* see Dudziak, *Cold War Civil Rights*.

37. Arriola, "Knocking Down the Schoolhouse Door," 195.

38. González, *Chicano Education in the Era of Segregation*, 14.

39. Ed Cray, *Chief Justice: A Biography of Earl Warren* (1997), 337, cited in Cho, "Redeeming Whiteness in the Shadow of Internment."

40. For this interpretation of Warren see Cho, "Redeeming Whiteness in the Shadow of Internment," and McWilliams, *The Education of Carey McWilliams*, esp. 107.

41. McWilliams, *The Education of Carey McWilliams*, 205.

42. See Cho, "Redeeming Whiteness in the Shadow of Internment." For studies that show consistency between Warren's California and Supreme Court stances, see Johnson, "Hernández v. Texas"; Pollack, *Earl Warren*; Valencia, "The Mexican American Struggle for Equal Educational Opportunity"; and White, *Earl Warren a Public Life*.

43. On Warren's action making illegal all California school segregation, see Wollenberg, *All Deliberate Speed*, 132. See too Valencia, "The Mexican American Struggle for Equal Educational Opportunity," 411, and Johnson, "Hernández v. Texas," 26. California's Supreme Court had already ruled, in 1890, that California public schools may not establish separate schools for children of African descent or exclude them from public schools established for white children. See *Wysinger v. Crookshank*, 83 Cal. 588, January 29, 1890.

44. On Ruíz's efforts, see, for example, Ruíz, letter to Warren, October 1, 1945, Folder 3, Box 16, Ruíz; Beach Vasey (Legislative Secretary for Warren's office), letter to Ruiz, October 3, 1945, Folder 3, Box 16, Ruíz; Press Release, April 30, 1945, Folder 3, Box 16, Ruíz, which discusses Manuel Ruiz's participation as the head of the lobby group that first pressed this bill, which L.A. assemblyman William H. Rosenthal initially wrote; Rosenthal, letter to Ruíz, June 8, 1945, Folder 3, Box 16, Ruíz; and various other documents in this folder. See too Woods, Augustus F. Hawkins, *Black Leadership in Los Angeles*, 42. See too García, "Americans All."

45. See Ruíz letter to Jack Tenney, July 24, 1946, Folder 4, Box 16, Ruíz.

46. See Johnson, "Hernandez v. Texas," 7.

47. Warren, *The Memoirs of Earl Warren*, 299.

48. Ibid., 4.

49. Ibid., 5.

50. Ibid., 6.

51. Ibid., 7.

52. See White, *Earl Warren a Public Life*, 153–54, and Schuparra, *Triumph of the Right*, 10–22.

53. Harvey, *Earl Warren*, 157–59. On the 1945 proposal as a national pathbreaker, see Pollack, *Earl Warren*, 100–101.

54. Inaugural Address of Governor Earl Warren, Governor of the State of California, January 6, 1947, Carton 6, Ford.

55. Governor Warren's statement to Governor's Council concerning Minority Employment, 1950(?), Incoming Corresp. LA Jewish Community Council Folder, Box 4, CFCU.

56. For more on Warren's history with FEPC in California, see Harvey, *Earl Warren*, 157–59, and Pollack, *Earl Warren*, 100–101.

57. Wilkins, with Matthews, *Standing Fast*, 213. Augustus Hawkins, on the other hand, was frustrated with what he saw as Warren's inaction on civil rights. Flamming, "Becoming Democrats," 295.

58. "First Negro Named Court Head," *Los Angeles Examiner* clippings, December 5, 1961.

59. Pitt, *Joseph Roos Oral History Interview*, 10.

60. Schippers, *Jack B. Tenney: California Legislator*, 1745.

61. Pollack, *Earl Warren*, 91. For further discussion of Warren's health-care initiatives, see Mitchell, "Impeding Earl Warren."

62. White, *Earl Warren: A Public Life*, 154.

63. Evidence suggests that California activists working on other issues, too, first tested many of the civil rights arguments that eventually shaped national policy. California activists were the first in the nation, for instance, to invalidate statewide antimiscegenation legislation. The 1948 *Perez v. Lippold* case became a precedent for the U.S. Supreme Court's 1967 *Loving v. Virginia* decision, which eliminated antimiscegenation laws nationwide. For more on *Perez v. Lippold*, see Brilliant, "Color Lines," 128–53; Pascoe, "Miscegenation Law, Court Cases, and Ideologies of 'Race' in Twentieth-Century America" and "Race, Gender, and the Privileges of Property."

64. For more on Mosk's career, see Congresswoman Nancy Pelosi, "Pelosi Pays Tribute to the Late Justice Stanley Mosk," Statement on the Floor of the U.S. House of Representatives, July 11, 2001, http://www.house.gov/pelosi/flmosk7–11–01.htm (accessed December 14, 2009); Gerald F. Uelmen, "Remembering Stanley Mosk," *Forum* (California Attorneys for Criminal Justice publication), undated, http://www.cacj.org/forum_articles_memory_stanley_mosk-p.htm (accessed April 18, 2007); and Wikipedia entry, "Stanley Mosk," http://en.wikipedia.org/wiki/Stanley_Mosk (accessed December 14, 2009).

65. See Taylor, *In Search of the Racial Frontier*, 272, and Flamming, "Becoming Democrats," 298.

66. According to historian Margaret Rose, the CSO was "an important bridge to the expanding options of the 1960s" such as political associations, government programs, unions, women's organizations, and others. Rose, "The Community Service Organization," 194–95.

67. See Chall, "Hope Mendoza Schechter."

68. "Fred Ross Helped Unionize Farm Workers," *San Francisco Chronicle*, October 1, 1992. See also "Fred Ross Helped Unionize Farm Workers," Obituary,

San Francisco Chronicle, October 1, 1992, Folder 8, Box 2, Ross. For Fred Ross's account of their meeting, see Ross, *Cesar Chavez at the Beginning*, 1–4.

69. Rose, "Gender and Civic Activism in Mexican American Barrios in California," 183.

70. Chávez, "Dolores Huerta and the United Farm Workers." Incidentally, Huerta and Chávez eventually left the CSO to form the United Farm Workers because the CSO wanted to remain an urban-oriented organization, while Chávez and Huerta wanted to focus more on field-workers as well.

71. These leaders included Cruz Reynoso and Herman Gallegos as well as Roybal and Chávez. See Gallegos interview with Dolores Huerta, citation from pages 13, 16, written transcript, in author's possession.

72. On CSO as a foundation for later Chicano activism, see Chávez, *Mi Raza Primero!*, 9, 41; Pitti, *The Devil in Silicon Valley*, 149, 170–72, 187; Pitti, "Quicksilver Community," chapter 6; and Rose, "The Community Service Organization," 194–95. See also Gómez-Quiñones, *Chicano Politics*, 54, 56, and Gutiérrez, *Walls and Mirrors*, 10.

Other Cold War activist groups with more internationalist and less anticommunist agendas also influenced later reform efforts including the civil rights movements and power movements of the 1960s. See, for instance, the discussion of the SCLC in Horne, *Black and Red*. Robert Self also discusses the connection between labor activism in the 1930s, 1940s, 1950s, and 1960s, arguing that Bobby Seale, Huey Newton, and others were influenced by earlier activism like that among East Bay dockworkers and railroad unions in the 1930s and 1940s. Self, *American Babylon*, 6.

CONCLUSION

1. For more on Japanese Americans' and African Americans' shifting residential patterns, see Kurashige, *The Shifting Grounds of Race*, 232, 233, 243, 268–69, 272–75, 280–81, chapter 10 passim. Kurashige discusses Japanese and African Americans' changing status from the early to mid-twentieth century, which led to different agendas, residential patterns, and so forth. On African Americans, see too Sides, "Working Away," chapter 5 passim, and *L.A. City Limits*. On Jews, see Vorspan and Gartner, *History of the Jews of Los Angeles*. On the Eastside, Mexican-origin and otherwise, see Sánchez, *Becoming Mexican American*, and "What's Good for Boyle Heights." For further discussion of the increasing separation between ethnic and racial groups in Los Angeles, see too Wild, *Street Meeting*.

2. See Brilliant, *The Color of America Has Changed*.

3. CRC, Meeting Minutes, January 27, 1950, Subcommittee: CSO 1949–1950 Folder, Section AII, Series III, CRC.

4. Ibid.

5. Roos, Letter to Baldwin (ACLU), September 16, 1953, Community Service Organization 1953 Folder, Box 70, Series IV, CRC.

6. Ross, letter to Roger N. Baldwin (Chairman of the national ACLU), January 4, 1951, Folder 1, Box 6, Ross; Roybal letter to Roger N. Baldwin, January 10,

1951, Folder 1, Box 6, Ross; CRC, Meeting Minutes, January 27, 1950, "Subcommittee: CSO 1949–1950" Folder, Section AII, Series III, CRC; Fred Herzberg, Letter to Rabbi Magnin, 28 April 1950, Subcommittee: CSO, 1949–1950 Folder, Section AII, Series III, CRC; Subcommittee on CSO meeting minutes, August 31, 1950, Subcommittee: CSO, 1949–1950 Folder, Section AII, Series II, CRC.

7. CRC, Meeting Minutes, August 31, 1950, Subcommittee: CSO 1949–1950 Folder, Section AII, Series III, CRC. Jewish community support for the CSO continued, as people like William Becker (a former organizer who worked with the prominent Chicano civil rights activist Ernesto Galarza in the National Farm Labor Union), used his influence as the chair of the California Jewish Labor Committee Adult Education Project to continue directing Jewish community money toward the CSO. Pitti, "Quicksilver Community," 441.

8. For a discussion of later coalitional politics to elect Bradley, see Gottlieb, Vallianatos, Freer, and Dreier, *The Next Los Angeles*; Kurashige, *The Shifting Grounds of Race*, 277–85; Sonenshein, "Coalition Building in Los Angeles"; and Sonenshein, *Politics in Black and White*.

9. Fewer than 39 percent of one Eastside district's eligible voters had voted in 1945, while in 1949 over 82 percent went to the polls. The CSO registered 15,000 Spanish-speaking people in the ninth district alone for that election. See Gutiérrez, *Walls and Mirrors*, 169, and Danny Feingold, "Common Threads," *L.A. Times*, October 21, 1998.

10. For more on ongoing police brutality in late 1950s and 1960s Los Angeles, see Kurashige, *The Shifting Grounds of Race*, 270.

11. Although California voters struck down this fair housing legislation a mere year later by passing Proposition 14 almost two to one, it ultimately prevailed when in 1966 the California Supreme Court, and in 1967 the U.S. Supreme Court struck Proposition 14 down as unconstitutional because it denied equal protection of the laws. For an in-depth discussion of fair housing campaigns and reactions in Los Angeles, see Kurashige, *The Shifting Grounds of Race*, esp. 234–36 and 260–67; Kurashige, "Transforming Los Angeles," 457–91; Hosang, "Racial Proposition"; and Hosang, "Remaking Liberalism in the Sunbelt West."

12. The Civil Rights Act prohibited discrimination in public facilities, in government, and in employment. The 1965 Voting Rights Act, which outlawed discriminatory voting practices like literacy tests and poll taxes, prohibiting the denial or abridgment of the right to vote, provides another example of the mid-century interracial Cold War activists' victory, though in a more southern- rather than western-specific vein.

13. For discussions of the protest movements see for instance, Chávez, "*Mi Raza Primero!*"; Collier-Thomas and Franklin, eds., *Sisters in the Struggle*; Fujino, *Heartbeat of Struggle*; Josephy, Nagel, and Johnson, eds., *Red Power*; Kurashige, *The Shifting Grounds of Race*, 267–77; López, *Racism on Trial*; Louie and Omatsu, eds., *Asian Americans*; Maeda, "Forging Asian American Identity"; Marable, *Race, Reform, and Rebellion*; Muñoz, *Youth, Identity, Power*; Pulido, *Black, Brown, Yellow and Left*; Theoharis, Woodard, and Payne, *Groundwork*; Wei, *The Asian American Movement*; and Woodard, *A Nation Within a Nation*.

Many of these protest movements involved both interracial cooperation as well as interethnic tensions and missed opportunities. Laura Pulido argues, for instance, that cooperation among Los Angeles communities on the left in the late 1960s and 1970s was difficult to sustain, in part because of the region's sprawl and segregation, which made working together challenging. See, for example, Araiza, "For Freedom of Other Men"; Ferreira, "All Power to the People"; and Pulido, *Black, Brown, Yellow and Left*, esp. 179.

For discussions of the Watts Riots, see Adler, "Watts"; Horne, "Black Fire"; Horne, *Fire This Time*; Kurashige, *The Shifting Grounds of Race*, 267–77; and Model, "The 1965 Watts Rebellion." For more on late twentieth-century and twenty-first-century reform movements in Los Angeles, see Gottlieb, Vallianatos, Freer, and Dreier, *The Next Los Angeles*.

14. A growing body of scholarship reevaluating mid-century "liberalism" focuses on this issue, arguing that liberals in California who supported the Rumford Act stifled working-class voices and hid minorities' role in the campaign in order to gain more white support in their attack of Proposition 14. See Hosang, "Racial Proposition"; Hosang, "Remaking Liberalism in the Sunbelt West"; and Kurashige, *The Shifting Grounds of Race*, esp. chapter 11 passim. For a similar take on black and white civil rights liberals' urban renewal efforts in mid-century Miami, specifically that liberal interracial activists' efforts reinforced and even worsened the poverty of "blighted" African Americans, see Connolly, "Sunbelt Civil Rights."

15. See, for instance, Carson, *In Struggle*; Horne, *Fire this Time*; Gómez-Quiñones, *Chicano Politics*, 54; Kurashige, *The Shifting Grounds of Race*, 267–77, 282–85; Marable, *Race, Reform, and Rebellion*; Pitti, *The Devil in Silicon Valley*, 149; Muñoz, *Youth, Identity, Power*; Pulido, *Black, Brown, Yellow and Left*; and Rose, "Gender and Civic Activism in Mexican American Barrios in California," 194–95.

16. See Brilliant, *The Color of America Has Changed*, chapter 8. See too Kurashige, *The Shifting Grounds of Race*.

17. Scholars of Asian-American history often argue the media largely fabricated these tensions. Nevertheless, a certain amount of Korean-African American tension was visible in the African American community's reaction to the shooting death of Latasha Harlins by the Korean immigrant Sun Da Ju. For discussions of surrounding issues, see Freer, "Black Korean Conflict," and Kurashige, *The Shifting Grounds of Race*, 291.

18. For discussions of the significance of Los Angeles's history, see, for instance, Davis, *City of Quartz*, and Engh, "At Home in the Heteropolis."

19. Brilliant, "Color Lines." For further discussions of the difficulties of coalition building between diverse racial and ethnic groups in Los Angeles in more recent history, see Acuña, *Anything but Mexican*; Moore, *To the Golden Cities*; Parker, "The Elusive Coalition"; and Sonenshein, *Politics in Black and White*. For a helpful discussion of even more contemporary tensions specifically between Mexican and African American communities in Los Angeles, see Camarillo, "Black and Brown in Compton." See too Kurashige, *The Shifting Grounds of Race*, 292, and Saito, *Race and Politics*.

20. This fissure among Latinos in particular manifested itself in the 2004 presidential election, when Latinos debated whether to support Democratic

candidate John Kerry or Republican candidate George W. Bush. Latino votes were split, revealing an increasing trend toward Latino support for the Republican Party, and away from the Democratic Party, the traditional party for minority groups like African Americans, Jews, and Latinos since the 1930s. Bush won 35 percent of the Latino vote in 2000, and even more, 44 percent in 2004. Asian American voters expressed less public tension over the issue, but an even greater proportion of that population supported Republicans, if less so than in earlier elections: approximately 45 percent of Asian-American voters supported President Bush and the Republican Party in 2004, whereas in 1992, George H. W. Bush claimed 62 percent of Asian-American votes. African Americans, on the other hand, have been consistently less split on the issue, generally voting Democratic. Fewer than 15 percent of African-American voters voted for the Republican Party in recent national elections (from 1980 to 2004). "Republican Party (United States)" entry, Wikipedia, http://en.wikipedia.org/wiki/Republican_Party_(United_States) (accessed December 14, 2009). See too Thomas Chen, "Why Asian Americans Voted for Obama," February 26, 2009, http://www.hcs. harvard.edu/~perspy/2009/02/why-asian-americans-voted-for-obama/(accessed December 14, 2009); James G. Gimpel, "Losing Ground or Staying Even: Republicans and the Politics of the Latino Vote," October 2004, Center for Immigration Studies, http://www.cis.org/articles/2004/back1004.html (accessed December 14, 2009).

In the 2008 presidential election, the Republican Party's inroads among Latinos diminished as that population largely supported Barack Obama (approximately 66–67 percent). African Americans also overwhelmingly mobilized behind Obama (95–96 percent). See Manzano, "Latinos in the Sunbelt: Political Implications of Demographic Change." Asian Americans gradually have been shifting away from the Republican Party and toward the Democratic Party, as Obama won 61–63 percent of Asian Americans' votes. Thomas Chen, "Why Asian Americans Voted for Obama," February 26, 2009, http://www.hcs.harvard. edu/~perspy/2009/02/why-asian-americans-voted-for-obama/(accessed December 14, 2009); Joe Von Kanel and Hal Quinley, "Exit Polls: Obama Wins Big among Young, Minority Voters," November 3, 2008, CNN Politics, http:// www.cnn.com/2008/POLITICS/11/04/exit.polls/ (accessed December 14, 2009); and Asian Americans for Obama, "CNN National Exit Polls," November 5, 2008, http://www.asianamericansforobama.com/cnn-national-exit-polls (accessed December 14, 2009). Jewish support of the Democratic Party in 2008 remained strong; Obama received 75–78 percent of American Jews' vote. See Shmuel Rosner, "Jews and the 2008 Election," *Commentary Magazine*, February 2009, http://www.commentarymagazine.com/viewarticle.cfm/jews-and-the-2008-election-14385 (accessed December 14, 2009).

21. Numerous newspaper articles and radio shows explore tensions between Latinos and African Americans over immigration and resources. For just a few examples, see "Blacks, Latinos and the Immigration Debate, March 31, 2005, National Public Radio, http://news.wnpr.org/templates/story/story.php?storyId=5314594 (accessed February 28, 2008); Earl Ofari Hutchinson, "Los Angeles School Brawls Expose Black-Latino Tension," April 27, 2005, New American Media (Pacific News Service project), http://news.ncmonline.com/news/view_article.html?article_id=00c83b0739520c4f380469df2c520743 (accessed December 14, 2009); and Earl Ofari

Hutchinson, "Old Civil Rights Groups Missing-in-Action as Immigrants Hit the Streets," March 27, 2006, Pacific News Service, http://news.pacificnews.org/news/view_article.html?article_id=b3543d592890b6a801a6c4a84d0f6d5f (accessed December 14, 2009). For a scholarly take on the issue, see Johnson, Farrell, and Guinn, "Immigration Reform and the Browning of America." For more on Asian and Latino participation in the 2006 immigration protests, see Barreto, Manzano, Rim, and Ramirez, "Mobilization, Participation, and *Solidaridad*."

Latino and Asian American populations, though, also have diverse internal opinions and stances on immigration. For instance, Mexican Americans at times have been among the staunchest proponents of tighter immigration policies, as scholars like David Gutiérrez have shown. See Gutiérrez, *Walls and Mirrors*.

22. See, for instance, various essays in Salzman and West, *Struggles in the Promised Land*.

23. See, for instance, the discussion on disagreements over desegregation between Asian-origin populations and others in San Francisco in the mid to late twentieth century in Brilliant, *The Color of America Has Changed*.

Bibliography

MANUSCRIPT COLLECTIONS

American Civil Liberties Union Collection. Department of Special Collections, Young Research Library, University of California, Los Angeles [ACLU]

Fletcher Bowron Collection, 1934–1970. Huntington Library. [Bowron]

California Federation for Civic Unity Records, 1945–1956. Bancroft Library, University of California, Berkeley [CFCU]

California Un-American Activities Committee Records, 1935–1977. California State Archives, Office of the Secretary of State [Also known as the Tenney Committee]

Civil Rights Congress Collection, Los Angeles, Late 1940's—1950's. Southern California Library for Social Studies and Research [Civil Rights Congress]

Bert N. Corona Papers, 1923–1984. Department of Special Collections, Green Library, Stanford University [Corona]

CSO Project, University of California San Diego (http://www.csoproject.org/) [CSO Project]

John Anson Ford Papers, 1928–1971. Huntington Library [Ford]

Ernesto Galarza Papers, 1936–1984. Department of Special Collections, Green Library, Stanford University [Galarza]

Hermán Gallegos Papers. Department of Special Collections, Green Library, Stanford University [Gallegos]

The Jewish Federation Council of Greater Los Angeles' Community Relations Committee Collection. Urban Archives Center, Oviatt Library, California State University, Northridge [CRC]

Jewish Secular Material Collection. Southern California Library for Social Studies and Research [Jewish Secular Material]

Los Angeles Committee for the Protection of the Foreign Born Files. Southern California Library for Social Studies and Research [LACPFB]

Los Angeles Examiner Clippings Files. Regional History Center, University of Southern California [*Los Angeles Examiner* Clippings]

Los Angeles Urban League Records, 1933–1945. Department of Special Collections, Young Research Library, University of California, Los Angeles [Los Angeles Urban League]

Alice Greenfield McGrath Papers, 1943–1990. Department of Special Collections, Young Research Library, University of California, Los Angeles [McGrath]

Carey McWilliams Papers, ca 1905–1980, 1319. Department of Special Collections, Young Research Library, University of California, Los Angeles [McWilliams, 1319]

Loren Miller Papers, 1876–2003. Huntington Library [Miller]

National Association for the Advancement of Colored People Collection. Library of Congress [NAACP LOC]

National Association for the Advancement of Colored People, Region I, Records, 1942–1986. Bancroft Library, University of California, Berkeley [NAACP]

Fred Ross Papers, 1910–1992. Department of Special Collections, Green Library, Stanford University [Ross]

Edward Ross Roybal Papers, 1953–1963. Department of Special Collections, Young Research Library, University of California, Los Angeles [Roybal]

Manuel Ruíz Papers, 1931–1986. Department of Special Collections, Green Library, Stanford University [Ruíz]

Earl Warren Papers, 1924–1953. California State Archives, Office of the Secretary of State [Warren]

GOVERNMENT DOCUMENTS

California Legislature Joint Fact-Finding Committee on Un-American Activities in California. *Report 1: 1943*. Senate of the State of California: Sacramento, 1943.

California Legislature Joint Fact-Finding Committee on Un-American Activities in California. *Report 2: 1945*. Senate of the State of California: Sacramento, 1945.

California Legislature Joint Fact-Finding Committee on Un-American Activities in California. *Fourth Report of the Senate Fact-Finding Committee on Un-American Activities. 1948: Communist Front Organizations*. Senate of the State of California: Sacramento, 1948.

Federal Emergency Relief Administration. *Unemployment Relief Census, October, 1933*, Report No. One, United States Summary. Washington, D.C.: U.S. Government Printing Office, 1934.

United States Bureau of the Census. *Twelfth Census of the United States Taken in the Year 1900, Population: Part I*. Washington, D.C.: U.S. Government Printing Office, 1901.

United States Bureau of the Census. *Thirteenth Census of the United States Taken in the Year 1910, Volume II: Population 1910*. Washington, D.C.: U.S. Government Printing Office, 1910.

United States Bureau of the Census. *Fourteenth Census of the United States Taken in the Year 1920, Vol.II: Population 1920, General Report and Analytical Tables*. Washington, D.C.: U.S. Government Printing Office, 1922.

United States Bureau of the Census. *Fifteenth Census of the United States 1930. Population, Vol. III, Part I: Reports by States, Showing the Composition and Characteristics of the Population for Countries, Cities, and Townships or Other Minor Civil Divisions*. U.S. Government Printing Office: Washington, D.C., 1932.

United States Bureau of the Census. *16th Census of the United States, 1940, Population: Nativity and Percentage of the White Population, Mother Tongue*. Washington, D.C.: U.S. Government Printing Office, 1943.

United States Bureau of the Census. *Sixteenth Census of the United States: 1940 Population, Vol. I, Number of Inhabitants.* Washington, D.C.: U.S. Government Printing Office, 1942.

United States Bureau of the Census. *Sixteenth Census of the United States 1940. Population, Vol. II: Characteristics of the Population, Part 1: United States Summary and Alabama-District of Columbia.* U.S. Government Printing Office: Washington, D.C., 1943.

United States Bureau of the Census. *17th Census of the Population: 1950, Vol. I, Number of Inhabitants.* Washington, D.C.: U.S. Government Printing Office, 1952.

United States Bureau of the Census. *A Report of the Seventeenth Decennial Census of the United States Census of the Population 1950. Vol. II: Characteristics of the Population, Part 5: California.* U.S. Government Printing Office: Washington, D.C., 1952.

United States Bureau of the Census. *U.S. Census of the Population: 1950—Special Reports: Persons of Spanish Surname, Vol. IV, Special Reports Part 3, Chapter C.* Washington, D.C.: U.S. Government Printing Office, 1953.

NEWSPAPERS AND PERIODICALS

California Eagle
Daily People's World
Jewish Daily Forward
LA Citizen News
Los Angeles Daily News
Los Angeles Examiner
Los Angeles Herald
Los Angeles Times
Rafu Shimpo
San Francisco Chronicle

ORAL HISTORY INTERVIEWS

Balter, Michael S. *Law and Social Conscience,* interview of Ben Margolis. University of California Los Angeles: Oral History Program, 1987.

Chall, Malca. Oral History Interview: *Hope Mendoza Schechter: Activist in the Labor Movement, the Democratic Party, and the Mexican-American Community,* conducted 1977–78. Bancroft Library Regional History Office, University of California Berkeley, 1980.

Cunningham, L. Craig and Elizabeth I. Dixon. *John Anson Ford and Los Angeles County Government.* University of California Los Angeles: Oral History Program, 1967.

de Graaf, Lawrence. Interview with Judge Loren Miller: *"Negroes in Los Angeles during the Depression.* California State University Fullerton Oral History Program, 29 April 1967.

Gallegos, Herman. *Interview with Dolores Huerta*. CSO Project, University of California San Diego (http://csoproject.org/), 29 January 2006.

Gardner Joel. *Honorable in All Things: Carey McWilliams*. University of California Los Angeles: Oral History Program, 1982.

Gardner, Joel. *Tradition's Chains Have Bound Us: Dorothy Healey*. University of California Los Angeles: Oral History Program, 1982.

Kutner, Eric and Gilbert Padilla. *Interview with Hector Tarango*. CSO Project, University of California San Diego (http://csoproject.org/),15 November 2005.

Mischel, Florence D. *A Passion for Justice: Seniel Ostrow*. University of California Los Angeles: Oral History Program, 1987.

Nunis, Doyce B. *My First Forty Years in California Politics 1922–1962*. University of California Los Angeles: Oral History Program, 1964.

Pitt, Leonard. *Joseph Roos Oral History Interview*. 18 December 1979, 7 January 1980, 28 January 1980, and 14 February 1980, The Jewish Federation Council of Greater Los Angeles' Community Relations Committee Collection, Urban Archives Center, Oviatt Library, California State University, Northridge.

Schippers, Jack B. *Jack B. Tenney: California Legislator*. University of California Los Angeles: Oral History Program, 1969.

Valenciana, Christine. *Mexican-American Repatriation during the Depression:* Interview with John Anson Ford. California State University Fullerton Oral History Program, 4 September 1971.

Vásquez, Carlos. *Oral History Interview Augustus F. Hawkins*. University of California Los Angeles: Oral History Program, for the California State Archives State Government Oral History Program, 1988.

Woods, Clyde. Augustus F. Hawkins: *Black Leadership in Los Angeles*. University of California Los Angeles: Oral History Program, 1992.

PUBLISHED WORKS

http://www.ajclosangeles.org/site/c.mlI0IfN1JyE/b.2026491/k.246B/Who_We_Are.htm [Accessed December 14, 2009]

http://csoproject.org/ [Accessed December 13, 2009]

"Pelosi Pays Tribute to the Late Justice Stanley Mosk," Statement on the Floor of the House, July 11, 2001, http://www.house.gov/pelosi/flmosk7–11–01.htm [Accessed December 14, 2009]

Wilkipedia entry, "Stanley Mosk," http://en.wikipedia.org/wiki/Stanley_Mosk [Accessed December 14, 2009]

The Brown Foundation for Educational Equity website, http://brownvboard.org/research/opinions/347us483.htm [Accessed December 14, 2009]

"Republican Party (United States)" entry, Wikipedia, http://en.wikipedia.org/wiki/Republican_Party_(United_States) [Accessed December 14, 2009]

"Blacks, Latinos and the Immigration Debate, 31 March 2005, National Public Radio, http://news.wnpr.org/templates/story/story.php?storyId=5314594 [Accessed February 28, 2008]

Abbott, Carl. *The Metropolitan Frontier: Cities in the Modern American West*. Tucson: University of Arizona Press, 1993.

Abel, Emily K. "From Exclusion to Expulsion: Mexicans and Tuberculosis in Los Angeles, 1914–1940." *Bulletin of the History of Medicine*, 77 no. 4: 823–849.
——. *Tuberculosis and the Politics of Exclusion: A History of Public Health and Migration to Los Angeles.* New Brunswick, NJ: Rutgers University Press, 2007.
Acuña, Rodolfo. *Anything But Mexican: Chicanos in Contemporary Los Angeles.* New York: Verso, 1996.
——. *A Community under Siege: A Chronicle of Chicanos East of the Los Angeles River, 1945–1975.* University of California, Los Angeles: Chicano Studies Research Center, Publications, 1984.
Allen, James, and Eugene Turner. *Changing Faces, Changing Places.* Northridge: Center for Geographical Studies, California State University, Northridge, 2002.
Almaguer, Tomás. *Racial Fault Lines: The Historical Origins of White Supremacy in California.* Berkeley: University of California Press, 1994.
Álvarez, Luis. *The Power of the Zoot: Youth Culture and Resistance during World War II.* Berkeley: University of California Press, 2008.
——. "Zoot Violence on the Home Front: Race, Riots, and Youth Culture during World War II." In *Mexican Americans & World War II*, ed. Maggie Rivas-Rodriguez, 141–175. Austin: University of Texas Press, 2005.
Álvarez, Luis and Daniel Widener. "A History of Black and Brown: Chicana/o-African American Cultural and Political Relations." *Aztlán: A Journal of Chicano Studies* 33, no. 1 (2008): 143–54.
Alvarez, Robert R., Jr. "The Lemon Grove Incident: The Nation's First Successful Desegregation Court Case." *Journal of San Diego History* 32, no. 2 (1986):116–35.
Anderson, Carol. "Bleached Souls and Red Negroes: The NAACP and Black Communists in the Early Cold War, 1948–1952." In *Window on Freedom: Race, Civil Rights, and Foreign Affairs 1945–1988*, ed. Brenda Gayle Plummer. Chapel Hill: University of North Carolina Press, 2003.
Anderson, E. Frederick. *The Development of Leadership and Organization Building in the Black Community of Los Angeles from 1900 through World War II.* Saratoga, CA: Century Twenty One Publishing, 1980.
Apodaca, Linda M. *Mexican American Women and Social Change: The Founding of the Community Service Organization in Los Angeles, an Oral History,* Working Paper Series No.27. Tucson: The University of Arizona, 1999.
Arnesen, Eric. "'No Graver Danger': Black Anticommunism, the Communist Party, and the Race Question." *Labor* 3, no. 4 (Winter 2006): 13–52.
Arredondo, Gabriela F. *Mexican Chicago: Race, Identity, and Nation, 1919–1939.* Champaign, IL: University of Illinois Press, 2008.
——. "Navigating Ethno-Racial Currents, Mexicans in Chicago, 1919–1939." *Journal of Urban History* 30 no. 3 (March 2004): 399–427.
Arriola, Christopher. "Knocking on the Schoolhouse Door: *Mendez v. Westminster*–Equal Protection, Public Education, and Mexican Americans in the 1940s." *La Raza Law Journal* 8, no. 2 (1995): 166–207.
Aschheim, Steven E. *Beyond the Border: The German-Jewish Legacy Abroad.* N.J.: Princeton University Press, 2007.
Asian Americans for Obama. "CNN National Exit Polls." November 5, 2008. Online. Available: http://www.asianamericansforobama.com/cnn-national-exit-polls. [Accessed December 14, 2009.]

Austin, Allan W. *From Concentration Camp to Campus: Japanese American Students and World War II.* Urbana, IL: University of Illinois Press, 2004.

Avrich, Paul. *Sacco and Vanzetti: The Anarchist Background.* Princeton: Princeton University Press, 1991.

Bahr, Ehrhard. *Weimar on the Pacific: German Exile Culture in Los Angeles and the Crisis of Modernism.* Berkeley: University of California Press, 2007.

Baldassare, Mark, ed. *The Los Angeles Riots: Lessons for the Urban Future.* Boulder, CO: Westview Press, 1994.

Balderrama, Francisco E., and Raymond Rodriguez. *Decade of Betrayal: Mexican Repatriation in the 1930s.* Albuquerque: University of New Mexico Press, 1995.

——. *In Defense of la Raza: The Los Angeles Mexican Consulate and the Mexican Community, 1929 to 1936.* Tucson: University of Arizona Press, 1982.

Barajas, Frank P. "Resistance, Radicalism and Repression on the Oxnard Plain: the Social Context of the Betabelero Strike of 1933." *Western Historical Quarterly* 35, no. 1 (Spring 2004): 29–52.

Barreto, Matt A., Sylvia Manzano, Kathy Rim and Ricardo Ramirez, "Mobilization, Participation, and *Solidaridad:* Latino Participation in the 2006 Immigration Protest Rallies." *Urban Affairs Review* 44, no. 5 (May 2009): 736–764.

Barrett, Edward L. *The Tenney Committee: Legislative Investigation of Subversive Activities in California.* Ithaca, New York: Cornell University Press, 1951.

Barrett, James R. and David Roediger. "In Between Peoples: Race, Nationality and the 'New Immigrant' Working Class." *Journal of American Ethnic History* 16, no. 3 (Spring 1997): 3–44.

Bass, Charlotta. *Forty Years: Memoirs from the Pages of a Newspaper.* Los Angeles: Bass Publishers, 1960.

Belknap, Michael R. *Cold War Political Justice: The Smith Act, the Communist Party, and American Civil Liberties.* Westport, CT: Greenwood Press, 1977.

Bell, Horace. *Reminiscences of a Ranger, or Early Times in Southern California.* Santa Barbara: Wallace Hubbard, 1927.

Biondi, Martha. *To Stand and Fight: The Struggle for Civil Rights in Postwar New York City.* Cambridge: Harvard University Press, 2003.

Birdwell, Michael E. *Celluloid Soldiers: Warner Bros.'s Campaign against Nazism.* New York: New York University Press, 1999.

Blakely, Allison. *Russia and the Negro: Blacks in Russian History and Thought.* Washington, D.C.: Howard University Press, 1986.

Blum, John Morton. *V was for Victory: Politics and American Culture during World War II.* New York: Harcourt Brace Jovanovich, 1976.

Bobo, Lawrence D., Melvin L. Oliver, James H. Johnson Jr., and Abel Valenzuela Jr., eds. *Prismatic Metropolis: Inequality in Los Angeles.* New York: Russell Sage Foundation, 2000.

Bodnar, John, Roger Simon, and Michael P. Weber. *Lives of their Own: Blacks, Italians, and Poles in Pittsburgh 1900–60.* Urbana: University of Illinois Press, 1981.

Borstelmann, Thomas. *The Cold War and the Color Line: American Race Relations in the Global Arena.* Cambridge: Harvard University Press, 2001.

Bracey, Jr., John H., and August Meier. "Allies or Adversaries? The NAACP, A. Philip Randolph and the 1941 March on Washington." *Georgia Historical Quarterly* 75, no. 1 (1991): 1–17.

Branch, Taylor. *Parting the Waters: America in the King Years, 1954–63.* New York: Simon and Schuster, 1988.

Brilliant, Mark. *The Color of America Has Changed: The Challenge of Racial Diversity to Racial Liberalism in California, 1941–1978.* New York: Oxford University Press, Forthcoming.

Brinkley, Alan. *The End of Reform: New Deal Liberalism in Recession and War.* New York: Knopf, 1995.

Broder, John M. "A Black-Latino Coalition Emerges in Los Angeles." April 24, 2005, *New York Times.* Online. Available: http://query.nytimes.com/gst/fullpage.html?res=9E0DE2DA1231F937A15757C0A9639C8B63&sec=&spo n=&pagewanted=print. [Accessed December 14, 2009.]

Broder, John M. "Latino Victor in Los Angeles Overcomes Division." May 19, 2005, *New York Times.* Online. Available: http://www.nytimes. com/2005/05/19/national/19angeles.html?_r=1&n=Top/Reference/ Times%20Topics/People/V/Villaraigosa,%20Antonio&oref=slogin. [Accessed December 14, 2009.]

Brodkin, Karen. *How Jews Became White Folks and What That Says about Race in America.* New Brunswick, NJ: Rutgers University Press, 1998.

Brooks, Charlotte. *Alien Neighbors, Foreign Friends: Asian Americans, Housing, and the Transformation of Urban California.* Chicago: University of Chicago Press, 2009.

———. "Sing Sheng vs. Southwood: Residential Integration in Cold War California." *Pacific Historical Review* 73, no. 3 (August 2004): 463–494.

Broussard, Albert S. *Black San Francisco: The Struggle for Racial Equality in the West, 1900–1954.* Lawrence, Kansas: The University Press of Kansas, 1993.

Buhle, Paul and Dave Wagner. *Radical Hollywood: The Untold Story behind America's Favorite Movies.* New York: The New Press, 2002.

Bulosan, Carlos. *America is in the Heart.* New York: Harcourt, Brace, and Company, 1943.

Burt, Kenneth C. "The Battle for Standard Coil: The United Electrical Workers, The Community Service Organization, and The Catholic Church In Latino East Los Angeles." In *American Labor and the Cold War: Grassroots Politics and Postwar Political Culture,* ed. Robert W. Cherny, William Issel, Kieran Walsh Taylor, 118–140. New Brunswick, NJ: Rutgers University Press, 2004.

———. "Latino Empowerment in Los Angeles: Postwar Dreams and Cold War Fears, 1948–1952." *Labor's Heritage* 8, no. 1 (Summer 1996): 6–25.

———. "The Power of a Mobilized Citizenry and Coalition Politics: the 1949 Election of Edward R. Roybal to the Los Angeles City Council." *Southern California Quarterly* 85, no. 4 (Winter 2003): 413–38.

———. *The Search for A Civic Voice: California Latino Politics.* Claremont, CA: Regina Books, 2007.

Camarillo, Albert. "Black and Brown in Compton: Demographic Change, Suburban Decline, and Intergroup Relations in a South Central Los Angeles Community, 1950 to 2000." In *Not Just Black and White: Historical and Contemporary Perspectives on Immigration, Race, and Ethnicity in the United*

States, ed. George Fredrickson and Nancy Foner. New York: Russell Sage Foundation, 2004.

——. *Chicanos in a Changing Society: from Mexican Pueblos to American Barrios in Santa Barbara and Southern California, 1848–1930.* Cambridge: Harvard University Press, 1979; 2ⁿᵈ ed. 1996.

——. "Mexicans and Europeans in American Cities: Some Comparative Perspectives 1900–1940." In *From "Melting Pot" to Multiculturalism: The Evolution of Ethnic Relations in the United States and Canada, Estratto Biblioteca Di Cultura 418,* ed. Valeria Gennaro Lerda, 253–62. Bulzoni Editore, 1990.

Cardoso, Lawrence A. *Mexican Emigration to the United States, 1897–1931: Socio-Economic Patterns.* Tucson: University of Arizona Press, 1980.

Carson, Clayborne. *In Struggle: SNCC and the Black Awakening of the 1960s.* Cambridge: Harvard University Press, 1981.

——. "Black-Jewish Universalism in the Era of Identity Politics." In *Struggles in the Promised Land: Toward a History of Black-Jewish Relations in the United States,* ed. Jack Salzman and Cornel West. New York: Oxford University Press, 1997.

Cash, Floris Loretta Barnett. *African American Women and Social Action: the Clubwomen and Volunteerism from Jim Crow to the New Deal, 1896–1936.* Westport, Conn.: Greenwood Press, 2001.

Caughey, John and Laree Caughey, eds. *Los Angeles: Biography of a City.* Berkeley: University of California Press, 1976.

Caute, David. *The Great Fear: The Anti-Communist Purge Under Truman and Eisenhower.* New York: Simon and Schuster, 1978.

Ceplair, Larry and Steven Englund. *The Inquisition in Hollywood: Politics in the Film Community, 1930–1960.* Garden City, New York: Anchor Press/ Doubleday, 1980.

Chafe, William H., ed. *The Achievement of American Liberalism: the New Deal and Its Legacies.* New York : Columbia University Press, 2003.

Cha-Jua, Sundiata Keita and Clarence Lang. "The 'Long Movement' as Vampire: Temporal and Spatial Fallacies in Recent Black Freedom Studies." *The Journal of African American History* 92, no. 2 (Spring 2007): 265–288.

Chambless, Timothy M. "Pro-Defense, Pro-Growth, and Anti-Communism: Cold War Politics in the American West." In *The Cold War American West, 1945–1989,* ed. Kevin J. Fernlund. Albuquerque: University of New Mexico Press, 1998.

Chan, Sucheng. *Asian Americans: an Interpretive History.* Boston: Twayne Publishers, 1991.

Chang, Edward T. and Russell C. Leong, eds. *Los Angeles: Struggles toward Multiethnic Community: Asian American, African American and Latino Perspectives.* Seattle: University of Washington Press, 1994.

Chang, Gordon. *Morning Glory, Evening Shadow: Yamato Ichihashi and His Internment Writings, 1942–1945.* Stanford: Stanford University Press, 1997.

Chávez, Alicia. "Dolores Huerta and the United Farm Workers." In *Latina Legacies: Identity, Biography, and Community,* ed. Vicki L. Ruiz and Virginia Sánchez Korrol, 243–244. New York: Oxford University Press, 2005.

Chávez, Ernesto. *"Mi Raza Primero!" (My People First!): Nationalism, Identity, and Insurgency in the Chicano Movement in Los Angeles, 1966–1978.* Berkeley: University of California Press, 2002.

Chen, Anthony S. "'The Hitlerian Rule of Quotas': Racial Conservatism and the Politics of Fair Employment Legislation in New York State, 1941–1945." *Journal of American History* 92, no. 4 (March 2006): 1238–64.

Chen, Thomas. "Why Asian Americans Voted for Obama." February 26, 2009. Online. Available: http://www.hcs.harvard.edu/~perspy/2009/02/why-asian-americans-voted-for-obama/. [Accessed December 14, 2009.]

Chen, Yong. *Chinese San Francisco, 1850–1943: A Trans-Pacific Community.* Stanford: Stanford University Press, 2000.

Cherny, Robert W., William Issel, Kieran Walsh Taylor, eds. *American Labor and the Cold War: Grassroots Politics and Postwar Political Culture.* New Brunswick, NJ: Rutgers University Press, 2004.

Chinese Historical Society of Southern California, *Linking our Lives: Chinese American Women of Los Angeles.* Los Angeles, CA: Chinese Historical Society of Southern California, 1984.

Cho, Sumi K. "Redeeming Whiteness in the Shadow of Internment: Earl Warren, *Brown*, and a Theory of Racial Redemption." In "Symposium: The Long Shadow of *Korematsu,*" *Boston College Law Review,* 40 (Dec. 1998) and *Boston College Third World Law Journal,* 19 (Fall 1998), 73–170.

Chuman, Frank F. *The Bamboo People: The Law and Japanese Americans.* Del Mar, CA: Publisher's Inc., c1976.

Chung, Sue Fawn. "Fighting for Their American Rights: A History of the Chinese American Citizens Alliance." In *Claiming America: Constructing Chinese American Identities during the Exclusion Era,* ed. K. Scott Wong and Sucheng Chan. Philadelphia: Temple University Press, 1998.

Clive, Alan. *State of War: Michigan in World War II.* Ann Arbor: University of Michigan Press, 1979.

Cohen, Lizabeth. *Making a New Deal: Industrial Workers in Chicago, 1919–1939.* New York: Cambridge University Press, 1990.

Collier-Thomas, Bettye and V.P. Franklin, eds. *Sisters in the Struggle: African American Women in the Civil Rights-Black Power Movement.* New York: New York University Press, 2001.

Connolly, Nathan. "Sunbelt Civil Rights: Urban Renewal and the Follies of Desegregation in Greater Miami." In *Sunbelt Rising: The Politics of Space, Place and Region in the American South and Southwest,* ed. Darren Dochuk and Michelle Nickerson. Philadelphia: University of Pennsylvania Press, forthcoming.

Dalfiume, Richard M. *Desegregation of the U.S. Armed Forces: Fighting on Two Fronts, 1939–1953.* Columbia, Missouri: University of Missouri Press, 1969.

D'Amelio, Dan A. "A Season of Panic: the Internments of World War II," *Italian Americana* 17, no. 2 (1999): 147–162.

Daniel, Clete. *Chicano Workers and the Politics of Fairness: the FEPC in the Southwest, 1941–1945.* Austin: University of Texas Press, 1991.

Daniels, Roger. *Asian America: Chinese and Japanese in the United States since 1850.* Seattle: University of Washington Press, 1988.

——. *Concentration Camps USA: Japanese Americans and World War II.* New York: Holt, Rinehart and Winston, 1971.

——. *Prisoners without Trial: Japanese Americans in World War II.* New York: Hill and Wang, 1993.

Daniels, Roger, Sandra C. Taylor, and Harry H.L. Kitano, eds. *Japanese Americans: From Relocation to Redress*. Salt Lake City, Utah: University of Utah Press, 1986.

Davis, Clark. *Company Men: White-Collar Life and Corporate Cultures in Los Angeles, 1892–1941*. Baltimore: Johns Hopkins University Press, 2000.

Davis, Mike. *City of Quartz: Excavating the Future in Los Angeles*. New York: Vintage Books, 1992.

———. "Sunshine and the Open Shop: Ford and Darwin in 1920s Los Angeles." In *Metropolis in the Making: Los Angeles in the 1920s*, ed. Tom Sitton and William Deverell. Berkeley: University of California Press, 2001.

de Graaf, Lawrence B.. Kevin Mulroy, and Quintard Taylor, eds. *Seeking El Dorado: African Americans in California*. Los Angeles: Autry Museum of Western Heritage, in association with the University of Washington Press, 2001.

de Genova, Nicholas ed. *Racial Transformations: Latinos and Asians Remaking the United States*. Durham: Duke University Press, 2006.

D'Emilio, John. *Sexual Politics, Sexual Communities: The Making of a Homosexual Minority in the United States, 1940–1970*. Chicago: The University of Chicago Press, 1983.

Deverell, William. "My America or Yours? Americanization and the Battle for the Youth of Los Angeles." In *Metropolis in the Making: Los Angeles in the 1920s*, ed. Tom Sitton and William Deverell. Berkeley: University of California Press, 2001.

———. *Whitewashed Adobe: the Rise of Los Angeles and the Remaking of its Mexican Past*. Berkeley: University of California Press, 2005.

Deverell, William and Douglas Flamming, "Race and Regional Identity: Black and White Boosters in Los Angeles, 1880–1930." in *Many Wests: Regional Consciousness in the American West*, ed. John Findlay and Richard White. Seattle: University of Washington Press, 1999.

Dias, Ric. "Cold War Cities in the American West." In *The Cold War American West, 1945–1989*, ed. Kevin J. Fernlund. Albuquerque: University of New Mexico Press, 1998.

Dinnerstein, Leonard. "Anti-Semitism Exposed and Attacked, 1945–1950." *American Jewish History*, 71 (September 1981).

Diner, Hasia R. *A Time for Gathering: The Second Migration, 1820–1880*. Baltimore: The Johns Hopkins University Press, 1992.

———. "Between Words and Deeds: Jews and Blacks in America, 1880–1935." In *Struggles in the Promised Land: Toward a History of Black-Jewish Relations in the United States*, ed. Jack Salzman and Cornel West. New York: Oxford University Press, 1997.

———. *In the Almost Promised Land: American Jews and Blacks, 1915–1935*. Baltimore, MD: The Johns Hopkins University Press, 1995.

Dochuk, Darren, *From Bible Belt to Sunbelt: Plain-folk Religion, Grassroots Politics, and the Rise of Evangelical Conservatism*. New York: W.W. Norton & Company, Inc., forthcoming 2010.

Dollinger, Marc. *Quest for Inclusion: Jews and Liberalism in Modern America*. Princeton: Princeton University Press, 2000.

Donner, Frank. *Protectors of Privilege: Red Squads and Police Repression in Urban America*. Berkeley: University of California Press, 1990.

Dower, John W. *War without Mercy: Race & Power in the Pacific War.* New York: Pantheon Books, 1986.

Dudziak, Mary L. *Cold War Civil Rights: Race and the Image of American Democracy.* Princeton, NJ: Princeton University Press, 2000.

Eisenberg, Ellen M. "Civil Rights and Japanese American Incarceration." In *California Jews*, ed. Ava F. Kahn and Marc Dollinger. Boston, MA: Brandeis University Press, 2003.

——. *The First to Cry Down Injustice? Western Jews and Japanese Removal during World War II.* Lanham, MD: Lexington Books, 2008.

Ellis, J. Ethan. *Republican Foreign Policy, 1921–1933.* New Brunswick, N.J.: Rutgers University Press, 1968.

Engh, S.J., Michael E. "At Home in the Heteropolis: Understanding Postmodern L.A." *American Historical Review* 105, no. 4 (December 2000): 1676–1682.

Escobar, Edward J. "Bloody Christmas and the Irony of Police Professionalism: The Los Angeles Police Department, Mexican Americans, and Police Reform in the 1950s." *Pacific Historical Review* 72, No.2 (May 2003): 171–199.

——. *Race, Police, and the Making of a Political Identity: Mexican Americans and the Los Angeles Police Department, 1900–1945.* Berkeley: University of California Press, 1999.

España-Maram, Linda. *Creating Masculinity in Los Angeles's Little Manila: Working-Class Filipinos and Popular Culture, 1920s-1950s.* New York: Columbia University Press, 2006.

Faderman, Lillian and Stuart Timmons. *Gay L.A.: A History of Sexual Outlaws, Power Politics, and Lipstick Lesbians.* New York: Basic Books, 2006.

Faragher, John Mack. "The Social Fabric of the American West." *The Historian*, 66, no. 3 (Sept 2004): 442–54.

Fernlund, Kevin J., ed. *The Cold War American West, 1945–1989.* Albuquerque: University of New Mexico Press, 1998.

Ferguson, Karen. *Black Politics in New Deal Atlanta.* Chapel Hill: University of North Carolina Press, 2002.

Fields, Barbara J. "Ideology and Race in American History." In *Region, Race, and Reconstruction: Essays in Honor of C. Vann Woodward*, ed. J. Morgan Kousser and James M. McPherson. New York: Oxford University Press, 1982.

Findlay, John and Richard White, eds. *Many Wests: Regional Consciousness in the American West.* Seattle: University of Washington Press, 1999.

Fine, Sidney. *Violence in the Model City: The Cavanaugh Administration, Race Relations, and the Detroit Riot of 1967.* Ann Arbor: University of Michigan Press, 1989.

Finks, P. David. *The Radical Vision of Saul Alinsky.* Ramsey, N.J.: Paulist Press, 1984.

Flamming, Douglas. "Becoming Democrats: Liberal Politics and the African American Community in Los Angeles, 1930–1965." In *Seeking El Dorado: African Americans in California*, ed. Lawrence B. de Graaf, Kevin Mulroy, and Quintard Taylor. Los Angeles: Autry Museum of Western Heritage, in association with the University of Washington Press, 2001.

——. *Bound for Freedom: Black Los Angeles in Jim Crow America.* Berkeley: University of California Press, 2005.

Fogelson, Robert M. *The Fragmented Metropolis: Los Angeles, 1850–1930.* Cambridge: Harvard University Press, 1967.

Foley, Neil. "Becoming Hispanic: Mexican Americans and the Faustian Pact with Whiteness." In *Reflexiones 1997: New Directions in Mexican American Studies*, ed. Neil Foley. Austin: The University of Texas Press, 1998.

———. "Over the Rainbow: Hernandez v. Texas, Brown v. Board of Education, and Black v. Brown." In *"Colored Men" and "Hombres Aqui": Hernandez v. Texas and the Emergence of Mexican-American Lawyering*," ed. Michael A. Olivas, 111–21. Houston: Arte Público Press, 2006.

———. *Quest for Equality: The Failed Promise of Black-Brown Solidarity*. Cambridge: Harvard University Press, 2010.

———. *The White Scourge: Mexicans, Blacks, and Poor Whites in Texas Cotton Culture*. Berkeley: University of California Press, 1997.

Ford, James W. *Communists in the Struggle for Negro Rights*. NY: New Century Publishers, 1945.

Ford, John Anson. *Thirty Explosive Years in Los Angeles County*. San Marino, CA: Huntington Library, San Marino, California, 1961.

Fox, Stephen. *America's Invisible Gulag: A Biography of German American Internment and Exclusion in World War II*. New York: Peter Lang, 2000.

Fraser, Steve and Gary Gerstle, eds. *The Rise and Fall of the New Deal Order, 1930–1980*. Princeton, N.J.: 1989.

Freer, Regina. "Black Korean Conflict." In *The Los Angeles Riots: Lessons for the Urban Future*, ed. Mark Baldassare, 175–203. Boulder, CO: Westview Press, 1994.

———. "L.A. Race Woman: Charlotta Bass and the Complexities of Black Political Development in Los Angeles." *American Quarterly* 56, no. 3 (September 2004): 607–632.

Fried, Richard M. *Nightmare in Red: The McCarthy Era in Perspective*. New York: Oxford University Press,1990.

Fujino, Diane C. *Heartbeat of Struggle: The Revolutionary Life of Yuri Kochiyama*. Minneapolis: University of Minnesota Press, 2005.

Gabler, Neil. *An Empire of their Own: How the Jews Invented Hollywood*. New York: Crown Publishers, Inc., 1988.

Gaines, Kevin. *American Africans: Black Expatriates and the Civil Rights Era*. Chapel Hill: University of North Carolina Press, 2006.

García, Mario T. "Americans All: The Mexican-American Generation and the Politics of Wartime Los Angeles, 1941–1945." *Social Science Quarterly* 65 (June 1984): 278–289.

———. *Mexican Americans: Leadership, Ideology, and Identity, 1930–1960*. New Haven: Yale University Press, 1989.

———. *Memories of Chicano History: The Life and Narrative of Bert Corona*. Berkeley: University of California Press, 1994.

García, Matt. "Memories of El Monte: Intercultural Dance Halls in Post-World War II Greater Los Angeles." In *Generations of Youth: Youth Cultures and History in Twentieth-century America*, ed. Joe Austin and Michael Willard. New York: New York University Press, 1998.

Garcilazo, Jeffrey M. "McCarthyism, Mexican Americans, and the Los Angeles Committee for Protection of the Foreign-Born, 1950–1954." *Western Historical Quarterly* 32, no. 3 (Autumn 2001): 273–295.

Gardner, Martha. *The Qualities of a Citizen: Women, Immigration, and Citizenship, 1870–1965*. Princeton, NJ: Princeton University Press, 2005.

Geary, Daniel. "Carey McWilliams and Antifascism, 1934–1943." *Journal of American History* 90, no. 3 (December 2003): 912–934.

Gimpel, James G. "Losing Ground or Staying Even: Republicans and the Politics of the Latino Vote." October 2004, Center for Immigration Studies. Online. Available: http://www.cis.org/articles/2004/back1004.html. [Accessed December 14, 2009.]

Girdner, Audrie and Anne Loftis. *The Great Betrayal: The Evacuation of the Japanese-Americans during World War II.* Toronto: The Macmillan Company, 1969.

Goldstein, Eric L. *The Price of Whiteness: Jews, Race, and American Identity.* Princeton, NJ: Princeton University Press, 2006.

Goluboff, Risa L. *The Lost Promise of Civil Rights.* Cambridge: Harvard University Press, 2007.

Gómez-Quiñones, Juan. *Chicano Politics: Reality and Promise, 1940–1990.* Albuquerque: University of New Mexico Press, 1990.

González, Gilbert G. *Chicano Education in the Era of Segregation.* Philadelphia: Balch Institute Press, 1990.

Gordon, Margaret S. *Employment Expansion and Population Growth: The California Experience: 1900–1950.* Berkeley and Los Angeles: University of California Press, 1954.

Gottlieb, Robert, Mark Vallianatos, Regina M. Freer, and Peter Dreier. *The Next Los Angeles: The Struggle for a Livable City.* Berkeley: University of California Press, 2006.

Greenberg, Cheryl. "Black and Jewish Reponses to Japanese Internment." *Journal of American Ethnic History* 14, n0.2 (1995): 3–37.

——. "Negotiating Coalition: Black and Jewish Civil Rights Agencies in the Twentieth Century." In *Struggles in the Promised Land: Toward a History of Black-Jewish Relations in the United States,* ed. Jack Salzman and Cornel West. New York: Oxford University Press, 1997.

——. *Troubling the Waters: Black-Jewish Relations in the American Century.* Princeton, N.J.: Princeton University Press, 2006.

Gregory, James N. *American Exodus: The Dust Bowl Migration and Okie Culture in California.* New York: Oxford University Press, 1989.

Griswold del Castillo, Richard. *The Los Angeles Barrio, 1850–1890.* Berkeley: University of California Press, 1979.

——. "The Los Angeles 'Zoot Suit Riots' Revisited: Mexican and Latin American Perspectives." *Mexican Studies/Estudios Mexicanos* 16, no. 2 (Summer 2000): 367–391.

Grodzins, Morton. *Americans Betrayed: Politics and the Japanese Evacuation.* Chicago: The University of Chicago Press, 1949.

Guglielmo, Thomas A. "Fighting for Caucasian Rights: Mexicans, Mexican Americans, and the Transnational Struggle for Civil Rights Legislation in World War II Texas." *Journal of American History,* 92, no. 4 (March 2006): 1212–1237.

——. *White on Arrival: Italians, Race, Color, and Power in Chicago, 1890–1945.* New York: Oxford University Press, 2003.

Gutiérrez, David G. *Walls and Mirrors: Mexican Americans Mexican Immigrants, and the Politics of Ethnicity.* Berkeley: University of California Press, 1995.

Hacker, Doug. "Aliens in Montana." *American History* 36, no. 2 (2001): 32–36.

Haglund, David G. *Latin America and the Transformation of U.S. Strategic Thought, 1936–1940.* Albuquerque: University of New Mexico Press, 1984.

Hall, Jacqueline Dowd. "The Long Civil Rights Movement and the Political Uses of the Past." *Journal of American History* 91, no. 4 (March 2005): 1233–1263.

Hart, Justin. "Making Democracy Safe for the World: Race, Propaganda, and the Transformation of U.S. Foreign Policy during World War II." *Pacific Historical Review,* 73, no. 1 (February 2004): 49–84.

Harvey, Richard B. *Earl Warren: Governor of California.* New York: Exposition Press, 1969.

Hayashi, Brian Masaru. *"For the Sake of Our Japanese Brethren": Assimilation, Nationalism, and Protestantism among the Japanese of Los Angeles, 1895–1942.* Stanford: Stanford University Press, 1995.

Haynes, John Earl. *Red Scare or Red Menace?: American Communism and Anticommunism in the Cold War Era.* Chicago: Ivan R. Dee, 1996.

Heale, M.J. *American Anticommunism: Combating the Enemy Within, 1830–1970.* Johns Hopkins University Press, 1990.

Healey, Dorothy Ray and Maurice Isserman. *California Red: A Life in the American Communist Party.* Urbana: University of Illinois Press, 1993.

Herman, Felicia. "Hollywood, Nazism and the Jews, 1933–41." *American Jewish History* 89, no. 1 (March 2001): 61–89.

——. "Jewish Leaders and the Motion Picture Industry." In *California Jews,* ed. Ava F. Kahn and Marc Dollinger, 102–08. Boston, MA: Brandeis University Press, 2003.

Higham, John. "Multiculturalism and Universalism: A History and Critique." *American Quarterly* 45, n0.2 (June 1993): 195–219.

——. *Strangers in the Land: Patterns of American Nativism, 1860–1925.* New Brunswick, N.J.: Rutgers University Press, 1955; reprint, New York: Atheneum, 1963, 2nd edition.

Hing, Bill Ong. *Making and Remaking Asian America through Immigration Policy, 1850–1990.* Stanford: Stanford University Press, 1993.

Hoffman, Abraham. *Unwanted Mexican Americans in the Great Depression: Repatriation Pressures 1929–1939.* Tucson: University of Arizona Press, 1974.

Hollinger, David. *Postethnic America: Beyond Multiculturalism.* New York: BasicBooks, 1995.

Honey, Maureen, ed., *Bitter Fruit: African American Women in World War II.* Columbia, Missouri: University of Missouri Press, 1999.

Honey, Michael K. "Operation Dixie, the Red Scare, and the Defeat of Southern Labor Organizing." In *American Labor and the Cold War: Grassroots Politics and Postwar Political Culture,* ed. Robert W. Cherny, William Issel, Kieran Walsh Taylor, 216–244. New Brunswick, NJ: Rutgers University Press, 2004.

Horne, Gerald. *Black and Red: W.E.B. DuBois and the Afro-American Response to the Cold War 1944–1963.* Albany, NY: State University of New York Press, 1986.

——. "Black Fire: 'Riot and 'Revolt' in Los Angeles, 1965 and 1992," in *Seeking El Dorado: African Americans in California,* ed. Lawrence B. de Graaf, Kevin Mulroy, and Quintard Taylor. Los Angeles: Autry Museum of Western Heritage in association with University of Washington Press, 2001.

——. *Fire This Time: The Watts Uprising and the 1960s.* Charlottesville: University Press of Virginia, 1995.

Horowitz, Daniel. *Betty Friedan and the Making of the Feminine Mystique: the American Left, the Cold War, and Modern Feminism.* Amherst, MA: University of Massachusetts Press, 1998.

Horwitt, Sanford D. *Let Them Call Me Rebel: Saul Alinsky—His Life and Legacy.* New York: Alfred A. Knopf, 1989.

Hosang, Daniel Martinez. "Remaking Liberalism in the Sunbelt West: California's 1964 Fair Housing Ballot Measure and the Politics of Racial Innocence." In *Sunbelt Rising: The Politics of Space, Place and Region in the American South and Southwest*, ed. Darren Dochuk and Michelle Nickerson. Philadelphia: University of Pennsylvania Press, forthcoming.

Hosokawa, Bill. *JACL: In Quest of Justice.* New York: William Morrow and Company, Inc., 1982.

Howe, Irving. *The World of Our Fathers.* New York: Harcourt Brace Jovanovich, 1976.

Hurewitz, Daniel. *Bohemian Los Angeles and the Making of Modern Politics.* Berkeley: University of California Press, 2007.

Hurt, R. Douglas. *The Dust Bowl: an Agricultural and Social History.* Chicago : Nelson-Hall, 1981.

Hutchinson, Earl Ofari. "Los Angeles School Brawls Expose Black-Latino Tension." April 27, 2005, *New American Media (Pacific News Service* project). Online. Available: http://news.ncmonline.com/news/view_article. html?article_id=00c83b0739520c4f380469df2c520743. [Accessed December 14, 2009.]

——. "Old Civil Rights Groups Missing-in-Action as Immigrants Hit the Streets." March 27, 2006, *Pacific News Service.* Online. Available: http://news. pacificnews.org/news/view_article.html?article_id=b3543d592890b6a801a6c 4a84d0f6d5f. [Accessed December 14, 2009.]

Ignatiev, Noel. *How the Irish Became White.* New York: Routledge, 1995.

Issel, William. "Jews and Catholics against Prejudice." In *California Jews*, ed. Ava F. Kahn and Marc Dollinger. Boston, MA: Brandeis University Press, 2003.

——. "Jews and Catholics Against Prejudice: Interfaith Cooperation in the San Francisco Civil Rights Campaign, 1940–1960," http://bss.sfsu.edu/issel/ jews%20catholics.htm

Jacobsen, Matthew Frye. *Special Sorrows: The Diasporic Imagination of Irish, Polish, and Jewish Immigrants in the United States.* Cambridge: Harvard University Press, 1995.

——. *Whiteness of a Different Color: European Immigrants and the Alchemy of Race.* Cambridge: Harvard University Press, 1998.

Janken, Kenneth R. "From Colonial Liberation to Cold War Liberalism: Walter White, the NAACP, and Foreign Affairs, 1941–1955." *Ethnic and Racial Studies* 21, no. 6 (November 1998): 1074–1095.

Japanese Chamber of Commerce of Southern California. *Japanese in Southern California: "A History of 70 Years."* Los Angeles: Japanese Chamber of Commerce of Southern California, 1960.

Johnson, Gaye Theresa. "Constellations of Struggle: Luisa Moreno, Charlotta Bass, and the Legacy for Ethnic Studies." *Aztlan: A Journal of Chicano Studies* 33, no. 1 (2008): 155–172.

Johnson, James H. Jr., Walter C. Farrell, Jr., and Chandra Guinn. "Immigration Reform and the Browning of America: Tensions, Conflicts and Community Instability in Metropolitan Los Angeles." International Migration Review 31, no. 4 (Special Issue: Immigrant Adaptation and Native-Born Responses in the Making of Americans, Winter, 1997):1055–1095.

Johnson, Kevin R. "Hernández v. Texas: Legacies of Justice and Injustice" (November 2004). UC Davis Law, Legal Studies Research Paper No. 19. Online. Available: http://ssrn.com/abstract=625403 [Accessed December 15, 2009]

Josephy, Alvin M., Jr., Joane Nagel, and Troy Johnson, eds. Red Power: the American Indians' Fight for Freedom. New York: American Heritage Press, 1971; reprint Lincoln: University of Nebraska Press, 1999.

Kahn, Ava F. and Marc Dollinger, eds. California Jews. Boston, MA: Brandeis University Press, 2003.

Kaplowitz, Craig A. LULAC, Mexican Americans, and National Policy. College Station, TX: Texas A&M University Press, 2005.

Kaufman, Jonathan. "Blacks and Jews: The Struggle in the Cities." In Struggles in the Promised Land: Toward a History of Black-Jewish Relations in the United States, ed. Jack Salzman and Cornel West. New York: Oxford University Press, 1997.

Kellogg, Charles Flint. NAACP: A History of the National Association for the Advancement of Colored People. Baltimore: The Johns Hopkins Press, 1967.

Kelley, Robin D.G. Hammer and Hoe: Alabama Communists during the Great Depression. Chapel Hill: University of North Carolina Press, 1990.

Kennedy, David M. Freedom from Fear: the American People in Depression and War, 1929–1945. New York: Oxford University Press, 1999.

Kessner, Thomas. The Golden Door: Italian and Jewish Immigrant Mobility in New York City, 1880–1915. New York: Oxford University Press, 1977.

Kitano, Harry H. L. and Roger Daniels, eds. Asian Americans: Emerging Minorities. Englewood Cliffs, NJ: Prentice Hall, 1988.

Klarman, Michael J. "How Brown Changed Race Relations: the Backlash Thesis." Journal of American History 81, no. 1 (1994): 81–118.

Klehr, Harvey. Communist Cadre: the Social Background of the American Communist Party Elite. Stanford: Stanford University Press, 1978.

Kleinman, Mark L. A World of Hope, a World of Fear: Henry A. Wallace, Reinhold Niebuhr, and American Liberalism. Columbus: Ohio State University Press, 2000.

Korstad, Robert and Nelson Lichtenstein. "Opportunities Found and Lost: Labor, Radicals, and the Early Civil Rights Movement." Journal of American History 75, no. 3 (1988): 786–811.

Krammer, Arnold. Undue Process: The Untold Story of America's German Alien Internees. Lanham, Md.: Rowman & Littlefield, 1997.

Kropp, Phoebe. California Vieja: Culture and Memory in a Modern American Place. Berkeley: University of California Press, 2006.

Kryder, Daniel. Divided Arsenal: Race and the American State during World War II. New York: Cambridge University Press, 2000.

Kurashige, Lon. Japanese American Celebration and Conflict: a History of Ethnic Identity and Festival in Los Angeles, 1934–1990. Berkeley: University of California Press, 2002.

Kurashige, Scott. *The Shifting Grounds of Race: Black and Japanese Americans in the Making of Multiethnic Los Angeles.* Princeton N.J.: Princeton University Press, 2008.

——. "The Many Facets of Brown: Integration in a Multiracial Society." *Journal of American History* 91, no 1 (June 2004): 56–68.

Kutler, Stanely I. *The American Inquisition: Justice and Injustice in the Cold War.* New York: Hill and Wang, 1982.

Kuznets, Simon Smith and Dorothy Swaine Thomas. *Population Redistribution and Economic Growth, United States, 1870–1950,* vol. I. Philadelphia: American Philosophical Society, 1957.

Lau, Peter F., ed. *From Grassroots to the Supreme Court: Exploration of* Brown v. Board of Education *and American Democracy.* Durham: Duke University Press, 2004.

Lawson, Steven F. and Charles Payne. *Debating the Civil Rights Movement: The View from the Nation in Debating the Civil Rights Movement, 1945–1968.* Lanham, MD: Rowman & Littlefield Publishers, Inc., 1998.

Leader, Leonard. *Los Angeles and the Great Depression.* New York: Garland Publishing, 1991.

Leonard, David J. "'The Little Fuehrer Invades Los Angeles': The Emergence of a Black-Jewish Coalition after World War II." *American Jewish History* 92, no. 1 (March 2004): 81–102.

Leonard, Karen Tsaksen. *Making Ethnic Choices: California's Punjabi Mexican Americans.* Philadelphia: Temple University Press, 1992.

Leonard, Kevin Allen. *The Battle for Los Angeles: Racial Ideology and World War II.* Albuquerque: University of New Mexico Press, 2006.

——. "'In the Interest of All Races': African Americans and Interracial Cooperation in Los Angeles during and after World War II." In *Seeking El Dorado: African Americans in California,* ed. Lawrence B. de Graaf, Kevin Mulroy, and Quintard Taylor. Los Angeles: Autry Museum of Western Heritage, in association with the University of Washington Press, 2001.

Leong, Karen J. "Foreign Policy, National Identity, and Citizenship: The Roosevelt White House and the Expediency of Repeal." *Journal of American Ethnic History* 2, no. 4 (summer 2003): 3–30.

Lerner, Michael. *Jews and Blacks: Let the Healing Begin.* New York: G. P. Putnam's Sons, 1995.

Leuchtenburg, William E. *Franklin D. Roosevelt and the New Deal, 1932–1940.* New York: Harper & Row, 1963.

Levy, David W. *FDR's Fireside Chats.* Norman: University of Oklahoma Press, 1992.

Liebman, Arthur. *Jews and the Left.* New York: Wiley, 1979.

Limerick, Patricia Nelson. "The Case of the Premature Departure: The Trans-Mississippi West and American History Textbooks." *Journal of American History* 78, no. 4 (March 1992): 1390–1391.

——. *The Legacy of Conquest: the Unbroken Past of the American West.* New York: W.W. Norton & Company, Inc., 1987.

López, Ian Haney. *Racism on Trial: the Fight for Chicano Justice.* Cambridge, MA: Belknap Press, 2004.

——. *White by Law: The Legal Construction of Race.* New York: NYU Press, 1996.

Lotchin, Roger W. *The Bad City in the Good War: San Francisco, Los Angeles, Oakland and San Diego*. Bloomington: Indiana University Press, 2003.

——. *Fortress California, 1910–1961: From Warfare to Welfare*. New York: Oxford University Press, 1992.

——. "The Impending Western Urban Past: an Essay on the Twentieth-Century West." In *Researching Western History: Topics in the Twentieth Century*, ed. Gerald D. Nash and Richard W. Etulain, ed. Albuquerque: The University of New Mexico, 1997.

Louie, Steve and Glenn K. Omatsu, eds. *Asian Americans: the Movement and the Moment*. Los Angeles, CA: UCLA Asian American Studies Center Press, 2001.

Lothrop, Gloria Ricci. "Unwelcome in Freedom's Land: the Impact of World War II on Italian Aliens in Southern California." *Southern California Quarterly* 81, no. 4 (1999): 507–544.

Lowitt, Richard. *The New Deal and the West*. Bloomington: Indiana University Press, 1984.

Lubin, Alex. "What's Love Got to Do with It? The Politics of Race and Marriage in the California Supreme Court's 1948 *Perez v. Sharp* Decision." Organization of American Historians *Magazine of History* 18 (July 2004): 31–34.

Macias, Anthony. "Bringing Music to the People: Race, Urban Culture, and Municipal Politics in Postwar Los Angeles." *American Quarterly* 56, no. 3 (September 2004): 693–717.

——. *Mexican American Mojo: Popular Music, Dance, and Urban Culture in Los Angeles, 1935–1968*. Durham, NC: Duke University Press, 2008.

MacLean, Nancy. *Freedom is Not Enough: the Struggle for the American Workplace*. Cambridge: Harvard University Press, 2006.

Manzano, Sylvia. "Latinos in the Sunbelt: Political Implications of Demographic Change." In *Sunbelt Rising: The Politics of Space, Place and Region in the American South and Southwest*, ed. Darren Dochuk and Michelle Nickerson. Philadelphia: University of Pennsylvania Press, forthcoming.

Marable, Manning. *Race, Reform, and Rebellion: the Second Reconstruction in Black America, 1945–1990*. Jackson, University Press of Mississippi Press: 1984; 1991 reprint.

Marks, Frederick W. III. *Wind Over Sand: The Diplomacy of Franklin Roosevelt*. Athens: University of Georgia Press, 1988.

Martin, Tony. "March on Washington Movement." *Journal of African-Afro-American Affairs* 3, no. 1 (1979): 63–69.

May, Elaine Tyler. *Homeward Bound: American Families in the Cold War Era*. New York: Basic Books, 1988.

May, Lary. *The Big Tomorrow: Hollywood and the Politics of the American Way* Chicago: University of Chicago Press, 2000.

——, ed. *Recasting America: Culture and Politics in the Age of the Cold War*. Chicago: University of Chicago Press, 1989.

Mayo, Louise A. *The Ambivalent Image: Nineteenth-Century America's Perception of the Jew*. Cranbury, NJ: Associated University Presses, Inc., 1988.

Mazón, Mauricio. *The Zoot-Suit Riots*. Austin: University of Texas Press, 1984.

McAuliffe, Mary Sperling. *Crisis on the Left: Cold War Politics and American Liberals, 1947–1954*. Amherst: The University of Massachusetts Press, 1978.

MacDougall, Curtis D. *Gideon's Army.* New York: Marzani & Munsell, 1965.

McDougal, Dennis. *Privileged Son: Otis Chandler and the Rise and Fall of the L.A. Times Dynasty.* Cambridge, MA: Perseus Publishing, 2001.

McGirr, Lisa. *Suburban Warriors: The Origins of the New American Right.* Princeton, N.J.: Princeton University Press, 2001.

McHaney, Sharon E. et al. "Detroit's 1943 Riot." *Michigan History* 77, no. 3 (1993): 34–39.

McLean, Adrienne L. *Being Rita Hayworth: Labor, Identity, and Hollywood Stardom.* Piscataway, NJ: Rutgers University Press, 2004.

McWilliams, Carey. *The Education of Carey McWilliams.* New York: Simon and Schuster, 1978.

———. *Factories in the Field: The Story of Migratory Farm Labor in California.* Santa Barbara: Peregrine Smith, 1935.

———. *It Can Happen Here: Active Anti-Semitism in Los Angeles.* Los Angeles: American League against War and Fascism and Jewish Anti-Nazi League of Southern California, 1935.

———. *North from Mexico: the Spanish-Speaking People of the United States.* Philadelphia: J. B. Lippincott Co., 1949; 2nd ed. New York: Greenwood Press, 1968.

———. *Southern California Country: An Island on the Land.* New York: Duell, Sloan, and Pearce, 1946.

Mechner, Jordan. "Chavez Ravine: A Los Angeles Story." Bullfrog Films, JAM Flicks, LLC, 2004.

Meriwether, James H. *Proudly We Can Be Africans: Black Americans and Africa, 1935–1961.* Chapel Hill: University of North Carolina Press, 1992.

Meyerowitz, Joanne, ed. *Not June Cleaver: Women and Gender in Postwar America, 1945–1960.* Philadelphia: Temple University Press, 1994.

Meyerson, Harold. "A City Hesitates at Political Change." June 8, 2001, *New York Times.* Online. Available: http://www.nytimes.com/2001/06/08/opinion/a-city-hesitates-at-political-change.html. [Accessed December 14, 2009.]

Miller, Loren. *The Petitioners: The Story of the Supreme Court of the United States and the Negro.* New York: Pantheon Books, 1966.

Mink, Gwendolyn. *The Wages of Motherhood: Inequality in the Welfare State, 1917–1942.* Ithaca, N.Y.: Cornell University Press, 1995.

Mitchell, Daniel J.B. "Impeding Earl Warren: California's Health Care Plan that Wasn't and What Might Have Been." *Journal of Health Politics, Policy and Law* 27.6 (2002) 947–976.

Model, Paul. "The 1965 Watts Rebellion: The Self-Definition of a Community." *Radical America* 24, no. 2 (1990): 74–88.

Modell, John. *The Economics and Politics of Racial Accommodation: The Japanese of Los Angeles, 1900–1942.* Urbana: The University of Illinois Press, 1977.

Mohl, Raymond A. *South of the South: Jewish Activists and the Civil Rights Movement in Miami, 1945–1960.* Gainesville: University Press of Florida, 2004.

Molina, Natalia. *Fit to be Citizens? Public Health and Race in Los Angeles, 1879–1939.* Berkeley: University of California Press, 2006.

Moore, Deborah Dash. *To the Golden Cities: Pursuing the American Jewish Dream in Miami and L.A.* New York: The Free Press, 1994.

———. *GI Jews: How World War II Changed a Generation.* Cambridge: Harvard University Press, 2004.

———. *At Home in America: Second Generation New York Jews.* New York: Columbia University Press, 1981.

Morehouse, Maggi M. *Fighting in the Jim Crow Army: Black Men and Women Remember World War II.* New York: Lanham, Rowman & Littlefield, 2000.

Mullins, William H. *Depression and the Urban West Coast, 1929–1933.* Bloomington: Indiana University Press, 1984.

Muñoz, Carlos. *Youth, Identity, Power: the Chicano Movement.* New York: Verso, 1989.

Munroy, Douglas. *Rebirth: Mexican Los Angeles from the Great Migration to the Great Depression.* Berkeley: UC Press, 1999.

Murase, Ichiro Mike. *Little Tokyo: One Hundred Years in Pictures.* Los Angeles: Visual Communications, 1983.

Naison, Mark. *Communists in Harlem during the Depression.* Urbana: University of Illinois Press, 1983.

Nash, Gary and Richard Etulain, eds. *Researching Western History: Topics in the Twentieth Century.* Albuquerque: The University of New Mexico, 1997.

Nash, Gerald D. *The American West in the Twentieth Century: A Short History of an Urban Oasis.* Englewood Cliffs: Prentice-Hall, 1973.

Navasky, Victor. *Naming Names.* New York: Penguin Books, 1982 edition; copyright The Viking Press, 1980.

Ngai, Mai. *Impossible Subjects: Illegal Aliens and the Making of Modern America.* Princeton, N.J.: Princeton University Press, 2003.

Niblo, Stephen R. *War, Diplomacy, and Development: The United States and Mexico, 1938–1954.* Wilmington, Del: Scholarly Resources, 1995.

Nickerson, Michelle. *Mothers of Conservatism: Women and the Postwar Right.* Princeton, N.J.: Princeton University Press, forthcoming.

Novick, Peter. *The Holocaust in American Life.* Boston: Houghton Mifflin, 1999.

Omi, Michael and Howard Winant. *Racial Formation in the United States: from the 1960s to the 1990s.* New York: Routledge, 1994, 2nd ed.

Pagán, Eduardo Obregón. *Murder at the Sleepy Lagoon: Zoot Suits, Race, & Riot in Wartime L.A.* Chapel Hill: University of North Carolina Press, 2003.

Orenstein, Dara. "Void for Vagueness: Mexicans and the Collapse of Miscegenation Law in California." *Pacific Historical Review,* 74 (Aug 2005): 367–408.

Orozco, Cynthia E. *No Mexicans, Women, or Dogs Allowed: the Rise of the Mexican American Civil Rights Movement.* Austin: University of Texas Press, 2009.

Parson, Don. *Making a Better World: Public Housing, the Red Scare, and the Direction of Modern Los Angeles.* Minneapolis: University of Minnesota Press, 2005.

Pascoe, Peggy. "Miscegenation Law, Court Cases, and Ideologies of 'Race' in Twentieth-Century America." *Journal of American History,* 83 (1): 44–69.

———. "Race, Gender, and the Privileges of Property: On the Significance of Miscegenation Law in the U.S. West." In *Over the Edge: Remapping the American West,* ed. V.J. Matsumoto and B. Allmendinger. Berkeley: University of California Press, 1999.

——. *What Comes Naturally: Miscegenation Law and the Making of Race in America.* New York: Oxford University Press, 2009.

Patterson, James T. *Grand Expectations: the United States, 1945–1974.* New York: Oxford University Press, 1996.

Perry, Louis B. and Richard S. Perry. *A History of the Los Angeles Labor Movement, 1911–1941.* Berkeley and Los Angeles: University of California Press, 1963.

Pesotta, Rose. *Bread upon the Waters.* Dodd, Mead & Company, 1944.

Pike, Fredrick B. *FDR's Good Neighbor Policy: Sixty Years of Generally Gentle Chaos.* Austin: University of Texas Press, 1995.

Pintar, Laurie. "Behind the Scenes: Bronco Billy and the Realities of Work in Open Shop Hollywood." In *Metropolis in the Making: Los Angeles in the 1920s,* ed. Tom Sitton and William Deverell. Berkeley: University of California Press, 2001.

Pitt, Leonard. *The Decline of the Californios: A Social History of the Spanish-Speaking Californians.* Berkeley: University of California Press, 1966.

——. *LA A to Z: An Encyclopedia of the City and County.* Berkeley: University of California Press, 1997.

Pitti, Stephen J. *The Devil in Silicon Valley: Northern California, Race, and Mexican Americans.* Princeton, N.J.: Princeton University Press, 2003.

Plummer, Brenda Gayle. *Rising Wind: Black Americans and U.S. Foreign Affairs, 1935–1960.* Chapel Hill: University of North Carolina Press, 1996.

——, ed. *Window on Freedom: Race, Civil Rights, and Foreign Affairs 1945–1988.* Chapel Hill: University of North Carolina Press, 2003.

Pollack, Jack Harrison. *Earl Warren: the Judge Who Changed America.* New Jersey: Prentice-Hall, 1979.

Pritchett, Wendell E. "A Local and National Story: The Civil Rights Movement in Postwar Washington, D.C." *History Now: American History Online* 8 (June 2006) [http://www.historynow.org/06_2006/historian3.html]

Pulido, Laura. *Black, Brown, Yellow and Left: Radical Activism in Los Angeles.* Berkeley: University of California Press, 2006.

Raineri, Vivian McGuckin. *The Red Angel: the Life and Times of Elaine Black Yoneda, 1906–1988.* New York: International Publishers Co., Inc., 1991.

Ramírez, Catherine S. *The Woman in the Zoot Suit: Gender, Nationalism, and the Cultural Politics of Memory.* Durham, North Carolina: Duke University Press, 2009.

Raphael, Marc Lee, Mark Dollinger, and Ava F. Kahn, ed. *Jewish Life in the American West: Perspectives on Migration, Settlement, and Community.* Los Angeles: Autry Museum of Western Heritage, 2002.

Rawls, James J. and Walton Bean. *California: an Interpretive History.* Boston: McGraw Hill, 1968; 7th ed. 1997.

Record, Wilson. *The Negro and the Communist Party.* Chapel Hill: University of North Carolina Press, 1951; 2nd ed. New York: Atheneum, 1971.

——. *Race and Radicalism: The NAACP and the Communist Party in Conflict.* Ithaca: Cornell University Press, 1964.

Richardson, Peter. *American Prophet: the Life & Work of Carey McWilliams.* Ann Arbor: University of Michigan Press, 2005.

Rischin, Moses and John Livingston. *Jews of the American West.* Detroit: Wayne State University Press, 1991.

Rischin, Moses. *The Jews of the West: the Metropolitan Years*. Berkeley: Western Jewish History Center, 1979.

Rivas-Rodriguez, Maggie, ed. *Mexican Americans and World War II*. Austin: University of Texas Press, 2005.

Robinson, Armstead L. and Patricia Sullivan, eds. *New Directions in Civil Rights Studies*. Charlottesville: University Press of Virginia, 1991.

Robinson, Greg. *By Order of the President: FDR and the Internment of Japanese Americans*. Cambridge, MA: Cambridge University Press, 2001.

Robinson, Toni and Greg Robinson. "The Limits of Interracial Coalitions: Méndez v. Westminster *Reexamined*." In *Racial Transformations: Latinos and Asians Remaking the United States*, ed. Nicholas De Genova. Durham, North Carolina: Duke University Press, 2006: 94–119.

Rodríguez, Clara E. *Heroes, Lovers, and Others: The Story of Latinos in Hollywood*. Smithsonian Books, Washington, 2004.

Roediger, David. *The Wages of Whiteness: Race and the Making of the American Working Class*. London: Verso, 1991.

Rogin, Michael. *Blackface, White Noise: Jewish Immigrants in the Hollywood Melting Pot*. Berkeley: University of California Press, 1998.

Romano, Renee. "No Diplomatic Immunity: African Diplomats, the State Department, and Civil Rights, 1961–1964." *Journal of American History* 87, No.2 (2000): 546–579.

Romo, Ricardo. *East Los Angeles: History of a Barrio*. Austin: University of Texas Press, 1983.

Rose, Margaret. "Gender and Civic Activism in Mexican American Barrios in California: The Community Service Organization, 1947–1962." In *Not June Cleaver: Women and Gender in Postwar America, 1945–1960*, ed. Joanne Meyerowitz. Philadelphia: Temple University Press, 1994.

Rosenberg, Jonathan. *How Far the Promised Land? World Affairs and the American Civil Rights Movement from the First World War to Vietnam*. Princeton, N.J.: Princeton University Press, 2005.

Rosner, Shmuel. "Jews and the 2008 Election." *Commentary Magazine*, February 2009. Online. Available: http://www.commentarymagazine.com/viewarticle. cfm/jews-and-the-2008-election-14385. [Accessed December 14, 2009.]

Ross, Fred. *Cesar Chavez at the Beginning: Conquering Goliath*. Keene, California: El Taller Grafico, 1989.

Ruiz, Vicki L. *Cannery Women, Cannery Lives: Mexican Women, Unionization, and the California Food Processing Industry, 1930–1950*. Albuquerque: University of New Mexico Press, 1987.

———. *From Out of the Shadows: Mexican Women in Twentieth-Century America*. New York: Oxford University Press, 1998.

———. "Luisa Moreno and Latina Labor Activism." In *Latina Legacies: Identity, Biography, and Community*, ed. Vicki L. Ruiz and Virginia Sánchez Korrol. New York: Oxford University Press, 2005: 178–84.

———. "Tapestries of Resistance: Episodes of School Segregation and Desegregation in the U.S. West." In *From Grassroots to the Supreme Court: Exploration of* Brown v. Board of Education *and American Democracy*, ed. Peter F. Lau. Durham: Duke University Press, 2004.

——. "Una Mujer Sin Fronteras: Luisa Moreno and Latino Labor Activism." *Pacific Historical Review,* 73 (Feb. 2004): 1–20.

Sachar, Howard M. *A History of the Jews in America.* New York: Alfred A. Knopf, 1992.

Salzman, Jack, and Cornel West, eds. *Struggles in the Promised Land: Toward a History of Black-Jewish Relations in the United States.* New York: Oxford University Press, 1997.

Sánchez, George J. " 'What's Good for Boyle Heights is Good for the Jews': Creating Multiracialism on the Eastside during the 1950s." *American Quarterly Special Edition, Los Angeles and the Future of Urban Cultures* 56, no. 3 (Sept 2004): 633–661.

——. *Becoming Mexican American: Ethnicity, Culture and Identity in Chicano Los Angeles, 1900–1945.* New York: Oxford University Press, 1993.

Saunders, Kay and Roger Daniels, eds. *Alien Justice: Wartime Internment in Australia and North America.* St. Lucia, Australia: University of Queensland Press, 2000.

Savage, Barbara Dianne. *Broadcasting Freedom: Radio, War, and the Politics of Race, 1938–1948.* Charlotte: University of North Carolina Press, 1999.

Saxton, Alexander. *The Indispensable Enemy: Labor and the Anti-Chinese Movement in California.* Berkeley: University of California Press, 1971.

Schary, Dore. *Heydey: an Autobiography.* Boston: Little, Brown and Company, 1979.

Schlesinger, Arthur. *The Vital Center: the Politics of Freedom.* New York: Houghton Mifflin Co., 1949.

Schrecker, Ellen. *Many are the Crimes: McCarthyism in America.* New Jersey: Princeton University Press, 1998.

Schultz, Debra L. *Going South: Jewish Women in the Civil Rights Movement.* New York: New York University Press, 2001.

Schuparra, Kurt. *Triumph of the Right: the Rise of the California Conservative Movement, 1945–1966.* Armonk, NY: M. E. Sharpe, 1988.

"Segregation in Public Schools—a Violation of 'Equal Protection of the Laws.' " *Yale Law* Journal 56 (1947): 1059–67.

"Segregation in Schools as a Violation of the XIVth Amendment." *Columbia Law Review* 47 (March 1947): 325–327.

Saito, Leland. *Race and Politics: Asian Americans, Latinos, and Whites in a Los Angeles Suburb.* Champaign, IL: University of Illinois Press, 1998.

Self, Robert O. *American Babylon: Race and the Struggle for Postwar Oakland.* Princeton, N.J.: Princeton University Press, 2003.

Shogan, Robert and Tom Craig. *The Detroit Race Riot: A Study in Violence.* Philadelphia: Chilton Books, 1964.

Sides, Josh A. *L.A. City Limits: African American Los Angeles from the Great Depression to the Present.* Berkeley: University of California Press, 2004.

——. " 'You Understand My Condition': The Civil Rights Congress in the Los Angeles African-American Community, 1946–1952." *Pacific Historical Review* 67, no. 4 (1998): 233–57.

Singh, Nikhil Pal. *Black is a Country: Race and the Unfinished Struggle for Democracy.* Cambridge: Harvard University Press, 2004.

Sitkoff, Harvard. "The Detroit Race Riot of 1943." *Michigan History* 53 (Fall 1969): 183–206.

——. *A New Deal for Blacks: The Emergence of Civil Rights as a National Issue.* New York: Oxford University Press, 1978.

——. *The Struggle for Black Equality, 1954–1992.* New York: Hill and Wang, 1993.

Sitton, Tom. *Los Angeles Transformed: Fletcher Bowron's Urban Reform Revival, 1938–1953.* Albuquerque: University of New Mexico Press, 2005.

Sitton, Tom and William Deverell, eds. *Metropolis in the Making: Los Angeles in the 1920s.* Berkeley: University of California Press, 2001.

Smith, Jack. "The Great Los Angeles Air Raid." In *Los Angeles: Biography of a City,* ed. John and Laree Caughey. Berkeley: University of California Press, 1976.

Somkin, Fred. "How Vanzetti Said Goodbye." *Journal of American History* 68, no. 2 (1981): 298–312.

Sonenshein, Raphael J. "Coalition Building in Los Angeles: The Bradley Years and Beyond." In *Seeking El Dorado: African Americans in California,* ed. Lawrence B. de Graaf, Kevin Mulroy, and Quintard Taylor. Los Angeles: Autry Museum of Western Heritage, in association with the University of Washington Press, 2001: 450–473.

——. *Politics in Black and White: Race and Power in Los Angeles.* Princeton, New Jersey: Princeton University Press, 1993.

Starr, Kevin. *The Dream Endures: California Enters the 1940s.* New York: Oxford University Press, 1997.

Stein, Walter J. *California and the Dust Bowl Migration.* Westport, Conn.: Greenwood Press, 1973.

Stephan, Alexander. *"Communazis": FBI Surveillance of German Emigrae Writers.* New Haven: Yale University Press, 2000, translated.

Stimson, Grace Heilman. *Rise of the Labor Movement in Los Angeles.* Berkeley: University of California Press, 1955.

Sugrue, Thomas. *The Origins of the Urban Crisis: Race and Inequality in Postwar Detroit.* Princeton, N.J.: Princeton University Press, 1996.

——. *Sweet Land of Liberty: the Forgotten Struggle for Civil Rights in the North.* New York: Random House, 2008.

Sullivan, Patricia. *Days of Hope: Race and Democracy in the New Deal Era.* Chapel Hill : University of North Carolina Press, 1996.

Svonkin, Stuart. *Jews against Prejudice: American Jews and the Fight for Civil Liberties.* New York: Columbia University Press, 1997.

Takahashi, Jere. *Nisei/Sansei: Shifting Japanese American Identities and Politics.* Philadelphia: Temple University Press, 1997.

Takaki, Ronald. *Double Victory: A Multicultural History of America in World War II.* Boston: Little, Brown and Company, 2000.

——. *Strangers from a Different Shore: A History of Asian Americans.* New York: Penguin Books, 1989.

Taylor, Quintard. *In Search of the Racial Frontier: African Americans in the American West, 1528–1990.* New York: W. W. Norton, 1998.

tenBroek, Jacobus, Edward Barnhart, and Floyd Matson. *Prejudice, War and the Constitution: Causes and Consequences of the Evacuation of the Japanese Americans in World War II.* Berkeley: University of California Press, 1954; reprint 1968.

Theoharis, Athan. *Seeds of Repression: Harry S. Truman and the Origins of McCarthyism.* Chicago: Quadrangle Books, 1971.

Theoharis, Jeanne. "Black Freedom Studies: Re-imagining and Redefining the Fundamentals." *History Compass* 4, no. 2 (2006).

——, Komozi Woodard and Charles Payne. *Groundwork: Local Black Freedom Movements in America.* New York: New York University Press, 2005.

Gaines, Kevin. *American Africans: Black Expatriates and the Civil Rights Era.* Chapel Hill: University of North Carolina Press, 2006.

Thernstrom, Stephan. *The Other Bostonians: Poverty and Progress in the American Metropolis, 1880–1970.* Cambridge: Harvard University Press, 1973.

Tolbert, Emory J. *The UNIA and Black Los Angeles: Ideology and Community in the American Garvey Movement.* Los Angeles: Center for Afro-American Studies, University of California, 1980.

Toll, William. *The Making of an Ethnic Middle Class: Portland Jewry over Four Generations.* Albany: State University of New York Press, 1982.

Tygiel, Jules. *The Great Los Angeles Swindle: Oil, Stocks, and Scandal during the Roaring Twenties.* New York: Oxford University Press, 1994.

Tyson, Timothy B. *Radio Free Dixie: Robert F. Williams and the Roots of Black Power.* Chapel Hill: University of North Carolina Press, 1999.

Uelmen, Gerald F. "Remembering Stanley Mosk." Undated, *Forum* (California Attorneys for Criminal Justice publication). Online. Available: *http://www.cacj.org/forum_articles_memory_stanley_mosk-p.htm.* [Accessed April 18, 2007.]

Underwood, Katherine. "Pioneering Minority Representation: Edward Roybal and the Los Angeles City Council, 1949–1962." *Pacific Historical Review* 66 (August 1997): 399–425.

Valencia, Richard. "The Mexican American Struggle for Equal Educational Opportunity in *Mendez v. Westminster:* Helping to Pave the Way for *Brown v. Board of Education.*" *The Teachers College Record* 107, no. 3 (March 2005): 389–423.

Vargas, Zaragosa. "In the Years of Darkness and Torment: The Early Mexican American Struggle for Civil Rights, 1945–1963." *New Mexico Historical Review* 76 (2001): 383–414.

——. *Labor Rights are Civil Rights: Mexican American Workers in Twentieth-Century America.* Princeton, N.J.: Princeton University Press, 2005.

Varzally, Allison. *Making a Non-White America: Californians Coloring outside Ethnic Lines, 1925–1955.* Berkeley: University of California Press, 2008.

von Eschen, Penny. *Race Against Empire: Black Americans and Anticolonialism 1937–1957.* Ithaca: Cornell University Press, 1997.

Von Kanel, Joe and Hal Quinley. "Exit polls: Obama Wins Big among Young, Minority Voters." November 3, 2008, CNN Politics. Online. Available: http://www.cnn.com/2008/POLITICS/11/04/exit.polls/. [Accessed December 14, 2009.]

Vorspan, Max and Lloyd P. Gartner. *History of the Jews of Los Angeles.* San Marino, California: The Huntington Library, 1970.

Waldinger, Roger and Mehdi Bozorgmehr, eds. *Ethnic Los Angeles.* New York: Russell Sage Foundation, 1996.

Wall, Wendy. *Inventing the "American Way": The Politics of Consensus from the New Deal to the Civil Rights Movement.* New York: Oxford University Press, 2008.

Walton, Richard J. *Henry Wallace, Harry Truman, and the Cold War.* New York: the Viking Press, 1976.

Waltzer, Kenneth. "The New History of American Communism." *Reviews in American History* (June 1983): 259–67.

Warren, Earl. *The Memoirs of Earl Warren.* New York: Doubleday and Company, 1977.

Webb, Clive. *Fight against Fear: Southern Jews and Black Civil Rights.* Athens: University of Georgia Press, 2001.

Weber, Devra. *Dark Sweat, White Gold: California Farm Workers, Cotton, and the New Deal.* Berkeley: University of California Press, 1994.

Weglyn, Michi. *Years of Infamy: The Untold Story of America's Concentration Camps.* New York: Morrow Quill Paperbacks, 1976.

Wei, William. *The Asian American Movement.* Philadelphia: Temple University Press, 1993.

Wenger, Beth S. *New York Jews and the Great Depression: Uncertain Promise.* New Haven: Yale University Press, 1996.

West, Elliott. "Expanding the Racial Frontier," *The Historian* 66, no. 3 (Sept 2004): 552–56.

——. "Reconstructing Race," *Western Historical Quarterly* 34 (Spring 2003): 6–26.

Whitaker, Matthew C. *Race Work: The Rise of Civil Rights in the Urban West.* Lincoln: University of Nebraska Press, 2005.

White, G. Edward. *Earl Warren a Public Life.* New York: Oxford University Press, 1982.

White, Richard. *"It's Your Misfortune and None of My Own": A History of the American West.* Norman, Oklahoma: University of Oklahoma Press, 1991.

——. "Race Relations in the American West." *American Quarterly* 38, no. 3 (1986): 396–416.

Whitfield, Stephen J. *The Culture of the Cold War.* Baltimore: Johns Hopkins University Press, 1991; 2nd edition, 1996.

Widener, Daniel. Black Arts West: Culture and Struggle in Postwar Los Angeles. Durham: Duke University Press, 2010.

——. "Perhaps the Japanese are to be Thanked? Asia, Asian Americans, and the Construction of Black California." *Positions: East Asia Cultures Critique,* 11.1 (2003), 135–181.

Wild, Mark. *Street Meeting: Multiethnic Neighborhoods in Early Twentieth-Century Los Angeles.* Berkeley: University of California Press, 2005.

Wilkerson, Doxey Alphonso. *Why Negroes are Joining the Communist Party.* NY: CPUSA, 1946.

Wilkins, Roy with Tom Mathews. *Standing Fast: the Autobiography of Roy Wilkins.* New York: the Viking Press, 1982.

Williams, William Appleman. *The Tragedy of American Diplomacy,* 2d ed., rev. and enl. New York: Dell Publishing, Delta Books, 1972.

Wollenberg, Charles. *All Deliberate Speed: Segregation and Exclusion in California Schools, 1855–1975.* Berkeley: University of California Press, 1976.

Wong, K. Scott and Sucheng Chan, eds. *Claiming America: Constructing Chinese American Identities during the Exclusion Era.* Philadelphia: Temple University Press, 1998.

Wood, Bryce. *The Making of the Good Neighbor Policy.* New York: Columbia University Press, 1961.

Woodard, Komozi. *A Nation Within a Nation: Amiri Baraka (LeRoi Jones) and Black Power Politics.* Chapel Hill, N.C.: University of North Carolina Press, 1999.

Woods, Jeff. *Black Struggle, Red Scare: Segregation and Anti-communism in the South, 1948–1968.* Baton Rouge: Louisiana State University, 2004.

Wunder, John R., Frances W. Kaye, and Vernon Carstensen, eds. *Americans View their Dust Bowl Experience.* Niwot, Colorado: University Press of Colorado, 1999.

Worster, Donald. *Dust Bowl: the Southern Plains in the 1930s.* New York: Oxford University Press, 1979.

Yoneda, Karl G. *Ganbatte: Sixty-year Struggle of a Kibei Worker.* Los Angeles: Resource Development and Publications, Asian American Studies Center, UCLA, 1983.

Yoo, David K. *Growing up Nisei: Race, Generation, and Culture among Japanese Americans of California, 1924–49.* Urbana: University of Illinois Press, 2000.

Young, William and David E. Kaiser. *Postmortem: New Evidence in the Case of Sacco and Vanzetti.* Amherst: University of Massachusetts Press, 1985.

Yu, Renqiu. *To Save China, To Save Ourselves: the Chinese Hand Laundry Alliance of New York.* Philadelphia: Temple University Press, 1992.

Yung, Judy. *Unbound Feet: a Social History of Chinese Women in San Francisco.* Berkeley: University of California Press, 1995.

Zamora, Emilio. *Claiming Rights and Righting Wrongs in Texas: Mexican Workers and Job Politics during World War II.* College Station: Texas A&M University Press, 2009.

——. "Mexico's Wartime Intervention on Behalf of Mexicans in the United States: A Turning of Tables." In *Mexican Americans & World War II*, ed. Maggie Rivas-Rodriguez. Austin: University of Texas Press, 2005): 221–243.

Zieger, Robert. *The CIO 1935–1955.* Chapel Hill: University of North Carolina Press, 1995.

UNPUBLISHED WORKS

Adler, Patricia Rae. "Watts: from Suburb to Black Ghetto." Ph.D. diss., University of Southern California, 1977.

Apodaca, Maria Linda. "They Kept the Home Fires Burning: Mexican-American Women and Social Change." Ph.D. diss., University of California Irvine, 1994.

Araiza, Lauren. "For Freedom of Other Men: Civil Rights, Black Power, and the United Farm Workers, 1965–1973." Ph.D. diss., University of California Berkeley, 2006.

Beltrán, Mary Caudle. "Bronze Seduction: The Shaping of Latina Stardom in Hollywood Film and Star Publicity." Ph.D. diss, The University of Texas at Austin, 2002.

Bernstein, Shana. "Against the Grain: The National Japanese American Student Relocation Council during World War II." Unpublished Research Paper, Stanford University, 1997.

Bond, J. Max. "The Negro in Los Angeles." Ph.D. diss., University of Southern California, 1936.

Brilliant, Mark. "Color Lines: Civil Rights Struggles on America's 'Racial Frontier,' 1945–1975." Ph.D. diss., Stanford University, 2002; forthcoming Oxford University Press.

Carson, Clayborne. "Reconceptualizing the Black Freedom Struggle at the Dawn of the Twenty-First Century." Paper Delivered at the Annual Meeting of the Organization of American Historians, April 28, 2001.

Chen, Wen-Hui Chung. "Chinese Socio-Cultural Patterns of the Chinese Community in Los Angeles." Ph.D. diss., University of Southern California, 1952.

de Graaf, Lawrence B. "Negro Migration to Los Angeles, 1930 to 1950." Ph.D. diss., University of California Los Angeles, 1962.

Ferreira, Jason. "All Power to the People: A Comparative History of Third World Radicalism in San Francisco, 1968–1980." Ph.D. diss., University of California Berkeley, 2003.

Fisher, James Adolphus. "A History of the Political and Social Development of the Black Community in California." Thesis, State University of New York at Stony Brook, 1971.

Flores, Rubén. "Social Science in the Southwestern Courtroom: A New Understanding of the Development of the NAACP's Legal Strategies in the School Desegregation Cases." B.A. Thesis, Princeton University, 1994.

Fukuoka, Fumiko. "Mutual Life and Aid Among the Japanese in Southern California with Special Reference to Los Angeles." M.A. thesis, University of Southern California, 1937.

Furmanovsky, Michael. "Communism as Jewish Radical Subculture: the Los Angeles Experience, 1920–1939." Paper Delivered at the Annual Meeting of the Organization of American Historians, April 26, 2001.

Hosang, Daniel Wei. "Racial Proposition: 'Genteel Apartheid' in Postwar California." Ph.D. diss.: University of Southern California, 2007.

Kurashige, Scott Tadao. "Transforming Los Angeles: Black and Japanese American Struggles for Racial Equality in the 20th Century." Ph.D. diss., University of California Los Angeles, 2000.

Leonard, Kevin Allen. "Years of Hope, Days of Fear: the Impact of World War II on Race Relations in Los Angeles (California)." Ph.D. diss., University of California Davis, 1992.

Long, Edward Robert. "Loyalty Oaths in California, 1947–1952: The Politics of Anti-Communism." Ph.D. diss., University of California, San Diego, 1981.

Louis, Kit King. "A Study of American-Born and American-Reared Chinese in Los Angeles." M.A. thesis, University of Southern California, 1931.

Lozano, Rosina. "The Struggle for Inclusion: A Study of the Community Service Organization in East Los Angeles, 1947–1951." B.A. thesis, Stanford University, 2000.

Maeda, Daryl. "Forging Asian American Identity: Race, Culture, and the Asian American Movement." Ph.D. Diss, University of Michigan, 2001.

Munroy, Douglas G. "Mexicanos in Los Angeles, 1930–1941: An Ethnic Group in Relation to Class Forces." Ph.D. diss., University of California Los Angeles, 1978.

Parker, Heather Rose. "The Elusive Coalition: African American and Chicano
    Political Organization and Interaction in Los Angeles, 1960–1973." Ph.D.
    diss., University of California, Los Angeles, 1996.
Pitti, Gina Marie. "To 'Hear about God in Spanish': Ethnicity, Church, and
    Community Activism in the San Francisco Archdiocese's Mexican American
    Colonias, 1942–1965," Ph.D. diss., Stanford University, 2003.
Pitti, Stephen. "Quicksilver Community: Mexican Migrations and Politics in the
    Santa Clara Valley, 1800–1960." Ph.D. diss., Stanford University, 1998.
Poulson, Norris. Who Would Have Ever Dreamed? Los Angeles, UCLA
    Department of Special Collections, 1966.
Romero, Tom I. Jr., "Of Race and Rights: Legal Culture, Social Change, and the
    Making of a Multiracial Metropolis, Denver, 1940–1975." Ph.D. diss.,
    University of Michigan, 2004.
Scobie, Ingrid. "Jack B. Tenney: Molder of Anti-Communist Legislation in
    California, 1940–1949." Ph.D. diss., University of Wisconsin, 1970.
Scott, Robin Fitzgerald. "The Mexican-American in the Los Angeles Area,
    1920–1950: From Acquiescence to Activity." Ph.D. diss., University of
    Southern California, 1971.
Sides, Josh A. "Working Away: African American Migration and Community in
    Los Angeles from the Great Depression to 1954." Ph.D. diss., University of
    California, Los Angeles, 1999.
Skinner, Byron Richard. "The Double 'V': the Impact of World War II on Black
    America." Ph.D. diss., University of California Berkeley, 1978.
Smith, Alonzo Nelson. "Black Employment in the Los Angeles Area, 1938–
    1948." Ph.D. diss., University of California Los Angeles, 1978.
Underwood, Katherine. "Process and Politics: Multiracial Electoral Coalition
    Building and Representation in Los Angeles' Ninth District, 1949–1962."
    Ph.D. diss., University of California San Diego, 1992.
Unrau, Harlan D. "The Double V Movement in Los Angeles during the Second
    World War: a Study in Negro Protest." M.A. thesis, California State College
    Fullerton, 1971.
Wall, Wendy. "The Idea of America: Democracy and the Dilemmas of
    Difference, 1935–1965." Ph.D. diss., Stanford University, 1998.
Wild, H. Mark. "A Rumored Congregation: Cross-Cultural Interaction in the
    Immigrant Neighborhoods of Early Twentieth-Century Los Angeles." Ph.D.
    diss., University of California, San Diego, 2000.
Zheng, Mei. "Chinese-Americans in San Francisco and New York City during
    the Anti-Japanese War: 1937–1945." M.A. thesis, University of California Los
    Angeles, 1990.

Index

Note: Page numbers followed by *"f"* denote figures.

Labor activism, 36–39
Labor Herald, 38
LACCCR. *See* Los Angeles County Conference for Community Relations (LACCCR)
LACCHR. *See* Los Angeles County Committee on Human Relations (LACCHR)
LACPFB. *See* Los Angeles Committee for the Protection of the Foreign Born (LACPFB)
Ladies' Aid Society, 27
LaGuardia, Fiorello, 76
Lang, María Durán. *See* Durán, Maria
Lardner, Ring, 88
Larkin, John, 33
Latin America
    Germany's economic control over, 67
    Soviet propaganda in, 6
Lawson, John Howard, 88
Lazarus, Emma, 113
League of United Latin American Citizens (LULAC), 43, 93, 145, 189, 214n17
League of Women Voters
    El Congreso's financial support for, 46
LeBerthon, Ted, 91
Lewis, Leon, 7, 50–51, 55, 81, 96
Liberals, 179–83
Little Tokyo, 21, 108, 109, 153
Lomax, Lucius, 97
López, Frank, 39, 88
Los Angeles, 16–27, 185–99, 211n2
    African Americans migration to, 30
    anti-Nazi rally in, 54f
    Asian-origin populations migration to, 30
    black children in schools, 20
    Chinese migration to, 30
    cooperative activism in, 185
    discrimination against Mexican-origin people, 66–72
    employment discrimination in, 21–22, 24, 31
    fears of an attack on, 64
    housing crisis in, 62

immigrant population in, 16–20, 19f
interracial civil rights activists at work in, 7
Japanese American Young Democrats in, 34
Japanese migration to, 30
Jewish migration to, 30
labor activism in, 36–39
local communist registration ordinance, 7
Mexican migration to, 30
Nazi activities in, 49–55
organized labor movement in, 22
population growth in, 16
restrictive housing covenants, 23–24
trade unionism in, 37
"white spot" of the nation, 22–23
Los Angeles Bar Association, 111
Los Angeles Catholic Interracial Council, 192
Los Angeles City Council, 103
Los Angeles Committee for American Unity
    Harry Braverman as chairman of, 149
Los Angeles Committee for the Protection of the Foreign Born (LACPFB), 8, 114
Los Angeles Community Chest, 113
Los Angeles Council for Civic Unity, 125–26, 161, 168
Los Angeles County, 103, 185
    repatriation program, 30–31
Los Angeles County Anti-Asiatic Society, 26
Los Angeles County Board of Supervisors, 63, 77, 78
Los Angeles County Committee for Interracial Progress, 78, 182
Los Angeles County Committee on Human Relations (LACCHR), 78, 167, 182
Los Angeles County Conference for Community Relations (LACCCR), 92, 126, 166, 167, 175
    CRC's support for, 167